READING POETRY

Harper & Row, Publishers

NEW YORK, EVANSTON, AND LONDON

READING POETRY

SECOND EDITION

Fred B. Millett

DIRECTOR EMERITUS OF THE HONORS COLLEGE
WESLEYAN UNIVERSITY

Arthur W. Hoffman

SYRACUSE UNIVERSITY

David R. Clark

UNIVERSITY OF MASSACHUSETTS

Reading Poetry, *Second Edition*

Library of Congress Catalog Card Number: 68-10198

Acknowledgments

W. H. AUDEN: "As I Walked Out One Evening" and "In Memory of W. B. Yeats" copyright 1940 by W. H. Auden. Reprinted from *The Collected Poetry of W. H. Auden* by permission of Random House, Inc. and Faber and Faber, Inc.

LEON O. BARRON: "The Foolish Cat That Died on Hallowe'en" and "Big Business" reprinted from *The Massachusetts Review* © 1960 and 1959, *The Massachusetts Review,* Inc.

ELIZABETH BISHOP: "The Fish" from *Poems North & South* by Elizabeth Bishop. Reprinted by permission of the publisher, Houghton Mifflin Company.

PHILIP BOOTH: "Heron" from *Letter from a Distant Land* by Philip Booth. Copyright © 1953 by Philip Booth. Reprinted by permission of the Viking Press, Inc. "The Owl" from *The Islanders* by Philip Booth. Copyright © 1960 by Philip Booth. Reprinted by permission of the Viking Press, Inc.

AUSTIN CLARKE: "Ancient Lights" and "The Scholar" from *Later Poems* (Dublin: The Dolmen Press, 1961). © Austin Clarke, 1961. Published by permission of Austin Clarke and The Dolmen Press, Ltd.

HART CRANE: "Voyages, II," "At Melville's Tomb," and "The River" from *The Collected Poems of Hart Crane*. By permission of Liveright, Publishers, N.Y. Copyright © Renewed, 1961, by Liveright Publishing Corp.

E. E. CUMMINGS: "Chansons Innocentes, I," copyright, 1923, by E. E. Cummings. Reprinted from his volume *Poems 1923–1954* by permission of Harcourt, Brace & World, Inc. and Faber and Faber, Ltd. "it's over a," copyright, 1944 by E. E. Cummings. Reprinted from his volume *Poems 1923–1954* by permission of Harcourt, Brace & World, Inc. "anyone lived in a pretty how town," copyright, 1939, 1940, by E. E. Cummings. From *50 Poems* by E. E. Cummings, by permission of Duell, Sloan and Pierce, affiliate of Meredith Press.

H. D. "Phaedra" from *The Collected Poems of H. D.*, published by Liveright, copyright, 1925, by Boni & Liveright, Inc.

WALTER DE LA MARE: "The Listeners," from *Collected Poems* by permission of the publishers, Henry Holt and Company, Inc. Copyright, 1941, by Walter de la Mare.

JAMES DICKEY: "Between Two Prisoners" and "Drowning with Others," copyright © 1960 by James Dickey. "A Dog Sleeping on My Feet," © 1962 by James Dickey. Poems reprinted from *Drowning with Others* by James Dickey, by permission of Wesleyan University Press.

RICHARD EBERHART: "Cancer Cells," "The Fury of Aerial Bombardment," and "The Groundhog" from *Collected Poems 1930–1960* by Richard Eberhart. © 1960 by Richard Eberhart. Reprinted by permission of Oxford University Press, N.Y. and Chatto and Windus, Ltd.

T. S. ELIOT: "Sweeney Among the Nightingales," "Marina," "Portrait of a Lady," and "Journey of the Magi" from *Collected Poems 1909–1962* by T. S. Eliot, copyright 1936, by Harcourt, Brace & World, Inc.; copyright, © 1963, 1964, by T. S. Eliot. Reprinted by permission of the publisher and Faber and Faber, Ltd.

KENNETH FEARING: "Portrait" reprinted by permission of Kenneth Fearing.

ROBERT FRANCIS: "Farm Boy After Summer," and "Cypresses," copyright © 1959 by Robert Francis. "Hide-and-Seek," "Swimmer," and "High Diver," copyright © 1953 by Robert Francis. "Pitcher" copyright © 1963 by Robert Francis. Poems reprinted from *The Orb Weaver* by Robert Francis, by permission of Wesleyan University Press.

ROBERT FROST: "Acquainted with the Night," "Stopping by Woods on a Snowy Evening," " 'Out, Out—,' " "House Fear," and "The Oft-Repeated Dream"; all from *Complete Poems of Robert Frost.* Copyright 1916, 1923, 1928, by Holt, Rinehart and Winston, Inc. Copyright 1944, 1951, © 1956 by Robert Frost. Reprinted by permission of Holt, Rinehart and Winston, Inc. and Jonathan Cape, Ltd. "After Apple-Picking" from *North of Boston* included in *Collected Poems of Robert Frost 1939.* Copyright, 1930, 1939 by Henry Holt and Company, Inc. Copyright, 1936, by Robert Frost.

THOMAS HARDY: "The Darkling Thrush" from *Collected Poems* by Thomas Hardy. Copyright, 1925, by The Macmillan Company. Used by permission of The Macmillan Company, publishers, the Trustees of the Hardy Estate, and Macmillan & Co., Ltd.

ANTHONY HECHT: "Samuel Sewall," reprinted with permission of The Macmillan Company from *Summoning of Stones* by Anthony Hecht. Copyright 1954 by Anthony Hecht.

GERARD MANLEY HOPKINS: "Pied Beauty," "The Windhover," and "Felix Randal" from *Poems of Gerard Manley Hopkins,* Third Edition, edited by W. H. Gardner. Copyright 1948 by Oxford University Press, Inc. Reprinted by permission of Oxford University Press, N.Y.

A. E. HOUSMAN: "On Wenlock Edge" from *A Shropshire Lad*—Authorized Edition—from *The Collected Poems of A. E. Housman.* Copyright 1939, 1940, © 1959 by Holt, Rinehart and Winston, Inc. Copyright © 1967 by Robert R. Symons. Reprinted by permission of Holt, Rinehart and Winston, Inc. "Epitaph on an Army of Mercenaries" from *The Collected Poems of A. E. Housman.* Copyright 1922 by Holt, Rinehart and Winston, Inc. Copyright 1950 by Barclays Bank Ltd. Reprinted by permission of Holdt, Rinehart and Winston, Inc. Permission granted by The Society of Authors as the literary representative of the Estate of the late A. E. Housman and Jonathan Cape, Ltd., publishers of A. E. Housman's *Collected Poems.*

BARBARA HOWES: "Death of a Vermont Farm Woman," "The Roses of Sa'adi," "El Desdichado," and "The Lost Wine" by permission of Barbara Howes.

TED HUGHES: "Meeting," "The Thought-Fox," and "The Jaguar" from *The Hawk in the Rain* by Ted Hughes. Copyright © 1957 by Ted Hughes. Reprinted by permission of Harper & Row, Publishers and Faber and Faber, Ltd.

DONALD JUSTICE: "Landscape with Little Figures," copyright © 1953 by Donald Justice; "Anniversaries" and "Counting the Mad," copyright © 1957 by Donald Justice; and "A Dream Sestina," copyright © 1959 by Donald Justice. Poems reprinted from *The Summer Anniversaries* by Donald Justice by permission of Wesleyan University Press.

RICHARD KELL: "Fishing Harbour towards Evening" and "The Swan" from *Control Tower.* Reprinted by permission of Richard Kell and Chatto and Windus, Ltd.

ARNOLD KENSETH: "Note upon a Manner of Living," "Elegy," and "O Stand Me Massive Then" from *Holy Merriment.* Copyright © 1942, 1946, 1959, 1960, 1963 by Arnold Kenseth. Reprinted by permission of The University of North Carolina Press.

THOMAS KINSELLA: "Downstream II," reprinted from *The Massachusetts Review,* © 1964, *The Massachusetts Review,* Inc. "Downstream II" is much shortened and changed from the poem in *Downstream* (Dublin: The Dolmen Press, 1962), © Thomas Kinsella, 1962. Reprinted by permission of Thomas Kinsella, *The Massachusetts Review,* and The Dolmen Press.

STANLEY KOEHLER: "Blue Umbrella" first appeared in *A Curious Quire,* © 1962 by The University of Massachusetts. Reprinted by permission of The Massachusetts Press. "Two by the Forsythia" first appeared in *The Sewanee Review.* Reprinted by permission of Stanley Koehler.

JOSEPH LANGLAND: "Crane" and "Sacrifice of a Gunnysack of Cats" reprinted from *The Wheel of Summer* by Joseph Langland. Copyright © 1959, 1963 by Joseph Langland and used with permission of the publishers, The Dial Press, Inc. "War" is reprinted with the permission of Charles Scribner's Sons from *The Green Town: Poems by Joseph Langland* (Copyright 1956 by Joseph Langland) *Poets of Today III.*

EDWIN H. LEMARE: "Moonlight and Roses" by Edwin H. Lemare, Ben Black, and Neil Moret. Copyright 1925, Villa Moret, Inc. Used by special permission.

DENISE LEVERTOV: "A Happening," "To the Snake," and "The Departure" from Denise Levertov, *With Green Eyes at the Back of Our Heads.* © 1958, 1959 by Denise Levertov Goodman. Reprinted by permission of New Directions Publishing Corporation.

ROBERT LOWELL: "Christmas Eve Under Hooker's Statue" from *Lord Weary's Castle,* copyright, 1944, 1946, by Robert Lowell. Reprinted by permission of Harcourt, Brace & World, Inc. and Faber and Faber, Ltd.

ARCHIBALD MACLEISH: "You, Andrew Marvell" from *The Collected Poems of Archibald Macleish.* Reprinted by permission of the publishers, Houghton Mifflin Company.

GEORGE MEREDITH: "Juggling Jerry," reprinted from *Poetical Works of George Meredith,* copyright 1912, by Charles Scribner's Sons; 1940, by William Meredith. Used by permission of Charles Scribner's Sons and Constable and Company, Ltd.

JOHN MONTAGUE: "The First Invasion of Ireland" by permission of John Montague.

MARIANNE MOORE: "Peter" and "Poetry" from *Selected Poems* by Marianne Moore. Copyright, 1935, by Marianne Moore. Used by permission of The Macmillan Company, publishers.

RICHARD MURPHY: "The Drowning of a Novice" from *Sailing to an Island.* © 1963 by Richard Murphy. Reprinted by permission of Richard Murphy, The Chilmark Press, Inc., and Faber and Faber, Ltd.

EZRA POUND: "In a Station of the Metro," "Envoi (1919)," "The Return," and "A Virginal" from Ezra Pound, *Personae.* Copyright 1926, 1954 by Ezra Pound. Reprinted by permission of the publishers, New Directions Publishing Corporation and Faber and Faber, Ltd.

JOHN CROWE RANSOM: "Here Lies a Lady of Beauty and High Degree," reprinted from *Selected Poems* by John Crowe Ransom, by permission of Alfred A. Knopf, Inc. Copyright, 1924, 1945, by Alfred A. Knopf, Inc. "The Tall Girl," "Winter Remembered," and "Bells for John Whiteside's Daughter," copyright 1922 by Alfred A. Knopf, Inc. and renewed 1952 by John Crowe Ransom. Reprinted from *Selected Poems,* Revised edition, by John Crowe Ransom, by permission of the publisher and Eyre and Spottiswoode, Ltd.

HENRY REED: "Naming of Parts" ("Lessons of the War") from *A Map of Verona and Other Poems,* copyright, 1947, by Henry Reed, Reprinted by permission of Harcourt, Brace & World, Inc. and Jonathan Cape, Ltd.

EDWIN ARLINGTON ROBINSON: "Eros Turannos" and "Flammonde," reprinted with permission of The Macmillan Company from *The Man Against the Sky* by Edwin Arlington Robinson. Copyright 1916 by The Macmillan Company, renewed 1944 by Ruth Nivison. "Mr. Flood's Party," reprinted with permission of The Macmillan Company from *Collected Poems* by Edwin Arlington Robinson. Copyright 1921 by Edwin Arlington Robinson, renewed 1949 by Ruth Nivison. The following poems by Edwin Arlington Robinson are reprinted with the permission of Charles Scribner's Sons: "Miniver Cheevy" (Copyright 1907 Charles Scribner's Sons: renewal copyright 1935) and "For a Dead Lady" from *The Town Down the River* (Copyright 1910 Charles Scribner's Sons; renewal copyright 1938 Ruth Nivison); and "Richard Cory" and "Luke Havergal" from *The Children of the Night.*

THEODORE ROETHKE: "My Papa's Waltz," copyright 1942 by Hearst Magazines, Inc.; "Child on Top of a Greenhouse," copyright 1946 by Editorial Publications, Inc.; "Big Wind," copyright 1947 by The United Chapters of Phi Beta Kappa; "A Field of Light," copyright 1948 by *The Tiger's Eye;* "Transplanting," copyright 1948 by Theodore Roethke; "Elegy for Jane," copyright 1950 by Theodore Roethke; "Song for the Squeeze-Box," copyright 1953 by Theodore Roethke; and "I Knew a Woman," copyright 1954 by Theodore Roethke. Poems from *The Collected Poems of Theodore Roethke.* Reprinted by permission of Doubleday & Company, Inc.

DELMORE SCHWARTZ: "In the naked bed, in Plato's cave," and "Socrates' ghost must haunt me now" by Delmore Schwartz from *In Dreams Begin Responsibilities.* Copyright 1938 by New Directions. Reprinted by permission of the publishers, New Directions Publishing Corporation.

KARL SHAPIRO: "Poet" and "Scyros," copyright 1942 by Karl Jay Shapiro. Reprinted from *Poems 1940–1953,* by Karl Jay Shapiro, by permission of Random House, Inc.

LOUIS SIMPSON: "The Green Shepherd," copyright © 1956 by Louis Simpson. Reprinted from *A Dream of Governors* by Louis Simpson by permission of Wesleyan University Press; first appeared in *The New Yorker.* "The Redwoods," copyright © 1961 by Louis Simpson; "The Troika," copyright © 1962 by Louis Simpson; "American Poetry" and "A Story about Chicken Soup," copyright © 1963 by Louis Simpson. Poems from *At the End of the Open Road* by Louis Simpson by permission of Wesleyan University Press.

DAME EDITH SITWELL: "Ass-Face," reprinted by permission of the publisher, The Vanguard Press from *The Collected Poems of Edith Sitwell.* Copyright, 1954, by Edith Sitwell. Also reprinted by permission of The Macmillan Company and David Higham Associates, Ltd.

ROBIN SKELTON: "Heron" and "A Ballad of Despair" by permission of Oxford University Press, London.

STEPHEN SPENDER: "I Think Continually of Those Who Were Truly Great" and "The Express" from *Poems by Stephen Spender.* Copyright 1934 and renewed 1961 by Stephen Spender. Reprinted from *Collected Poems 1929–1953,* by Stephen Spender, by permission of Random House, Inc. and Faber and Faber, Ltd.

JAMES STEPHENS: "The Main-Deep," reprinted with permission of The Macmillan Company from *Collected Poems* by James Stephens. Copyright 1925, 1926 by The Macmillan Company, renewed 1953, 1954 by James Stephens. Used by permission of The Macmillan Company, Mrs. Iris Wise, and Macmillan & Co., Ltd.

WALLACE STEVENS: "Peter Quince at the Clavier," reprinted from

Harmonium by Wallace Stevens, by permission of Alfred A. Knopf, Inc. Copyright, 1923, 1931, by Alfred A. Knopf, Inc.

DYLAN THOMAS: "In My Craft or Sullen Art," "A Refusal to Mourn . . . ," and "Do Not Go Gentle into that Good Night" by Dylan Thomas from *The Collected Poems of Dylan Thomas.* Copyright 1953 by Dylan Thomas, © 1957 by New Directions. Reprinted by permission of the publishers, New Directions Publishing Corporation, J. M. Dent & Sons, Ltd., and the Trustees for the Copyrights of the late Dylan Thomas.

ROBERT G. TUCKER: "Prayer," reprinted from *The Massachusetts Review* © 1961, by *The Massachusetts Review,* Inc. "Song In and Out of a Country Churchyard" first appeared in *A Curious Quire* © by The University of Massachusetts. Reprinted by permission of The University of Massachusetts Press.

RICHARD WEBER: "On an Italian Hillside," reprinted from *Six Irish Poets,* edited by Robin Skelton (London, Oxford University Press, 1962), by permission of Richard Weber.

RICHARD WILBUR: "Ceremony," copyright 1949, by Richard Wilbur; first published in *The New Yorker;* "Museum Piece," "Year's-End," "The Pardon," copyright, 1950 by Richard Wilbur. Poems reprinted from his volume *Ceremony and Other Poems* by permission of Harcourt, Brace & World, Inc. and Faber and Faber, Ltd. "Advice to a Prophet," copyright © 1959 by Richard Wilbur, first published in *The New Yorker.* Reprinted from his volume *Advice to a Prophet and Other Poems* by permission of Harcourt, Brace & World, Inc. and Faber and Faber, Ltd. "Exeunt" from *Things of this World,* © 1956 by Richard Wilbur. Reprinted by permission of Harcourt, Brace & World, Inc. Also reprinted from *Poems 1943–1956,* by permission of Faber and Faber, Ltd.

WILLIAM CARLOS WILLIAMS: "Poem," "The Red Wheelbarrow," "The Botticellian Trees," and "This Is Just to Say" by William Carlos Williams from *The Collected Earlier Poems of William Carlos Williams.* Copyright 1938, 1951 by William Carlos Williams. Reprinted by permission of the publisher, New Directions Publishing Corporation and Macgibbon & Kee, Ltd.

JAMES WRIGHT: "Complaint," copyright © 1958 by James Wright; "Paul," copyright © 1951 by James Wright; and "Old Man Drunk," copyright © 1959 by James Wright. Poems reprinted from *Saint Judas* by James Wright, by permission of Wesleyan University Press,

"A Blessing," copyright © 1961; "A Dream of Burial," "Milkweed," and "Autumn Begins in Martins Ferry, Ohio," copyright © 1962 by James Wright. Poems reprinted from *The Branch Will Not Break* by James Wright by permission of Wesleyan University Press.

ELINOR WYLIE: "Velvet Shoes," reprinted from *Collected Poems of Elinor Wylie,* by permission of Alfred A. Knopf, Inc. Copyright, 1921, 1932, by Alfred A. Knopf, Inc.

WILLIAM BUTLER YEATS: "The Wild Swans at Coole" from *Collected Poems* by William Butler Yeats. Copyright 1917, by Margaret C. Anderson; 1919 by The Macmillan Company. Used by permission of The Macmillan Company, publishers, Mrs. Yeats, and Macmillan & Co., Ltd. "On a Political Prisoner," "The Second Coming," and "A Prayer for My Daughter," reprinted with permission of The Macmillan Company from *Later Poems from Michael Robartes & Dancer* by William Butler Yeats. Copyright 1924 by The Macmillan Company, renewed 1952 by Bertha Georgie Yeats. "The Magi" and "To a Friend whose Work has come to Nothing," reprinted with permission of The Macmillan Company from *Responsibilities,* by William Butler Yeats. Copyright 1916 by The Macmillan Company, renewed 1944 by Bertha Georgie Yeats. "Leda and the Swan" and "Sailing to Byzantium," reprinted with permission of The Macmillan Company from *The Tower* by William Butler Yeats. Copyright 1928 by The Macmillan Company, renewed 1956 by Bertha Georgie Yeats. "The Cold Heaven" and "That the Night Come," reprinted with permission of The Macmillan Company from *The Green Helmet and Other Poems* by William Butler Yeats. Copyright 1912 by The Macmillan Company, renewed 1940 by Bertha Georgie Yeats. "John Kinsella's Lament for Mrs. Mary Moore." reprinted with permission of The Macmillan Company from *Last Poems and Plays* by William Butler Yeats. "From the 'Antigone,'" "Mohini Chatterjee," "'I am of Ireland,'" and "Lullaby," reprinted with permission of The Macmillan Company from *Collected Poems* by William Butler Yeats. Copyright 1933 by The Macmillan Company, renewed 1961 by Bertha Georgie Yeats. All poems also reprinted from *Collected Poems of W. B. Yeats,* by permission of Mr. M. B. Yeats and Macmillan & Co., Ltd. "The Only Jealousy of Emer – 'A woman's beauty,'" reprinted with permission of The Macmillan Company from *Collected Plays* by William Butler Yeats. Copyright 1934 and renewed 1952 by The Macmillan Company. Also reprinted from *The Variorum Edition of the Poems of W. B. Yeats,* edited by Peter Allt and Russell K. Alspach, by permission of Mr. M. B. Yeats and Macmillan & Co., Ltd.

Contents

Expression of Emotion in Poetry: Manner and Content 200

Ideas in Poetry 243

Preface

THIS revision of Fred B. Millett's *Reading Poetry* is a new and enlarged edition. The major sections of the original edition remain in the structure: the discursive chapters on topics such as rhythm and sound-pattern, a group of poems and exercises, and the directions for the analysis of a poem; a substantial anthology of poems has been added as a final section. A chapter on denotation, connotation, and allusion has been added to the discursive chapters, and the treatment of some topics in the original chapters has been reconsidered and revised. The section of poems and exercises has been expanded; more poems have been included and a greater variety of exercises supplied. The part, "Directions for the Analysis of a Poem" is substantially unchanged.

The editors wish especially to thank Joyce Hoffman for many hours of assistance in reading proof. Rosalind Clark cut out and arranged the texts of a great many poems. William Deadwyler helped with proofreading and the checking of texts. Mrs. Edith Markert did much patient xeroxing. Students in English 160 at Syracuse University and in English 64 (Spring, 1964) at the University of Massachusetts have contributed to the reshaping of the text. Work done on the revision during the summer has been made pleasant for one of the editors by the Edwin Gustafsons.

Fred Millett has accorded us most generous freedom in the revision; it is for him as teacher and friend, with respect and affection, that we have made the book.

ARTHUR W. HOFFMAN
DAVID R. CLARK

To the Teacher

THE purpose of this book is to train young people in the intensive reading of literature. I have spent all my adult life teaching English, but only within the last decade have I come to the conclusion that we, as teachers, can help young students most by training them in the technique of close reading. Most of them will learn to read rapidly without our help, although every English course should furnish some guidance to the acquisition of this important skill. But, unless we train students to read intensively, no one will, and their understanding and appreciation of literature will always be superficial.

Emphasis on the intensive reading of literature may help to keep primary the most appropriate and meaningful approach to literature, the aesthetic, the study of a work of art as a work of art and not as a footnote to biography, social or literary history, philosophy, or ethics. Until recent years, most introductory literature courses have favored the historical approach. If, in many colleges and universities, the introductory survey course has given way to courses in literary types or literary analysis, the reason is that teachers have come to feel that for young people the historical emphasis is less meaningful and valuable than the aesthetic.

This book is designed, as the title indicates, to set forth a method of literary analysis. To that end, it consists of four easily distinguishable and separable portions: a series of chapters outlining the technical elements essential to literary analysis; a group of selections for close study; directions, commentaries, and questions designed to embody an analytical procedure; and an anthology of poems. The book, therefore, may be used in a number of ways. You may wish to treat it simply as a collection of readings and use the theoretical chapters merely for reference, if your students show little or no interest in discussing the theory of literary technique. If, on the other hand, your students have a flair for discussing critical terms and literary processes, you may emphasize the theoretical chapters and use the readings to test your theoretical findings. With a responsive class, you may feel justified in making full use of the "Directions for the Analysis of a Poem."

These directions for the analysis of imaginative literature embody an elaborate analytical procedure, and, at first, you may feel that they are not only elaborate but pedantic. They are included for two reasons: first, because they set forth the process of analysis I used in my own classes; and, second, because students carry out these directions with great gusto and intelligence and with profit to them and myelf. *You* will, of course, feel perfectly free to use any or all of these directions, or to ignore them completely.

You will certainly find errors in this book. Of these, I should be glad to hear. You will also disagree with some of the ideas and emphases, but perhaps you may enjoy arguing with me behind my back or to my face. I have always found it more stimulating to teach a book which gave me a chance to conduct a running argument with the unseen author than to teach a book compact of gospel truth. If you feel—as you may well do—that either literary theory or technical analysis is overemphasized, the close study of the texts included will make a rich and rewarding course. After all, what matters is the literature itself.

If your students find the study of this book profitable, you may feel sure that you have given them a training that they will probably get nowhere else. They will never again read a literary work quite superficially. They will always be more observant than they would otherwise have been of at least some of the sources of a work's skill and excellence.

FRED B. MILLETT

PART I

Seven Discursive Chapters

The Substance of Poetry

The traditional purposes of poetry are "to teach and to delight." The pendulum swings historically between these two, never coming to rest at either extreme and resisting by the continuity of its movement efforts to convert "and" to "or," the impulse of the puritan or hedonist to establish one-half of the proposition as the whole. The good poet, even at his most serious, is having fun with words, and at his most playful is saying things worth listening to. As children, we have all been close to some forms of poetry, and as adults we are likely, in the role of parents, to come back to the same poems with a new perspective—songs of innocence and songs of experience. The adult advantage is obvious only if the perspective of experience includes a sufficient recollection of the perspective of innocence. Take the following familiar rhyme, for example.

DR. FOSTER

Doctor Foster went to Gloucester,
In a shower of rain;
He stepped in a puddle up to his middle,
And never went there again.

To a child, there is something wonderful about a puddle, the bigger the better, and an adult stepping into a puddle and going in up to his waist is a delicious (and perhaps not entirely innocent) idea. An adult is more likely to think that, besides being funny, the episode has some bearing on the mess the roads are in, the negligence of the highway department, and the extreme but perhaps not altogether unjustified reaction of an individual to these dismaying conditions. The good doctor is eccentric, but his provocation is very wet and considerable. The rueful, somber, or even morose reflections of some adults will not, however, obscure the playful character of the piece: the fun of finding a rhyme for Foster, the unusual rhyming of a person with a place, the persistent double rhymes coming close together, the joke of the missed rhyme ("puddle"/"middle") that goes with the misstep, the emphasis and firmness of rhythm that characterize Dr. Foster's entering the puddle as well as his decisiveness upon emerging.

A poet not only plays with words but also endures the effort of wrestling with words until they say, or come close to saying, what he seriously and passionately wants to get said. Poetry is the most thoroughly developed craft and art of language; the resources are there if the poet can learn how to use them. Poetry is the highest form of play in language—it is the game at its most sophisticated and most serious. That is why its rhythms were in our bedrooms as children and will probably be spoken over our graves.

Some poetry has a dazzling simplicity. Ben Jonson's famous lyric is an example.

TO CELIA

Drink to me only with thine eyes,
  And I will pledge with mine;
Or leave a kiss but in the cup
  And I'll not look for wine.
The thirst that from the soul doth rise   5
  Doth ask a drink divine;
But might I of Jove's nectar sup,
  I would not change for thine.

Simplicity, of course, in poems as in people, may mask a great deal of complexity. To *create* simplicity can be the most arduous and sophisticated of all tasks.

Some poetry impresses us immediately as formidably complex. Take, for example, the following stanza in the second of Hart Crane's poems entitled "Voyages."

> Take this Sea, whose diapason knells
> On scrolls of silver snowy sentences,
> The sceptred terror of whose sessions rends
> As her demeanors motion well or ill,
> All but the pieties of lovers' hands.

The range of poetry, in subject and in style, is extraordinarily wide, from beyond the rocket's venture to beneath the psychiatrist's probing, from the outward facts of landscape to the scenes and forms that rise in the recesses of consciousness, from a vocabulary and diction that a child may read and understand to a special language into which we must slowly and laboriously initiate our understanding, sequences and tangles of metaphor, riddling, mysterious and arcane, runic and doubtfully decipherable.

There is the further question of whether the poet is making us know something hitherto unknown or making us *see* something we have always known. Is his material basically familiar or unfamiliar? Has his main problem been to make us experience something not experienced before or to make us tolerate having another look at something we have seen many times over? Consider the following examples, the first a poem by Robert Frost and the second some lines from a poem by Samuel Taylor Coleridge.

ACQUAINTED WITH THE NIGHT

Robert Frost

I have been one acquainted with the night.
I have walked out in rain—and back in rain.
I have outwalked the furthest city light.

I have looked down the saddest city lane.
I have passed by the watchman on his beat 5
And dropped my eyes, unwilling to explain.

I have stood still and stopped the sound of feet
When far away an interrupted cry
Came over houses from another street,

But not to call me back or say good-by; 10
And further still at an unearthly height,
One luminary clock against the sky

Proclaimed the time was neither wrong nor right.
I have been one acquainted with the night.

From KUBLA KHAN
Samuel Taylor Coleridge

In Xanadu did Kubla Khan
  A stately pleasure-dome decree:
Where Alph, the sacred river, ran
Through caverns measureless to man
  Down to a sunless sea. 5
So twice five miles of fertile ground
With walls and towers were girdled round:
And there were gardens bright with sinuous rills,
Where blossomed many an incense-bearing tree;
And here were forests ancient as the hills, 10
Enfolding sunny spots of greenery.

The material of Frost's poem is recognizable, familiar, closely affiliated with everyday experience. The indicated subjective mood of the speaker may be more special and unusual than the outward scene in which he takes his walk, but even the subjective side of his experience is directly familiar to most of us and, by way of what we have heard others tell, or read about, or seen in a movie, the basic materials and main features of the poem are familiar to all of us.

Coleridge's lines, on the other hand, represent quite a different reach of poetic material. We know right away that we are in a strange and exotic landscape, not a place we go by on the way to the grocery store or the dry-cleaner's. We are likely to be unsure whether what we are confronting represents an actual person and place—actual but remote in space and time—or whether this is a fantastic realm of the imagination. The pleasure-dome, the sacred river, the measureless caverns, and the sunless sea all contribute to our sense of strangeness, of all but utter divorce from what we familiarly and reassuringly recognize and know. On the other hand, we do recognize here a kind of scene that we have encountered in prose fiction, in the movies, perhaps on the late-late show. Furthermore, for all the exoticism of the description, rivers, caverns, fertile ground, forests, spots of greenery are basically familiar; the very strange is a distortion, a twist on the familiar—we could not get to it without bases in familiar experience to start from. It is worth remarking, too, that Frost's poem and Coleridge's poem, widely different in their materials, are both versions of an inner voyage.

The range of experience in the Frost and Coleridge poems is very considerable, yet neither poem presents material that is strikingly ugly or disgusting. It should be emphasized that all experience can be the material of poetry, any kind of experience, the repulsive as well as the attractive, the ugly and the beautiful. Take a look at the poem Richard Eberhart makes of his experience of a dead groundhog (p. 358) or of his vision of cancer cells.

THE CANCER CELLS

Today I saw a picture of the cancer cells,
Sinister shapes with menacing attitudes.
They had outgrown their test-tube and advanced,
Sinister shapes with menacing attitudes,
Into a world beyond, a virulent laughing gang. 5
They looked like art itself, like the artist's mind,
Powerful shaker, and the taker of new forms.
Some are revulsed to see these spiky shapes;
It is the world of the future too come to.
Nothing could be more vivid than their language, 10

Lethal, sparkling and irregular stars,
The murderous design of the universe,
The hectic dance of the passionate cancer cells.
O just phenomena to the calculating eye,
Originals of imagination. I flew 15
With them in a piled exuberance of time,
My own malignance in their racy, beautiful gestures
Quick and lean: and in their riot too
I saw the stance of the artist's make,
The fixed form in the massive fluxion. 20

I think Leonardo would have in his disinterest
Enjoyed them precisely with a sharp pencil.

These materials are just as valid for a poet to use as a Grecian urn, a nightingale, or a beautiful woman. Such, at any rate, is the prevailing modern view; too much of the world we know would be excluded and the poet would become a half-man if his songs did not include pain, anguish, and ugliness, as well as pleasure, delight, and beauty.

This view of the material of poetry, however, should not obscure the fact that poets may, from time to time, deliberately focus on a limited subject or set of subjects and, further, establish limits of style within which they will usually treat such subjects. The developments of such literary conventions (i.e., agreements, tacit or expressed) can lead to some very fine poetry, poetry of a fineness very difficult to achieve in any other way. We do need to insist, however, that the burden of the evidence supports the view that there are no *inherently* poetic materials and there are no materials that are *inherently* unpoetic.

Types of Structure

Apart from the quite primitive matter—primitive and of prime importance—of whether the substance of a poem is basically familiar or unfamiliar to the reader, and apart from whether the material is attractive, neutral, or repulsive, there is the further choice made by the poet of different types of structure, or modes of presentation. By structure here we mean certain facts of the interior character of the poem, *not* its external shape (number of lines, length of lines, arrangement of rhymes, etc.).

A poem, like a human being or any other organism, must have both these elements to give it identity and continuity—an internal structure that constitutes, we may say, the skeletal element of the creation and an external shape that gives the creature a specific and differentiated contour. Just as we have the structures and shapes of cats, fish, monkeys, birds, lions, and men in the world of living creatures, so we have, in the world of poems, such structures and shapes as elegies, lyrics, epics, pastorals, and ballads. The poet may tell a story, describe a scene, present a feeling or idea, or advance an argument for an attitude or idea; these types of structure or modes of presentation we may label, respectively, narrative, descriptive, expository, and argumentative. In most poems two or more types of structure are present in combination, but in many poems one type dominates.

In the simplest narrative poem, the indispensable elements are the problem, the turning point, the climax, and the denouement. In most such narrative poems, there will also be an element of exposition,[1] although in the folk ballad this element is very frequently minimized. We may test the validity of these assertions by studying an example of a simple narrative poem such as the folk ballad "Sir Patrick Spens" (p. 99). In this ballad, as in many folk ballads, the element of exposition is almost nonexistent. It is, at any rate, limited to the first three stanzas of this poem, which tell us that an unnamed king directed Sir Patrick Spens to undertake a sea voyage. Out of this bare exposition rises the problem of the poem: Will Sir Patrick succeed or fail in carrying out the commission the king has given him? The tragic denouement of the ballad is foreshadowed in Sir Patrick's reaction to the king's orders. There is relatively little development of the problem that rises out of the situation roughly sketched by the first three stanzas, and the climax is implied rather than stated. What we are given—in the most imaginatively telling lines of the poem—are the tragic consequences of the storm, the turning point in the narrative, and its climactic incident.

In a ballad such as "Edward" (p. 115), the narrative elements are even less elaborately developed. In this ballad, which takes the form of a dramatic dialogue between a mother and a son, a series of questions and answers involving rigid formula-like repetitions with slight variations (a stylistic device characteristic of the ballad and known as incremental repetition), we learn that a son has killed his father and that he has killed him because the mother wanted him killed. We learn nothing about the situation out of which this problem arose; the problem itself—shall the hero carry out the mother's demand that he kill his father—is not implied until the next to the last stanza. We are never told why the father was killed. We get no direct indication of the character of either the mother or the father. What we do get, again by implication, is the feeling of horror that the son now feels at the crime he has committed and his feeling of revulsion at the (utterly unexplained) unnaturalness of his

[1] *Exposition* is the part of a narrative that gives the background of the characters and the initial dramatic situation. Be careful to recognize the distinction between *exposition* as a term for part of a narrative structure and *expository* as a designation for one of the four major types of structure.

mother's conduct. But the atmosphere of the ballad from its very beginning is so sinister and threatening, the emotion felt by the hero is so violent, the suspense as to what the situation really is is so adroitly preserved, our imagination is so powerfully aroused both by what is and by what is not told us that this ballad deserves its reputation as one of the finest in the rich store of English folk poetry.

The simple narrative structure of "The Eve of St. Agnes" (p. 120) is closely akin to that of a short story. Here are not only the indispensable elements we have seen in the ballads on which we have just commented, but also a more detailed exposition, a development, both favorable and unfavorable, both before and after the climax, a turning point, and a clearly depicted climax. In this "literary" romance, as distinct from the folk ballad, the setting is described in superb detail. The amazing selectivity of "Edward" produces a great sense of power and shock; Keats' narrative moves like an action depicted in tapestry on an intricate field threaded with black and gold.

Since no extended narrative poems are included in this book, we need not discuss in any detail the structure of such poems as Milton's *Paradise Lost* or Spenser's *The Faerie Queene*. There are, however, no structural elements in either of these long poems that are essentially different from those in briefer narratives.

Although description—as a type of poetic structure—appears more frequently as a subordinate than as the predominant element, there are some poems, usually rather brief, in which the descriptive element is primary. In such poems the poet is concerned with presenting a scene in words, with conveying all the sensory richness of his subject without depending upon the interest of event or character. If there are relatively few purely descriptive poems of very high quality, the reasons are perhaps that the medium of words is less efficient than the medium of painting in the communication of visual experience and that extended description is very likely to pall on readers unless there is at least a slight admixture of the narrative element, that is, the element of action.

A poem that comes quite close to being purely descriptive is James Stephens' "The Main-Deep."

THE MAIN-DEEP

The long-rólling,
Steady-póuring,
Deep-trenchéd
Green billów:

The wide-topped, 5
Unbróken,
Green-glacid,
Slow-sliding,

Cold-flushing,
—On—on—on— 10
Chill-rushing,
Hush—hushing,

. . . Hush—hushing . . .

This short poem is remarkable for its rich sensory variety. Notice how many different senses are enlisted in the account and how many facets of our complex visual sensation are engaged. The present active participles, thickly present but carefully chosen, make the whole description move. Even the punctuation, down to a differentiation so slight as that between a hyphen and a dash (line 11 and line 12), serves to indicate the continuity, the sequence, and the pace in time, and the avoidance of a final period implies the on-going of a process the main features of which have been described. Poetry involves the sequence of words in time, and it is arguable that a narrative structure, however rudimentary, is therefore always present no matter what the dominant type of structure may be. In this case, the main "character" is a large green wave out at sea; we are introduced to the wave and watch while something happens to it. The height of the wave's career is about midway in the second stanza and the wave's subsidence, decline, and distancing in space begin with line 8 and continue to the end of the poem. Elements of narrative akin to climax and descending action with denouement incomplete are present. Yet this is very clearly a predominantly descriptive poem, extraordinarily accurate in the way a painter might be accurate; the poem, however, enlists senses other than the visual to a degree and with a sharpness not readily achieved in a painting. Moreover, by the sequence of words in time, the poem has an analogue of motion; the description is not of a state but of a process and our directed movement from word to word animates in a way that a painter must stretch his art even partially to emulate.

A third, and very common, type of poetic structure is expository. The method of exposition may be applied to either emotions or ideas or, as is more usual, to a combination of the two. In a combination of the two it is generally not difficult to decide whether the poet is primarily concerned with the exposition of emotion or of ideas. Since the material of lyric poetry is usually feeling or emotion, it is not surprising that the structure of many lyric poems is expository. As an example of expository structure, let us use one of the finest of Byron's short lyrics.

SO, WE'LL GO NO MORE A-ROVING

So, we'll go no more a-roving
  So late into the night,
Though the heart be still as loving,
  And the moon be still as bright.

For the sword outwears its sheath, 5
  And the soul wears out the breast,
And the heart must pause to breathe,
  And Love itself have rest.

Though the night was made for loving,
  And the day returns too soon, 10
Yet we'll go no more a-roving
  By the light of the moon.

The feeling precipitated in this lyric is one that is much easier to feel than to name. It is a complex feeling, a feeling of weariness, if not satiety, that is contrasted sharply with the vivid memory of passionate love in a congenial setting to produce a profound and moving melancholy. The structure of the poem is nicely calculated to communicate this subtle and mature feeling. The melancholy emotion is suggested, but not stated, in the first stanza, with its abnegation of the joys of roving; the second stanza gives the reasons for the abnegation (argumentative structure in the form of argument by analogy appears here); the final stanza repeats the emotion boldly through adroit variations of the language and mood of the first stanza.

The expository type of structure is also appropriate in poems devoted to the expression of ideas rather than feelings. Walter Savage Landor's short lyric, "Past Ruin'd Ilion," in which he is more intent on communicating an idea than on expressing an emotion, is an excellent illustration of this variety of expository structure.

Past ruin'd Ilion Helen lives,
  Alcestis rises from the shades;
Verse calls them forth; 'tis verse that gives
  Immortal youth to mortal maids.

Soon shall Oblivion's deepening veil   5
  Hide all the peopled hills you see,
The gay, the proud, while lovers hail
  These many summers you and me.

A major theme of this poem is the power of poetry to make its subjects immortal. The presentation of this idea has an orderliness characteristic of the poet. The first two lines give two illustrations of the truth of the theme (if, for you, Helen lives but Alcestis does not, look up Alcestis in a good classical dictionary); the third and fourth lines state the theme. The fifth and sixth lines express the converse of the proposition which is the subject of the poem, and the seventh and eighth lines apply the proposition—prophetically—to the poet and his beloved.

In the fourth type of poetic structure—the argumentative—the poet states a proposition and then gives reasons for the acceptance of the proposition or proof of its "truthfulness"; he may conclude with a restatement of the proposition. Arthur Hugh Clough's "Say Not the Struggle Nought Availeth" is an excellent example of argumentative structure.

> Say not the struggle nought availeth,
>   The labour and the wounds are vain,
> The enemy faints not, nor faileth,
>   And as things have been they remain.
>
> If hopes were dupes, fears may be liars; 5
>   It may be, in yon smoke concealed,
> Your comrades chase e'en now the fliers,
>   And, but for you, possess the field.
>
> For while the tired waves, vainly breaking,
>   Seem here no painful inch to gain, 10
> Far back, through creeks and inlets making,
>   Comes silent, flooding in, the main.
>
> And not by eastern windows only,
>   When daylight comes, comes in the light,
> In front, the sun climbs slow, how slowly, 15
>   But westward, look, the land is bright.

In this poem the proposition is that an apparent defeat may really be a victory. The first stanza is devoted to the poet's protest against confusing an apparent defeat with a real victory. In each of the three following stanzas, he gives a "reason" for the rejection of the view of which he disapproves. Each of the reasons takes the form of an argument by analogy (a form of argument, incidentally, that is logically more reputable than it is commonly said to be). Each of these stanzas, moreover, carries out the antithesis, implicit in the proposition, between an apparent defeat and a real victory. Thus, the second stanza contrasts the man who in his blindness has given up the fight, and his comrades, who at the very moment of his failure of nerve are winning it. The third stanza contrasts the apparent inability of the waves to make an impression on a forbidding coast with the power of the total ocean to make deep inroads into the land. The final stanza contrasts the light as seen by one who looks only toward the east with the light that illumines the land for one who, with a larger hopefulness, looks toward the west. One of the memorable moments of World War II came when, as Britain's desperate fortunes moved toward a turning point, Winston Churchill vigorously growled this last stanza at the members of the British parliament.

The four basic types of poetic structure admit of a large number of possible combinations. As a matter of fact, it is the rather rare poem that, though predominantly narrative, descriptive, expository, or argumentative, does not contain subordinate elements of one or more of the other types of structure. Let us take as an example of a poem that combines two types of structure skillfully one of Wordsworth's finest sonnets.

COMPOSED UPON WESTMINSTER BRIDGE, SEPTEMBER 3, 1802

Earth has not anything to show more fair:
Dull would he be of soul who could pass by
A sight so touching in its majesty:
This City now doth, like a garment, wear
The beauty of the morning; silent, bare, 5
Ships, towers, domes, theatres, and temples lie
Open unto the fields, and to the sky;
All bright and glittering in the smokeless air.
Never did sun more beautifully steep
In his first splendor, valley, rock, or hill; 10
Ne'er saw I, never felt, a calm so deep!
The river glideth at his own sweet will:
Dear God! the very houses seem asleep;
And all that mighty heart is lying still!

In this sonnet Wordsworth is more concerned with expressing the feeling aroused in him by the sight of London from Westminster Bridge than with giving the reader a picture of London from that point of view. To further his dual purpose, the fusion of the expository and the descriptive methods is appropriate, and his treatment of each of these elements is affected by the presence of the other.

In considering the structure of this poem, we must realize that the title is a part of the poem (compare the importance of the title in Stephens' "The Main-Deep") and that without it, the poem would be a less lucid structure. The title gives us, as the poem itself does not, the poet's physical point of view, Westminster Bridge. You are thereby informed that this is not any bridge across any river in any city, but a specific bridge across the Thames in London. The title further gives us the exact date of this experience. An awareness of any personal significance the date "September 3, 1802" had for Wordsworth would add to your understanding of the poem. But even if you know nothing of the background of the poem, the date is not without significance, for it warns you to eliminate from your associations with the poem any knowledge you may have of the London of other times and to attempt to re-create, with the poet's assistance, the less industrial, less colossally urban London of 1802.

The first three lines of the sonnet give nothing in the way of the basic pattern of Wordsworth's picture; instead, they suggest the feeling that Wordsworth had and the feeling he hoped you would have by the time you finished reading the poem sympathetically. The fourth and fifth lines of the poem contain two elements essential to the basic pattern of the poem: city and morning. The subject of the poem is now clear—the feeling aroused by the view of the city of London from Westminster Bridge on the morning of September 3, 1802. Once this subject has been made clear, the other details are filled in; the details, in accordance with Wordsworth's total purpose, are amazingly few and bare: ships, towers, domes, theaters, temples. Two aspects of the scene are emphasized in lines 8–10 and 12–14. In lines 8–10 the quality and effect of the light are described. The air is smokeless; the sunlight is the fresh and sharp light of early morning ("sun . . . in his first splendor"); in consequence, the entire city is "bright and glittering." In line 11 he returns to a direct statement of his feeling at the moment and of the depth of that calm feeling in comparison with similar feelings aroused by similar scenes. In lines 12–14 the poet emphasizes the quiet of early morning by his descriptive details; the incomparable calm of the scene is not only felt but seen by the poet. The river, the only moving element, glides; the movement of water is not modified, disrupted, artificially altered or impelled by boat traffic; the river does not rush turbulently. The city, which in the simile in line 4 was almost personified, *is* personified here; the houses are asleep; the throbbing heart of the great city is as nearly stilled as that of a giant motionless in sleep.

Thus far we have been considering the types of structure that poets have found convenient for the efficient communication of their feelings, emotions, and ideas. But a poem, like an organism, has not only an internal structure, a kind of skeletal base, but also an external shape that has an integral relationship to its structure. The internal structure furnishes a rough notion of the size of the living poem, just as the skeleton of a mouse or an elephant gives us a general but by no means exact notion of the size of the living creature. The external shape of the poem is determined by the metrics of the poem and, in the case of a rhymed poem, by its rhyme scheme. It is these elements of poetry that we shall discuss next, and, in the course of this discussion, you will do well to bear in mind that, whatever other functions meter and rhyme may have, they bear the responsibility of creating sharply and clearly the external shape of the poem.

Rhythm in Poetry

Poetry is language measured and supercharged. The measuring or metering of language is itself one way of supercharging, but many of the devices used to gain special power—metaphor, for example—have nothing to do with measure or meter. The degree of emphasis upon modes of measurement or upon devices for supercharging is one index to the major styles and periods of English poetry.

Probably the most obvious difference between poetry and prose is the more regular rhythm of a great deal of poetry, that is, the pattern made by the number and the arrangement of stressed and unstressed, accented and unaccented, syllables. Rhythm is, to be sure, one of the elements of attractive or excellent prose, but rhythm in prose, if it approaches the rhythm of regular verse or even of the best "free" verse, is likely to have an unpleasant effect. Thus, when Dickens in his more highly emotional prose passages falls into a series of iambic pentameters, the reader is likely to resent this unconscious approximation of prose to verse. On the other hand, the prose of Walter Pater's famous interpretation of Leonardo da Vinci's "Mona Lisa" has such a marked rhythm—not to mention its other poetic characteristics—that William Butler Yeats divided this passage into its obvious rhythmic units and printed it as the opening "poem" in his *Oxford Book of Modern Verse.* But the rhythm of Pater's prose is so subtle and elaborate as to avoid the effect of too great regularity.

You can feel immediately the rhythmic patterns of such traditional nursery rhymes as "Hickory, Dickery Dock," or

"Doctor Foster Went to Gloucester," or such folk rhymes as "Thirty Days Hath September." But even though the rhythmic element in these verses is felt immediately and deeply, the untutored reader would be unable to describe with any accuracy the particular rhythm to which he had responded. A method for describing rhythm is an indispensable part of your equipment as a student of poetry.

For our purposes, a visual analysis of meter is more important than a verbal description of the metrical patterns. The basis of rhythm in Latin and Greek verse is the brevity or the length of the syllable; in French verse, it is the syllable itself; and in English verse, it is the accent or the absence of accent, the stress or the lack of stress, combined with the number of syllables, that determines the meter or measure. If, for example, we read aloud the first stanza of that familiar poem, Thomas Gray's "Elegy Written in a Country Churchyard," in such a way as to bring out as clearly as possible the meaning of the lines, we shall find that, more or less unconsciously, we express ten syllables in each line and we stress certain syllables. In a reading of the following stanza, those syllables with the [—] mark over them would be stressed. Then if we place [u] over the syllables that are not to be stressed, we are on our way to bringing out the rhythmic pattern of the lines.

u — u — u — u — u —
The curfew tolls the knell of parting day,

u — u — — — u u u —
The lowing herd wind slowly o'er the lea,

u — u — u — u — u —
The plowman homeward plods his weary way,

u — u — u — u u u —
And leaves the world to darkness and to me.

At this point, you may very well object that if *you* were reading this stanza, the resulting pattern of stresses would not coincide with the one shown here. Such an objection is perfectly legitimate. Since the author is not usually at hand to read his verses for us, the best we can do is to read them as intelligently as possible, and any two readers, trained or untrained, may very well arrive at varying, although probably not widely varying, results. Even the author's own reading (or recording) of a poem may not give the beat and stresses exactly as he wants them, or he may change his mind from time to time. The author's version, in any case, is often only one among several good versions. It is possible to prefer Siobhan McKenna's version of a Yeats poem to the poet's own reading; the important thing is to become aware of the bases of choice that underlie various versions.

In the process of scansion one must aim at representing as accurately as possible the emphasis that brings out most clearly the meaning of the lines. For instance, in the example given above, some readers might feel that the second and fourth lines have exactly the same arrangement of stressed and unstressed syllables as the first and third. Such a reading, however, does not do full justice to certain words which are of great importance for the meaning of the stanza and emphasizes words which are relatively unimportant. To accent "o'er" in the second line or "and" in the fourth line seems to ignore the sense of these lines. Moreover, the analysis of meter has been made meaningless and distasteful to generations of students because many teachers have regarded metrics as a Procrustean bed into which the poem must be forced. If metrical analysis is regarded as an index to your rhythmic sensibility, you may very well find it not a burdensome and meaningless exercise, but a challenge to your powers of observation and taste.

If we assume for the moment that this reading of these lines is a defensible one, we observe that the first and the third lines have an identical rhythmical pattern and that the second and fourth lines vary slightly from this pattern. Here we see one of the essentials of effective rhythm, that is, the interplay between regularity and irregularity. It might be possible by diligent search to discover four lines of good verse that would show no variation from the metrical norm established by the first line of the four, but such a search would have to be a very patient one, because, as one can tell by tapping out any familiar succession of drumbeats, a certain degree of irregularity undoubtedly heightens the total effect of the rhythm. What the poet's and the reader's ears seem to demand is, first, the establishment of a recognizable rhythmical pattern, and, then, the dexterous interplay of variations within the pattern. Dexterity in the handling of rhythm may be said to reside in the avoidance of too little variation or too frequent variation. The effect of the first is monotony; the effect of the second is perplexity, that is, a feeling of uncertainty as to whether or not there is any basic rhythmic pattern.

If we wish to put into words the effects we have indicated by the symbols [—] and [ᵕ], we shall have to come to terms with the traditional language of English metrics. The unit of meter is the foot, and the foot is made up of a particular number and order of stressed and unstressed syllables.[1] The most frequently encountered foot in English metrics is made up of an unaccented syllable followed by an accented syllable; a foot of this type is called an iambus, and a line in which a majority of the feet are of this type is called an iambic line. The types of feet that are commonly used in the meters or measures of English poetry are the following (the words in parentheses are the adjectival forms). Irregularity or variation may be produced by using a combination of types within a line, for example, by introducing a trochee in an iambic pattern.

ᵕ —	iambus (iambic)
— ᵕ	trochee (trochaic)
ᵕ ᵕ —	anapest (anapestic)
— ᵕ ᵕ	dactyl (dactylic)

The following types of feet are *not* used to create normative patterns of rhythm but occur as substitutions; they provide the irregularity, or much of it, in the rhythms which the basic feet establish.

1 A considerable number of students do not recognize a syllable when they see one. *The American College Dictionary* defines a syllable as "a segment of speech uttered with a single impulse of air pressure from the lungs, and consisting of one sound of relatively great sonority, with or without one or more subordinated sounds," and as "a character or set of characters representing (more or less exactly) such an element of speech." This or any other reliable dictionary will indicate the correct division of a word into syllables.

— — spondee (spondaic)
u u pyrrhic (pyrrhic)
u — u amphibrach (amphibrachic)

A line of poetry may be further described in terms of the number of feet it contains. We speak of a line of one foot as monometer, of two feet as dimeter, of three feet as trimeter, of four feet as tetrameter, of five feet as pentameter, and of six feet as hexameter.

In order to visualize the division of a line of English verse into its units, it is customary to draw a vertical line between one foot and the next. Thus, the first stanza of Gray's "Elegy" might be marked as follows:

u — u — u — u — u —
The cur|few tolls| the knell| of part|ing day,
u — u — — — u u u —
The low|ing herd|wind slow|ly o'er| the lea,
u — u — u — u — u —
The plow|man home|ward plods| his wear|y way,
u — u — u — u u u —
And leaves| the world| to dark|ness and| to me.

In this analysis of the rhythmic pattern, seventeen of the feet are iambic; three are variations from the iambic. Each of these variations from the iambic norm involves the substitution of one of the other feet named above for an iambic foot. Thus, in the second line, the third foot is a spondee rather than an iambus, and the fourth foot of that line is a pyrrhic rather than an iambus; the fourth foot of the fourth line is also a pyrrhic rather than an iambus.

One further refinement in the treatment of stresses needs to be mentioned. The usual discussion of metrics assumes that all stressed syllables are stressed equally; observation of anyone's reading of a line of verse will reveal the error of this assumption. The rhythmic effect of a line is achieved, not merely by varying the order and the number of the stressed and unstressed syllables but by varying the intensity of the stress upon the stressed syllables. Since no satisfactory formal system for differentiating intensity of a stress seems to have been worked out, here is an easy and usable scheme to follow. If we assume that a normally stressed syllable bears three times the weight of an unstressed syllable, we may use a superior number [4] for a heavily stressed syllable and a superior number [2] for a lightly stressed syllable.

It is well to reserve these markings for quite unusual stresses, whether strong or weak. The following couplet from Pope's "Windsor Forest" can serve to illustrate both of these special markings.

> See! from| the Brake| the whir|ring Pheas|ant springs,
>
> And mounts| exult|ing on| trium|phant Wings.

The case for the [4] marking of "See" in the first line is obvious. In the second line, "on" might well be marked as unstressed; the word is relatively unimportant, but in Pope's poetry the iambic norm is firmly present, and to disappoint the rhythmic expectation completely with respect to stress is a debatable decision in this context. Accordingly, one way to describe the situation would be to mark "on" with a [2]—an unusually light stress.

Actually, this system oversimplifies the real situation, since it has been demonstrated that some unusually stressed syllables bear *seven* times the weight of an unstressed syllable. The ingenious person may, however, be left to devise a system that represents with greater accuracy the variations in intensity of stress.

The following criteria are helpful in establishing the marking of stressed and unstressed elements and they suggest, too, some reflections on the bases of English metrics: (1) pronunciation; (2) normal rhythmical expectation; (3) rhetorical importance. Pronunciation is the first criterion and is seldom overridden by considerations presented by the other two. Pronunciation dictates the number of syllables and the quantity ("numbers" is one of the older terms for meter); and in all cases of words of more than one syllable, pronunciation has a very strong influence in determining what is to be stressed and what is not to be stressed. The emphases and rhythms accepted and daily expressed in speech are of the highest importance to the poet because they may be made to coincide with or to deviate from a normal verse rhythm. For example, the words "avenge" and "slaughtered" on the basis of pronunciation would have the metrical character of an iambus (avenge) and of a trochee (slaughtered). A poet could make them coincide with a metrical pattern or use them to introduce variation. Milton located them so that their pronunciation coincided with the normal expectation of his iambic pentameter line:

> Avenge,| O Lord,| Thy slaugh|tered saints| whose bones

But in the following alteration of the line the pronunciation of "slaughtered" would vary from the rhythm of an iambic pattern:

> Slaughtered| Thy Saints!|—O Lord,| avenge| their bones

while the pronunciation of "avenge" would coincide with an iambic verse rhythm.

Consider another example. At the agonizing moment when King Lear enters carrying the body of Cordelia, he expresses his anguish and sense of irrecoverable loss in the line

> Never,| never,| never,| never,| never.

Pronunciation dictates the whole line in which the expected iambic pentameter pattern is completely overturned. So far as speech goes, the line is perfectly easy, but in the context of iambic pentameter expectation, normal pronunciation here becomes the vehicle of a drastic overturn and reversal.

EXERCISE

> *Mother,* good night. *Indeed* this *counselor*
> Is now most still, most *secret,* and most grave
> Who was in life a *foolish prating* knave.

• • •

Nothing at all, yet all that is I see.

. . .

The King shall drink to *Hamlet's better* breath,
And in the cup an *union* shall he throw
Richer than that which four *successive* kings
In *Denmark's* crown have worn. Give me the cups.

1. In the above lines from *Hamlet*, in which instances does the pronunciation of the italicized words coincide with the iambic pentameter expectation?
2. In which instances does the pronunciation differ from the metric expectation?

The second criterion in establishing stressed and unstressed elements is normal rhythmical expectation. It should be regarded as much more tentative and provisional in importance, frequently subordinate to the third criterion, rhetorical importance. A high proportion of English poetry has been written in iambic rhythms, especially in the ten-syllable iambic line (iambic pentameter). We expect iambic pentameter rhythm not only in Shakespeare's plays but also in much of Donne's poetry, in Milton's *Paradise Lost*, in the poetry of Dryden and Pope, in Wordsworth's *The Prelude*, and in many of the longer poems of the Romantic and Victorian periods. Yet the treatment of this normal rhythm is amazingly varied. In Shakespeare's plays, for example, since one objective is to make language convey something of the effect of speech, the verse rhythm is not rigorously or mechanically observed. There are types of verse—those designed for chanting, for instance—in which a rigorous beat might have very high priority. More frequently, however, and this holds true for a great deal of twentieth-century poetry, a regular rhythmical expectation is disappointed almost as often as it is fulfilled, and the rationale of the scansion depends considerably on rhetorical importance.

To illustrate, suppose we apply all three criteria, one after the other, to the first line of W. B. Yeats' "Sailing to Byzantium" (see p. 267 for the complete poem).

That is| no count|ry for |old men.| The young

Pronunciation determines the marking of the word country (— ∪) and, applying the second criterion to a line of ten syllables (and other lines in the poem affirm this norm and make it quite clear), we would have the following scansion:

∪ — ∪ — ∪ — ∪ — ∪ —
That is| no coun|try for |old men.| The young

So far as the word "country" is concerned, pronunciation and rhythmical expectation coincide. Applying the third criterion, however, the rest of the line would probably be altered to produce the following marking:

— ∪ — — ∪ ∪ — — ∪ —
That is| no coun|try for |old men.| The young

The third criterion recognizes that certain words in our language are not ordinarily of any great importance (e.g., articles such as a, an, the and prepositions such as in, on, for). In the line we are examining, "the" is not a problem since the second and third criteria coincide in evaluating its importance; on the basis of an iambic expectation, "The" is not stressed and on the basis of rhetorical importance "the" does not call for stress. The marking of "for" as unstressed means a judgment that, on the grounds of the third criterion, "for" has little importance, not even enough to rate the expected iambic stress. Other words in the line, however, are given stress even though doing so involves overruling the second criterion; these words are "That" and "no" and "old." Stressing these words follows from a judgment that they are important based on their context. One makes the determination of importance not only on the basis of a word's general importance but also on the basis of the word's indicated importance in a specific context. Some of the decisions about importance can be based on the evidence of the line alone; here, for example, the direct contrast of "old" to "young" suggests stress on both. The full force and logic of this decision, however, depends upon the contrast between age and youth developed as a central motif of the whole poem.

EXERCISE

Try your hand at applying these criteria to the following passages:

> Of man's first disobedience, and the fruit
> Of that forbidden tree, whose mortal taste
> Brought death into the world, and all our woe,
> With loss of Eden . . .

. . .

> Achilles' wrath, to Greece the direful spring
> Of woes unnumbered, heavenly goddess, sing!

. . .

> Then die, that she
> The common fate of all things rare
> May read in thee;
> How small a part of time they share
> That are so wondrous sweet and fair!

. . .

> Come all you young fellows that follow the sea,
> Now pray pay attention and listen to me,
> I'm a deep-water sailor just come from Hong Kong,
> If you give me some whiskey I'll sing you a song.
> As I was a-walking down Paradise Street,
> A pretty young damsel I chanced for to meet.

1. Which stresses in these lines are supported by normal pronunciation of individual words?
2. Do the stresses that are supported by pronunciation seem particularly important in any of these cases?

Consider the rhythms that appear in the following examples:

Farewell, farewell! but this I tell
To thee, thou Wedding-Guest!
He prayeth well, who loveth well
Both man and bird and beast.

He prayeth best, who loveth best 5
All things both great and small;
For the dear God who loveth us,
He made and loveth all.

• • •

Was this the face that launch'd a thousand ships,
And burnt the topless towers of Ilium?

• • •

If I could dwell
Where Israfel
  Hath dwelt, and he where I,
He might not sing so lordly well
  A mortal melody, 5
While a bolder note than this might swell
  From my lyre within the sky.

• • •

For thy sweet love remembered such wealth brings
That then I scorn to change my state with kings.

• • •

Ye marshes, how candid and simple and nothing-
  withholding and free
Ye publish yourselves to the sky and offer yourselves to the sea!

1. Does a pattern of rhythmical expectation develop in each of these examples? If so, what is the pattern?
2. Where a pattern does develop, are there deviations from it? Do the variations seem justified? What are some of the effects that the variations produce?

Read the following lines with special attention to the criterion of rhetorical importance. Except for the last line of the last quotation, the lines belong to patterns in which iambic pentameter is the normal expectation.

Put out the light, and then put out the light.
(Othello, as he prepares to kill Desdemona)

• • •

Know then thyself, presume not God to scan;
The proper study of Mankind is Man.

• • •

Roll on, thou deep and dark blue Ocean—roll!
Ten thousand fleets sweep over thee in vain.

• • •

Up rose the sun and up rose Emilyë.

• • •

Sleep after toil, port after stormy seas,
Ease after war, death after life does greatly please.
(Conrad chose these lines by Spenser for his epitaph.)

1. Scan these lines and underscore the variations from iambic pentameter.
2. In which instances are considerations of rhetorical importance the main basis for variations from the regular pattern?

There is one other element in rhythmic pattern which requires explanation—pauses, whether within or at the end of a line. If there is a marked pause at the end of a line of verse, the line is said to be *end-stopped;* if there is little or no pause at the end of a line of verse, the line is said to be a *run-on* line. A line that ends with a comma or a semicolon or a dash is usually an end-stopped line; a line that ends with a period is always an end-stopped line. The use of pauses is another means by which the poet may introduce an element of variety into his rhythmic pattern. If he wishes to secure an effect of regularity or to maintain the integrity of the line of verse as a line or to emphasize rhymes, he will use many end-stopped lines; if he wishes to blur or to obscure the effect of the line as a unit or to play down the rhymes, he will use run-on lines. In the poetry of Dryden and Pope, end-stopping is quite emphatically the norm; in Gray's "Elegy," which is classical in form and style but somewhat romantic in spirit, the end-stopping is fairly constant although it is not as marked as it is in the poetry of Pope. In Shakespeare's early plays, there is usually a great deal of end-stopping, as a passage from *A Midsummer Night's Dream* will show.

These are |the for|geries |of jeal|ousy:///
And nev|er, since| the mid|dle sum|mer's spring,/
Met we| on hill,| in dale,| forest| or mead,/
By pav|ed foun|tain or| by rush|y brook,/
Or in| the beach|ed mar|gent of |the sea,/
To dance| our ring|lets to| the whist|ling wind,/
But with| thy brawls| thou hast| disturb'd| our sport.///

In a play of Shakespeare's maturity, like *Macbeth,* the end-stopping gives way to a large number of run-on lines. In this instance, we may feel that the change exhibits both taste and skill, particularly if we consider that it allows for greater freedom and variety in the organization of dramatic speech. However, we might praise a poet for learning to reduce the number of run-on lines in his poetry, if the change reflected less verbal sprawl and greater precision in the use of language.

In addition to the pause at the end of a line, the poet may also introduce a pause somewhere within the line; such a pause is called a *caesura.* Normally such a pause is likely to occur near the middle of a four- or five-foot line, but in order to avoid monotony or to emphasize the word or phrase preceding or following the caesura, the poet may shift the caesura toward the beginning or the end of the line. Consider the emphasis Yeats gets on "The young," in the line we have scanned, by employing a heavy caesura late in the line.

That is no country for old men.///The young 0

The following system can be used to mark caesuras, run-on lines, and end-stopped lines:

run-on line	0
light caesura light end-stop	/
normal caesura normal end-stop	//
heavy caesura heavy end-stop	///

To illustrate the application of this system for the visual analysis of meter, we may utilize a familiar passage from Shakespeare's *Macbeth*. The meter here is unrhymed iambic pentameter; the verse is written to be spoken. We shall not then be surprised to see that Shakespeare has used or omitted a pause at the end of a line or within the line to give the verse a more colloquial movement than that of Gray's brooding meditative stanza. We shall not be surprised, further, to find that Shakespeare has introduced a rather large number of variations in feet; in other words, although the verse is basically iambic, the proportion of substitutions for normal feet is far higher than it is in Gray's stanza.

u — u u u — u u u — u
Tomor|row and| tomor|row and| tomorrow|//

— u u — u — u — u —
Creeps in| this pet|ty pace|/ from day| to day|//

u u — — u u u u — u —
To the last| sylla|ble of| record|ed time;|///

And all| our yes|terdays|// have light|ed fools|0
The way| to dust|y death.|/// Out,// out,|/ brief cand|le,//
Life's but| a walk|ing shad|ow;// a| poor play|er,//
That struts| and frets| his hour| upon| the stage,|/
And then| is heard| no more;|/// it is| a tale|0
Told by| an id|iot,// full| of sound| and fury,|//
Signi|fying| nothing.|///

Here we encounter another rhythmic element that was not apparent in the first stanza of Gray's "Elegy"—the occurrence of an extra syllable at the end of the first, fifth, sixth, and ninth lines. This unaccented extra-metrical syllable is called a feminine ending, and, in the division into feet, may often be accommodated as the last element of an amphibrach. A line which does not have this extra syllable is said to have a masculine ending. Here is another resource for the poet whose ear is rhythmically sensitive, another means by which he can achieve variety. The skill with which Shakespeare utilizes the feminine ending for these purposes has, indeed, been taken to mark the increasing maturity of his use of blank verse.

EXERCISE

Caesuras, end-stops, and run-ons are important in the following examples:

> The grave's a fine and private place,
> But none, I think, do there embrace.
>
> . . .
>
> At the round earth's imagined corners, blow
> Your trumpets, angels, and arise, arise

From death you numberless infinities
Of souls, and to your scattered bodies go.

• • •

Stop!—for thy tread is on an Empire's dust!

• • •

Earth has not anything to show more fair:
Dull would he be of soul who could pass by
A sight so touching in its majesty:
This City now doth like a garment, wear
The beauty of the morning; silent, bare, 5
Ships, towers, domes, theatres, and temples lie
Open unto the fields, and to the sky;
All bright and glittering in the smokeless air.

1. Which caesuras are strongest and most obvious in these passages? Describe the effect produced in two or three cases.
2. Which lines are most clearly and insistently run-on? What makes them so? How do the run-on lines relate to and affect the tone and import of what is being said?
3. Where are the heaviest end-stops? Do the heavy end-stops make any difference to the impact of the rhymes?

Before we conclude our discussion of meter, we must take into account two important types not yet considered. For the last century or more, poets have introduced more and more audacious variations into the metrical patterns of their verse. These experiments have taken two major directions, resulting in what we may call irregular meter and free verse.

In poems with irregular meter, the poet emphasizes variety rather than regularity by changing at will the length of successive lines and the number of lines in successive parts of the poem, and by using rhymes in such a way as not to create a regularly recurring sound-pattern. Of the poems included in this book, Wordsworth's "Ode: Intimations of Immortality" (p. 269), Coleridge's "Dejection" (p. 280), Arnold's "Dover Beach" (p. 244), Frost's "After Apple-Picking" (p. 175), H. D.'s "Phaedra" (p.

166), and Eliot's "Portrait of a Lady" (p. 168) belong to this class as a glance at their line-lengths and arrangements of rhymes will show.

The first three stanzas of Wordsworth's "Intimations" ode, for example, show the following order of feet per line and of rhymes: I, 542455326, ababacdds; II, 333443446, aabcbcdxd (in which *x*, "go," is paired with the internal rhyme "know"); III, 5335535555324 3472, abbccadaadeffeegeg. Despite these irregularities in the number of feet per line and the order of the rhymes, the stanzas have a satisfactory effect of recurrence and pattern because all the lines can be scanned without difficulty, certain line lengths are frequently repeated, and all the lines end in rhyme. But the number of variations the poet allows himself gives his poem a fluidity of form that Herrick does not permit himself in "Corinna's Going A-Maying" (p. 253). Similarly, lines 10–20 of Frost's "After Apple-Picking" (p. 175), have the following arrangement of feet per line and of rhymes: 55552525535, abacdddcefe. Lines 14–16, which show the widest variation in line length, are tied together by a recurrent rhyme, ddd. Furthermore, lines of five feet are so frequent and the rhymes are placed so close together that the effect of neither the meter nor the sound-pattern is obscured. Eliot's "Portrait of a Lady" (p. 168) is an even more audacious experiment with the potentialities of irregular meter. The first thirteen lines might be analyzed as follows:

Among| the smoke| and fog| of a |Decem|ber af|ternoon| 7x

You have| the scene| arrange| itself|—as it| will seem| to do—| 7a

With "I| have saved| this af|ternoon| for you";| 5a

And four| wax can|dles in| the dark|ened room,| 5b

Four rings| of light| upon| the ceil|ing o|verhead,| 6c

An at|mosphere| of Jul|iet's tomb| 4b

Prepared| for all| the things| to be said,| or left| unsaid.| 6c

We have| been, let| us say,| to hear| the la|test Pole| 6d

Transmit| the Pre|ludes, through| his hair| and fing|ertips.| 6e

"So in|timate,| this Cho|pin, that| I think| his soul| 6d

Should be re|surrect|ed on|ly a|mong friends| 5x

Some two| or three,| who will| not touch| the bloom| 5b

That is rubbed| and ques|tioned in| the con|cert room."| 5b

Here the groupings of lines of five and six feet supply the experience of expectation and fulfillment that is fundamental to a satisfactory metrical system, while the lines of four and seven feet enhance the sense of variation. The effect of regularity is heightened by the fact that nearly all the lines rhyme and that of the seventy-three feet in this passage, fifty-three are iambic.

Free verse departs even more widely from regularity of meter and ventures even more boldly than irregular meter in the direction of variety. Free verse is unrhymed, and, therefore, dispenses with the slight effect of cohesion given by the irregular rhyme schemes in the poems we have just analyzed. Two examples of free verse are Eliot's "Journey of the Magi" and Auden's "In Memory of W. B. Yeats" (Part I). If we analyze passages from these two poems, some of the possible metrical characteristics of free verse may become clear. The first ten lines of Eliot's "Journey of the Magi" might be scanned as follows:

'A cold| coming| we had| of it,| 4

Just the |worst time| of the year| 3

For a jour|ney, and such| a long| journey:| 4

The ways| deep and |the weath|er sharp,| 4

The ve|ry dead| of winter.'| 3

And the cam|els galled,| sore-foot|ed, refrac|tory,| 5

Lying| down in| the melt|ing snow.| 4

There were| times we| regretted| 3

The sum|mer pal|aces| on slopes,| the ter|races,| 6

And the silk|en girls| bringing| sherbet.| 4

Here, the predominance of lines of four feet establishes the normal rhythm of the passage, to which the occasional shorter or longer lines make an agreeable variation. An effect of regularity is further secured by the use of twenty iambic feet out of the forty feet in this passage; four lines, however, end on an unstressed syllable, and in three cases the stress in the terminal iambic foot is weak (these three might well be marked as pyrrhic feet). The age and weariness of the speaker and, in the last three lines, the remembered relaxations of sensory well-being are suitably expressed in this falling away of stress at the end of phrases and lines. The quantitative range (i.e., range in the number of syllables per line) is from seven to twelve syllables—"free" but not radically "free."

In the first eleven lines of Auden's "In Memory of W. B. Yeats" the quantitative range is considerably greater, from four to sixteen syllables per line, and the extremes of the range occur in successive lines (lines 9 and 10):

He dis|appeared| in the dead| of winter:|

The brooks| were froz|en, the air|ports almost| deserted,|

And snow| disfig|ured the pub|lic statues;|

The mer|cury sank| in the mouth| of the dy|ing day.|

O all| the in|struments| agree| 5

The day| of his death| was a dark| cold day.|

Far from| his illness|

The wolves| ran on| through the ev|ergreen for|ests,

The peas|ant riv|er was un|tempted by| the fashion|able quays;|

By mourn|ing tongues| 10

The death| of the po|et was kept| from his po|ems.

The division into feet, in a passage such as this, is aimed at showing up such regularities in stress pattern as may be present, especially when those regularities are easily translatable into normal types of feet. Of the forty-four feet marked above, eighteen are iambic and fifteen anapestic. It would be misleading to say that either the iambic or the anapestic rhythm is the norm of the passage; however, it would be still more misleading to say that the stress pattern is free in the sense of utterly random. On the contrary, and even allowing for variation in the division into feet at some points, there are notable regularities. There is unusual agreement, for example, in the stress patterns of lines 1–3; the patterns of line 1 and 3 are identical and line 2 follows the same pattern except for the addition of three terminal syllables. There is also, throughout the whole passage, an unusually persistent resort to iambic form at the beginning of the line (nine times in eleven); consequently, the trochaic beginning of "Far from his illness" (line 7) is firm and clear—enough pattern has been developed in the initial position for this functional variation to be effective. The spondee on "cold day" at the end of line 6 is similarly effective; this is the only line in the passage that ends in a spondee, and more than half the lines end on an unstressed syllable.

In concluding the discussion of meter, one all-important warning should be sounded. If you learn to apply sensitively the method of visual analysis outlined in this chapter, you will have learned to observe and to feel something of the subtlety with which a skillful poet uses rhythm and meter. If, however, you merely make a visual analysis of the meter, you will have failed, in a very fundamental respect, to understand the significance of rhythm. Rhythm and the possible variations upon it may, to be sure, be interesting and effective in and of themselves; they may have an intrinsic value. But in good poetry —as distinct perhaps from good or bad verse—rhythm is not merely an end in itself but a means to an end, and that end you must keep in mind constantly. That end is the utilization of the rhythm to heighten the effect of what the poet is trying to communicate. In other words, meter, like every other technical element of poetic style, must be seen functionally, that is, in relation to the total purpose of the poem. We are interested in describing rhythm as it *measures,* but we are also interested very much in the way rhythm emphasizes qualities and topics, the way it *supercharges* meanings. Every type of meter, like every type of musical rhythm, has its character, and, if there is a discrepancy between the character of the metrical pattern and the otherwise evident tone and meaning, then the rhythm will detract from rather than contribute to the total effect of the poem. When you have completed a visual analysis of the meter of a poem, you should rise above the details that you have brought into view and ask yourself questions such as: Is the basic rhythm of this poem appropriate to the subject matter of the poem? Are the local variations in rhythm intelligently related to meaning?

One of the most reliable bases for discriminating between good poetry and indifferent or bad verse is the writer's treatment of rhythm. Words strung together by unvaried and unsubtle rhythm, with no discernible functional justification for an obvious beat, do not deserve to be called poetry. The reader who has had relatively little experience with poetry may be persuaded by obvious and resounding rhythm that he is reading a poem and not just an effective piece of verse. But the ultimate test of poetry, as of all other excellent imaginative writing, is its ability to arouse in us a recurrent favorable interest, and an obvious rhythm is likely to strike harshly upon the ear if it is experienced over and over again. Mark Twain quotes a horrendous example of the torture that a maddeningly obvious rhythm can inflict.

> Punch, brother, punch with care
> Punch in the presence of the passenjare

The following famous lines by Byron are a somewhat more elevated illustration:

> The Assyrian came down like the wolf on the fold,
> And his cohorts were gleaming in purple and gold;
> And the sheen of their spears was like stars on the sea,
> When the blue wave rolls nightly on deep Galilee.

Justification of this rhythm as functional is fairly easy at some points in the passage but very difficult at others.

Perhaps the major function of the meter of a poem is to assist in establishing the dominant tone of a poem. Just as we are accustomed to think of certain musical rhythms as martial or languorous, solemn or lively, funereal or jocose, so the metrical rhythms of poetry tend to take on a fairly distinct character. It is the business of the poet to select a rhythm that is appropriate to the subject he is treating and one that is calculated to invest the subject with the tonal aura he wishes it to have.

Just as dactylic hexameter was the inevitable meter for epic narrative in Greek and Latin, so iambic pentameter has proved to be the most satisfactory rhythm for sustained narrative or dramatic poetry in English. Indeed, iambic rhythms are a normal expectation in English poetry in general, possibly because the linguistic character of the total English vocabulary makes it readily amenable to such rhythms. On the other hand, the very fact that, in English literature, so much has been expressed—and often so greatly expressed—in iambic rhythms establishes a convention or set of conventions with respect to what these rhythms can do, and though a poet will want to avoid mere imitation, he will also, in some ways and on some occasions, want his expression to be a continuation of that of his poetic predecessors. The choice of rhythm can be one mode for achieving such a continuity of expression.

EXERCISE

Here are some examples in which you can test your perception of various rhythms.

The splendor falls on castle walls
  And snowy summits old in story:
The long light shakes across the lakes,
  And the wild cataract leaps in glory.

• • •

Piping down the valleys wild,
Piping songs of pleasant glee,
On a cloud I saw a child,
And he laughing said to me:

"Pipe a song about a Lamb!" 5
So I piped with merry cheer.
"Piper, pipe that song again";
So I piped: he wept to hear.

• • •

Dr. Foster went to Gloucester
In a shower of rain;
He stepped in a puddle
Up to his middle
And never went there again.

• • •

From too much love of living,
  From hope and fear set free,
We thank with brief thanksgiving
  Whatever gods may be
That no life lives for ever; 5
That dead men rise up never;
That even the weariest river
  Winds somewhere safe to sea.

1. Compare the rhythms employed in two or three of these examples.
2. In which of these examples do you regard the rhythms as most appropriate to the indicated tone and content? Why? Least appropriate? Why?

Sound-Pattern in Poetry

Just as a word of more than one syllable has rhythm or as a word of any length may constitute an element in a pattern of rhythm, so a spoken word has, as one of its essential aspects, sound. Accordingly, a line of poetry or a complete poem may be regarded not only as a simple or complicated pattern of rhythm but also as a simple or complicated pattern of sounds. From one point of view, the printed word or the printed poem is nothing but a series of conventional symbols intended to suggest to the initiated reader a series of sounds. It is only because we live in a period of civilization when thousands of words reach us daily in the form of printed symbols that we are inclined to overlook the more primitive experience of the word as a conventional combination of sounds.

The element of sound-pattern in poetry is of inestimable importance, because it is one of the most reliable means—perhaps only slightly less reliable than the element of rhythm—by which the poet casts his spell over us and persuades us to attend to a subject that seems important to him and to feel toward it as he wishes us to feel. The writers of advertising copy are very much aware that sound-patterns can be manipulated to affect attitudes and that the effects are perhaps all the more potent because some of the means by which they are produced are subtle and often go unrecognized.

Sounds and sound-patterns, apart from such volume and pitch of sound as may be physically painful or damaging to the eardrum, are probably not inherently agreeable or disagreeable. They become pleasant or unpleasant by association with meaning. A French woman is said to have maintained that the most beautiful English word she knew was cellar-door; her choice could scarcely have been dictated by the English meaning of the word, but it might well have been considerably determined by the not very different sound of the French *je t'adore,* well known as music to a woman's ears, yet scarcely music divorced from meaning.

The sounds we can make are, of course, quite various, and the major types are produced in physically different ways by the speech apparatus of vocal cords, throat, mouth, lips, tongue, and teeth. Some sounds are physically more difficult to produce than others, but the physical ease or difficulty entailed in producing a given sound is not necessarily an index to the sound's pleasant or unpleasant quality. Browning's famous line

Irks care the crop-full bird? Frets doubt the maw-crammed beast?

is unpleasant enough, but the means by which the unpleasant effect is produced are complex. The words are hammered out with great stress in a scarcely relieved rhythm.

— — u — — — — — u — —

Irks care| the crop|-full bird?| Frets doubt| the maw-|crammed

—

beast?|

An unusual grammatical arrangement, in which questions are not signalized in the usual way, forces the reader to dwell on the opening verbs ("Frets itch the nice baby?" would reproduce much of the same awkwardness but with a quite different sound-pattern). These features together with the meanings of "irks" and "frets" and "maw-crammed" rather than inherent unpleasantness of sound account for the generally unpleasant effect.

It has been traditional to suppose that some words imitate directly the sound associated with the thing or quality or action designated; the phenomenon is called *onomatopoeia.* So, for example, bees buzz, dogs bow-wow and cats meow. These words, however, are attached by strong and early conditioning to the act of imitating particular sounds; how direct any such imitation is may be considered with some skepticism if we note that in

French dogs bark *biff-biff* and in Japanese *yan-yan,* and even within English there is the usual range from bow-wow to woof-woof to arf-arf. It is to be conceded, of course, that there are widely different dogs and that every dog, whether or not he has his day, does have his bark, but it seems likely that the supposedly directly imitative, onomatopoetic words are actually well-established, strongly conditioned signals standing for particular meanings plus sounds but not really very close in their imitation. In any case, the number of such words is decidedly limited, and they play an inconsiderable part in the sound-pattern of poetry.

What sound devices do poets employ then? What effects can be achieved by way of sounds and by what means? Probably the most basic device in the sound-pattern of poetry is repetition, and a little observation will convince the reader that this device, though elementary, is used frequently in all poetry from the most primitive to the most sophisticated. Consider the following series of examples.

> *Lully, lulley! lully, lulley!*
> *The faucon hath borne my make away!*
> He bare him up, he bare him down,
> He bare him into an orchard brown.
>
> faucon: falcon
> make: mate

In this medieval lyric, the italicized lines are a refrain, repeated in its entirety after the couplets making up the body of the poem, and, as is apparent in this example, there is a good deal of repetition in the body of the poem.

In the following passages we have italicized the repetitions or very near repetitions.

From THE LIE
Sir Walter Ralegh

> *Tell* fortune *of* her blindness;
> *Tell* nature *of* decay;

Tell friendship *of* unkindness;
Tell justice *of* delay:
And if they will reply, 5
Then give them all the lie.

From THE GOOD MORROW
John Donne

Whatever *dies* was not mix'd equally;
If our two *loves* be one, or thou and I
Love so alike that *none can* slacken, *none can die.*

From SAILING TO BYZANTIUM
William Butler Yeats

Once out *of* nature I shall never take
My bodily *form* from any natural thing,
But such a *form* as Grecian *gold*smiths make
Of hammered *gold* and *gold* enamelling
To keep a drowsy Emperor awake; 5
Or set upon a *gold*en bough to sing
To lords and ladies *of* Byzantium
Of what is past, *or* passing, *or* to come.

From the lullaby, the nursery rhyme, and the sophisticated ballad through staccato imperatives such as those of Ralegh, the carefully stressed distinctions and consequences of Donne, to the gold that Yeats hammers into his symbolic Byzantium, repetition is a fundamental device, capable of an astonishing variety of effects. It is the kind of device that a child can recognize yet one that will often tax the resources of the mature critic and cause him to despair of giving an adequate account of the effects produced. It is a device that the attentive student will not neglect to notice because it is often a very helpful cue to basic themes and motifs of a poem.

EXERCISE

There lived a wife at Usher's Well,
  And a wealthy wife was she;
She had three stout and stalwart sons,
  And sent them o'er the sea.

They hadna been a week from her, 5
A week but barely ane,
Whan word came to the carline wife
  That her three sons were gane.

They hadna been a week from her,
  A week but barely three, 10
Whan word came to the carline wife
  That her sons she'd never see.

carline: old woman

1. This example involves the characteristic ballad device of *incremental repetition,* i.e., repetition with addition of a new element. What motifs do the repetitions themselves emphasize? What role do these repetitions play in the over-all sound-pattern?
2. What additions to the story are pointed up by being attached to repetitions?

LULLABY

Beloved, may your sleep be sound
That have found it where you fed.
What were all the world's alarms
To mighty Paris when he found
Sleep upon a golden bed 5
That first dawn in Helen's arms?

Sleep, beloved, such a sleep
As did that wild Tristram know
When, the potion's work being done,
Roe could run or doe could leap 10

Under oak and beechen bough,
Roe could leap or doe could run;

Such a sleep and sound as fell
Upon Eurotas' grassy bank
When the holy bird, that there 15
Accomplished his predestined will,
From the limbs of Leda sank
But not from her protecting care.

Look up relevant information about Paris, Tristram, Eurotas, and Leda.

1. Circle the repetitions in these stanzas. Which of the poem's themes are emphasized by repetition?
2. Does repetition have a special function in a lullaby? Is such a function actually relevant here?
3. Do the sounds emphasized in the repeated words appear elsewhere in the poem?

The second most obvious element in sound-pattern is rhyme; indeed, some readers might feel that the kind of sound-pattern we know as rhyme is the most obvious pattern the poet uses. Rhyme in its normal form involves both identity of sound and difference of sound; the difference in sound is at the front of the rhyme pair and the identity at the back. The sound repeated may be a vowel sound (be/me, bay/may) or it may be a vowel sound plus a terminal consonantal sound or sounds (bear/hair or breaths/deaths).[1] These are called true or exact rhymes. When the vowel sounds are close but not identical, and especially when they are surrounded by strengthened consonant similarity, the rhyme is called a slant rhyme or off-rhyme. Some examples of slant rhyme are: love/move, boat/bait, light/late. It is worth remarking that rhyme is one of several poetic devices we shall encounter involving the principle of a combination of

[1] When the final syllable of the rhymed words bears a stress, the rhyme is called a masculine rhyme. When the rhyming syllables are followed by identical unstressed endings, the rhyme is called a feminine rhyme (smarting/darting). If the rhyme words are identical in sound but divergent in meaning (bear/bare), the rhyme is called a rich rhyme.

likeness and unlikeness. This principle extends to the nature of rhyme pairs in which the words related by rhyme may be notably like or unlike each other in meaning. Consider, for example, the nature of the meanings related in the following rhymes:

> If Time improve our Wit as well as Wine,
> Say at what age a Poet grows divine?
>
> Great Friend of LIBERTY! in *Kings* a Name
> Above all Greek, above all Roman Fame.
>
> This told, I joy, but then no longer glad,
> I send them back again, and straight grow sad.
>
> If this be error and upon me proved,
> I never writ, nor no man ever loved.
>
> And when she sees her Friend in deep despair,
> Observes how much a Chintz exceeds Mohair.

Although rhyme, like rhythm, may be interesting in itself, it may also be of use in relation to the line or the stanza. As we shall see, the auditory element in the rhyme word is usually repeated not only in another rhyme word but in the sound-pattern of the passage in which it occurs. Moreover, the pattern made by the rhyme words or the order in which the rhymes are repeated is one of the means by which the poet may give his poem the formal element that we know as the stanza. The other element that in regular verse contributes to the formation of a stanza is, of course, the meter.

EXERCISE

Consider the rhymes in the following examples.

> 'Tis with our judgments as our watches, none
> Go just alike yet each believes his own.

• • •

O wild West Wind, thou breath of Autumn's being,
Thou, from whose unseen presence the leaves dead
Are driven, like ghosts from an enchanter fleeing.

• • •

Let not a pyramid give you or me hopes,
Since not a pinch of dust remains of Cheops.

• • •

St. Agnes' Eve—Ah, bitter chill it was!
The owl, for all his feathers, was a-cold;
The hare limp'd trembling through the frozen grass,
And silent was the flock in woolly fold.

• • •

Farewell, farewell! but this I tell . . .

1. Which rhymes in the examples above are true or exact? Which are slant or off-rhyme?
2. Which of the rhymes are masculine? Which are feminine?
3. Are there any internal rhymes? Any rich rhymes?

Alliteration is usually defined as the repetition of initial consonantal sounds; the word sounds should be emphasized because we are not talking about how words are spelled but how they are pronounced: *city* and *court* do not alliterate, but *court* and *country* do; *city* and *silent* are an alliterative pair as are *court* and *king* or *king* and *queen*. Alliterative linkages serve basically to call attention to the items linked. The items linked may be variously related in meaning, but it is useful to recognize that the relationship is often either *conjunctive* (one term goes with and reenforces or adds to the meaning of the other) or *disjunctive* (one term opposes, undercuts, or ironically reduces the other). Thus we have once again the combination of likeness and unlikeness, and the terms disjunctive and conjunctive can usefully be applied to the description of meaning-relations in rhyme pairs. Alliterations of these two basic types (as well as others not clearly belonging to either category, neither obviously like nor obviously unlike) are frequent in the fabric of our language.

"Are we *mice* or *men?*" is a good example of disjunctive alliteration. "Where there's a *man* there's a *Marlboro*" is a good example of alliteration that the cigarette manufacturer hopes will work conjunctively. That the conjunction may indeed be effective and influential is demonstrated by current efforts legally to curb advertisements carrying the kind of implication with respect to cigarettes presented in this alliterative linkage.

Along with alliteration we should also consider the broader picture of consonant similarity in medial and final positions. Consider the alliteration in the seductive sound-pattern of Keats' line in "The Eve of St. Agnes."

> And still she slept an azure-lidded sleep,

We can point to the recurrent initial *s* sound in still, slept, and sleep. Extending our consideration to consonance at other positions within or at the end of words, we would notice that the repetitions of *l* and *p* in this group of words is of the greatest importance in the sound-pattern of the line. Effects produced by repetition of the same (or related) medial or final sounds as well as initial consonant sounds should not be overlooked.[2] The phrase "or related" is needed because not a little of the subtle beauty of this line arises not merely from the repetition of the identical *s* sound but also from the use of the closely related sounds *sh* and *z* and of the related sounds *d, t,* and *p.*[3]

EXERCISE

> The groves of Eden, vanished now so long,
> Live in description and look green in song.

• • •

2 Slant rhyme already described (p. 47), is a special form of consonance; slant rhyme is consonance occurring between words located in the rhyme position. Modern poets have made a great deal of use of slant rhyme.

3 The basis of the relationship of sounds is physiological, that is, sounds produced in the same or almost the same portion of the mouth and throat are considered related. Related sounds, by reason of their common physiological origin, have a similar character, as suggested by the names of certain sounds such as labials, dentals, and fricatives.

The good grey guardians of art
Patrol the halls on spongy shoes,
Impartially protective, though
Perhaps suspicious of Toulouse.

Toulouse: Toulouse-Lautrec

• • •

Hasten, while they are true,—sleep, death, desire,
Close round one instant in one floating flower.

1. Mark the instances of alliteration in the above examples. Are there any notable instances of conjunctive alliteration? Any cases of disjunctive alliteration?
2. In which of the above examples do consonants in medial or final positions extend and support alliterated consonants?

One other major element in sound-pattern remains to be considered, namely, assonance. Assonance is commonly defined as the recurrence of identical or related vowels. Here again, the basis of the relationship is physiological. Vowels that are produced in the same or about the same part of the mouth or throat are felt to be related; such sounds are the sound of *a* in *mate* and the sound of *e* in *feet,* on the one hand, and the sounds of *a* in *bar* and of *o* in *note.* These vowels, it should be observed, are the traditional long vowels. Short vowels fall into similarly closely related groups; on the one hand, the *e* in *met* and the *i* in *hit,* and on the other hand, the *a* in *at,* the *o* in *hot,* and the *u* in *but.*

Let us look now at the assonance in Keats' line

And still she slept an azure-lidded sleep.

We are struck at once by the repetition of the short *i* sound in still and lidded, and the short *a* sound in and, an, and azure. We should also note the repetition of the long *e* sound in she and sleep. The vowel *u* is the only one that does not enter into the amazing sound-pattern of this line. If we combine the results of our analysis of the alliteration and assonance in this line and consider the propriety of it to the effect of softness and delicacy that Keats wanted to produce, we shall come close to establishing one of the major sources of its beauty.

EXERCISE

From THE RAPE OF THE LOCK
Alexander Pope

Whatever spirit, careless of his charge,
His post neglects, or leaves the fair at large,
Shall feel sharp vengeance soon o'ertake his sins,
Be stopped in vials, or transfixed with pins;
Or plunged in lakes of bitter washes lie, 5
Or wedged whole ages in a bodkin's eye:
Gums and pomatums shall his flight restrain,
While clogged he beats his silken wings in vain;
Or alum styptics with contracting power
Shrink his thin essence like a rivelled flower. 10

washes: liquid cosmetics
bodkin: needle
pomatums: perfumed hair-dressing
alum styptics: astringents causing contraction of tissues and small blood vessels

The speaker in this passage is Ariel, a mythical guardian spirit. He is exhorting his fellow spirits to watch carefully over their charge, a beautiful young woman.

1. Read the passage aloud, emphasizing the vowel sounds.
2. Underscore the frequently repeated vowel sounds.
3. To what extent is a particular vowel sound repeated here in association with a single basic theme?

Let us look now at the features of sound-pattern we have discussed as they occur in the stanza from Gray's "Elegy," the meter of which we have already analyzed.

> The Curfew tolls the knell of parting day,
> The lowing herd wind slowly o'er the lea;
> The plowman homeward plods his weary way,
> And leaves the world to darkness and to me.

We note the occurrence of alliteration in day and darkness; lowing, lea, and leaves; wind, weary, way, and world; and parting, plowman, and plods. Extending our consideration to medial and final consonance, we see the intricacy of the sound-pattern in this stanza. Thus, we see the *l*-sound running through the stanza in tolls, knell, lowing, slowly, lea, plowman, plods, and leaves. This is perhaps the most significant consonant pattern in the whole stanza. Noteworthy also is the recurrence of *d* in day, herd, wind, homeward, plods, world, and darkness.

The most striking examples of assonance in this stanza are the recurrence of the vowel sounds in the masculine rhymes day/way and lea/me. These sounds are not repeated, however, within the stanza unless we wish to relate the *ea* in lea and leaves to the sound *ea* in weary. But apart from the vowel sounds in the rhyme words, there is a significant instance of assonance within the stanza, the repetition of the sound of *o* in tolls, lowing, slowly, and homeward.

Perhaps you wonder whether the complex sound-patterns that can be discovered in good and bad poetry alike are introduced by the poet deliberately. In the light of what we know of the ways in which a poet works, the answer to this question must be that most trying of all answers, "Yes and no." One of the gifts of the good poet is a good ear, that is, an ear that selects either consciously or unconsciously a sound-pattern that furthers his effect. In any case, the deliberateness of the poet's intention is irrelevant. The sound-pattern, once seen and felt, is forevermore a part of your experience of the poem.

As with metrics, there must be a functional relationship between the sound-pattern and the total effect of the poem. Is the sound-pattern appropriate to the total experience the poem is creating? Does it contribute to the mood and tone of the poem or does it tend to destroy it? Is the sound-pattern so obtrusive or so persistent or so engrossing that it tends to attract too much attention to itself and interfere with the meaning of the whole poem? The sound-pattern should be used to emphasize a meaning or to relate meanings.

In a poet as sensitive to sound as Swinburne, the sound-pattern tended to become an end in itself and not a means to an end, and some of his later poems are hardly more than coruscations of sounds with less than a modicum of meaning. In the following stanza, for example, there is a serious disproportion between substance and form:

What light, what shadow, diviner than dawn or night,
Draws near, makes pause, and again—or I dream—draws near?
More soft than shadows, more strong than the strong sun's light,
More pure than moonbeams—yea, but the rays run sheer
As far from the sun through the dusk of the pinewood, clear 5
And constant; yea, but the shadow itself is bright
That the light clothes round with love that is one with fear.

The observation we made earlier of the relationship between obvious metrics and inferior poetic quality can be extended to include sound-pattern. You should be on guard against a "poem" whose sound-pattern is painfully obvious.

Diction in Poetry: Image and Abstraction

We have now discussed two of the major elements of style in poetry: meter and sound-pattern. The third element to be considered is diction. Diction normally relates to the choice of words and the further choice of ways of arranging them. A great deal of critical analysis of poetry has been focused on recognizing whether the words chosen by a poet are concrete and specific in their reference or abstract and general. Words of the former sort are referred to as images or image-bearing words (collectively, we speak of a poet's imagery[1]). When a critic comments on the vividness of a writer's diction, he is frequently talking loosely about imagery without, perhaps, being quite clear as to why some words are vivid and some are not. Imagery is the result of the evocation, with varying degrees of clarity, of mental reproductions, representations, or imitations of sense perceptions. If, for instance, you speak or read the word orange and dwell on it, you will experience almost immediately not a sense perception of a certain color but a more or less vivid imitation or representation of that color. If you persist in dwelling on the word, you will probably get other images, of smell or taste or shape or even touch. Of course, you may get the image of taste or smell before you get the image of color.

There are, then, as many kinds of images as there as senses: images of sight, smell, taste, touch, and sound. In addition to

[1] In much contemporary criticism, "imagery" means not only concrete language but figurative language in general and sometimes a hash and ragout of other things besides. For analytic purposes, it is useful to carry out a separate consideration of the figurative character of language (see pp. 65–82).

these five senses, psychologists have demonstrated a sixth sense which they have somewhat awkwardly named kinesthetic, a term which they apply to the sensation of tension or relaxation. Such images—of greatest importance in the contribution of imagery to poetic style—are evoked by words like dive, sprawl, stretch, yawn, or tumble. More broadly, a kinesthetic image may be that of any sensation arising from the tensed or relaxed muscles, joints, and tendons of the body or from related disturbances in the sense of balance. Kinesthetic images are most commonly carried by verbs.

If we analyze sight images closely, we can distinguish a number of kinds: color, size, shape, position, and movement. These sight images may be illustrated, respectively, by such words as blue, mountain, cat, near, and dive. The last illustration also makes it clear that certain words may evoke not merely different kinds of sight images but also distinct kinds of images. From the word dive, for example, certain readers will get a visual image, others a kinesthetic image. Most readers will probably get a complex image of sight, more specifically of movement, and of muscular tension. It is convenient also to assign sensations of temperature, complex as they are and variously conveyed, to the separate category of thermal sensation.

Psychologists have made some use of a classification of persons as predominantly visual-minded or predominantly auditory-minded. If they had been interested in pushing their observations further, it is possible that they would have discovered that there are not only these two types of image-making persons but also persons who find it easier to evoke one of the other four basic types of images. It would be interesting, for instance, to try to ascertain whether athletes evoke muscular images more easily than nonathletic persons. Almost certainly, musicians are more likely to be able to evoke auditory images with ease than persons who "have no ear."

In the analysis of imagery, there is one easy error that you must train yourself to avoid—namely, the confusion of the images *evoked* by a word with the images *involved in the associations aroused* by a word. The concept of association is, of course, another term the psychologists have made available to students of literature. Association is the ability to bring up from experience and memory circumstances that are relevant (or apparently irrelevant) to some word that refers to a person, place, object, or experience. "Free association" means, as the phrase suggests, the unrestrained evocation of relevant or irrelevant remembered circumstances. With a little practice, you can learn to activate sometimes very startling series of associations to any series of words that you may select or that may be selected for you.

This consideration of free association may help us to see why care is necessary to distinguish between the images immediately evoked by a word and the images involved in associations. The poet, in his use of image-making words, assumes, and is safe in assuming, that most of his audience have a normal capacity for experiencing sense perceptions and, similarly, have a normal, though admittedly differentiated, capacity for evoking images of sense perceptions. If he uses such words as scarlet, bloom, tight, heliotrope, velvet, gouge (with the additional definition provided by a specific context), he is safe in assuming that readers who know the language and who have normal sensory equipment will evoke similar, though of course not identical, images. However, the poet, can utilize the associations of his readers only to a certain point; in the first place, he does not know what these associations are and, in the second place, even if he does know something of the probable associations of a limited audience, he cannot depend on the associations that his poem will evoke in a larger audience.

The good reader, then, will develop, among other powers, skill in distinguishing between the images evoked by the words in a poem and the images involved in the personal associations those words have for him. To give excessive weight to one's private associations with the poet's words detracts from the poem's character as a public event and a form of communication that can be discussed with the likelihood of substantial areas of agreement.

Another error in the analysis of imagery is the failure to distinguish between the image suggested by a word when it stands alone and the image suggested by the word in a particular context. For instance, the image aroused by the word red, when it is alone, will not be the same as those which are aroused when it is associated with other words such as apple, sunset, beets, or barn. Even more clearly, the word frosted arouses a distinctly different set of images when it is associated with cake and when it is associated with breath. Obviously, in the analysis of imagery in either poetry or prose, we are concerned primarily with the images that arise from a word in a particular context.

These theoretical considerations may be clarified by an analysis of the imagery in the opening stanza of Keats' "The Eve of St. Agnes." Concrete words, words that are image-bearing, are italicized. These words are classified according to categories of imagery in the list following the stanza.

St. Agnes' Eve—Ah, *bitter chill* it was!
The *owl,* for all his *feathers,* was *a-cold;*
The *hare limp'd trembling through* the *frozen grass,*
And *silent* was the *flock in woolly fold:*
Numb were the *Beadsman's fingers,* while he *told* 5
His *rosary,* and while his *frosted breath,*
Like pious *incense from* a *censer* old
Seem'd *taking flight* for heaven, without a death,
Past the sweet *Virgin's picture,* while his *prayer* he *saith.*

1a Sight-color
owl, feathers, hare, grass, woolly, fingers, frosted breath

1b Sight-size
owl, feathers, hare, grass, flock, fold, beadsman's, fingers, rosary, censer, Virgin's picture

1c Sight-shape
owl, feathers, hare, grass, flock, fold, beadsman's, fingers, rosary, censer, Virgin's picture

1d Sight-position
through (line 3), in (line 4), from (line 7)

1e Sight-movement (or expressed lack of movement)

limp'd, trembling, told his rosary, taking flight, past the picture

2 Sound (or expressed absence of sound)
silent, told his rosary, prayer he saith

3 Touch
woolly, numb

4 Kinesthetic sensation of tension or relaxation
limp'd, trembling, numb

5 Smell
incense

6 Taste
———

7 Thermal
bitter chill, a-cold, frozen, numb, frosted

The predominance of sight imagery is readily apparent. The sense of sight is so basic and complex, so various in its recognitions, that it is quite usual for sight imagery to constitute half or more than half of all the imagery in a poem with the remaining imagery divided among all the other senses. Keats' stanza is one of the most brilliant communications of the sense of cold that English poetry affords, especially because of the variety of means by which the sensation is conveyed ranging from the direct and rather generalized suggestion of temperature in "bitter chill" through the gingerly movement of the hare over the harsh and frosted grass and on to the numbness of the beadsman's fingers and his visible breath. Then there is the owl, whose coldness is sharpened by the contrast of feathers, and the lambs huddled silent in their woolly coats also enhance by contrast the suggested coldness. It is surprising that so much of the communication of cold begins in sight images, but we can also recognize that kinesthetic effects are partly blended with sight-movement words and with words that are directly thermal. Unquestionably the most vivid images in this stanza are those tactile and kinesthetic images which build up the dominant impression of piercing cold. By comparison, the sound images, "silent," "told," "rosary," "prayer," "saith," the olfactory image, "incense," and the visual images are rather dim. It will also be observed that, just as sounds may be used for either pleasant or unpleasant effects, so images may be used. Here, in the main, the images are—as Keats intended them to be—unpleasant.

This stanza is a good example of poetry heavily dependent upon concrete, image-bearing words, but one should not conclude that the mere presence of a great deal of imagery is a reliable index of good poetry. Some fine poems are highly charged with imagery; some fine poems have relatively little imagery. When we pick out and classify the images in a poem we are performing a *descriptive* operation, not an operation that is in itself *evaluative*.

Suppose we consider some of the instances in which words that are not concrete, not image-bearing, have a significant part to play. In the stanza we have just inspected, "pious incense" is a good example of the sharp juxtaposition of an abstract with a concrete word, a juxtaposition in which both words may actually gain in vividness. There are times when vividness of diction comes about as the result of the fusion or the clash of abstract and concrete words. One of Shakespeare's habits of style is the arrangement that critics call the doublet. Hamlet, for example, is described as

> the expectancy and *rose* of the fair state.

Hamlet charges his mother with

> Such an act
> That blurs the grace and *blush* of modesty.

The italicized image-bearing word in each case seems to take on increased vividness as a result of the abstract word with which it is yoked in the doublet as well as by contrast with other abstract words close at hand. In some cases the yoking of abstract and concrete words in the doublet reflects the Latin and Germanic components of our language. Whatever the etymology of the terms juxtaposed, however, it is often true that the rose is redder and the blush deeper as the result of the abstraction with which it is paired.

EXERCISE

IN A STATION OF THE METRO
Ezra Pound

The apparition of these faces in the crowd;
Petals on a wet, black bough.

ON THE GRASSHOPPER AND CRICKET
John Keats

The poetry of earth is never dead:
When all the birds are faint with the hot sun,
And hide in cooling trees, a voice will run
From hedge to hedge about the new-mown mead;
That is the grasshopper's—he takes the lead 5
In the summer luxury,—he has never done
With his delights; for when tired out with fun
He rests at ease beneath some pleasant weed.
The poetry of earth is ceasing never:
On a lone winter evening, when the frost 10
Has wrought a silence, from the stove there shrills
The cricket's song, in warmth increasing ever,
And seems to one in drowsiness half lost,
The grasshopper's among some grassy hills.

1. Identify and classify the images in these two poems.
2. What role do non-image-bearing words play in these two poems?

EPITAPH ON AN ARMY OF MERCENARIES
A. E. Housman

These, in the day when heaven was falling,
The hour when earth's foundations fled,

Followed their mercenary calling
And took their wages and are dead.

Their shoulders held the sky suspended; 5
They stood, and earth's foundations stay;
What God abandoned, these defended,
And saved the sum of things for pay.

1. To what extent does this poem rely on image-bearing words for its effects?
2. What features of this poem's diction contribute significantly to its effectiveness?

A poet like Donne works a great deal with a technical, scientific, philosophical vocabulary the terms of which are generally nonsensory, abstract, not image-bearing. As a consequence, Donne's images when they do come often strike with astonishing force. Ordinary images can, by such manipulation, become highly effective, and images which are vivid in their own right may, by such stylistic maneuvering, become overwhelmingly powerful. Consider the following examples.

Pleasure or business, our souls admit
For their first mover, and are *whirled* by it.

Wilt Thou forgive that sin which I did shun
A year or two, but *wallowed* in a score?

Our two souls, therefore, which are one,
Though I must go, endure not yet
A breach, but an expansion,
Like *gold* to *airy thinness beat*.

Imagery is perhaps the most reliable technical means by which the poet may give you the experience which his poem aims to create. The experience of imagery is not that of a vague feeling or emotion; it is almost physiological. Through the power of the poet's words, the symbols with which the literary artist works, the poem becomes an experience enmeshed in our sense organs and in those deeper sensations that are muscular and even visceral. Nonsensory language—language that is intellectual and abstract—has great powers too, and when wielded together with imagery may serve to keep us aware of the complexity of human nature and the various dimensions of man. When Donne says that his spirit will never be chaste unless ravished by God, he is trading profitably with two worlds—the world of intense physical sensation and the world of sophisticated theological thought.

Imagery is one of the technical means by which the poet gives his subject the tone he wishes the reader to associate with it and eliminates tones that do not suggest his own feeling for the subject. Broadly speaking, images, taken by themselves, give the reader either a pleasant or an unpleasant feeling, and by the accumulation of normally pleasant or unpleasant images the poet can build up an aura that determines the reader's feeling about the subject of the poem. Naïve or sentimental readers are inclined to think that poetry should confine itself to the accumulation of pleasant images, and if you consider the "lyric" of almost any popular song in the romantic vein, you will discover that it is constructed out of the pleasant but vapid verbal debris of romantic poetry. Thus, the lyric of the well-known "Moonlight and Roses," if separated from the elementary melody, is seen to be unbearably banal.

Moonlight and roses
Bring wonderful mem'ries of you
My heart reposes
In beautiful thoughts so true
June light discloses
Love's olden dreams sparkling a-new
Moonlight and roses
Bring mem'ries of you.

Readers of such a "lyric" will find it difficult to understand why any poet should ever write such a line as Shakespeare's

Than unswept stone besmeared with sluttish time

where "unswept," "sluttish," and, especially, "besmeared" all evoke powerfully unpleasant images. Similarly, when Shakespeare wants to contrast the real beauty of his dark mistress with the unreal beauty of the blonde mistresses of other poets, he piles up decidedly unpleasant images with a perhaps excessive boldness.

> My mistress' eyes are nothing like the sun;
> Coral is far more red than her lips' red;
> If snow be white, why then her breasts are dun;
> If hairs be wires, black wires grow on her head.

But you will find that the serious poet expresses unpleasant feelings as well as pleasant, and, if necessary, uses deliberately unpleasant images to create the tone that expresses his attitude most vividly.

Figures and Symbols in Poetry

Recognition that the words a poet employs are, in varying proportions and arrangements, concrete and abstract, image-bearing and non-image-bearing, is an important step in the description and analysis of a poem. Another important step is recognition of instances in which the arrangement of these words or their logical implication constitutes a "figure of speech" and of instances in which their character or patterning is such as to constitute a symbol.

For purposes of analyzing the figurative aspects of a poem's language, it will be useful to be able to recognize two major types of figures, the simile and the metaphor, and two special forms in which the major types often occur, personification (including animation) and metonymy.

A simile is an expressed comparison between two entities belonging to different classes of entities.

> Blue were her eyes as the fairy-flax,

> Like as the waves make toward the pebbled shore,
> So do our minutes hasten to their end;

> Haply I think on thee,—and then my state
> Like to the lark at break of day arising
> From sullen earth, sings hymns at heaven's gate.

In a simile, the two things compared are linked grammatically by the conjunction *as* or *like* or sometimes *than*.[1]

[1] These conjunctions, to be sure, do not always introduce similes; the student must decide whether or not the conjunction introduces a comparison between one entity and another entity of a *different* order. Thus, "He is as tall as I" is not a simile.

It is the business of the poet to suggest rather than to state the aspects of the two things compared which are relevant and appropriate to the comparison. Thus, in the lines Robert Burns adapted from an old folk song,

> O, my Luve's like a red, red rose,
> That's newly sprung in June:
> O, my Luve's like a melodie
> That's sweetly play'd in tune.

he does not want us to think of the thorniness of the rose but of its freshness and its beauty of color; he does not want us to think of the melody of a rollicking drinking song but of a melody that is sweetly played and which, therefore, will suggest the delightful harmoniousness of the personality of his beloved. One of the most famous similes in twentieth-century poetry is T. S. Eliot's

> When the evening is spread out against the sky
> Like a patient etherized upon a table.

The first line alone does no more than hint that the evening is a distinctly unattractive one. Even the effect of the word "patient" might have been softened by some such phrase as "lying snugly in the sun." But instead of characterizing the evening directly as horridly pale and grim, the poet leads the reader from "spread" to "patient" and then to the particular state in which this unhappy patient finds himself.

EXERCISE

SONNET 73
William Shakespeare

That time of year thou mayst in me behold
When yellow leaves, or none, or few, do hang
Upon those boughs which shake against the cold,

Bare ruined choirs where late the sweet birds sang.
In me thou see'st the twilight of such day 5
As after sunset fadeth in the west,
Which by and by black night doth take away,
Death's second self, that seals up all in rest.
In me thou see'st the glowing of such fire,
That on the ashes of his youth doth lie 10
As the deathbed whereon it must expire,
Consumed with that which it was nourished by.
This thou perceiv'st, which makes thy love more strong,
To love that well which thou must leave ere long.

1. Identify the similes in this poem. (Remember that to qualify as a simile the comparison must be between entities of *different* orders.)
2. Identify the metaphors in the poem.
3. Re-read and reconsider this poem after you have read the discussion of symbolism in the latter part of this chapter.

The simile then is one means by which the poet can suggest the feelings and the associations which he wishes his reader to have. It invests the subject with a rich suggestiveness which is completely lacking in direct prose statements such as "The girl I love is very beautiful" or "The appearance of the evening sky was peculiarly unpleasant." The simile then is not merely a stylistic ornament; it is one of the most reliable means to the poet's goal, namely, the communication to the reader of the totality of the experience embodied in the poem.

It is customary to make a distinction between the simple or undeveloped simile and the extended or developed simile (also called the Homeric simile). The Homeric simile often becomes a matter of interest in itself and may be like a short poem embedded in a larger structure. Homer enriched *The Iliad* tremendously by the introduction of a large number of extended similes which not only clarify the first element in the comparison but frequently offer an effective contrast to it, since the first element of the comparisons in *The Iliad* is usually martial and the second element is frequently domestic, pastoral, or natural.

The Homeric simile became one of the conventions of the

classical epic. The following lines are an amusing example of Milton's deliberate use of this stylistic device.

PARADISE LOST
(Book I, ll. 192–210)
John Milton

Thus Satan, talking to his nearest mate,
With head uplift above the wave, and eyes
That sparkling blazed; his other parts besides
Prone on the flood, extended long and large,
Lay floating many a rood; in bulk as huge 5
As whom the fables name of monstrous size,
Titanian, or Earth-born, that warred on Jove;
Briareos or Typhon, whom the den
By ancient Tarsus held; or that sea-beast
Leviathan, which God of all his works, 10
Created hugest that swim the ocean stream.
Him haply slumbering on the Norway foam,
The pilot of some small night-foundered skiff,
Deeming some island, oft, as seamen tell,
With fixèd anchor in his scaly rind 15
Moors by his side under the lee, while night
Invests the sea, and wishèd morn delays:
So stretched out huge in length the arch-fiend lay
Chained on the burning lake. . . .

The metaphor, as distinct from the simile, is an *implied* and not an *expressed* comparison, or, to put it another way, the metaphor fuses the two elements in the comparison whereas the simile keeps the elements distinct. Instead of saying "The wisteria drips like rain," a poet using metaphor fuses the idea of the pendant blossoms of the wisteria and the dripping character of rain and says, "dripping wisteria"; the wisteria blossom becomes, for the moment of the fusion, a kind of dripping lavender rain. In a simile the basic statement is, "*x* is like *y*," but in a metaphor the basic statement is, "*x* is *y*." A simile is logically possible, but metaphor presents a logical impossibility. Our awareness of the logical incongruity is no doubt part of the reason that metaphor seems, on many occasions, more intense than simile. Both forms of statement can be powerful; the nature of the effect depends on the particular entities brought together as well as on whether the elements are kept distinct or fused. Figurative effects derive their power from content as well as from mode. Both of these figures make large demands upon the poetic imagination of the poet and the reader, and it is not surprising that so acute an analyst as Aristotle concluded that the capacity for producing such figures is "a sign of genius, since it implies an intuitive perception of the similarity in dissimilars."[2] It is worth noticing that in considering these poetic devices we come once more to the principle of things at once both like and unlike. One of the central powers of poetry is the power to relate and connect.

EXERCISE

EXEUNT

Richard Wilbur

Piecemeal the summer dies;
At the field's edge a daisy lives alone;
A last shawl of burning lies
On a gray field-stone.

All cries are thin and terse; 5
The field has droned the summer's final mass;
A cricket like a dwindled hearse
Crawls from the dry grass.

1. What figures of speech are employed in this poem?
2. What special type of figure is present in lines 1, 2, 3, and 6?

[2] In translation, Aristotle is represented as making this statement about metaphor, but it seems clear from the context that Aristotle did not mean to exclude simile from his assertion.

Considerable light may be thrown on the character and quality of a poem if we raise the question, "What are the general sources of the material for the similes and metaphors in the poem?" Quite simply, the source of a poem's similes is experience, real or imaginary; more elaborately, we may break down experience into the following useful categories: man, nature, man-made things, human society (institutions, ceremonies, and rituals), and the world of the supernatural. In Donne's famous lines,

> Ride ten thousand days and nights
> Till age *snow* white hairs on thee,

the metaphor is obviously from the world of nature. The extraordinary freshness and vividness of this metaphor, as compared to the banal simile, "His hair is white as snow," arises in part from the fact that Donne has embedded his metaphor in a verb, "snow," and thus has speeded up the process by which age turns the hair white. The metaphor gains, furthermore, from the context that suggests the impossible feat of a ride that lasts ten thousand days and nights and that ends with the rider old and white-haired.

In Bacon's fine sentence (of which the rhythm and the sound-pattern are as worthy of observation as the metaphors), "For a crowd is not company, and faces are but a gallery of pictures, and talk but a tinkling cymbal, where there is no love," the metaphors "gallery of pictures" and "tinkling cymbal" are from the realm of man-made things, in this case, the world of the arts.

In the lines

> Can the mole
> Take a census of the stars?

the metaphor "take a census," which emphasizes the immense distance between the mole and the stars, is from the realm of social institutions.

In the horrifying phrase

> For war is eating now

the seemingly harmless metaphor from the world of men or animals suggests in its context the concept of war as a monster devouring human flesh. Here we encounter personification, a specialized figure of speech which may occur in the form of simile or metaphor. In a figure of this type the subject which is not a person is treated as though it were a person. Thus, through the metaphor "eating," war becomes a monster devouring human flesh. The scrupulous student may wish to make a further distinction between animation and personification, reserving the term personification for instances in which specifically human qualities are assigned to something inanimate or abstract. An example of personification in this stricter form, involving a specifically human quality, may be found in the opening line of a famous sonnet by Donne:

Death, be not proud . . .

Most similes and metaphors are accepted almost without question. Some, indeed, have been used for so long and so frequently that they are worn out; they have become what we call dead metaphors. But a great deal of metaphor is casually and vividly alive in day-to-day speech, in serious discourse, or in moments of excitement: "Kill the ump! That was a rotten call—he missed the tag a mile. You must be blind, ump!" Much of this, one hopes, is metaphor. It is worth noticing that sometimes, when called to account for such vivid statements, we say, apologetically, "It was just a figure of speech. I didn't actually mean it." In certain respects metaphor can reduce the sheer force of words. The word "rotten" may be powerfully image-bearing in some contexts, but when used in metaphors such as the one just cited, its image-bearing properties are somewhat reduced. The following sequence provides further illustration of the point: (1) the green grass; (2) the green wave of Dartmouth men; (3) green recruits. The image-bearing capacity of the word "green" is perhaps more fully operative in the nonfigurative statement (1) than in either of the metaphoric statements (2 or 3). "Green recruits" is an example of dead metaphor. Or consider the following series: (1) a raw carrot; (2) a raw day; (3) a raw deal.

Does the image-bearing property of "raw" fade in the second case? Does it disappear? Does the image disappear in the third instance?

We readily accept the time-honored similes and metaphors of great classical and romantic poetry. In English metaphysical poetry of the seventeenth century and in certain kinds of twentieth-century poetry, some of which has been deeply influenced by the earlier metaphysical poetry, you may find yourself rejecting, or accepting reluctantly, similes and metaphors that strike you as far-fetched or preposterous. The elements are linked in the same grammatical form, but they seem to be drawn together over a great distance or, because of their normal associations, to collide harshly when brought together, to yield their analogic characteristics slowly and grudgingly. Donne's lines

> Go and catch a falling star,
> Get with child a mandrake root,

are in the metaphysical style because of the imaginative distance between the catchable object (implied) and a falling star, and between a woman (implied) and the root of the mandrake which is shaped roughly like a human being. If he had written

> Go and catch a meadow-lark,
> Get with child a chimpanzee,

the distance between the elements would have been great but not so audaciously extravagant as in the metaphors we have cited.

Let us now consider the figures of speech we have been discussing as they occur in two poems.

SONNET 65

William Shakespeare

Since *brass,* nor *stone,* nor *earth,* nor *boundless sea,*
But sad *mortality o'er-sways their power,*

How with this *rage* shall *beauty hold a plea,*
Whose *action* is no stronger *than a flower?*
O! how shall *summer's honey breath hold out* 5
Against the *wreckful siege* of *batt'ring* days,
When rocks *impregnable* are not so stout
Nor *gates of steel* so strong, but Time *decays?*
O fearful meditation! where, alack,
Shall *Time's best jewel* from *Time's chest lie hid?* 10
Or what strong hand can *hold his swift foot back?*
Or who his *spoil* of beauty can *forbid?*
O, none, unless this *miracle* have might,
That *in black ink* my love shall still *shine bright.*

"Hold a plea" and "action," it should be observed, are terms which in Shakespeare's day were immediately recognized as the language of the law and of courts. In the contest between beauty and time, in legal and other metaphors, the figure of personification is several times involved. Of the italicized figures, "flower," "honey," "decay," and probably "shine bright" are from the general world of nature. A most brilliantly audacious metaphor comes from the physical activity of man. In the line

Or what strong hand can hold his swift foot back?

we get the fused picture of a man attempting to run while another powerful, if not gigantic, being restrains the striving foot. This picture, rich in kinesthetic imagery, supplies an extraordinarily forceful comparison with the unpreventable flight of time. The other metaphors, by and large, refer to activities of man more serious than a footrace. "Boundless," at least glances at the human recognition of physical and legal bounds; "o'ersways their power" refers to political power; and the general metaphor developed in the series "hold out," "siege," "batt'ring," and "gates of steel" refers to the social institution of warfare. The "siege" metaphor is carried on by that of "spoil," since one of the likely meanings is that of the plundered property acquired in the despoiling of a captured city. A final metaphor from the field of man's activities is built up through the series of words "jewel," "chest," and "lie hid." "Shine bright," the concluding metaphor, is striking. It takes its rise, perhaps, from the glossiness of black ink in the broad strokes of a pen. There is the tension of contrast between "black ink" and "shine bright" and perhaps ultimately between night and day, darkness and sunlight. And "black ink" is here a metaphor of the part for the whole, the merest physical part of the act of writing put for the whole expressive power of language.

This fine metaphor is an example of the special form called *metonymy*. Metonymy means basically an "altered naming," that is, the part stands for the whole, or an attribute or strongly associated idea is named instead of the thing itself. The use of a part for the whole occurs, for example, in the statement that a factory "employs *hands*." In the phrase "the King's *Rifles*" an attribute or strongly associated idea, the habitually present implement, is named instead of the thing itself, a regiment of soldiers. To cite another familiar example, "Mr. Throckmorton is the lawyer for the *Crown*" is an instance in which one physical appurtenance of sovereign authority stands for the whole majesty of authority and for the public interest in the prosecutive side of the system of law.

Let us turn now to a poem that is unmistakably in the metaphysical tradition.

A VALEDICTION: FORBIDDING MOURNING
John Donne

As virtuous men pass mildly away,
  And *whisper to their souls,* to go,
Whilst some of their sad friends do say,
  The breath goes now, and some say, No:

So let us *melt,* and make no noise, 5
  No *tear-floods,* nor *sigh-tempests* move,
T'were *profanation* of our joys
  To tell the *laity* our love.

Moving of th' earth brings harms and fears,
  Men reckon what it did and meant, 10
But *trepidation of the spheres,*
  Though greater far, is innocent.

Dull sublunary lovers' love
  (Whose *soul is sense*) cannot admit
Absence, because it doth remove 15
  Those things which *elemented* it.

But we by a love, so much *refined*
  That our selves know not what it is,
Inter-assurèd of the mind,
  Care less, eyes, lips, and hands to miss. 20

Our two souls therefore, which are one,
  Though I must go, endure not yet
A *breach,* but an *expansion,*
  Like gold to airy thinness beat.

If they be two, they are two so 25
  As stiff twin compasses are two;
Thy soul the *fixed foot,* makes no show
  To move, but doth, if *th' other* do.

And though it in the *center sit,*
  Yet when the other far doth *roam,* 30
It *leans,* and *hearkens* after it,
  And *grows erect* as that *comes home.*

Such wilt thou be to me who must
  Like th' other *foot, obliquely run;*
Thy *firmness* makes my *circle* just, 35
  And makes me *end,* where I *begun.*

Both Shakespeare and Donne are expressing fundamentally familiar emotions, the first, the distress evoked by an acute awareness of the transience of the beauty of the beloved, and the second, the emotions a lover experiences as he faces a period of necessary absence from his beloved. But, despite the familiarity of the content of these poems, it is immediately obvious that the figures that Donne utilizes (here italicized) to enhance his expression of the lover's emotions differ in degree, if not in kind, from those that Shakespeare has utilized. Donne's figures involve a greater distance between the elements compared than Shakespeare's do, or, in other words, the elements compared are less obviously comparable than the elements in Shakespeare's metaphors and similes. There are three similes in Donne's poem, and each of them seems more surprising or strange than any of Shakespeare's figures. The first element in each of these three similes is the lovers' parting, which is after all the subject of this poem. The lovers' parting is compared, first, to the separation of virtuous men's souls from their bodies at death; second, to the beating out of a sheet of gold leaf to the degree of airy thinness; and, finally, to a compass drawing a circle. If we say that the strangeness or remoteness or extravagance of the similes increases as the poem goes on, and that Donne seems to be luring the reader to accept more and more audacious operations of his imagination, we should also notice that the climax of this audacity, the third simile, is in certain respects the most prosaic. A draftsman's compass is a relatively familiar rather than an exotic item, but its employment usually has nothing whatever to do with intensities of feeling. Accordingly, in this context, the compass drawing a circle comes as a surprise. There is intellectual and imaginative ingenuity in the way the simile is developed and explicated. Most of the metaphors in the last three stanzas have the function of expanding and developing the basic simile, and the metaphors from other areas of human experience, "roam" and "comes home"—warm and familiar metaphors—serve to emotionalize the geometry of the simile. Such emotionalizing could imperil the main point of the poem were it not so firmly within the unemotional simile. The calm control and certain accuracy expressed in the compass are what the speaker wants his beloved to achieve, and beyond what he is recommending to her he seems to be trying to persuade himself into the same sure control and achieved calm.

Several of the other metaphors call for a brief comment.

"Tear-floods" and "sigh-tempests," almost banal metaphors, are given a certain freshness by the form, the compound words. But these relatively familiar metaphors are contrasted immediately with the more unusual metaphors implied in "profanation" and "laity." Here, the lovers, with some audacity, are compared with sacred beings who are set off by their spiritual distinction and subtlety from the laity, the less spiritual beings. This superior status of the lovers is reenforced by the comparison that is developed in the next two stanzas. The comparison of the movement of the lovers in parting with an earthquake, "Moving of th'earth," and with the movement of the heavenly bodies, "trepidation of the spheres," serves to build up his conception of the lovers as much more than sublunary, as, indeed, supermundane. The metaphor "elemented" implies, in context, that the lovers are made of a finer essential substance than others, and probably the Pythagorean idea of a superior and celestial fifth element or quintessence is being employed here.

A word, finally, must be said for the role that symbols play in poetry, since, just as the figures that we have been discussing are commonly thought of as characteristic of poetry rather than of prose, so symbols perhaps tend to be more heavily stressed in poetry than in prose. Any discussion of symbolism in poetry can be immediately perplexed by the bewildering variety of meanings that the term has acquired in various disciplines, in addition to the varieties of symbols that occur in poetry. Suppose we begin with some quite obvious and conventional examples and move on from them to some of the major patterns of symbolism that persistently appear in English poetry. We all recognize flags as national symbols, the cross as a religious symbol; a white flag relates to a truce in fighting; a white handkerchief tied to the handle of a car door is in the process of development as a symbol of distress and need for assistance on the highway.

Two of the most basic traditional symbolic patterns in poetry are the seasonal cycle and the diurnal cycle. It would be hard to overstate how pervasive the symbols in these cycles are in all the poetry you read.

Here are some examples of the symbolism of the seasonal

cycle. Chaucer expresses the symbolic connection between the stirrings of life in external nature and the beginnings of human restlessness, movement, and pilgrimage.

> Whan that *Aprille* with his shoures soote
> The droghte of March hath perced to the roote, . . .
> Thanne longen folk to goon on pilgrimages.

> shoures: showers
> soote: sweet
> droghte: drought

Robert Burns links his love to the freshness of a flower and the beginning of summer.

> O my Luve's like a red, red, rose,
> That's *newly sprung in June.*

Shakespeare's Macbeth reflects on the condition of his life in his elder years and the declining turn of his fortunes. (Some scholars think the correct reading is "*May* of life.")

> My way of life
> Is fall'n into the *sear, the yellow leaf.*

Shakespeare's Cleopatra speaks of Antony's later years, passionately praising his generosity.

> For his bounty,
> There was *no winter in 't, an autumn 't was*
> That grew the more by *reaping.*

And here are some examples of the symbolism of the diurnal cycle. Wordsworth makes a statement of his early, excited response to the promise of the French revolution.

> Bliss was it in that *dawn* to be alive
> And to be young was very heaven.

Tennyson expresses a vision of death and attitudes toward death in "Crossing the Bar."

> *Twilight* and *evening* bell,
> And after that the *dark!*
> And may there be no sadness of farewell,
> When I embark.

Pope, in his lines to Robert Harley, Earl of Oxford, a statesman in retirement, links the passing day with the later years of life.

> Ev'n now she shades thy *evening* walk with bays,
> (No hireling she, no prostitute to praise)
> Ev'n now, observant of *the parting ray,*
> Eyes the *calm sunset* of thy *various day.*

she: the Muse, poetic imagination

Tennyson dramatizes Ulysses in his old age, summoning his old shipmates to one more voyage.

> Death closes all: but something ere the end,
> Some work of noble note, may yet be done,
> Not unbecoming men that strove with Gods.
> The *lights begin to twinkle* from the rocks:
> The *long day wanes:* the slow *moon climbs:* the deep 5
> Moans round with many voices. Come, my friends,
> 'Tis not *too late* to seek a newer world.

Not infrequently these two basic symbolisms, seasonal and diurnal, are active together, the movement from spring through summer to autumn and winter allied with and reenforced by the movement from dawn to dark.

In Keats' "To Autumn" (p. 179), for example, the movement is from the earlier phases and circumstances of autumn to the completion of the harvest and the repose that follows; at the same time, the three major parts of the poem present a movement from sunlit mid-day or afternoon to evening and sunset.

EXERCISE

STOPPING BY WOODS ON A SNOWY EVENING

Robert Frost

Whose woods these are I think I know.
His house is in the village though;
He will not see me stopping here
To watch his woods fill up with snow.

My little horse must think it queer 5
To stop without a farmhouse near
Between the woods and frozen lake
The darkest evening of the year.

He gives his harness bells a shake
To ask if there is some mistake. 10
The only other sound's the sweep
Of easy wind and downy flake.

The woods are lovely, dark and deep,
But I have promises to keep,
And miles to go before I sleep, 15
And miles to go before I sleep.

1. Do figures of speech play any part in this poem? Are there any similes? Any metaphors? Any personifications?
2. What symbolism is there in the poem? How are the symbols interrelated? In what ways does symbolism affect the expression of the poem's themes?

It may be useful, finally, to extend our consideration of symbolism by looking at the symbolic patterns in two very diverse poems, Robinson's "Flammonde" (p. 162) and Keats' "La Belle Dame sans Merci" (p. 117).

Robinson's poem is written in a style that is rather bare of figures, although such metaphors as are used are extremely effective. But this portrait of a personality has meaning for us beyond its literal significance, because it is made by the use of symbols to "stand for" a type of person and experience that is not unique. The fundamental pattern of the symbols is suggested by the most brilliant metaphor in the poem, the phrase "Prince of Castaways." We have here a fusion of two series of antithetical symbols. One set refers to the noble characteristics of Flammonde, and the second to his ambiguously ignoble characteristics. These series run through the poem and give it its symbolic structure. The first series is built up by the expressions "firm address and foreign air," "something royal in his walk," "held his head as one by kings accredited," "graciously," "courtesy," "his mien distinguished any crowd," and "firm in every look and limb." Set against this series are the expressions which establish and emphasize the mysterious flaw in the character of Flammonde: "borrowed," "mischance," "banished," "played a part," "satanic kink," "broken link," "surface of a shield," "ethical unrest." But what is most remarkable about the manipulation of the symbols here is the success Robinson has in fusing them into the portrait of a mysterious but comprehensible and credible personality.

A somewhat less obvious manipulation of symbols may be discovered in Keats' "La Belle Dame sans Merci." If this is more than a charming fairy story, a literary ballad about an "Other-World Mistress," the reason is to be found in the symbols and the pattern that Keats has made of them. Here, too, there are antithetical groups of symbols, one emphasizing the beauty of the "Other-World Mistress" and the other, her destructiveness. Each series of symbols is built up with incomparable skill. The first is created out of such words as "a faery's child/Her hair was long, her foot was light," "a faery's song," "roots of relish sweet," "honey," "wild," "manna dew," "elfin grot," "I love thee true." The antithetical series is created out of the description of the lady's victim in the first three stanzas and the last by such phrases as "pale kings and princes," "pale warriors, death-pale," "starved lips in the gloam," and "horrid warning."

What we get, then, through the symbolic pattern of this poem is a highly imaginative expression of man's ambivalent attitude toward woman, the fascination that she has for him and the primitive and perhaps unconscious fear aroused in him by his awareness of her power over him. What begins by seeming to be an innocuous fairy tale turns out to be the perfect embodiment of something that is fundamental to man's conscious and unconscious experience. So, a work of art, when it is closely studied, may be seen to embody a wealth of significance. Here indeed, as in every successful work of art, are infinite riches in a little room.

Denotation, Connotation, and Allusion

Scientists, engineers, and mathematicians seek forms of statement that will say one thing and say it precisely. In order to achieve this objective they devise a language, a form of communication, in which ambiguity and associative coloration are kept to a minimum. They are likely to employ a wordless language ($E = mc^2$) because most words have several meanings and many words are inevitably charged wih powerful associations. The possible dictionary meanings of a word are its *denotations*; the associations naturally attached to a word are its *connotations.* "Dear," for example, means "held in affection" but it also means "expensive"; both of these meanings are denotations of this word. In some statements it is hard to be sure which denotation of a word is operative. "The toy was very *cheap*" may mean simply that it did not cost much, but it may also mean that it was flimsy and badly made. The language of words is full of such ambiguity of denotation, and the scientist characteristically, and for very good reasons, seeks to avoid ambiguity. The poet, on the other hand, welcomes ambiguity because he often wants to say two or more things at once. The pun is one familiar form of such denotative ambiguity. Consider, for example, Shakespeare's Mercutio, describing his mortal wound.

No, 'tis not so deep as a well nor so wide as a church door, but 'tis enough, 'twill serve. Ask for me tomorrow and you shall find me a *grave* man.

(*Romeo and Juliet,* III, i)

By the use of denotative ambiguity, Shakespeare conveys not only the seriousness of the wound but also Mercutio's attitude toward mortality.

In addition to the complex denotative character of words there is the aura of associations, the connotations that many words have. Take, for example, this powerful line from Pope's *The Dunciad.*

> And the fresh vomit run for ever green.
> (II, 156)

"Fresh," "for ever," and "green" are denotatively acceptable here with little ambiguity. But the connotations of "fresh," "for ever," and "green" are in the main very strongly associated with positive values—in the realm of nature, in pledges of romantic and patriotic fidelity, in the language of the Bible and of church liturgy. "Vomit" is abominably subversive in this context; it overturns the connotations of three of the fairest expressions in the language.

EXERCISE

Octavius Caesar, in Shakespeare's *Antony and Cleopatra,* describes his rival Mark Antony (not unmeritorious and by some deeply beloved) as follows:

> You shall find there
> A man who is the abstract of all faults
> That all men follow. (I, iv)

1. What denotative ambiguities or uncertainties do these lines present?
2. Are the dual possibilities merely confusing or do both possibilities contribute effectively to the general purport?
3. Is the denotative ambiguity here chiefly in the meaning of individual words or in the relations of words?

The following lines occur near the beginning of Pope's savage satiric portrait of Sporus in "An Epistle to Dr. Arbuthnot".

Yet let me flap this bug with gilded wings,
This painted child of dirt that stinks and stings.

1. Which words here degrade the person under attack directly and chiefly by their denotative meaning?
2. In which instances are the force and range of the attack significantly assisted by the connotations of words?

Denotation and connotation take a special form when a poet includes in his poem reference to other works of literature. Such reference or *allusion* occurs in a great variety of ways, ranging from explicit to implicit, overt to covert, and clearly deliberate to probably unintentional. It may be argued that, after about twenty-five hundred years of poetry in the tradition of our western culture, there is no such thing as a nonallusive poem. In choice of theme, form, rhythm, verbal character, and factual details the poet will remind some of his readers of other poets and other poems. Some poets usually suppose that you have read a great deal. It is hard to imagine a poet who could be seriously opposed to reading. A poem by Richard Eberhart will serve as an example of some of the range and kinds of allusion.

THE FURY OF AERIAL BOMBARDMENT

You would think the fury of aerial bombardment
Would rouse God to relent; the infinite spaces
Are still silent. He looks on shock-pried faces.
History, even, does not know what is meant.

You would feel that after so many centuries 5
God would give man to repent; yet he can kill
As Cain could, but with multitudinous will,
No farther advanced than in his ancient furies.

Was man made stupid to see his own stupidity?
Is God by definition indifferent, beyond us all? 10
Is the eternal truth man's fighting soul
Wherein the Beast ravens in its own avidity?

Of Van Wettering I speak, and Averill,
Names on a list, whose faces I do not recall
But they are gone to early death, who late in school 15
Distinguished the belt feed lever from the belt holding pawl.

The most explicit and overt kind of allusion occurs in line 7; we are expected to recognize Cain as the biblical character (Genesis 4), traditionally the first murderer, who slew his brother, Abel. A far less explicit allusion occurs in the same line in the word "multitudinous." "Multitudinous" is not the sort of word that we all use daily; we might manage to get through a thousand breakfast-table conversations without using it at all. When and where does this unusual word occur? Has it ever occurred in any famous discussions or statements? If we know Shakespeare, we will think of Macbeth considering the guilt and stain of murder on his hand, and how, immersed in the sea, instead of being cleansed, that hand

will rather
The *multitudinous* seas incarnadine,
Making the green one red.
(*Macbeth,* II, ii)

Eberhart, reflecting on man's capaciousness in murder, thinks not only of Cain, the biblical prime murderer, but also of the tormented Shakespearean murderer, Macbeth. The Bible and Shakespeare are frequent sources of allusion, and so is the literature of Greece and Rome, both as history and as fiction, especially as mythology. Classical allusion is present in Eberhart's title, in the first line, and in the eighth line; there is a denotative ambiguity about the word "fury." On the one hand, "fury" means the physical and emotional violence of aerial bombing; on the other hand, with some assistance from "ancient" in line 8, we are jogged into remembering the classical myth of the Furies. It would be better to say myths because there are several stories and concepts associated with these beings. In general, they were thought of as ministers of divine vengeance.

They inflicted wars and pestilence upon earth to punish guilty men. It seems probable that Eberhart, in his title, by way of the denotative ambiguity of "Fury," is bringing this role of the Furies into a modern context. The most famous action of the Furies is their pursuit of Orestes who killed his mother, Clytemnestra, and her paramour, Aegisthus, to avenge their murder of his father, Agamemnon (see Aeschylus, the *Oresteia*). Along with the crimes of Cain and of Macbeth, Eberhart seems to be alluding to this chain of murders in Greek tragedy.

We may wonder, once we have recognized an allusion, just how far we should go into it. In the *Eumenides,* the final play of the tetralogy called the *Oresteia,* the Furies' vengeful pursuit of the guilty Orestes ends in the shrine of Apollo, the patron god of Orestes, and they are converted for the future into spirits of justice, benevolence, and grace. Is this conclusion of the cycle in the Greek plays pertinent to the modern poem? Eberhart's poem does, at any rate, persistently ask whether murder after murder, war after war is to be the continuing destiny of man. Once we have recognized the basic allusion, we are bound to ponder the extent and limits of its relevance. That allusion, skillfully employed, can, at a stroke, considerably enlarge the dimensions of a poem would seem to be beyond dispute.

PART II

Directions for the Analysis of a Poem

I. "Factual" Values

Summarize the poem in not more than two or three sentences. What elements in the poem as summarized seem familiar to you? Are they familiar through your personal experience of them, through your reading of imaginative or nonimaginative literature, or through their presentation in some artistic medium other than literature?

What elements in the poem as summarized seem unfamiliar to you? Why do they seem unfamiliar?

In the handling of the familiar elements in the poem, which details seem to you to be the most telling, the most vivid? Why?

In the handling of the unfamiliar elements in the poem, has the author succeeded in giving you a lively imaginative experience of these elements? Why or why not?

Does the "factual" value of the poem reside in the skillful presentation of familiar or unfamiliar material?

II. Psychological Values

A. Sensory

What is the general proportion of image-making to abstract words? Are the image-making words notably vivid in their impact, or are they routine images? Are the images strongly pleasurable, neutral, or decidedly repulsive?

B. Emotional

Make a list, with brief comments, presenting the succession of feelings and emotions that you experience as you read the poem again and again.

Are the feelings and emotions impressive for their variety or their intensity or both? Is the order in which the feelings and emotions are experienced psychologically satisfying? Why or why not?

To what extent is the succession of feelings and emotions that you experience identical with those of the character created by the poet or the character that is apparently expressing himself in the poem? Why? What is the attitude of the poet toward the character expressing himself in the poem? How do you know? What effect on your experience of the poem does the apparent attitude of the author have? Why?

C. Empathetic

To what extent do you find it possible to accept as your own the feelings and emotions, the attitudes and the ideas expressed in the poem? If your acceptance of them is easy, what are the reasons for it? If your acceptance of them is incomplete or difficult, why? What elements in the poem compensate for the absence of a complete acceptance?

D. Analytical

Does one of the important values of the poem inhere in the author's analysis of the personality expressing itself in the poem or of the person's state of mind? Why or why not? Is the absence of any author's analysis offset by the stimulus the poem offers you to make your own analysis of a character or to infer what his state of mind or his motivation is? Would the poem be made more effective by more or less author's analysis? Why?

III. Technical Values

A. Structure

1. Narrative. If the structure is obviously narrative, analyze it in terms of its exposition, development, turning point, climax, development, and denouement, or such of these structural elements as appear in the poem.
2. Descriptive. If the structure is obviously descriptive, discuss the basic pattern and the relationship of the details to the basic pattern.
3. Expository
   a. If the poem consists primarily in the exposition of feelings and emotions, make an outline showing the succession of feelings and emotions presented, and

write a discussion of the outline in terms of the number of feelings and emotions presented, the order of the presentation, the reasons for the order, and the effectiveness of the order.

b. If the poem consists primarily in an exposition of ideas, make an outline showing the succession of ideas presented, and discuss it in terms of the number of ideas presented, the order in which they are presented, and the effectiveness of the order of presentation.

4. Argumentative. If the poem is primarily argumentative, state the thesis and outline the arguments in support of it, and discuss the number and order of the arguments, the reasons for the order, and the persuasiveness with which the argument is conducted.
5. Combined. If the structure is a combination of two or more of the types listed above, make an outline of the structure of the poem and discuss its organization in terms of the dominant type of structure, the subordinate types of structure, the effectiveness of the structure as a whole.
6. Relationship to the form of the poem. What relationship exists between the inner structure of the poem as just analyzed and the shape as determined by the meter (and the rhyme scheme, if any)? Does the structure assist in clarifying the shape or the shape assist in clarifying the structure? Why or why not?

B. Style

1. Meter

a. Regular meter. Make a visual analysis of the meter by the following method:

(I). Indicate the meter of the poem by the use of the following symbols: [∪], unstressed; [—], stressed; [|], division between feet.

(II). If a stressed syllable is lightly stressed, mark it with a superior number [2]; if a stressed syllable is heavily stressed, mark it with a superior number [4]. Reserve these markings for genuinely unusual stresses.

(III). Mark the caesuras, the end-stopped lines, and the run-on lines using the following symbols: [0], run-on lines; [/], slight pause; [//], normal pause; [///] heavy pause.

Write a discussion of the metrics of the poem, covering the following topics: the number, nature, and placement of the variations from the rhythmic norm; the light and heavy stresses; the placement of the major pauses and the use of run-on lines; the propriety and the effectiveness of the metrics in relationship to the subject and the tone of the poem.

b. Irregular meter or free verse. If the poem is in irregular meter or free verse, analyze it in accordance with the instructions in (I), (II), and (III) above, and discuss the following aspects of the meter: the degree of regularity attained through the repeated use of a particular type of foot or of a series of similar feet; the degree of regularity attained through the repeated use of lines of the same or approximately the same length; the attainment or the failure to attain a satisfactory balance between regularity or irregularity; the particularly light or particularly heavy stresses; the placement of the major pauses and the use of run-on lines; the propriety and effectiveness of the meter in relation to the subject and the tone of the poem.

2. Sound-Pattern. Make a visual analysis of the sound-pattern of the poem by the following method:
   a. Circle and link together significantly repeated words.
   b. Underscore and link together the final consonants (if any) in the rhyme words (if any).
   c. Overscore and link together the vowels in the rhyme words (if any).
   d. Underscore and link together the significant alliterations (including those in the rhyme words).
   e. Overscore and link together the significant assonances (including those in rhyme words).

   Write a discussion of the sound-pattern of the poem covering the following topics: the purpose and effect of repetitions; the obtrusiveness or the unobtrusiveness of the rhyme scheme (if any) and its relationship to the structure of the poem; the contribution of alliteration to the effectiveness of the poem, with attention to whether conjunctive or disjunctive types of alliteration are present; the contribution of assonance to the effectiveness of the poem.

3. Diction. Make a list identifying and classifying the image-making words in the poem using the following symbols:

1a Sight-color	3 Touch
1b Sight-size	4 Kinesthetic sensation of tension or relaxation
1c Sight-shape	5 Smell
1d Sight-position	6 Taste
1e Sight-movement (or lack of movement)	7 Thermal
2 Sound (or absence of sound)	

Write a discussion of diction covering the following topics: the proportion of image-bearing to abstract terms; the dominant type of imagery; the quality of the imagery (vivid or routine); the involvement or noninvolvement of the images in figurative language. Toward what general emphasis on the part of the poet do these considerations point, intellectual discourse or sensory presentation? What kind of poem do they go toward making?

4. Metaphors and similes. Make a visual analysis of the metaphors and similes in the poem by underscoring the metaphors with a single line and the similes with a double line.

Write a discussion of the metaphors and similes in the poem covering the following: a carefully detailed discrimination of the elements involved in the comparisons; the sources of the elements in comparisons; notice of any special types of simile or metaphor (animation, personification, metonymy); the quality (freshness, banality, oddity, propriety) of the figurative language; the amount of figurative language and an evaluation of its importance to the effectiveness of the poem.

IV. Symbolical Values

What are the major symbols in the poem: persons, objects, actions, terms?

What sort of pattern results from the relationship the poet has built up among the symbols? Do any of the recurrent symbol patterns appear: the seasonal cycle, the diurnal, water/dryness, light/dark?

What point or themes does the pattern of symbols emphasize?

Do you think the author is successful in making clear to you the significance the symbols have for him? Why or why not?

V. Ideational Values

State briefly the major themes which the symbols contribute to expressing. Are the major themes made explicit by the author or have they been left implicit? If they are left implicit, how do you know what they are? How sure are you of what the major themes are? Why?

Does the entire poem seem relevant to the major themes? If there are passages in it that seem irrelevant, can their presence in the poem be justified? Why or why not?

What is the author's attitude toward the major themes? Is his attitude communicated explicitly or implicitly? By what means is the attitude communicated? What is the dominant tone of the story? What are the subordinate tones, if any? Is the combination of tones harmonious, effectively inharmonious, or ineffectively inharmonious? Why?

What ethical values, if any, are suggested by the poem? What philosophical values, if any, are suggested? How important are the ethical and philosophical values in your final evaluation of the poem? Why?

Do you consider that the poem was or was not deserving of the exhaustive analysis you have given it? Why?

PART III

Poems and Questions

Narrative in Poetry

SIR PATRICK SPENS

Anonymous

The king sits in Dumferling toune,
  Drinking the blude-reid wine,
"O whar will I get guid sailor,
  To sail this schip of mine?"

Up and spak an eldern knicht, 5
  Sat at the kings richt kne:
"Sir Patrick Spens is the best sailor
  That sails upon the se."

The king has written a braid letter,
  And signd it wi his hand, 10
And sent it to Sir Patrick Spens,
  Was walking on the sand.

The first line that Sir Patrick red,
  A loud lauch lauchèd he;
The next line that Sir Patrick red, 15
  The teir blinded his ee.

"O wha is this has don this deid,
  This ill deid don to me,
To send me out this time o' the yeir,
  To sail upon the se! 20

"Mak hast, mak haste, my mirry men all,
  Our guid schip sails the morne:"
"O say na sae, my master deir,
  For I feir a deadlie storme.

"Late late yestreen I saw the new moone 25
  Wi the auld moone in hir arme,
And I feir, I feir, my dear master,
  That we will cum to harme."

O our Scots nobles wer richt laith
  To weet their cork-heild schoone; 30
Bot lang owre a' the play wer playd,
  Thair hats they swam aboone.

O lang, lang may their ladies sit,
  Wi thair fans into their hand,
Or eir they se Sir Patrick Spens, 35
  Cum sailing to the land.

O lang, lang may the ladies stand,
  Wi thair gold kems in their hair,
Waiting for thair ain deir lords,
  For they'll se thame na mair. 40

Haf owre, haf owre to Aberdour,
  It's fiftie fadom deip,
And thair lies guid Sir Patrick Spens,
  Wi the Scots lords at his feit.

1. Summarize the narrative content of this poem.
2. What important facts in the action are not revealed? Does the omission of these facts increase or diminish the effectiveness of the poem?
3. What effect do the sudden shifts of scene and point of view have?
4. What do you regard as the major themes of this poem? What evidence in the poem points to these themes as you conceive them?
5. What is the meaning of the following lines.

Late late yestreen I saw the new moone
Wi the auld moone in hir arme?

6. Does the dialect contribute to or detract from the effect of the poem? Why?

MICHAEL

A Pastoral Poem

William Wordsworth

If from the public way you turn your steps
Up the tumultuous brook of Green-head Ghyll,
You will suppose that with an upright path
Your feet must struggle; in such bold ascent
The pastoral moutains front you, face to face. 5
But, courage! for around that boisterous brook
The mountains have all opened out themselves,
And made a hidden valley of their own.
No habitation can be seen; but they
Who journey thither find themselves alone 10
With a few sheep, with rocks and stones, and kites
That overhead are sailing in the sky.
It is in truth an utter solitude;
Nor should I have made mention of this Dell
But for one object which you might pass by, 15
Might see and notice not. Beside the brook
Appears a straggling heap of unhewn stones!
And to that simple object appertains
A story—unenriched with strange events,
Yet not unfit, I deem, for the fireside, 20
Or for the summer shade. It was the first
Of those domestic tales that spake to me
Of shepherds, dwellers in the valleys, men
Whom I already loved;—not verily
For their own sakes, but for the fields and hills 25

Where was their occupation and abode.
And hence this Tale, while I was yet a Boy
Careless of books, yet having felt the power
Of Nature, by the gentle agency
Of natural objects, led me on to feel 30
For passions that were not my own, and think
(At random and imperfectly indeed)
On man, the heart of man, and human life.
Therefore, although it be a history
Homely and rude, I will relate the same 35
For the delight of a few natural hearts;
And, with yet fonder feeling, for the sake
Of youthful poets, who among these hills
Will be my second self when I am gone.

Upon the forest-side in Grasmere Vale 40
There dwelt a Shepherd, Michael was his name;
An old man, stout of heart, and strong of limb.
His bodily frame had been from youth to age
Of an unusual strength: his mind was keen,
Intense, and frugal, apt for all affairs, 45
And in his shepherd's calling he was prompt
And watchful more than ordinary men.
Hence had he learned the meaning of all winds,
Of blasts of every tone; and oftentimes,
When others heeded not, he heard the South 50
Make subterraneous music, like the noise
Of bagpipers on distant Highland hills.
The Shepherd, at such warning, of his flock
Bethought him, and he to himself would say,
"The winds are now devising work for me!" 55
And, truly, at all times, the storm, that drives
The traveller to a shelter, summoned him
Up to the mountains: he had been alone
Amid the heart of many thousand mists,
That came to him, and left him, on the heights. 60

So lived he till his eightieth year was past.
And grossly that man errs, who should suppose
That the green valleys, and the streams and rocks,
Were things indifferent to the Shepherd's thoughts.
Fields, where with cheerful spirits he had breathed 65
The common air; hills, which with vigorous step
He had so often climbed; which had impressed
So many incidents upon his mind
Of hardship, skill or courage, joy or fear;
Which, like a book, preserved the memory 70
Of the dumb animals, whom he had saved,
Had fed or sheltered, linking to such acts
The certainty of honourable gain;
Those fields, those hills—what could they less? had laid
Strong hold on his affections, were to him 75
A pleasurable feeling of blind love,
The pleasure which there is in life itself.

His days had not been passed in singleness.
His Helpmate was a comely matron, old—
Though younger than himself full twenty years. 80
She was a woman of a stirring life,
Whose heart was in her house: two wheels she had
Of antique form; this large, for spinning wool;
That small, for flax; and, if one wheel had rest,
It was because the other was at work. 85
The Pair had but one inmate in their house,
An only Child, who had been born to them
When Michael, telling o'er his years, began
To deem that he was old,—in shepherd's phrase,
With one foot in the grave. This only Son, 90
With two brave sheep-dogs tried in many a storm,
The one of an inestimable worth,
Made all their household. I may truly say,
That they were as a proverb in the vale
For endless industry. When day was gone, 95

And from their occupations out of doors
The Son and Father were come home, even then,
Their labour did not cease; unless when all
Turned to the cleanly supper-board, and there,
Each with a mess of pottage and skimmed milk, 100
Sat round the basket piled with oaten cakes,
And their plain home-made cheese. Yet when the meal
Was ended, Luke (for so the Son was named)
And his old Father both betook themselves
To such convenient work as might employ 105
Their hands by the fire-side; perhaps to card
Wool for the Housewife's spindle, or repair
Some injury done to sickle, flail, or scythe,
Or other implement of house or field.

Down from the ceiling, by the chimney's edge, 110
That in our ancient uncouth country style
With huge and black projection overbrowed
Large space beneath, as duly as the light
Of day grew dim, the Housewife hung a lamp;
An aged utensil, which had performed 115
Service beyond all others of its kind.
Early at evening did it burn—and late,
Surviving comrade of uncounted hours,
Which, going by from year to year, had found,
And left, the couple neither gay perhaps 120
Nor cheerful, yet with objects and with hopes,
Living a life of eager industry.
And now, when Luke had reached his eighteenth year,
There by the light of this old lamp they sate,
Father and Son, while far into the night 125
The Housewife plied her own peculiar work,
Making the cottage through the silent hours
Murmur as with the sound of summer flies.
This light was famous in its neighbourhood,
And was a public symbol of the life 130

That thrifty Pair had lived. For, as it chanced,
Their cottage on a plot of rising ground
Stood single, with large prospect, north and south,
High into Easedale, up to Dunmail-Raise,
And westward to the village near the lake; 135
And from this constant light, so regular
And so far seen, the House itself, by all
Who dwelt within the limits of the vale,
Both old and young, was named THE EVENING STAR.

Thus living on through such a length of years, 140
The Shepherd, if he loved himself, must needs
Have loved his Helpmate; but to Michael's heart
This son of his old age was yet more dear—
Less from instinctive tenderness, the same
Fond spirit that blindly works in the blood of all— 145
Than that a child, more than all other gifts
That earth can offer to declining man,
Brings hope with it, and forward-looking thoughts,
And stirrings of inquietude, when they
By tendency of nature needs must fail. 150
Exceeding was the love he bare to him,
His heart and his heart's joy! For oftentimes
Old Michael, while he was a babe in arms,
Had done him female service, not alone
For pastime and delight, as is the use 155
Of fathers, but with patient mind enforced
To acts of tenderness; and he had rocked
His cradle, as with a woman's gentle hand.

And in a later time, ere yet the Boy
Had put on boy's attire, did Michael love, 160
Albeit of a stern unbending mind,
To have the Young-one in his sight, when he
Wrought in the field, or on his shepherd's stool
Sate with a fettered sheep before him stretched

Under the large old oak, that near his door 165
Stood single, and, from matchless depth of shade,
Chosen for the Shearer's covert from the sun,
Thence in our rustic dialect was called
The CLIPPING TREE, a name which yet it bears.
There, while they two were sitting in the shade, 170
With others round them, earnest all and blithe,
Would Michael exercise his heart with looks
Of fond correction and reproof bestowed
Upon the Child, if he disturbed the sheep
By catching at their legs, or with his shouts 175
Scared them, while they lay still beneath the shears.

And when by Heaven's good grace the boy grew up
A healthy Lad, and carried in his cheek
Two steady roses that were five years old;
Then Michael from a winter coppice cut 180
With his own hand a sapling, which he hooped
With iron, making it throughout in all
Due requisites a perfect shepherd's staff,
And gave it to the Boy; wherewith equipt
He as a watchman oftentimes was placed 185
At gate or gap, to stem or turn the flock;
And, to his office prematurely called,
There stood the urchin, as you will divine,
Something between a hindrance and a help;
And for this cause not always, I believe, 190
Receiving from his Father hire of praise;
Though nought was left undone which staff, or voice,
Or looks, or threatening gestures, could perform.

But soon as Luke, full ten years old, could stand
Against the mountain blasts; and to the heights, 195
Not fearing toil, nor length of weary ways,
He with his Father daily went, and they
Were as companions, why should I relate

That objects which the Shepherd loved before
Were dearer now? that from the Boy there came 200
Feelings and emanations—things which were
Light to the sun and music to the wind;
And that the old Man's heart seemed born again?

Thus in his Father's sight the Boy grew up:
And now, when he had reached his eighteenth year, 205
He was his comfort and his daily hope.

While in this sort the simple household lived
From day to day, to Michael's ear there came
Distressful tidings. Long before the time
Of which I speak, the Shepherd had been bound 210
In surety for his brother's son, a man
Of an industrious life, and ample means;
But unforeseen misfortunes suddenly
Had prest upon him; and old Michael now
Was summoned to discharge the forfeiture, 215
A grievous penalty, but little less
Than half his substance. This unlooked-for-claim,
At the first hearing, for a moment took
More hope out of his life than he supposed
That any old man ever could have lost. 220
As soon as he had armed himself with strength
To look his trouble in the face, it seemed
The Shepherd's sole resource to sell at once
A portion of his patrimonial fields.
Such was his first resolve; he thought again, 225
And his heart failed him. "Isabel," said he,
Two evenings after he had heard the news,
"I have been toiling more than seventy years,
And in the open sunshine of God's love
Have we all lived; yet, if these fields of ours 230
Should pass into a stranger's hand, I think
That I could not lie quiet in my grave.

Our lot is a hard lot; the sun himself
Has scarcely been more diligent than I;
And I have lived to be a fool at last 235
To my own family. An evil man
That was, and made an evil choice, if he
Were false to us; and, if he were not false,
There are ten thousand to whom loss like this
Had been no sorrow. I forgive him;—but 240
'Twere better to be dumb than to talk thus.

"When I began, my purpose was to speak
Of remedies and of a cheerful hope.
Our Luke shall leave us, Isabel; the land
Shall not go from us, and it shall be free; 245
He shall possess it, free as is the wind
That passes over it. We have, thou know'st,
Another kinsman—he will be our friend
In this distress. He is a prosperous man,
Thriving in trade—and Luke to him shall go, 250
And with his kinsman's help and his own thrift
He quickly will repair this loss, and then
He may return to us. If here he stay,
What can be done? Where every one is poor,
What can be gained?"

At this the old Man paused, 255
And Isabel sat silent, for her mind
Was busy, looking back into past times.
There's Richard Bateman, thought she to herself,
He was a parish-boy—at the church-door
They made a gathering for him, shillings, pence, 260
And halfpennies, wherewith the neighbours bought
A basket, which they filled with peddlar's wares;
And, with this basket on his arm, the lad
Went up to London, found a master there,
Who, out of many, chose the trusty boy 265
To go and overlook his merchandise

Beyond the seas; where he grew wondrous rich,
And left estates and monies to the poor,
And, at his birth-place, built a chapel floored
With marble, which he sent from foreign lands. 270
These thoughts, and many others of like sort,
Passed quickly through the mind of Isabel,
And her face brightened. The old Man was glad,
And thus resumed:—"Well, Isabel! this scheme
These two days has been meat and drink to me. 275
Far more than we have lost is left us yet.
We have enough—I wish indeed that I
Were younger;—but this hope is a good hope.
Make ready Luke's best garments, of the best
Buy for him more, and let us send him forth 280
To-morrow, or the next day, or to-night:
If he *could* go, the Boy should go to-night."

Here Michael ceased, and to the fields went forth
With a light heart. The Housewife for five days
Was restless morn and night, and all day long 285
Wrought on with her best fingers to prepare
Things needful for the journey of her son.
But Isabel was glad when Sunday came
To stop her in her work: for, when she lay
By Michael's side, she through the last two nights 290
Heard him, how he was troubled in his sleep:
And when they rose at morning she could see
That all his hopes were gone. That day at noon
She said to Luke, while they two by themselves
Were sitting at the door, "Thou must not go: 295
We have no other Child but thee to lose,
None to remember—do not go away,
For if thou leave thy Father he will die."
The Youth made answer with a jocund voice;
And Isabel, when she had told her fears, 300
Recovered heart. That evening her best fare

Did she bring forth, and all together sat
Like happy people round a Christmas fire.

With daylight Isabel resumed her work;
And all the ensuing week the house appeared 305
As cheerful as a grove in Spring: at length
The expected letter from their kinsman came,
With kind assurances that he would do
His utmost for the welfare of the Boy;
To which, requests were added, that forthwith 310
He might be sent to him. Ten times or more
The letter was read over; Isabel
Went forth to show it to the neighbours round;
Nor was there at that time on English land
A prouder heart than Luke's. When Isabel 315
Had to her house returned, the old Man said,
"He shall depart to-morrow." To this word
The Housewife answered, talking much of things
Which, if at such short notice he should go,
Would surely be forgotten. But at length 320
She gave consent, and Michael was at ease.

Near the tumultuous brook of Green-head Ghyll,
In that deep valley, Michael had designed
To build a Sheep-fold; and, before he heard
The tidings of his melancholy loss, 325
For this same purpose he had gathered up
A heap of stones, which by the streamlet's edge
Lay thrown together, ready for the work.
With Luke that evening thitherward he walked:
And soon as they had reached the place he stopped, 330
And thus the old Man spake to him:—"My son,
Tomorrow thou wilt leave me: with full heart
I look upon thee, for thou art the same
That wert a promise to me ere thy birth,
And all thy life has been my daily joy. 335

I will relate to thee some little part
Of our two histories: 'twill do thee good
When thou art from me, even if I should touch
On things thou canst not know of.—After thou
First cam'st into the world—as oft befalls 340
To new-born infants—thou didst sleep away
Two days, and blessings from thy Father's tongue
Then fell upon thee. Day by day passed on,
And still I loved thee with increasing love.
Never to living ear came sweeter sounds 345
Than when I heard thee by our own fireside
First uttering, without words, a natural tune;
While thou, a feeding babe, didst in thy joy
Sing at thy Mother's breast. Month followed month,
And in the open fields my life was passed 350
And on the mountains; else I think that thou
Hadst been brought up upon thy Father's knees.
But we were playmates, Luke: among these hills,
As well thou knowest, in us the old and young
Have played together, nor with me didst thou 355
Lack any pleasure which a boy can know."
Luke had a manly heart; but at these words
He sobbed aloud. The old Man grasped his hand,
And said, "Nay, do not take it so—I see
That these are things of which I need not speak. 360
—Even to the utmost I have been to thee
A kind and a good Father: and herein
I but repay a gift which I myself
Received at others' hands; for, though now old
Beyond the common life of man, I still 365
Remember them who loved me in my youth.
Both of them sleep together: here they lived,
As all their Forefathers had done; and, when
At length their time was come, they were not loth
To give their bodies to the family mould. 370

I wished that thou shouldst live the life they lived,
But, 'tis a long time to look back, my Son,
And see so little gain from threescore years.
These fields were burthened when they came to me;
Till I was forty years of age, not more 375
Than half of my inheritance was mine.
I toiled and toiled; God blessed me in my work,
And till these three weeks past the land was free.
—It looks as if it never could endure
Another Master. Heaven forgive me, Luke, 380
If I judge ill for thee, but it seems good
That thou shouldst go."
At this the old Man paused;
Then, pointing to the stones near which they stood,
Thus, after a short silence, he resumed:
"This was a work for us; and now, my Son, 385
It is a work for me. But, lay one stone—
Here, lay it for me, Luke, with thine own hands.
Nay, Boy, be of good hope;—we both may live
To see a better day. At eighty-four
I still am strong and hale;—do thou thy part; 390
I will do mine.—I will begin again
With many tasks that were resigned to thee:
Up to the heights, and in among the storms,
Will I without thee go again, and do
All works which I was wont to do alone, 395
Before I knew thy face.—Heaven bless thee, Boy!
Thy heart these two weeks has been beating fast
With many hopes; it should be so—yes—yes—
I knew that thou couldst never have a wish
To leave me, Luke; thou hast been bound to me 400
Only by links of love: when thou art gone,
What will be left to us!—But I forget
My purposes. Lay now the corner-stone,
As I requested; and hereafter, Luke,

When thou art gone away, should evil men 405
Be thy companions, think of me, my Son,
And of this moment; hither turn thy thoughts,
And God will strengthen thee: amid all fear
And all temptation, Luke, I pray that thou
May'st bear in mind the life thy Fathers lived, 410
Who, being innocent, did for that cause
Bestir them in good deeds. Now, fare thee well—
When thou return'st, thou in this place wilt see
A work which is not here: a covenant
'Twill be between us; but, whatever fate 415
Befall thee, I shall love thee to the last,
And bear thy memory with me to the grave."

The Shepherd ended here; and Luke stooped down,
And, as his Father had requested, laid
The first stone of the Sheep-fold. At the sight 420
The old Man's grief broke from him; to his heart
He pressed his Son, he kissed him and wept;
And to the house together they returned.
—Hushed was that House in peace, or seeming peace,
Ere the night fell:—with morrow's dawn the Boy 425
Began his journey, and, when he had reached
The public way, he put on a bold face;
And all the neighbours, as he passed their doors,
Came forth with wishes and with farewell prayers,
That followed him till he was out of sight. 430

A good report did from their Kinsman come,
Of Luke and his well-doing: and the Boy
Wrote loving letters, full of wondrous news,
Which, as the Housewife phrased it, were throughout
"The prettiest letters that were ever seen." 435
Both parents read them with rejoicing hearts.
So, many months passed on: and once again
The Shepherd went about his daily work

With confident and cheerful thoughts; and now
Sometimes when he could find a leisure hour 440
He to that valley took his way, and there
Wrought at the Sheep-fold. Meantime Luke began
To slacken in his duty; and, at length,
He in the dissolute city gave himself
To evil courses: ignominy and shame 445
Fell on him, so that he was driven at last
To seek a hiding-place beyond the seas.

There is a comfort in the strength of love;
'Twill make a thing endurable, which else
Would overset the brain, or break the heart: 450
I have conversed with more than one who well
Remember the old Man, and what he was
Years after he had heard this heavy news.
His bodily frame had been from youth to age
Of an unusual strength. Among the rocks 455
He went, and still looked up to sun and cloud,
And listened to the wind; and, as before,
Performed all kinds of labour for his sheep,
And for the land, his small inheritance.
And to that hollow dell from time to time 460
Did he repair, to build the Fold of which
His flock had need. 'Tis not forgotten yet
The pity which was then in every heart
For the old Man—and 'tis believed by all
That many and many a day he thither went, 465
And never lifted up a single stone.

There, by the Sheep-fold, sometimes was he seen
Sitting alone, or with his faithful Dog,
Then old, beside him, lying at his feet.
The length of full seven years, from time to time, 470
He at the building of this Sheep-fold wrought,
And left the work unfinished when he died.

Three years, or little more, did Isabel
Survive her Husband: at her death the estate
Was sold, and went into a stranger's hand. 475
The Cottage which was named the EVENING STAR
Is gone—the ploughshare has been through the ground
On which it stood; great changes have been wrought
In all the neighbourhood:—yet the oak is left
That grew beside their door; and the remains 480
Of the unfinished Sheep-fold may be seen
Beside the boisterous brook of Green-head Ghyll.

1. Analyze the structure of the poem in terms of exposition, problem, development, turning point, climax, development, and denouement. Why does Wordsworth devote a good many lines to the exposition?
2. Summarize the content of this poem in two or three sentences. Does the content of the poem seem to warrant the extended presentation Wordsworth has given it? Why or why not?
3. What are the basic traits of the character of Michael? By what means are these traits brought out in the poem and emphasized?
4. Do you find it easy to accept the fact of Luke's deterioration? Why or why not?
5. Compare the imagery of nine lines of this poem with the imagery of a stanza in Keats' poem, "The Eve of St. Agnes" (p. 120). Are the differences in the amount and kind of imagery justified in terms of the purposes of the two poets?
6. Wordsworth held that poetry should be written in "a selection of language really used by men." To what extent has he achieved this objective in this poem?
7. Of what symbolic value are the lamp in the window and the sheep-fold? Of the two symbols which is the more successful? Why?

EDWARD
Anonymous

'Why dois your brand sae drap wi bluid,
Edward, Edward,
Why dois your brand sae drap wi bluid,
And why sae sad gang yee O?'
'O I hae killed my hauke sae guid, 5
Mither, mither,

O I hae killed my hauke sae guid,
  And I had nae mair bot hee O.'

'Your haukis bluid was nevir sae reid,
                    Edward, Edward, 10
Your haukis bluid was nevir sae reid,
  My deir son I tell thee O.'
'O I hae killed my reid-roan steid,
                    Mither, mither,
O I hae killed my reid-roan steid 15
  That erst was sae fair and frie O.'

'Your steid was auld, and ye hae got mair,
                    Edward, Edward,
Your steid was auld, and ye hae got mair,
  Sum other dule ye drie O.' 20
'O I hae killed my fadir deir,
                    Mither, mither,
O I hae killed my fadir deir,
  Alas, and wae is mee O!'

'And whatten penance wul ye drie for that? 25
                    Edward, Edward,
And whatten penance wul ye drie for that?
  My deir son, now tell me O.'
'Ile set my feit in yonder boat,
                    Mither, mither, 30
Ile set my feit in yonder boat,
  And Ile fare ovir the sea O.'

'And what wul ye doe wi your towirs and your ha,
                    Edward, Edward?
And what wul you doe wi your towirs and your ha, 35
  That were sae fair to see O?'
'Ile let thame stand tul they doun fa,
                    Mither, mither,
Ile let thame stand tul they doun fa,
  For here nevir mair maun I bee O.' 40

'And what wul ye leive to your bairns and your wife,
Edward, Edward?
And what wul ye leive to your bairns and your wife,
Whan ye gang ovir the sea O?
'The warldis room, late them beg thrae life, 45
Mither, mither,
The warldis room, late them beg thrae life,
For thame nevir mair wul I see O.'

'And what wul ye leive to your ain mither deir,
Edward, Edward? 50
And what wul ye leive to your ain mither deir?
My deir son, now tell me O.'
'The curse of hell frae me sall ye beir,
Mither, mither,
The curse of hell frae me sall ye beir, 55
Sic counseils ye gave to me O.'

1. Summarize the content of this poem in two or three sentences. What essential elements in the story must the reader supply? Is the responsibility that is thrown on the reader justifiable? Why or why not?
2. What is gained by the use of the question and answer method of narration? What is lost? Are the losses compensated for by the gains in this poem? Why or why not?
3. What purpose is served by the repetition of the "burden" ("Edward, Edward"; "Mither, mither")? Discuss the effect on the rhythm and the tone of the final O's in this poem.
4. By what means does the poet initiate interest and create and maintain suspense? By what means are interest and suspense sustained after the turning point at the end of the third stanza?
5. Why is the poem effective despite the sketchiness with which plot and characterization are treated?

LA BELLE DAME SANS MERCI

A Ballad

John Keats

O what can ail thee, knight-at-arms,
Alone and palely loitering?

The sedge has wither'd from the lake,
 And no birds sing.

O what can ail thee, knight-at-arms! 5
 So haggard and so woe-begone!
The squirrel's granary is full,
 And the harvest's done.

I see a lilly on thy brow,
 With anguish moist and fever dew, 10
And on thy cheeks a fading rose
 Fast withereth too.

I met a lady in the meads,
 Full beautiful—a faery's child,
Her hair was long, her foot was light, 15
 And her eyes were wild.

I made a garland for her head,
 And bracelets too, and fragrant zone;
She look'd at me as she did love,
 And made sweet moan. 20

I set her on my pacing steed,
 And nothing else saw all day long,
For sidelong would she bend, and sing
 A faery's song.

She found me roots of relish sweet, 25
 And honey wild, and manna dew,
And sure in language strange she said—
 'I love thee true.'

She took me to her elfin grot,
 And there she wept, and sigh'd full sore, 30
And there I shut her wild wild eyes
 With kisses four.

And there she lulled me asleep,
  And there I dream'd—Ah! woe betide!
The latest dream I ever dream'd 35
  On the cold hill side.

I saw pale kings and princes too,
  Pale warriors, death-pale were they all;
They cried—'La Belle Dame sans Merci
  Hath thee in thrall!' 40

I saw their starved lips in the gloam,
  With horrid warning gaped wide,
And I awoke and found me here,
  On the cold hill's side.

And this is why I sojourn here, 45
  Alone and palely loitering,
Though the sedge has wither'd from the lake,
  And no birds sing.

1. Compare the following aspects of this poem, written by a great poet, and "Sir Patrick Spens," an anonymous folk ballad: the nature of the subject matter, the treatment of the narrative elements, the meter, the diction, the emotions aroused in the reader. Do you consider it fair or unfair to compare these two poems? Why or why not?
2. What does Keats gain by making the first and the last stanzas almost identical? What does he gain by the changes he introduces in the last stanza?
3. Study the words what are repeated in this poem. Is the amount of repetition excessive? Why or why not?
4. Make an analysis of the meter of the first two, fifth and sixth and the last two stanzas. Has Keats achieved a satisfactory balance between regularity and variety? Make a metrical analysis of the fourth lines of the stanzas, and discuss the effects Keats gets through his variations in this short line.
5. Outline the feelings and emotions experienced by the knight who recounts his adventures. Does this sequence of feelings have an important bearing on what you conceive the poet's purpose to be in this poem?

THE EVE OF ST. AGNES

John Keats

St. Agnes' Eve—Ah, bitter chill it was!
The owl, for all his feathers, was a-cold;
The hare limp'd trembling through the frozen grass,
And silent was the flock in woolly fold:
Numb were the Beadsman's fingers, while he told 5
His rosary, and while his frosted breath,
Like pious incense from a censer old,
Seem'd taking flight for heaven, without a death,
Past the sweet Virgin's picture, while his prayer he saith.

His prayer he saith, this patient, holy man; 10
Then takes his lamp, and riseth from his knees,
And back returneth, meagre, barefoot, wan,
Along the chapel aisle by slow degrees:
The sculptur'd dead, on each side, seem to freeze,
Emprison'd in black, purgatorial rails: 15
Knights, ladies, praying in dumb orat'ries,
He passeth by; and his weak spirit fails
To think how they may ache in icy hoods and mails.

Northward he turneth through a little door,
And scarce three steps, ere Music's golden tongue 20
Flatter'd to tears this aged man and poor;
But no—already had his deathbell rung;
The joys of all his life were said and sung:
His was harsh penance on St. Agnes' Eve:
Another way he went, and soon among 25
Rough ashes sat he for his soul's reprieve,
And all night kept awake, for sinners' sake to grieve.

That ancient Beadsman heard the prelude soft;
And so it chanc'd, for many a door was wide,
From hurry to and fro. Soon, up aloft, 30

The silver snarling trumpets 'gan to chide:
The level chambers, ready with their pride,
Were glowing to receive a thousand guests:
The carved angels, ever eager-eyed,
Star'd, where upon their heads the cornice rests, 35
With hair blown back, and wings put cross-wise on their breasts.

At length burst in the argent revelry,
With plume, tiara, and all rich array,
Numerous as shadows haunting fairily
The brain, new-stuff'd, in youth, with triumphs gay 40
Of old romance. These let us wish away,
And turn, sole-thoughted, to one Lady there,
Whose heart had brooded, all that wintry day,
On love, and wing'd St. Agnes' saintly care,
As she had heard old dames full many times declare. 45

They told her how, upon St. Agnes' Eve,
Young virgins might have visions of delight,
And soft adorings from their loves receive
Upon the honey'd middle of the night,
If ceremonies due they did aright; 50
As, supperless to bed they must retire,
And couch supine their beauties, lily white;
Nor look behind, nor sideways, but require
Of Heaven with upward eyes for all that they desire.

Full of this whim was thoughtful Madeline: 55
The music, yearning like a God in pain,
She scarcely heard: her maiden eyes divine,
Fix'd on the floor, saw many a sweeping train
Pass by—she heeded not at all: in vain
Came many a tiptoe, amorous cavalier, 60
And back retir'd; not cool'd by high disdain,
But she saw not: her heart was otherwhere:
She sigh'd for Agnes' dreams, the sweetest of the year.

She danc'd along with vague, regardless eyes,
Anxious her lips, her breathing quick and short: 65
The hallow'd hour was near at hand: she sighs
Amid the timbrels, and the throng'd resort
Of whisperers in anger, or in sport;
'Mid looks of love, defiance, hate, and scorn,
Hoodwink'd with faery fancy; all amort, 70
Save to St. Agnes and her lambs unshorn,
And all the bliss to be before to-morrow morn.

So, purposing each moment to retire,
She linger'd still. Meantime, across the moors,
Had come young Porphyro, with heart on fire 75
For Madeline. Beside the portal doors,
Buttress'd from moonlight, stands he, and implores
All saints to give him sight of Madeline,
But for one moment in the tedious hours,
That he might gaze and worship all unseen; 80
Perchance speak, kneel, touch, kiss—in sooth such things have been.

He ventures in: let no buzz'd whisper tell:
All eyes be muffled, or a hundred swords
Will storm his heart, Love's fev'rous citadel:
For him, those chambers held barbarian hordes, 85
Hyena foemen, and hot-blooded lords,
Whose very dogs would execrations howl
Against his lineage: not one breast affords
Him any mercy, in that mansion foul,
Save one old beldame, weak in body and in soul. 90

Ah, happy chance! the aged creature came,
Shuffling along with ivory-headed wand,
To where he stood, hid from the torch's flame,
Behind a broad hall-pillar, far beyond
The sound of merriment and chorus bland: 95
He startled her; but soon she knew his face,

And grasp'd his fingers in her palsied hand,
Saying, 'Mercy, Porphyro! hie thee from this place;
'They are all here tonight, the whole blood-thirsty race!

'Get hence! get hence! there's dwarfish Hildebrand; 100
'He had a fever late, and in the fit
'He cursed thee and thine, both house and land:
'Then there's that old Lord Maurice, not a whit
'More tame for his gray hairs—Alas me! flit!
'Flit like a ghost away.'—'Ah, Gossip dear, 105
'We're safe enough; here in this arm-chair sit,
'And tell me how'—'Good saints! not here, not here;
'Follow me, child, or else these stones will be thy bier.'

He follow'd through a lowly arched way,
Brushing the cobwebs with his lofty plume, 110
And as she mutter'd 'Well-a—well-a-day!'
He found him in a little moonlight room,
Pale, lattic'd, chill, and silent as a tomb.
'Now tell me where is Madeline,' said he,
'O tell me, Angela, by the holy loom 115
'Which none but secret sisterhood may see,
'When they St. Agnes' wool are weaving piously.'

'St. Agnes! Ah! it is St. Agnes' Eve—
'Yet men will murder upon holy days:
'Thou must hold water in a witch's sieve, 120
'And be liege-lord of all the Elves and Fays,
'To venture so: it fills me with amaze
'To see thee, Porphyro!—St. Agnes' Eve!
'God's help! my lady fair the conjuror plays
'This very night: good angels her deceive! 125
'But let me laugh awhile, I've mickle time to grieve.'

Feebly she laugheth in the languid moon,
While Porphyro upon her face doth look,
Like puzzled urchin on an aged crone

Who keepeth clos'd a wond'rous riddle-book, 130
As spectacled she sits in chimney nook.
But soon his eyes grew brilliant, when she told
His lady's purpose; and he scarce could brook
Tears, at the thought of those enchantments cold
And Madeline asleep in lap of legends old. 135

Sudden a thought came like a full-blown rose,
Flushing his brow, and in his pained heart
Made purple riot: then doth he propose
A stratagem, that makes the beldame start:
'A cruel man and impious thou art: 140
'Sweet lady, let her pray, and sleep, and dream
'Alone with her good angels, far apart
'From wicked men like thee. Go, go!—I deem
'Thou canst not surely be the same that thou didst seem.

'I will not harm her, by all saints I swear,' 145
Quoth Porphyro: 'O may I ne'er find grace
'When my weak voice shall whisper its last prayer,
'If one of her soft ringlets I displace,
'Or look with ruffian passion in her face:
'Good Angela, believe me by these tears; 150
'Or I will, even in a moment's space,
'Awake, with horrid shout, my foemen's ears,
'And beard them, though they be more fang'd than wolves and
bears.'

'Ah! why wilt thou affright a feeble soul?
'A poor, weak, palsy-stricken, churchyard thing, 155
'Whose passing-bell may ere the midnight toll;
'Whose prayers for thee, each morn and evening,
'Were never missed.' Thus plaining, doth she bring
A gentler speech from burning Porphyro;
So woeful, and of such deep sorrowing, 160
That Angela gives promise she will do
Whatever he shall wish, betide her weal or woe.

Which was, to lead him, in close secrecy,
Even to Madeline's chamber, and there hide
Him in a closet, of such privacy 165
That he might see her beauty unespied,
And win perhaps that night a peerless bride,
While legion'd fairies pac'd the coverlet,
And pale enchantment held her sleepy-eyed.
Never on such a night have lovers met, 170
Since Merlin paid his Demon all the monstrous debt.

'It shall be as thou wishest,' said the Dame:
'All cates and dainties shall be stored there
'Quickly on this feast-night: by the tambour frame
'Her own lute thou wilt see: no time to spare, 175
'For I am slow and feeble, and scarce dare
'On such a catering trust my dizzy head.
'Wait here, my child, with patience; kneel in prayer
'The while: Ah! thou must needs the lady wed,
'Or may I never leave my grave among the dead.' 180

So saying, she hobbled off with busy fear.
The lover's endless minutes slowly pass'd;
The dame return'd, and whisper'd in his ear
To follow her; with aged eyes aghast
From fright of dim espial. Safe at last, 185
Through many a dusky gallery, they gain
The maiden's chamber, silken, hush'd, and chaste;
Where Porphyro took covert, pleas'd amain.
His poor guide hurried back with agues in her brain.

Her falt'ring hand upon the balustrade, 190
Old Angela was feeling for the stair,
When Madeline, St. Agnes' charmed maid,
Rose, like a mission'd spirit, unaware:
With silver taper's light, and pious care,
She turn'd, and down the aged gossip led 195
To a safe level matting. Now prepare,

Young Porphyro, for gazing on that bed;
She comes, she comes again, like ring-dove fray'd and fled.

Out went the taper as she hurried in;
Its little smoke, in pallid moonshine, died: 200
She clos'd the door, she panted, all akin
To spirits of the air, and visions wide:
No uttered syllable, or, woe betide!
But to her heart, her heart was voluble,
Paining with eloquence her balmy side; 205
As though a tongueless nightingale should swell
Her throat in vain, and die, heart-stifled, in her dell.

A casement high and triple-arch'd there was,
All garlanded with carven imag'ries
Of fruits, and flowers, and bunches of knot-grass, 210
And diamonded with panes of quaint device,
Innumerable of stains and splendid dyes,
As are the tiger-moth's deep-damask'd wings;
And in the midst, 'mong thousand heraldries,
And twilight saints, and dim emblazonings, 215
A shielded scutcheon blush'd with blood of queens and kings.

Full on this casement shone the wintry moon,
And threw warm gules on Madeline's fair breast,
As down she knelt for heaven's grace and boon;
Rose-bloom fell on her hands, together prest, 220
And on her silver cross soft amethyst,
And on her hair a glory, like a saint:
She seem'd a splendid angel, newly drest,
Save wings, for heaven:—Porphyro grew faint:
She knelt, so pure a thing, so free from mortal taint. 225

Anon his heart revives: her vespers done,
Of all its wreathed pearls her hair she frees;
Unclasps her warmed jewels one by one;
Loosens her fragrant boddice; by degrees
Her rich attire creeps rustling to her knees: 230

Half-hidden, like a mermaid in sea-weed,
Pensive awhile she dreams awake, and sees,
In fancy, fair St. Agnes in her bed,
But dares not look behind, or all the charm is fled.

Soon, trembling in her soft and chilly nest, 235
In sort of wakeful swoon, perplex'd she lay,
Until the poppied warmth of sleep oppress'd
Her soothed limbs, and soul fatigued away;
Flown, like a thought, until the morrow-day;
Blissfully haven'd both from joy and pain; 240
Clasp'd like a missal where swart Paynims pray;
Blinded alike from sunshine and from rain,
As though a rose should shut, and be a bud again.

Stol'n to this paradise, and so entranced,
Porphyro gazed upon her empty dress, 245
And listen'd to her breathing, if it chanced
To wake into a slumberous tenderness;
Which when he heard, that minute did he bless,
And breath'd himself: then from the closet crept,
Noiseless as fear in a wide wilderness, 250
And over the hush'd carpet, silent, stept,
And 'tween the curtains peep'd, where, lo!—how fast she slept.

Then by the bed-side, where the faded moon
Made a dim, silver twilight, soft he set
A table, and, half anguish'd, threw thereon 255
A cloth of woven crimson, gold, and jet:—
O for some drowsy Morphean amulet!
The boisterous, midnight, festive clarion,
The kettle-drum, and far-heard clarinet,
Affray his ears, though but in dying tone:— 260
The hall-door shuts again, and all the noise is gone.

And still she slept an azure-lidded sleep,
In blanched linen, smooth, and lavender'd,
While he from forth the closet brought a heap

Of candied apple, quince, and plum, and gourd; 265
With jellies soother than the creamy curd,
And lucent syrops, tinct with cinnamon;
Manna and dates, in argosy transferr'd
From Fez; and spiced dainties, every one,
From silken Samarcand to cedar'd Lebanon. 270

These delicates he heap'd with glowing hand
On golden dishes and in baskets bright
Of wreathed silver: sumptuous they stand
In the retired quiet of the night,
Filling the chilly room with perfume light.— 275
'And now, my love, my seraph fair, awake!
'Thou art my heaven, and I thine eremite:
'Open thine eyes, for meek St. Agnes' sake,
'Or I shall drowse beside thee, so my soul doth ache.'

Thus whispering, his warm, unnerved arm 280
Sank in her pillow. Shaded was her dream
By the dusk curtains:—'twas a midnight charm
Impossible to melt as iced stream:
The lustrous salvers in the moonlight gleam;
Broad golden fringe upon the carpet lies: 285
It seem'd he never, never could redeem
From such a stedfast spell his lady's eyes;
So mus'd awhile, entoil'd in woofed phantasies.

Awakening up, he took her hollow lute,—
Tumultuous,—and, in chords that tenderest be, 290
He play'd an ancient ditty, long since mute,
In Provence call'd, 'La belle dame sans mercy:'
Close to her ear touching the melody;—
Wherewith disturb'd, she utter'd a soft moan:
He ceased—she panted quick—and suddenly 295
Her blue affrayed eyes wide open shone:
Upon his knees he sank, pale as smooth-sculptured stone.

Her eyes were open, but she still beheld,
Now wide awake, the vision of her sleep:
There was a painful change, that nigh expell'd 300
The blisses of her dream so pure and deep
At which fair Madeline began to weep,
And moan forth witless words with many a sigh;
While still her gaze on Porphyro would keep;
Who knelt, with joined hands and piteous eye, 305
Fearing to move or speak, she look'd so dreamingly.

'Ah, Porphyro!' said she, 'but even now
'Thy voice was at sweet tremble in mine ear,
'Made tuneable with every sweetest vow;
'And those sad eyes were spiritual and clear: 310
'How chang'd thou art! how pallid, chill, and drear!
'Give me that voice again, my Porphyro,
'Those looks immortal, those complainings dear!
'Oh, leave me not in this eternal woe,
'For if thou diest, my Love, I know not where to go.' 315

Beyond a mortal man impassion'd far
At these voluptuous accents, he arose,
Ethereal, flush'd, and like a throbbing star
Seen 'mid the sapphire heaven's deep repose;
Into her dream he melted, as the rose 320
Blendeth its odour with the violet,—
Solution sweet: meantime the frost-wind blows
Like Love's alarum pattering the sharp sleet
Against the window-panes; St. Agnes' moon hath set.

'Tis dark: quick pattereth the flaw-blown sleet: 325
'This is no dream, my bride, my Madeline!'
'Tis dark: the iced gusts still rave and beat:
'No dream, alas! alas! and woe is mine!
'Porphyro will leave me here to fade and pine.—
'Cruel! what traitor could thee hither bring? 330

'I curse not, for my heart is lost in thine,
'Though thou forsakest a deceived thing;—
'A dove forlorn and lost with sick unpruned wing.'

'My Madeline! sweet dreamer! lovely bride!
'Say, may I be for aye thy vassal blest? 335
'Thy beauty's shield, heart-shap'd and vermeil-dyed?
'Ah, silver shrine, here will I take my rest
'After so many hours of toil and quest,
'A famish'd pilgrim,—saved by miracle.
'Though I have found, I will not rob thy nest 340
'Saving of thy sweet self; if thou think'st well
'To trust, fair Madeline, to no rude infidel.

'Hark! 'tis an elfin-storm from faery land,
'Of haggard seeming, but a boon indeed:
'Arise—arise! the morning is at hand;— 345
'The bloated wassailers will never heed:—
'Let us away, my love, with happy speed;
'There are no ears to hear, or eyes to see,—
'Drown'd all in Rhenish and the sleepy mead:
'Awake! arise! my love, and fearless be, 350
'For o'er the southern moors I have a home for thee.'

She hurried at his words, beset with fears,
For there were sleeping dragons all around,
At glaring watch, perhaps, with ready spears—
Down the wide stairs a darkling way they found.— 355
In all the house was heard no human sound.
A chain-droop'd lamp was flickering by each door;
The arras, rich with horseman, hawk, and hound,
Flutter'd in the besieging wind's uproar;
And the long carpets rose along the gusty floor. 360

They glide, like phantoms, into the wide hall;
Like phantoms, to the iron porch they glide;

Where lay the Porter, in uneasy sprawl,
With a huge empty flaggon by his side:
The wakeful bloodhound rose, and shook his hide, 365
But his sagacious eye an inmate owns:
By one, and one, the bolts full easy slide:—
The chains lie silent on the footworn stones;—
The key turns, and the door upon its hinges groans.

And they are gone: aye, ages long ago 370
These lovers fled away into the storm.
That night the Baron dreamt of many a woe,
And all his warrior-guests, with shade and form
Of witch, and demon, and large coffin-worm,
Were long be-nightmar'd. Angela the old 375
Died palsy-twitch'd, with meagre face deform;
The Beadsman, after thousand aves told,
For aye unsought for slept among his ashes cold.

1. Summarize the narrative content of the poem in two or three sentences.
2. Discuss the structure of the poem in terms of its exposition, development, turning point, climax, development, and denouement. Could this pattern of incidents be presented effectively in prose? Why or why not?
3. Porphyro's problem at his first appearance is very different from his problem in the climax of the poem. Is this shift in the character of the problem an advantage to the poem? Why or why not?
4. Make an analysis of the imagery of one of the stanzas according to the method outlined in "Directions for the Analysis of a Poem" (p. 95). Why is the imagery an important contributing element to the effectiveness of this stanza? Why is imagery an important contributing element to the effectiveness of the whole poem? How does imagery affect the narrative?
5. What do the first three stanzas and the last stanza contribute to the effect of the poem?
6. Critics have disagreed as to the appropriateness of the Spenserian stanza for narrative poetry. In the light of your study of this poem, do you think Keats was well advised to choose this metric-stanzaic form for this poem? Why?

SWEENEY AMONG THE NIGHTINGALES

T. S. Eliot

ὤμοι, πέπληγμαι καιρίαν πληγὴν ἔσω.

Apeneck Sweeney spreads his knees
Letting his arms hang down to laugh,
The zebra stripes along his jaw
Swelling to maculate giraffe.

The circles of the stormy moon 5
Slide westward toward the River Plate,
Death and the Raven drift above
And Sweeney guards the hornèd gate.

Gloomy Orion and the Dog
Are veiled; and hushed the shrunken seas; 10
The person in the Spanish cape
Tries to sit on Sweeney's knees

Slips and pulls the table cloth
Overturns a coffee-cup,
Reorganized upon the floor 15
She yawns and draws a stocking up;

The silent man in mocha brown
Sprawls at the window-sill and gapes;
The waiter brings in oranges
Bananas figs and hothouse grapes; 20

The silent vertebrate in brown
Contracts and concentrates, withdraws;
Rachel *née* Rabinovitch
Tears at the grapes with murderous paws;

She and the lady in the cape 25
Are suspect, thought to be in league;

Therefore the man with heavy eyes
Declines the gambit, shows fatigue,

Leaves the room and reappears
Outside the window, leaning in, 30
Branches of wistaria
Circumscribe a golden grin;

The host with someone indistinct
Converses at the door apart,
The nightingales are singing near 35
The Convent of the Sacred Heart,

And sang within the bloody wood
When Agamemnon cried aloud,
And let their liquid siftings fall
To stain the stiff dishonoured shroud. 40

Epigraph. "Ay me, I am struck a mortal blow and deep within"—Agamemnon's outcry as he is being stabbed to death by his wife, Clytemnestra (Aeschylus, *Agamemnon,* 1343)

Line 4. maculate: spotted
Line 6. River Plate: the Rio de la Plata in South America
Line 8. the hornèd gate: In the *Aeneid* (VI, 892 ff.) true dreams come through the gate of horn, false dreams through the ivory gate; *hornèd,* however, seems to mean "equipped with horns" more naturally than "made of horn."
Line 35. nightingales: see the story of Philomela

1. List the characters who are introduced.
2. Summarize, in two or three sentences, the story of what happened to Sweeney.
3. In what respects does Sweeney differ from Agamemnon? Is Sweeney in any way like Agamemnon? Consult a good classical dictionary for details of the Agamemnon story.
4. If Sweeney is both like and unlike Agamemnon, is it possible that what happens to him is similarly ambiguous? Outline the poem's narrative. If you see an alternative story, outline that also.
5. What are the chief metrical characteristics of the poem?
6. Discuss the types of imagery employed and their importance to the poem's themes.

THE LISTENERS

Walter de la Mare

"Is there anybody there?" said the Traveller,
  Knocking on the moonlit door;
And his horse in the silence champed the grasses
  Of the forest's ferny floor:
And a bird flew up out of the turret, 5
  Above the Traveller's head:
And he smote upon the door again a second time;
  "Is there anybody there?" he said.
But no one descended to the Traveller;
  No head from the leaf-fringed sill 10
Leaned over and looked into his grey eyes,
  Where he stood perplexed and still.
But only a host of phantom listeners
  That dwelt in the lone house then
Stood listening in the quiet of the moonlight 15
  To that voice from the world of men:
Stood thronging the faint moonbeams on the dark stair,
  That goes down to the empty hall,
Hearkening in an air stirred and shaken
  By the lonely Traveller's call. 20
And he felt in his heart their strangeness,
  Their stillness answering his cry,
While his horse moved, cropping the dark turf,
  'Neath the starred and leafy sky;
For he suddenly smote on the door, even 25
  Louder, and lifted his head:—
"Tell them I came, and no one answered,
  That I kept my word," he said.
Never the least stir made the listeners,
  Though every word he spake 30
Fell echoing through the shadowiness of the still house

From the one man left awake:
Ay, they heard his foot upon the stirrup,
And the sound of iron on stone,
And how the silence surged softly backward, 35
When the plunging hoofs were gone.

1. What elements of plot are present in this poem? What elements are suggested? How is the treatment of the elements of plot influenced by the purpose of the poet as you conceive it? Is the balance between incident and mood satisfactory? Why or why not?
2. Who are "the listeners"? How do you know? Who is the "Traveller"? What is the object of his quest?
3. Is the effect of the poem dependent on, or independent of, your personal belief or disbelief in "spirits"? Give the reasons for your answer.
4. Would you regard "man's courage in facing the cryptic riddle of life" as a satisfactory statement of the theme of this poem? Why or why not?
5. Make an analysis of the meter, the sound-pattern, and the imagery of ten lines. Which of these three elements of style seems to contribute most to the creation of the atmosphere of this poem?

THE HAYSTACK IN THE FLOODS
William Morris

Had she come all the way for this,
To part at last without a kiss?
Yea, had she borne the dirt and rain
That her own eyes might see him slain
Beside the haystack in the floods? 5

Along the dripping leafless woods,
The stirrup touching either shoe,
She rode astride as troopers do;
With kirtle kilted to her knee,
To which the mud splash'd wretchedly; 10
And the wet dripp'd from every tree
Upon her head and heavy hair,
And on her eyelids broad and fair;

The tears and rain ran down her face.

By fits and starts they rode apace, 15
And very often was his place
Far off from her; he had to ride
Ahead, to see what might betide
When the roads cross'd; and sometimes, when
There rose a murmuring from his men, 20
Had to turn back with promises;
Ah me! she had but little ease;
And often for pure doubt and dread
She sobb'd, made giddy in the head
By the swift riding; while, for cold, 25
Her slender fingers scarce could hold
The wet reins; yea, and scarcely, too,
She felt the foot within her shoe
Against the stirrup: all for this,
To part at last without a kiss 30
Beside the haystack in the floods.

For when they near'd that old soak'd hay,
They saw across the only way
That Judas, Godmar, and the three
Red running lions dismally 35
Grinn'd from his pennon, under which
In one straight line along the ditch,
They counted thirty heads.

So then
While Robert turn'd round to his men,
She saw at once the wretched end, 40
And, stooping down, tried hard to rend
Her coif the wrong way from her head,
And hid her eyes; while Robert said:
"Nay love, 'tis scarcely two to one;
At Poictiers where we made them run 45
So fast—why, sweet my love, good cheer,

The Gascon frontier is so near,
Nought after this."
But: "O," she said
"My God! my God! I have to tread
The long way back without you; then 50
The court at Paris; those six men;
The gratings of the Chatelet;
The swift Seine on some rainy day
Like this, and people standing by,
And laughing, while my weak hands try 55
To recollect how strong men swim.
All this, or else a life with him,
For which I should be damned at last;
Would God that this next hour were past!"

He answer'd not, but cried his cry, 60
"St. George for Marny!" cheerily;
And laid his hand upon her rein.
Alas! no man of all his train
Gave back that cheery cry again;
And, while for rage his thumb beat fast 65
Upon his sword-hilt, some one cast
About his neck a kerchief long,
And bound him.
Then they went along
To Godmar; who said: "Now, Jehane,
Your lover's life is on the wane 70
So fast, that, if this very hour
You yield not as my paramour,
He will not see the rain leave off—
Nay, keep your tongue from gibe and scoff,
Sir Robert, or I slay you now." 75

She laid her hand upon her brow,
Then gazed upon the palm, as though
She thought her forehead bled, and "No,"

She said, and turn'd her head away,
As there were nothing else to say, 80
And everything were settled: red
Grew Godmar's face from chin to head:
"Jehane, on yonder hill there stands
My castle, guarding well my lands:
What hinders me from taking you, 85
And doing that I list to do
To your fair wilful body, while
Your knight lies dead?"

A wicked smile
Wrinkled her face, her lips grew thin,
A long way out she thrust her chin: 90
"You know that I should strangle you
While you were sleeping; or bite through
Your throat, by God's help—ah!" she said,
"Lord Jesus, pity your poor maid!
For in such wise they hem me in, 95
I cannot choose but sin and sin,
Whatever happens: yet I think
They could not make me eat or drink,
And so should I just reach my rest."
"Nay, if you do not my behest, 100
O Jehane! though I love you well,"
Said Godmar, "would I fail to tell
All that I know?" "Foul lies," she said.
"Eh? lies, my Jehane? by God's head,
At Paris folks would deem them true! 105
Do you know, Jehane, they cry for you,
'Jehane the brown! Jehane the brown!
Give us Jehane to burn or drown!'—
Eh—gag me Robert!—sweet my friend,
This were indeed a piteous end 110
For those long fingers, and long feet,

And long neck, and smooth shoulders sweet;
An end that few men would forget
That saw it—So, an hour yet:
Consider, Jehane, which to take 115
Of life or death!"

So, scarce awake,
Dismounting, did she leave that place,
And totter some yards: with her face
Turned upward to the sky she lay,
Her head on a wet heap of hay, 120
And fell asleep: and while she slept,
And did not dream, the minutes crept
Round to the twelve again; but she,
Being waked at last, sigh'd quietly,
And strangely childlike came, and said: 125
"I will not." Straightway Godmar's head,
As though it hung on strong wires, turn'd
Most sharply round, and his face burn'd.

For Robert—both his eyes were dry,
He could not weep, but gloomily 130
He seem'd to watch the rain; yea, too,
His lips were firm; he tried once more
To touch her lips; she reach'd out, sore
And vain desire so tortured them,
The poor gray lips, and now the hem 135
Of his sleeve brushed them.

With a start
Up Godmar rose, thrust them apart;
From Robert's throat he loosed the bands
Of silk and mail; With empty hands
Held out, she stood and gazed, and saw 140
The long bright blade without a flaw
Glide out from Godmar's sheath, his hand
In Robert's hair; she saw him bend

Back Robert's head; she saw him send
The thin steel down; the blow told well, 145
Right backward the knight Robert fell,
And moan'd as dogs do, being half dead,
Unwitting, as I deem: so then
Godmar turn'd grinning to his men,
Who ran, some five or six, and beat 150
His head to pieces at their feet.

Then Godmar turn'd again and said:
"So Jehane, the first fitte is read!
Take note, my lady, that your way
Lies backward to the Chatelet!" 155
She shook her head and gazed awhile
At her cold hands with a rueful smile,
As though this thing had made her mad.

This was the parting that they had
Beside the haystack in the floods. 160

1. Summarize the content of this poem in not more than two or three sentences. What events prior to the beginning of the action of the poem are implied? Do you think the poet was well advised to present the expository material solely by implication? Was he well advised to foreshadow the nature of the denouement in the opening stanzas? Why?
2. The setting of both "The Eve of St. Agnes" and "The Haystack in the Floods" is medieval. Compare the means by which the two poets attempt to invest their stories with a medieval atmosphere. Which poet creates the more realistic effect? Why?
3. What happened at the battle of Poitiers (line 45)? Who are "those six men" (line 51)? What is the Chatelet (line 52)? What is meant by Jehane's reference to swimming in the Seine (lines 53–56)?
4. What elements in the basic situation in this poem tend to make it melodramatic? By what means has Morris attempted to minimize the melodramatic elements in his situation? To what extent has he succeeded?
5. Make a metrical analysis of twenty lines of the poem. Has Morris succeeded in attaining a satisfactory balance between regularity and variety in his treatment of the meter? Is the meter appropriate to the subject and tone of the poem? Why?

JOURNEY OF THE MAGI

T. S. Eliot

'A cold coming we had of it,
Just the worst time of the year
For a journey, and such a long journey:
The ways deep and the weather sharp,
The very dead of winter.' 5
And the camels galled, sore-footed, refractory,
Lying down in the melting snow.
There were times we regretted
The summer palaces on slopes, the terraces,
And the silken girls bringing sherbet. 10
Then the camel men cursing and grumbling
And running away, and wanting their liquor and women,
And the night-fires going out, and the lack of shelters,
And the cities hostile and the towns unfriendly
And the villages dirty and charging high prices: 15
A hard time we had of it.
At the end we preferred to travel all night,
Sleeping in snatches,
With the voices singing in our ears, saying
That this was all folly. 20

Then at dawn we came down to a temperate valley,
Wet, below the snow line, smelling of vegetation;
With a running stream and a water-mill beating the darkness,
And three trees on the low sky,
And an old white horse galloped away in the meadow. 25
Then we came to a tavern with vine-leaves over the lintel,
Six hands at an open door dicing for pieces of silver,
And feet kicking the empty wine-skins.
But there was no information, and so we continued
And arrived at evening, not a moment too soon 30
Finding the place; it was (you may say) satisfactory.

All this was a long time ago, I remember,
And I would do it again, but set down
This set down
This: were we led all that way for 35
Birth or Death? There was a Birth, certainly,
We had evidence and no doubt. I had seen birth and death,
But had thought they were different; this Birth was
Hard and bitter agony for us, like Death, our death.
We returned to our places, these Kingdoms, 40
But no longer at ease here, in the old dispensation,
With an alien people clutching their gods.
I should be glad of another death.

The first five lines are adapted from a sermon preached before James I on Christmas Day, 1621, by Bishop Lancelot Andrewes on the text of Matthew 2:1-2. The passage adapted is as follows: "It was no summer progress. A cold coming they had of it at this time of the year, just the worst time of the year to take a journey, and especially a long journey in. The ways deep, the weather sharp, the days short, the sun farthest off *in solstitio brumali,* the very dead of winter."

1. What is the nature of the structure of the poem: narrative, descriptive, expository, argumentative, or a combination of some of these types of structure? How is the structure of the poem designed to carry out the poet's purpose?
2. Outline the succession of feelings and emotions expressed or suggested by the Magus who is speaking. Make an analysis of the diction sufficiently detailed to explain the major changes in tone throughout the poem. Where is the diction most concrete? Where is it most abstract?
3. Make a metrical analysis of enough of the poem to show by what means Eliot has sustained the rhythms established by the quotation with which the poem begins.
4. What are the major symbols in the poem? Are they persons, actions, things, or terms? Discuss the play on words in birth/Birth and death/Death in the final stanza of the poem.

BETWEEN TWO PRISONERS

James Dickey

I would not wish to sit
In my shape bound together with wire,
Wedged into a child's sprained desk
In the schoolhouse under the palm tree.
Only those who did could have done it. 5

One bled from a cut on his temple,
And sat with his yellow head bowed,
His wound for him painfully thinking.
A belief in words grew upon them
That the unbound, who walk, cannot know. 10

The guard at the window leaned close
In a movement he took from the palm tree,
To hear, in a foreign tongue,
All things which cannot be said.
In the splintering clapboard room 15

They rested the sides of their faces
On the tops of the desks as they talked.
Because of the presence of children
In the deep signs carved in the desk tops,
Signs on the empty blackboard 20

Began, like a rain, to appear.
In the luminous chalks of all colors,
Green face, yellow breast, white sails
Whose wing feathers made the wall burn
Like a waterfall seen in a fever, 25

An angel came boldly to light
From his hands casting green, ragged bolts
Each having the shape of a palm leaf.

Also traced upon darkness in chalk
Was the guard at the rear window leaning 30

Through the red, vital strokes of his tears.
Behind him, men lying with swords
As with women, heard themselves sing,
And woke, then, terribly knowing
That they were a death squad, singing 35

In its sleep, in the middle of a war.
A wind sprang out of the tree.
The guard awoke by the window,
And found he had talked to himself
All night, in two voices, of Heaven. 40

He stood in the sunlit playground
Where the quiet boys knelt together
In their bloodletting trusses of wire,
And saw their mussed, severed heads
Make the ground jump up like a dog. 45

I watched the small guard be hanged
A year later, to the day,
In a closed horse stall in Manila.
No one knows what language he spoke
As his face changed into all colors, 50

And gave off his red, promised tears,
Or if he learned blindly to read
A child's deep, hacked hieroglyphics
Which can call up an angel from nothing,
Or what was said for an instant, there, 55

In the tied, scribbled dark, between him
And a figure drawn hugely in chalk,
Speaking words that can never be spoken
Except in a foreign tongue,
In the end, at the end of a war. 60

This poem seems to present an incident from World War II. Two soldiers, probably American, are imprisoned in a schoolhouse. They are bound with wire and are sitting at the undersized school desks. Unable to move, they find comfort in talk during the night, before their execution. Understandably their talk has something to do with their fears and hopes in the face of death. The palm tree outside the window becomes, in their near hallucinated state, the figure of an angel such as might be drawn in chalk on the blackboard of a schoolroom. The Japanese guard listens sympathetically, though not understanding English, until he falls asleep, and their words go on in his ears as if they were his own thoughts ("The guard awoke by the window,/and found he had talked to himself/All night, in two voices, of Heaven."). The voices have made the other members of the death squad dream that they were singing in their sleep. The prisoners are decapitated that morning. A year later this guard has been captured by the Americans, and the poet witnesses his execution. Such is your editors' tentative reading of this poem. The poem may or may not be based on an actual occurrence, but in either case, the incident would necessarily be transformed by the poet in terms of the special meaning it had for him.

1. Comment on the significance of the setting. Why does it suit the poet's purpose that the prisoners should be forced to sit at the desks of children and to have the illusion of seeing a child's chalk-drawn angel become real?
2. Except for the bare act of execution itself (which is not exactly a friendly gesture), is there any expression or feeling of enmity between prisoners and captors?
3. What do you make of the description of the sleeping death-squad as "men lying with swords/As with women"? Does this phrase emphasize that they are trained and hardened veterans, or that in sleep they forget the war, or what?
4. Why is the knowledge that they are a death-squad "singing/In its sleep, in the middle of a war" a terrible knowledge?
5. The guard and the death squad all are asleep, while the prisoners talk all night communicating to the sleepers the mood of their talking. Why does the poet have the prisoners gain this ascendancy over their captors through this unconscious influence, and why does

he want the same "words that can never be spoken/Except in a foreign tongue" to echo in the captors' minds?

6. In stanza 9, what effect is gained by having the execution take place in a playground, by calling the prisoners "quiet boys," and by speaking of their "mussed" heads?
7. Comment on the last three stanzas of the poem and try to summarize what the poet is saying in the total poem.
8. It would have been easy for the poet to have the Japanese guard understand English, or for us at least to overhear the actual words of the prisoners. Why does he avoid giving the actual content of their talk?
9. Is there a verse from the New Testament especially appropriate to this poem which might conceivably have been in the poet's mind?

Characterization in Poetry

JUGGLING JERRY

George Meredith

Pitch here the tent, while the old horse grazes:
  By the old hedge-side we'll halt a stage.
It's nigh my last above the daisies:
  My next leaf'll be man's blank page.
Yes, my old girl! and it's no use crying: 5
  Juggler, constable, king, must bow.
One that outjuggles all's been spying
  Long to have me, and he has me now.

We've traveled time to this old common:
  Often we've hung our pots in the gorse. 10
We've had a stirring life, old woman,
  You, and I, and the old grey horse.
Races, and fairs, and royal occasions,
  Found us coming to their call:
Now they'll miss us at our stations: 15
  There's a Juggler outjuggles all!

Up goes the lark, as if all were jolly!
  Over the duck-pond the willow shakes.
Easy to think that grieving's folly,
  When the hand's firm as driven stakes! 20
Aye, when we're strong, and braced, and manful,

Life's a sweet fiddle: but we're a batch
Born to become the Great Juggler's han'ful:
Balls he shies up, and is safe to catch.

Here's where the lads of the village cricket: 25
I was a lad not wide from here:
Couldn't I whip off the bail from the wicket?
Like an old world those days appear!
Donkey, sheep, geese, and thatched ale-house—I know them!
They are old friends of my halts, and seem, 30
Somehow, as if kind thanks I owe them:
Juggling don't hinder the heart's esteem.

Juggling's no sin, for we must have victual:
Nature allows us to bait for the fool.
Holding one's own makes us juggle no little: 35
But, to increase it, hard juggling's the rule.
You that are sneering at my profession,
Haven't you juggled a vast amount?
There's the Prime Minister, in one Session,
Juggles more games than my sins'll count. 40

I've murdered insects with mock thunder:
Conscience, for that, in men don't quail.
I've made bread from the bump of wonder:
That's my business, and there's my tale.
Fashion and rank all praised the professor: 45
Aye! and I've had my smile from the Queen:
Bravo, Jerry! she meant: God bless her!
Ain't this a sermon on that scene?

I've studied men from my topsy-turvy
Close, and, I reckon, rather true. 50
Some are fine fellows: some, right scurvy:
Most, a dash between the two.
But it's a woman, old girl, that makes me

Think more kindly of the race:
And it's a woman, old girl, that shakes me 55
When the Great Juggler I must face.

We two were married, due and legal:
Honest we've lived since we've been one.
Lord! I could then jump like an eagle:
You danced bright as a bit o' the sun. 60
Birds in a May-bush we were! right merry!
All night we kiss'd, we juggled all day.
Joy was the heart of Juggling Jerry!
Now from his old girl he's juggled away.

It's past parsons to console us: 65
No, nor no doctor fetch for me:
I can die without my bolus;
Two of a trade, lass, never agree!
Parson and Doctor!—don't they love rarely
Fighting the devil in other men's fields! 70
Stand up yourself and match him fairly:
Then see how the rascal yields!

I, lass, have lived no gipsy, flaunting
Finery while his poor helpmate grubs:
Coin I've stored, and you won't be wanting: 75
You shan't beg from the troughs and tubs.
Nobly you've stuck to me, though in his kitchen
Many a Marquis would hail you Cook!
Palaces you could have ruled and grown rich in,
But your old Jerry you never forsook. 80

Hand up the chirper! ripe ale winks in it;
Let's have comfort and be at peace.
Once a stout draught made me light as a linnet.
Cheer up! the Lord must have his lease.
May be—for none see in that black hollow— 85

It's just a place where we're held in pawn,
And, when the Great Juggler makes as to swallow,
It's just the sword-trick—I ain't quite gone!

Yonder came smells of the gorse, so nutty,
Gold-like and warm: it's the prime of May. 90
Better than mortar, brick and putty,
Is God's house on a blowing day.
Lean me more up the mound; now I feel it:
All the old heath-smells! Ain't it strange?
There's the world laughing, as if to conceal it, 95
But He's by us, juggling the change.

I mind it well, by the sea-beach lying,
Once—it's long gone—when two gulls we beheld,
Which, as the moon got up, were flying
Down a big wave that sparked and swelled. 100
Crack, went a gun: one fell: the second
Wheeled round him twice, and was off for new luck:
There in the dark her white wing beckon'd:—
Drop me a kiss—I'm the bird dead-struck!

1. What are the basic traits of the character described in this poem? Show how the character's account of his boyhood, his profession, and his experience with his wife and with other people are used as characterizing devices. Show how the character's professional experience has conditioned his view of other men.
2. What are the elements in the complex tone of the poem? What is the dominant tone? Is the total tone appropriate to this particular dying man? Why or why not?
3. Does the diction of the poem seem appropriate or inappropriate to the speaker? Why or why not? Cite particular examples in support of your judgment. What elements in the poem give it its rustic earthy flavor?
4. Was the choice of the meter and the rhyme scheme well advised? Why or why not?
5. What is the poet's attitude toward this character? How has he made his attitude evident?

PORTRAIT

Kenneth Fearing

The clear brown eyes, kindly and alert, with 12-20 vision give
confident regard to the passing world through R. K. Lambert
& Company lenses framed in gold;
His soul, however, is all his own;
Arndt Brothers necktie and hat (with feather) supply a touch
of youth.

With his soul his own, he drives, drives, chats and drives,
The first and second bicuspids, lower right, replaced by bridge-
work, while two incisors have porcelain crowns; 5

(Render unto Federal, state and city Caesar, but not unto time;
Render nothing unto time until Amalgamated Death serves
final notice, in proper form;

The vault is ready;
The will has been drawn by Clagget, Clagget, Clagget & Brown;
The policies are adequate, Confidential's best, reimbursing for
disability, partial or complete, with double indemnity should
the end be a pure and simple accident) 10

Nothing unto time,
Nothing unto change, nothing unto fate,
Nothing unto you, and nothing unto me, or to any other known
or unknown party or parties, living or deceased;

But Mercury shoes, with special arch supports, take much of the
wear and tear;
On the course, a custombuilt driver corrects a tendency to slice;
15

Love's ravages have been repaired (it was a textbook case) by
Drs. Schultz, Lightner, Mannheim, and Goode,
While all of it is enclosed in excellent tweed, with Mr. Baumer's
personal attention to the shoulders and the waist;

And all of it now roving, chatting amiably through space in a Plymouth 6,
With his soul (his own) at peace, soothed by Walter Lippmann, and sustained by Haig & Haig.

1. What traits of the subject of this poem are emphasized by the poet? What contrasting pattern do these traits fall into? Of what use is this contrasting pattern in establishing Fearing's attitude toward his subject?
2. Since this is a satirical poem and since satire implies a standard of values in accordance with which judgment is passed on the subject of satire, what is the standard by which this man is judged? Does the judgment seem to you to be fair? Valuable? Why?
3. Study the repetitions in this poem. What do these repetitions contribute to the effect that Fearing is trying to get?
4. Since this poem is metrically freer than any other poem we have studied, what devices has the poet used to distinguish the poem from prose? Do you think the selection is prose or poetry? Why?

ULYSSES

Alfred, Lord Tennyson

It little profits that an idle king,
By this still hearth, among these barren crags,
Matched with an agèd wife, I mete and dole
Unequal laws unto a savage race,
That hoard, and sleep, and feed, and know not me. 5
I cannot rest from travel; I will drink
Life to the lees. All times I have enjoyed
Greatly, have suffered greatly, both with those
That loved me, and alone; on shore, and when
Through scudding drifts the rainy Hyades 10
Vext the dim sea. I am become a name;
For always roaming with a hungry heart
Much have I seen and known,—cities of men,
And manners, climates, councils, governments,
Myself not least, but honored of them all; 15
And drunk delight of battle with my peers,

Far on the ringing plains of windy Troy.
I am a part of all that I have met;
Yet all experience is an arch wherethro'
Gleams that untraveled world whose margin fades 20
For ever and for ever when I move.
How dull it is to pause, to make an end,
To rust unburnished, not to shine in use!
As though to breathe were life! Life piled on life
Were all too little, and of one to me 25
Little remains; but every hour is saved
From that eternal silence, something more,
A bringer of new things; and vile it were
For some three suns to store and hoard myself,
And this gray spirit yearning in desire 30
To follow knowledge like a sinking star,
Beyond the utmost bound of human thought.
  This is my son, mine own Telemachus,
To whom I leave the scepter and the isle—
Well-loved of me, discerning to fulfil 35
This labor, by slow prudence to make mild
A rugged people, and through soft degrees
Subdue them to the useful and the good.
Most blameless is he, centered in the sphere
Of common duties, decent not to fail 40
In offices of tenderness, and pay
Meet adoration to my household gods,
When I am gone. He works his work, I mine.
  There lies the port; the vessel puffs her sail:
There gloom the dark, broad seas. My mariners, 45
Souls that have toiled and wrought, and thought with me—
That ever with a frolic welcome took
The thunder and the sunshine, and opposed
Free hearts, free foreheads—you and I are old;
Old age hath yet his honor and his toil. 50
Death closes all; but something ere the end,

Some work of noble note, may yet be done,
Not unbecoming men that strove with Gods.
The lights begin to twinkle from the rocks:
The long day wanes; the slow moon climbs; the deep 55
Moans round with many voices. Come, my friends,
'Tis not too late to seek a newer world.
Push off, and sitting well in order smite
The sounding furrows; for my purpose holds
To sail beyond the sunset, and the baths 60
Of all the western stars, until I die.
It may be that the gulfs will wash us down;
It may be we shall touch the Happy Isles,
And see the great Achilles, whom we knew.
Though much is taken, much abides; and though 65
We are not now that strength which in old days
Moved earth and heaven, that which we are, we are;
One equal temper of heroic hearts,
Made weak by time and fate, but strong in will
To strive, to seek, to find, and not to yield. 70

1. Who was Ulysses? (Read a summary of the plot of Homer's *Odyssey*.)
2. What are the basic traits of Ulysses as Tennyson conceives him? How do his attitudes toward his wife, his son, his people, his mariners, and his experience contribute to a revelation of these basic traits?
3. Read the account of Ulysses in Canto 26 of Dante's "Inferno." To what extent does Dante's conception of Ulysses agree with Tennyson's conception? Which of the two poets seems to you to suggest the circumstances of Ulysses' death more effectively? Why?
4. Make an analysis of the structure of the poem. Of what significance is the division of the poem into three parts? How does the structure of the poem contribute to the elucidation of the character of Ulysses and his situation?
5. Show how the meter and diction assist in investing this poem with its heroic tone.
6. Make a study of the kinesthetic imagery in this poem. Is the emphasis on this type of imagery appropriate? Why or why not?
7. Which do you think interested Tennyson more—the presentation of his conception of Ulysses or the setting forth of a view of life? Give the reasons for your conclusion.

MY LAST DUCHESS

Ferrara

Robert Browning

That's my last Duchess painted on the wall,
Looking as if she were alive. I call
That piece a wonder, now: Frà Pandolf's hands
Worked busily a day, and there she stands.
Will't please you sit and look at her? I said 5
"Frà Pandolf" by design, for never read
Strangers like you that pictured countenance,
The depth and passion of its earnest glance,
But to myself they turned (since none puts by
The curtain I have drawn for you, but I) 10
And seemed as they would ask me, if they durst,
How such a glance came there; so, not the first
Are you to turn and ask thus. Sir, 'twas not
Her husband's presence only, called that spot
Of joy into the Duchess' cheek: perhaps 15
Frà Pandolf chanced to say "Her mantle laps
Over my lady's wrist too much," or "Paint
Must never hope to reproduce the faint
Half-flush that dies along her throat": such stuff
Was courtesy, she thought, and cause enough 20
For calling up that spot of joy. She had
A heart—how shall I say?—too soon made glad,
Too easily impressed; she liked whate'er
She looked on, and her looks went everywhere.
Sir, 'twas all one! My favour at her breast, 25
The dropping of the daylight in the West,
The bough of cherries some officious fool
Broke in the orchard for her, the white mule
She rode with round the terrace—all and each
Would draw from her alike the approving speech, 30

Or blush, at least. She thanked men,—good! but thanked
Somehow—(I know not how)—as if she ranked
My gift of a nine-hundred-years-old name
With anybody's gift. Who'd stoop to blame
This sort of trifling? Even had you skill 35
In speech—which I have not—to make your will
Quite clear to such an one, and say, "Just this
Or that in you disgusts me; here you miss,
Or there exceed the mark"—and if she let
Herself be lessoned so, nor plainly set 40
Her wits to yours, forsooth, and made excuse,
—E'en then would be some stooping; and I choose
Never to stoop. Oh sir, she smiled, no doubt,
Whene'er I passed her; but who passed without
Much the same smile? This grew; I gave commands; 45
Then all smiles stopped together. There she stands
As if alive. Will 't please you rise? We'll meet
The company below, then. I repeat,
The Count your master's known munificence
Is ample warrant that no just pretence 50
Of mine for dowry will be disallowed;
Though his fair daughter's self, as I avowed
At starting, is my object. Nay, we'll go
Together down, sir. Notice Neptune, though,
Taming a sea-horse, thought a rarity, 55
Which Claus of Innsbruck cast in bronze for me!

1. Which components of a narrative structure are of major importance in this poem?
2. Which details are of prime importance in characterizing the Duchess? the Duke?
3. Does the person to whom the Duke is speaking have a significant role in the poem?
4. Discuss the psychological values of this poem (see pp. 91–92 and pp. 485–487).
5. What metrical form does Browning employ? Mark the end-stopped and run-on lines. Does the use of rhyme seem a sensible choice in

this poem? (Most of Browning's dramatic monologues are unrhymed.)

6. What symbols are there in the poem? Make a one-paragraph statement of the major themes of the poem incorporating your view of the poem's symbolism.

FELIX RANDAL

Gerard Manley Hopkins

Felix Randal the farrier, O he is dead then? my duty all ended,
Who have watched his mould of man, big-boned and hardy-handsome
Pining, pining, till time when reason rambled in it and some
Fatal four disorders, fleshed there, all contended?

Sickness broke him. Impatient he cursed at first, but mended 5
Being anointed and all; though a heavenlier heart began some
Months earlier, since I had our sweet reprieve and ransom
Tendered to him. Ah well, God rest him all road ever he offended!

This seeing the sick endears them to us, us too it endears.
My tongue had taught thee comfort, touch had quenched thy tears, 10
Thy tears that touched my heart, child, Felix, poor Felix Randal;

How far from then forethought of, all thy more boisterous years,
When thou at the random grim forge, powerful amidst peers,
Didst fettle for the great grey drayhorse his bright and battering sandal!

1. There is a basic contrast in this poem between Felix Randal in health and in mortal illness. What two phases in the attitude of Randal to his illness and approaching death does the poet distinguish? How does the second of these attitudes assist in reconciling Randal, the poet, and the reader to the basic conflict in the poem?
2. Outline the succession of attitudes of the speaker, a ministering

priest, to the subject of this poem. Is the order of the attitudes effective? Why? Was the poet well advised in his emphasis on the attitude expressed in the last three lines of the poem? Why?

3. Make an analysis of the sound-pattern of the poem. Of what structural value is the rhyme scheme? Why is the sound-pattern an important element in the total effect of the poem?
4. This poem is metrically more unconventional than any poem that we have studied, because it is written in accordance with a system that differs in a number of important respects from either the traditional meters of English poetry or from free verse. Hopkins' system—which he called "sprung-rhythm"—although it inevitably involves accented and unaccented syllables, permits almost any number of heavily accented syllables to a line, and even four or five unaccented syllables to a foot. In making an analysis of the meter of this poem, mark the stressed syllables first, and then the unstressed syllables. In dividing the lines into feet, do not include more than one stressed syllable in a foot (except for spondees), but feel free to include almost any number of unaccented syllables in a foot with one heavily stressed syllable. What effects does Hopkins get by means of his metrical system which could not be achieved using the traditional system?

THE BISHOP ORDERS HIS TOMB AT ST. PRAXED'S CHURCH

Rome, 15—

Robert Browning

Vanity, saith the preacher, vanity!
Draw round my bed: is Anselm keeping back?
Nephews—sons mine . . . ah God, I know not! Well—
She, men would have to be your mother once,
Old Gandolf envied me, so fair she was! 5
What's done is done, and she is dead beside,
Dead long ago, and I am Bishop since,
And as she died so must we die ourselves,
And thence ye may perceive the world's a dream.
Life, how and what is it? As here I lie 10
In this state-chamber, dying by degrees,
Hours and long hours in the dead night, I ask
"Do I live, am I dead?" Peace, peace seems all.

Saint Praxed's ever was the church for peace;
And so, about this tomb of mine. I fought 15
With tooth and nail to save my niche, ye know:
—Old Gandolf cozened me, despite my care;
Shrewd was that snatch from out the corner South
He graced his carrion with, God curse the same!
Yet still my niche is not so cramped but thence 20
One sees the pulpit o' the epistle-side,
And somewhat of the choir, those silent seats,
And up into the aery dome where live
The angels, and a sunbeam's sure to lurk:
And I shall fill my slab of basalt there, 25
And 'neath my tabernacle take my rest,
With those nine columns round me, two and two,
The odd one at my feet where Anselm stands:
Peach-blossom marble all, the rare, the ripe
As fresh-poured red wine of a mighty pulse. 30
—Old Gandolf with his paltry onion-stone,
Put me where I may look at him! True peach,
Rosy and flawless: how I earned the prize!
Draw close: that conflagration of my church
—What then? So much was saved if aught were missed! 35
My sons, ye would not be my death? Go dig
The white-grape vineyard where the oil-press stood,
Drop water gently till the surface sink,
And if ye find . . . Ah God, I know not, I! . . .
Bedded in store of rotten fig-leaves soft, 40
And corded up in a tight olive-frail,
Some lump, Ah God, of *lapis lazuli*,
Big as a Jew's head cut off at the nape,
Blue as a vein o'er the Madonna's breast . . .
Sons, all have I bequeathed you, villas, all, 45
That brave Frascati villa with its bath,
So, let the blue lump poise between my knees,
Like God the Father's globe on both his hands

Ye worship in the Jesu Church so gay,
For Gandolf shall not choose but see and burst! 50
Swift as a weaver's shuttle fleet our years:
Man goeth to the grave, and where is he?
Did I say basalt for my slab, sons? Black—
'Twas ever antique-black I meant! How else
Shall ye contrast my frieze to come beneath? 55
The bas-relief in bronze ye promised me,
Those Pans and Nymphs ye wot of, and perchance
Some tripod, thyrsus, with a vase or so,
The Saviour at his sermon on the mount,
Saint Praxed in a glory, and one Pan 60
Ready to twitch the Nymph's last garment off,
And Moses with the tables . . . but I know
Ye mark me not! What do they whisper thee,
Child of my bowels, Anselm? Ah, ye hope
To revel down my villas while I gasp 65
Bricked o'er with beggar's mouldy travertine
Which Gandolf from his tomb-top chuckles at!
Nay, boys, ye love me—all of jasper, then!
'Tis jasper ye stand pledged to, lest I grieve,
My bath must needs be left behind, alas! 70
One block, pure green as a pistachio-nut,
There's plenty jasper somewhere in the world—
And have I not Saint Praxed's ear to pray
Horses for ye, and brown Greek manuscripts,
And mistresses with great smooth marbly limbs? 75
—That's if ye carve my epitaph aright,
Choice Latin, picked phrase, Tully's every word,
No gaudy ware like Gandolf's second line—
Tully, my masters? Ulpian serves his need!
And then how I shall lie through centuries, 80
And hear the blessed mutter of the mass,
And see God made and eaten all day long,
And feel the steady candle-flame, and taste

Good strong thick stupefying incense-smoke!
For as I lie here, hours of the dead night, 85
Dying in state and by such slow degrees,
I fold my arms as if they clasped a crook,
And stretch my feet forth straight as stone can point,
And let the bedclothes, for a mortcloth, drop
Into great laps and folds of sculptor's-work: 90
And as yon tapers dwindle, and strange thoughts
Grow, with a certain humming in my ears,
About the life before I lived this life,
And this life too, popes, cardinals and priests,
Saint Praxed at his sermon on the mount, 95
Your tall pale mother with her talking eyes,
And new-found agate urns as fresh as day,
And marble's language, Latin pure, discreet,
—Aha, ELUCESCEBAT quoth our friend?
No Tully, said I, Ulpian at the best! 100
Evil and brief hath been my pilgrimage.
All *lapis,* all, sons! Else I give the Pope
My villas! Will ye ever eat my heart?
Ever your eyes were as a lizard's quick,
They glitter like your mother's for my soul, 105
Or ye would heighten my impoverished frieze,
Piece out its starved design, and fill my vase
With grapes, and add a vizor and a Term,
And to the tripod ye would tie a lynx
That in his struggle throws the thyrsus down, 110
To comfort me on my entablature
Whereon I am to lie till I must ask
"Do I live, am I dead?" There, leave me, there!
For ye have stabbed me with ingratitude
To death—ye wish it—God, ye wish it! Stone— 115
Gritstone, a-crumble! Clammy squares which sweat
As if the corpse they keep were oozing through—
And no more *lapis* to delight the world!

Well, go! I bless ye. Fewer tapers there,
But in a row: and, going, turn your backs 120
—Ay, like departing altar-ministrants,
And leave me in my church, the church for peace,
That I may watch at leisure if he leers—
Old Gandolf, at me, from his onion-stone,
As still he envied me, so fair she was! 125

Line 1. the preacher: see Ecclesiastes 1:2
Line 72. Tully: Marcus Tullius Cicero
Line 99. *elucescebat:* "he was famous"; Cicero would write *elucebat.*

1. In what period did Browning's Bishop live? How do you know? What were the Bishop's major interests? What light do they throw on his character? Look up the meanings of the following terms: onion-stone, lapis lazuli, jasper, travertine, mortcloth, thyrsus, term.
2. What are the basic traits of the Bishop's character? Do these traits form a pattern of personality that is consistent? Intelligible? Individual? What light is thrown on the Bishop's character by his attitudes toward the other persons mentioned?
3. What are the specific Christian and Pagan references in the poem? What is the significance of their juxtaposition and their interplay?
4. Make a metrical analysis of ten lines of "Ulysses" and ten lines of this poem. Which of the poets introduces the greater number of variations from the metrical norm? Which of the poets more nearly achieves the movement of actual speech? How?
5. Although Browning's attitude toward his subject is much less overt than Tennyson's, try to discover Browning's attitude and the evidence that points to it.

FLAMMONDE

Edwin Arlington Robinson

The man Flammonde, from God knows where,
With firm address and foreign air,
With news of nations in his talk
And something royal in his walk,
With glint of iron in his eyes, 5
But never doubt, nor yet surprise,

Appeared, and stayed, and held his head
As one by kings accredited.

Erect, with his alert repose
About him, and about his clothes, 10
He pictured all tradition hears
Of what we owe to fifty years.
His cleansing heritage of taste
Paraded neither want nor waste;
And what he needed for his fee 15
To live, he borrowed graciously.

He never told us what he was,
Or what mischance, or other cause,
Had banished him from better days
To play the Prince of Castaways. 20
Meanwhile he played surpassing well
A part, for most, unplayable;
In fine, one pauses, half afraid
To say for certain that he played.

For that, one may as well forego 25
Conviction as to yes or no;
Nor can I say just how intense
Would then have been the difference
To several, who, having striven
In vain to get what he was given, 30
Would see the stranger taken on
By friends not easy to be won.

Moreover, many a malcontent
He soothed and found munificent;
His courtesy beguiled and foiled 35
Suspicion that his years were soiled;
His mien distinguished any crowd,
His credit strengthened when he bowed;

And women, young and old, were fond
Of looking at the man Flammonde. 40

There was a woman in our town
On whom the fashion was to frown;
But while our talk renewed the tinge
Of a long-faded scarlet fringe,
The man Flammonde saw none of that, 45
And what he saw we wondered at—
That none of us, in her distress,
Could hide or find our littleness.

There was a boy that all agreed
Had shut within him the rare seed 50
Of learning. We could understand,
But none of us could lift a hand.
The man Flammonde appraised the youth,
And told a few of us the truth;
And thereby, for a little gold, 55
A flowered future was unrolled.

There were two citizens who fought
For years and years, and over nought;
They made life awkward for their friends,
And shortened their own dividends. 60
The man Flammonde said what was wrong
Should be made right; nor was it long
Before they were again in line,
And had each other in to dine.

And these I mention are but four 65
Of many out of many more.
So much for them. But what of him—
So firm in every look and limb?
What small satanic sort of kink
Was in his brain? What broken link 70

Withheld him from the destinies
That came so near to being his?

What was he, when we came to sift
His meaning, and to note the drift
Of incommunicable ways 75
That make us ponder while we praise?
Why was it that his charm revealed
Somehow the surface of a shield?
What was it that we never caught?
What was he, and what was he not? 80

How much it was of him we met
We cannot ever know; nor yet
Shall all he gave us quite atone
For what was his, and his alone;
Nor need we now, since he knew best, 85
Nourish an ethical unrest:
Rarely at once will nature give
The power to be Flammonde and live.

We cannot know how much we learn
From those who never will return, 90
Until a flash of unforeseen
Remembrance falls on what has been.
We've each a darkening hill to climb;
And this is why, from time to time
In Tilbury Town, we look beyond 95
Horizons for the man Flammonde.

1. What are the basic traits of Flammonde? Make an analysis of the structure of the poem, and show how it is designed to bring out these traits.
2. Analyze the meter of the first, fourth, eighth, and twelfth stanzas of this poem. Does Robinson introduce a sufficient number af variations to prevent monotony? Was the meter well chosen? Why?
3. How do you think that Flammonde would describe himself? Discuss the effectiveness of the metaphor, "Prince of Castaways."

4. Does the poem seem to you to be rich or poor in imagery? Analyze enough of the imagery of the poem to justify your opinion as to its amount and quality. Are the amount and kind of imagery appropriate to Robinson's purpose as you conceive it?
5. Does the poem show a considerable or a slight gift for the analysis of character? Why?
6. What are the opposed feelings aroused by Flammonde? How does this opposition contribute to the basic irony of the poem?
7. Of what symbolical value was Flammonde to the community for which the poet is the spokesman?

PHAEDRA

H. D.

Think, O my soul,
of the red sand of Crete;
think of the earth; the heat
burnt fissures like the great
backs of the temple serpents; 5
think of the world you knew;
as the tide crept, the land
burned with a lizard-blue
where the dark sea met the sand.

Think, O my soul— 10
what power has struck you blind—
is there no desert-root, no forest-berry
pine-pitch or knot of fir
known that can help the soul
caught in a force, a power, 15
passionless, not its own?

So I scatter, so implore
Gods of Crete, summoned before
with slight craft;

ah, hear my prayer: 20
Grant to my soul
the body that it wore,

trained to your thought,
that kept and held your power,
as the petal of black poppy, 25
the opiate of the flower.

For art undreamt in Crete,
strange art and dire,
in counter-charm prevents my charm
limits my power: 30
pine-cone I heap,
grant answer to my prayer.

No more, my soul—
as the black cup, sullen and dark with fire,
burns till beside it, noon's bright heat 35
is withered, filled with dust—
and into that noon-heat
grown drab and stale,
suddenly wind and thunder and swift rain,
till the scarlet flower is wrecked 40
in the slash of the white hail.

The poppy that my heart was,
formed to bind all mortals,
made to strike and gather hearts
like flame upon an altar, 45
fades and shrinks, a red leaf
drenched and torn in the cold rain.

1. Read an account of the life of Phaedra in a classical dictionary. What particular elements in the character of Phaedra is the poet emphasizing in this poem?
2. Structurally, the poem is in three parts. What is the nature of these parts, and what is the reason for the order in which they appear? Why does the poet italicize the second part of the poem?
3. Make an analysis of the imagery of the poem. How does it bring out the primitiveness of Phaedra's character in contrast to the sophisticated culture with which she is unhappily involved?
4. Make a metrical analysis of the meter of the first, fourth, and seventh

stanzas. By what metrical means does the poet achieve a certain degree of regularity in this poem in free verse?
5. How does the imagery of the last two stanzas contribute to the tone of the poem? Is this tone appropriate? Why?

PORTRAIT OF A LADY

T. S. Eliot

Thou hast committed—
Fornication: but that was in another country,
And besides, the wench is dead.
—The Jew of Malta

I

Among the smoke and fog of a December afternoon
You have the scene arrange itself—as it will seem to do—
With "I have saved this afternoon for you";
And four wax candles in the darkened room,
Four rings of light upon the ceiling overhead, 5
An atmosphere of Juliet's tomb
Prepared for all the things to be said, or left unsaid.
We have been, let us say, to hear the latest Pole
Transmit the Preludes, through his hair and fingertips.
"So intimate, this Chopin, that I think his soul 10
Should be resurrected only among friends
Some two or three, who will not touch the bloom
That is rubbed and questioned in the concert room."
—And so the conversation slips
Among velleities and carefully caught regrets 15
Through attenuated tones of violins
Mingled with remote cornets
And begins.
"You do not know how much they mean to me, my friends,
And how, how rare and strange it is, to find 20
In a life composed so much, so much of odds and ends,
[For indeed I do not love it . . . you knew? You are not blind!

How keen you are!]
To find a friend who has these qualities,
Who has, and gives 25
Those qualities upon which friendship lives.
How much it means that I say this to you—
Without these friendships—life, what *cauchemar!*"

Among the windings of the violins
And the ariettes 30
Of cracked cornets
Inside my brain a dull tom-tom begins
Absurdly hammering a prelude of its own,
Capricious monotone
That is at least one definite "false note." 35
—Let us take the air, in a tobacco trance,
Admire the monuments
Discuss the late events,
Correct our watches by the public clocks.
Then sit for half an hour and drink our bocks. 40

II

Now that lilacs are in bloom
She has a bowl of lilacs in her room
And twists one in her fingers while she talks.
"Ah, my friend, you do not know, you do not know
What life is, you who hold it in your hands"; 45
(Slowly twisting the lilac stalks)
"You let it flow from you, you let it flow,
And youth is cruel, and has no remorse
And smiles at situations which it cannot see."
I smile, of course, 50
And go on drinking tea.
"Yet with these April sunsets, that somehow recall
My buried life, and Paris in the Spring,
I feel immeasurably at peace, and find the world
To be wonderful and youthful, after all." 55

The voice returns like the insistent out-of-tune
Of a broken violin on an August afternoon:
"I am always sure that you understand
My feelings, always sure that you feel,
Sure that across the gulf you reach your hand. 60

You are invulnerable, you have no Achilles' heel.
You will go on, and when you have prevailed
You can say: at this point many a one has failed.
But what have I, but what have I, my friend,
To give you, what can you receive from me? 65
Only the friendship and the sympathy
Of one about to reach her journey's end.

I shall sit here, serving tea to friends. . . ."

I take my hat: how can I make a cowardly amends
For what she has said to me? 70
You will see me any morning in the park
Reading the comics and the sporting page.
Particularly I remark
An English countess goes upon the stage.
A Greek was murdered at a Polish dance, 75
Another bank defaulter has confessed.
I keep my countenance,
I remain self-possessed
Except when a street piano, mechanical and tired
Reiterates some worn-out common song 80
With the smell of hyacinths across the garden
Recalling things that other people have desired.
Are these ideas right or wrong?

III

The October night comes down; returning as before
Except for a slight sensation of being ill at ease 85
I mount the stairs and turn the handle of the door

And feel as if I had mounted on my hands and knees.
"And so you are going abroad; and when do you return?
But that's a useless question.
You hardly know when you are coming back, 90
You will find so much to learn."
My smile falls heavily among the bric-à-brac.

"Perhaps you can write to me."
My self-possession flares up for a second;
This is as I had reckoned. 95
"I have been wondering frequently of late
(But our beginnings never know our ends!)
Why we have not developed into friends."
I feel like one who smiles, and turning shall remark
Suddenly, his expression in a glass. 100
My self-possession gutters; we are really in the dark.

"For everybody said so, all our friends,
They all were sure our feelings would relate
So closely! I myself can hardly understand.
We must leave it now to fate. 105
You will write, at any rate.
Perhaps it is not too late.
I shall sit here, serving tea to friends."

And I must borrow every changing shape
To find expression . . . dance, dance 110
Like a dancing bear,
Cry like a parrot, chatter like an ape.
Let us take the air, in a tobacco trance—

Well! and what if she should die some afternoon,
Afternoon gray and smoky, evening yellow and rose; 115
Should die and leave me sitting pen in hand
With the smoke coming down above the housetops;
Doubtful, for a while
Not knowing what to feel or if I understand

Or whether wise or foolish, tardy or too soon . . . 120
Would she not have the advantage, after all?
This music is successful with a "dying fall"
Now that we talk of dying—
And should I have the right to smile?

Epigraph. These lines are from Marlowe's play, *The Jew of Malta.* The first three words are the beginning of an accusation by a corrupt friar. The rest is the quick retort of the cynical Jew, Barabas, who sees no need to keep faith in dealings with Christians since they do not live up to their professions and consider it no sin to cheat a heathen or a heretic.

Line 15. velleities: the weakest form of desire
Line 28. *cauchemar:* nightmare
Line 30. ariettes: short airs

1. What is the relationship between the epigraph and the poem?
2. Is the title of the poem appropriate? Why or why not? Is the poet more interested in the Lady or the speaker? Which is the central problem in the poem, the speaker's relationship to the Lady or the speaker's relationship to himself? How does one of these relationships throw light on the other?
3. What are the basic elements in the character of the Lady? By what methods of characterization does the poet reveal them? What are the basic elements in the character of the speaker? By what methods does the poet reveal them?
4. Make an analysis of the "irregular meter" of twenty lines of the poem. Has Eliot achieved a satisfactory balance between regularity and irregularity of meter? Was Eliot well advised to use rhyme in this poem? Why?
5. Study the figures drawn from music. What is the function of these figures in relation to the structure of the poem?
6. Discuss the analytical value of the poem, that is, the skill or lack of skill with which character is analyzed.
7. What are the major symbols in the poem? To what major themes does the pattern composed by these symbols point?

Description in Poetry

WINTER

William Shakespeare

When icicles hang by the wall,
  And Dick the shepherd blows his nail,
And Tom bears logs into the hall,
  And milk comes frozen home in pail,
When blood is nipp'd and ways be foul, 5
Then nightly sings the staring owl;
      "Tu-who!
Tu-whit, tu-who!" a merry note,
While greasy Joan doth keel the pot.
When all aloud the wind doth blow, 10
  And coughing drowns the parson's saw,
And birds sit brooding in the snow,
  And Marian's nose looks red and raw;
When roasted crabs hiss in the bowl,
Then nightly sings the staring owl: 15
      "Tu-who!
Tu-whit, tu-who!" a merry note,
While greasy Joan doth keel the pot.

Line 9. keel: cool, or cool by skimming

1. Make an analysis of the imagery and show what type of imagery predominates in each stanza. What is the effect of the imagery in

the final line of each stanza? What effect is created by the juxtaposition of the owl's song and the final line?
2. What are the major themes of the poem? Are the extent and nature of the treatment appropriate to the themes? Why or why not?

SPRING

William Shakespeare

When daisies pied and violets blue
  And lady-smocks all silver-white
And cuckoo-buds of yellow hue
  Do paint the meadows with delight,
The cuckoo then on every tree, 5
Mocks married men; for thus sings he,
  "Cuckoo!
Cuckoo, cuckoo!" O word of fear,
Unpleasing to a married ear!

When shepherds pipe on oaten straws, 10
  And merry larks are ploughmen's clocks;
When turtles tread, and rooks, and daws,
  And maidens bleach their summer smocks,
The cuckoo then, on every tree,
Mocks married men; for thus sings he, 15
  "Cuckoo!
Cuckoo, cuckoo!" O word of fear,
Unpleasing to a married ear!

1. What is the connotation of the cuckoo's song?
2. Make an analysis of the imagery and compare it with that of "Winter." Which poem seems to you to be the more successful in achieving the poet's purpose? Why?
3. Make an analysis of the metrics and the sound-pattern of the poem. What elements in either the meter or the sound-pattern make the poem suitable for singing?
4. Compare the refrains of the two songs and indicate which of the two refrains fulfills its function the more successfully. Give the reasons for your judgment.
5. These songs occur together in the last scene of Shakespeare's *Love's*

Labour's Lost. They are introduced by a comic character, Don Armado, "a fantastical Spaniard," who has just presented for the pleasure of the sophisticated Princess and her companions a "pageant" of characters from ancient and Biblical history, enacted absurdly by a rustic cast. By way of introducing these songs, he says: "Will you hear the dialogue that the two learned men have compiled in praise of the owl and the cuckoo? It should have followed at the end of our show. . . . This side, Hiems, Winter, this Ver, the Spring, the one maintained by the owl, the other by the cuckoo." What effect does knowledge of the context of these songs have on your interpretation of them?

AFTER APPLE-PICKING

Robert Frost

My long two-pointed ladder's sticking through a tree
Toward heaven still,
And there's a barrel that I didn't fill
Besides it, and there may be two or three
Apples I didn't pick upon some bough. 5
But I am done with apple-picking now.
Essence of winter sleep is on the night,
The scent of apples: I am drowsing off.
I cannot rub the strangeness from my sight
I got from looking through a pane of glass 10
I skimmed this morning from the drinking trough
And held against the world of hoary grass.
It melted, and I let it fall and break.
But I was well
Upon my way to sleep before it fell, 15
And I could tell
What form my dreaming was about to take.
Magnified apples appear and disappear,
Stem end and blossom end,
And every fleck of russet showing clear. 20
My instep arch not only keeps the ache,
It keeps the pressure of a ladder-round.

I feel the ladder sway as the boughs bend.
And I keep hearing from the cellar bin
The rumbling sound 25
Of load on load of apples coming in.
For I have had too much
Of apple-picking: I am overtired
Of the great harvest I myself desired.
There were ten thousand thousand fruit to touch, 30
Cherish in hand, lift down, and not let fall.
For all
That struck the earth,
No matter if not bruised or spiked with stubble,
Went surely to the cider-apple heap 35
As of no worth.
One can see what will trouble
This sleep of mine, whatever sleep it is.
Were he not gone,
The woodchuck could say whether it's like his 40
Long sleep, as I describe its coming on,
Or just some human sleep.

1. Does the poem have any marked analytical interest, that is, does the poet make any attempt to interest us in the kind of man whose experience is set forth here?
2. Outline the feelings and emotions aroused by this poem. Discuss the effectiveness of the variety and the arrangement of these feelings and emotions.
3. Analyze the meter of the first ten and the last ten lines of the poem. What justification can you see for the variation in the lengths of the lines? Make an analysis of the rhyme scheme. Is there any relationship between the rhyme scheme and the meter of the poem?
4. Discuss the contribution of the diction, meter, metaphors, and similes to the colloquial quality of the poem.
5. If you think that the poem has any symbolical value, what are the major symbols and to what ideas does the pattern of symbols point?

VELVET SHOES
Elinor Wylie

Let us walk in the white snow
  In a soundless space;
With footsteps quiet and slow,
  At a tranquil pace,
  Under veils of white lace. 5

I shall go shod in silk,
  And you in wool,
White as a white cow's milk,
  More beautiful
  Than the breast of a gull. 10

We shall walk through the still town
  In a windless peace;
We shall step upon white down,
  Upon silver fleece,
  Upon softer than these. 15

We shall walk in velvet shoes:
  Wherever we go
Silence will fall like dews
  On white silence below.
  We shall walk in the snow. 20

1. What is the predominant tone of this poem? If there are subordinate or contrasting tones, what are they?
2. Make an analysis of the imagery in this poem. To which sense is a particular appeal made? Does this particular sense appeal enhance the effect of the poem? Why or why not?
3. Discuss the metaphors and similes in this poem by pointing out their sources and considering their freshness and their propriety.
4. Make an analysis of the meter and sound-pattern of the poem. How does the sound-pattern emphasize the meter? How does the poet utilize end-stopped and run-on lines to get an effect of variety? Has she achieved a satisfactory balance between regularity and variety? Do you think that the meter and the rhyme scheme were well chosen? Why or why not?

CYPRESSES

Robert Francis

At noon they talk of evening and at evening
Of night, but what they say at night
Is a dark secret.

Somebody long ago called them the Trees
Of Death and they have never forgotten. 5
The name enchants them.

Always an attitude of solitude
To point the paradox of standing
Alone together.

How many years they have been teaching birds 10
In little schools, by little skills,
How to be shadows.

Known near the Mediterranean since classical antiquity, the Italian cypress is a tapering tree thickly covered with shining green leaves. It grows to 90 feet. As E. S. Harrar writes in the *Encyclopedia Britannica,* "The tree grows straight, or nearly so, and has a gloomy and forbidding but wonderfully stately aspect. With advancing age its foliage becomes almost black. . . . The cypress, which is incapable of developing stump sprouts once the tree is cut down, was regarded as a symbol of the dead, and perhaps for that reason is sacred to Pluto." When his friend Cyparissus died, Apollo changed him to a cypress tree and said that henceforward this tree should shade the graves of loved persons.

1. Count the number of stresses in each line, and discuss the relevance of this rhythmical pattern to the subject. Does it relate to the shape of the tree? To the significance of the tree?
2. Explain stanza 1 in detail as a description of sound and as a description of color. To whom are the cypresses talking? Characterize their conversation.
3. What do the associations with silence and with progressive darkness suggest about the nature of the dark secret?
4. Explain the semantical ambiguity in the word "enchants" (line 6) and comment on its relevance here.

5. Is there a semantical ambiguity in "point" in line 8?
6. Comment on the phrase "attitude of solitude." Is there anything paradoxical about putting these two words together?
7. Comment on the images evoked by the line "In little schools, by little skills."
8. In what sense have the cypresses taught the birds to be shadows?
9. Do you feel that the details given in these four stanzas have a unifying thread beyond simply describing the cypresses? Demonstrate this.
10. Do you feel that these stanzas are in an inevitable order? Or could you shift their order?
11. For somber trees of death which strike an attitude of solitude, these cypresses betray a considerable social sense. They talk all day in stanza 1, are enchanted by what someone called them long ago in stanza 2, strike an attitude to point a paradox in stanza 3, and are busily teaching school in stanza 4. What does the poet have in mind by this characterization? Does "the paradox of standing/Alone together" in the face of death have anything to do with it?

TO AUTUMN

John Keats

Season of mists and mellow fruitfulness,
  Close bosom-friend of the maturing sun;
Conspiring with him how to load and bless
  With fruit the vines that round the thatch-eves run;
To bend with apples the mossed cottage-trees, 5
  And fill all fruit with ripeness to the core;
    To swell the gourd, and plump the hazel shells
With a sweet kernel; to set budding more,
  And still more, later flowers for the bees,
  Until they think warm days will never cease, 10
    For Summer has o'er-brimmed their clammy cells.

Who hath not seen thee oft amid thy store?
  Sometimes whoever seeks abroad may find
Thee sitting careless on a granary floor,
  Thy hair soft-lifted by the winnowing wind; 15
Or on a half-reaped furrow sound asleep,

Drowsed with the fume of poppies, while thy hook
Spares the next swath and all its twinèd flowers:
And sometimes like a gleaner thou dost keep
Steady thy laden head across a brook; 20
Or by a cyder-press, with patient look,
Thou watchest the last oozings hours by hours.

Where are the songs of Spring? Ay, where are they?
Think not of them, thou hast thy music too,—
While barrèd clouds bloom the soft-dying day, 25
And touch the stubble-plains with rosy hue;
Then in a wailful choir the small gnats mourn
Among the river sallows, borne aloft
Or sinking as the light wind lives or dies;
And full-grown lambs loud bleat from hilly bourn; 30
Hedge-crickets sing: and now with treble soft
The red-breast whistles from a garden-croft;
And gathering swallows twitter in the skies.

Line 28. sallows: willows
Line 30. bourn: region
Line 32. croft: a small, enclosed piece of land

1. Make an analysis of the imagery of the poem. What is the dominant type of imagery in the first stanza? In the second stanza? In the third stanza? Discuss the relationship of the type of imagery emphasized and the phase of autumn depicted in each stanza.
2. Discuss the effectiveness or ineffectiveness of the personification of autumn in this poem.
3. What traditional symbols are employed in the poem?
4. Make an analysis of the sound-pattern of the third stanza. Which of the lines makes the most effective use of alliteration and assonance? Study the nature of the rhymes, and consider to what extent they contribute to the effect of the poem.
5. What is the major feeling evoked in each stanza of the poem? If there are subordinate or contrasting feelings, what are they? Are the feelings evoked by this poem a significant element in its effect? Why?

VOYAGES, II

Hart Crane

And yet this great wink of eternity,
Of rimless floods, unfettered leewardings,
Samite sheeted and processioned where
Her undinal vast belly moonward bends,
Laughing the wrapt inflections of our love; 5

Take this Sea, whose diapason knells
On scrolls of silver snowy sentences,
The sceptred terror of whose sessions rends
As her demeanors motion well or ill,
All but the pieties of lovers' hands. 10

And onward, as bells off San Salvador
Salute the crocus lustres of the stars,
In these poinsettia meadows of her tides,—
Adagios of islands, O my Prodigal,
Complete the dark confessions her veins spell. 15

Mark how her turning shoulders wind the hours,
And hasten while her penniless rich palms
Pass superscription of bent foam and wave,—
Hasten, while they are true,—sleep, death, desire,
Close round one instant in one floating flower. 20

Bind us in time, O Seasons clear, and awe.
O minstrel galleons of Carib fire,
Bequeath us to no earthly shore until
Is answered in the vortex of our grave
The seal's wide spindrift gaze toward paradise. 25

1. What general comment would serve to characterize the diction of this poem? How many words do you need to look up in a dictionary? Are there any words your dictionary does not give?

2. What elements are compared in the various metaphors of the first stanza?
3. Point out the places in the poem where personification is the figure of speech.
4. Is this poem heavily symbolic? What traditional symbols are present? Are any of these symbols specifically allusive?
5. What does "wrapt" (line 5) mean? Do you think the poet has made a mistake in his choice of this word?
6. What is the dominant tone of the poem? How is it established and carried out? What is the tone of the last stanza?

PIED BEAUTY

Gerard Manley Hopkins

Glory be to God for dappled things—
  For skies of couple-colour as a brinded cow;
    For rose-moles all in stipple upon trout that swim;
Fresh-firecoal chestnut-falls; finches' wings;
  Landscape plotted and pieced—fold, fallow, and plough; 5
    And áll trádes, their gear and tackle and trim.

All things counter, original, spare, strange;
  Whatever is fickle, freckled (who knows how?)
    With swift, slow; sweet, sour; adazzle, dim;
He fathers-forth whose beauty is past change: 10
          Praise him.

1. What is the significance of the title?
2. State the major themes of the poem. By what means does the poet emphasize these themes?
3. What effect is gained by the change from the specific diction of the first stanza to the relatively abstract diction of the second stanza?
4. Make an analysis of the meter of the poem in accordance with the directions given for the metrical analysis of "Felix Randal" (p. 157). Which poem shows freer use of Hopkins's metrical system?
5. Make an analysis of the sound-pattern and the imagery of the poem. Does the imagery or the sound-pattern contribute more to the effect of the poem? Why?
6. Comment on the effect of the short concluding line and the major pause that precedes it.

THE WILD SWANS AT COOLE

William Butler Yeats

The trees are in their autumn beauty,
The woodland paths are dry,
Under the October twilight the water
Mirrors a still sky;
Upon the brimming water among the stones 5
Are nine-and-fifty swans.

The nineteenth autumn has come upon me
Since I first made my count;
I saw, before I had well finished,
All suddenly mount 10
And scatter wheeling in great broken rings
Upon their clamorous wings.

I have looked upon those brilliant creatures,
And now my heart is sore.
All's changed since I, hearing at twilight, 15
The first time on this shore,
The bell-beat of their wings above my head,
Trod with a lighter tread.

Unwearied still, lover by lover,
They paddle in the cold 20
Companionable streams or climb the air;
Their hearts have not grown old;
Passion or conquest, wander where they will,
Attend upon them still.

But now they drift on the still water, 25
Mysterious, beautiful;
Among what rushes will they build,
By what lake's edge or pool

Delight men's eyes when I awake some day
To find they have flown away? 30

1. Is this poem predominantly descriptive or expository in structure? Give the reasons for your answer.
2. Analyze the structure of this poem with particular attention to the times indicated for the description and exposition. What does Yeats gain by the particular time sequence he has adopted, especially by the reference to the future in the last four lines of the final stanza?
3. Was Yeats well advised to use figures as definite as "nine-and-fifty" and "nineteenth"? Why or why not?
4. Classify the images in this poem. What type of imagery seems to you to predominate? Is the predominant type of imagery appropriate to Yeats' purpose as you see it? Why or why not?
5. Analyze the meter and the rhyme scheme of the poem. Has Yeats achieved a satisfactory balance between regularity and irregularity in his use of meter? Is the degree of emphasis on the rhyme scheme satisfactory? Why or why not? Do you consider the failure of the last two lines of the first stanza to rhyme a technical flaw? Why or why not?
6. Read Keats' "Ode to a Nightingale" (p. 226), and compare Yeats' attitude to the swans and Keats' attitude to the nightingale. Which attitude is the more realistic? Why?

DOWNSTREAM II

Thomas Kinsella

Drifting to meet us on the darkening stage
A pattern shivered; whorling in its place
Another held us in a living cage
Then broke to its reordered phase of grace.

Again in the mirrored night—a liquid mask— 5
We sank our oars, bowing both in team;
The ripples scattered, dying, to their task

Under ghost alders stooped above the seam
Of calm and current, mowing like the blind.
We gave our frail craft to the hungry stream, 10

Grazing the near reeds, letting the banks unwind
In stealth on either hand. The Wood's dark door
Opened and shut; the clean sky fell behind;

The channel shrank. Thick slopes from shore to shore
Lowered a matted arch and moved out roots, 15
Full of slant pike, over the river-floor;

The black cage closed about us. Furred night-brutes
Stopped in the rat-trails, twitching their tiny brushes,
Or plopped in the reeds, astir between the shoots.

Then I remembered how among those bushes 20
A man one night fell sick and left his shell
Collapsed, half-eaten, like a rotted thrush's

To frighten stumbling children. "You could tell,"
My co-shadow murmured, "by the hands
He died in trouble." Then the cold of hell, 25

A limb-lightness, a terror in the glands,
Pierced again as when that story first
Froze my blood: the soil of other lands

Drank lives that summer with a body thirst,
While nerveless by the European pit 30
—Ourselves through seven hundred years accurst—

We gazed on barren earth obscurely lit
By tall chimneys flickering in their pall,
The haunt of swinish man—each day a spit

That, turning, sweated war, each night a fall 35
Back to the evil dream where rodents ply,
Man-rumped, sow-headed, busy with whip and maul,

Among nude herds of the damned. It seemed that I,
Coming to conscience on that lip of dread,
Still dreamed, impervious to calamity, 40

Imagining a formal drift of the dead
  Stretched calm as effigies on velvet dust,
  Scattered on starlit slopes with arms outspread

And eyes of silver—when that story thrust
  Pungent horror and an actual mess 45
  Into my very face, and taste I must!

Then hungry joy and sickening distress
  Met in union by the brimming flood
  And Night devoured a hopeless loneliness . . .

Like mortal jaws, the alleys of the wood 50
  Fell-to behind us, caged upon a ghost
  That glimmered, hidden, with my gift of blood,

Spreadeagled on a rack of leaves, almost
  Remembering. It searched among the skies,
  Calmly encountering the starry host, 55

Meeting their silver eyes with silver eyes
  —An X of wavering flesh, a skull of light
  That dimmed in our wake and guttered to a close.

Then the current, pausing in its flight,
  Swerved on pliant muscle; we were sped 60
  Through sudden calm into a pit of night:

The Mill-Hole, whose rocky fathoms fed
  On moss and pure depth and the cold fin
  Turning in its heart. The river bed

Called to our flesh from under the watery skin 65
  And, breathless, our shell trembling across the abyss,
  We shipped our oars in dread. Now, deeper in,

Sheathed in obscurity, a quiet hiss
  Fluttered against the rock, a folded crest
  Shifted in sleep, betraying with feathered kiss 70

A soul of white with darkness for a nest;
Some creature wore the night so tranquilly
I lifted up my eyes. There without rest

The phantoms of the overhanging sky
Occupied their stations and descended; 75
But, for an instant, to the starlit eye,

The slow, downstreaming dead, it seemed, were blended
One with those silver hordes, and briefly shared
Their order, glittering. And then impended

A barrier of rock that turned and bared 80
A varied barrenness as toward its base
We glided—blotting heaven as it towered—

Searching the darkness for a landing place.

This poem is a description of a trip downstream by boat at night. There are two men together. The stream winds into a thick woods where the trees shut off the view of the sky and the channel narrows. The noise of animals in the rat trails alongside the stream reminds the speaker "how among those bushes/A man one night fell sick" and died, and his gnawed and rotted body frightened children who stumbled upon it. Being at the very spot, this woods, makes the speaker relive the thrill of fear and distress which the incident first made him feel.

It was during World War II that the incident occurred: "the soil of other lands/Drank lives that summer with a body thirst." But the war and death were not fully real to the speaker, an Irishman (Ireland remained neutral throughout the war) and very young at the time (Thomas Kinsella was only 16 when the war ended). The Irish had been through seven hundred years accurst—the seven hundred years of English rule. Free since 1922 and unwilling to endanger her shores by siding with her former oppressor, the little country perched on the edge of Europe watched the conflict with an objectivity, if not a detachment, unavailable to the participants.

While nerveless by the European pit

• • •

We gazed on barren earth obscurely lit
By tall chimneys flickering in their pall,
The haunt of swinish man—each day a spit

That, turning, sweated war, each night a fall
Back to the evil dream where rodents ply,
Man-rumped, sow-headed, busy with whip and maul,

Among nude herds of the damned.

The "European pit" suggests sitting on the edge of a pit watching rats fighting at the bottom of it. I suppose the "tall chimneys" refer to factories in regions like the English Midlands, frantically (and in some cases greedily) turning out war products. In the lines which follow, the image of rats in a pit merges with the image of rat-shaped demons punishing man. The picture evoked is worthy of Dante's "Inferno," and one should note that the rhyme scheme of "Downstream" is the one made famous in Dante's poem, *terza rima:* aba bcb cdc, etc. Since the poet speaks of "swinish man" and the rodent-demons are "man-rumped, sow-headed," it would seem that the concept is one of the brutishness of men being punished by the brutishness of other men in war.

The boy knew that soldiers were dying everywhere, but his thought of death was still an immature one. He had vaguely accepted death as the customary thing that happens to old people and to soldiers. Death as he had conceived it was distanced by a formal funereal quality which protected his young emotions.

. . . It seemed that I,
Coming to conscience on that lip of dread,
Still dreamed, impervious to calamity,

Imagining a formal drift of the dead
Stretched calm as effigies on velvet dust,
Scattered on starlit slopes with arms outspread

And eyes of silver . . .

The "formal drift" of the dead (down the river of time one supposes) suggests a funereal procession; "effigies" suggests tombs; and "velvet dust" suggests the lining of coffins. So death to this young boy was not a raw fact. He was shielded from the thought of it by all the traditional trappings with which society wraps death to make it bearable. But suddenly the incident of the man dying in this woods and being half-eaten by rats forced the raw fact of death into the boy's consciousness.

> . . . that story thrust
> Pungent horror and an actual mess
> Into my very face, and taste I must!

The next three lines give us the effect on the boy of this coming, in war time, to a vivid consciousness of the reality of death. These lines are powerful but puzzling, and tantalizingly brief.

> Then hungry joy and sickening distress
> Met in union by the brimming flood
> And Night devoured a hopeless loneliness . . .

First of all the lines present a vicarious reliving by the boy of the event of the man's death. "Hungry joy" would apply quite literally to the appetite of the rats, and "sickening distress" to the condition of the dying man. This appetite and this condition did meet in union by the "brimming flood" of the river. The stricken man no doubt felt a "hopeless loneliness" which ended as that night of his death passed: "And Night devoured a hopeless loneliness. . . ." The word "devoured" would apply literally as well as metaphorically since the body was found half-eaten.

But this stanza does not present merely the reenactment of the man's death in the boy's mind, or even the boy's vicarious reliving of that death as if it were his own. It presents as well the consequence, the effect which this experience had on the boy, his reaction to it. Thus the "sickening distress" is not only the stricken man's illness but also the boy's fear, disgust, and pity on hearing the story. His "hungry joy" is more difficult to account for. The awareness of death, for a youth, may, however, be an initiation into life. This death is real; the youth is at last living real life. This horror is not the conventional death which his elders have told the youth about or which he has had to face only when protected by the formality of funerals. The direct facing of death may make life more vivid, more immediate, more genuine, and may give a tremendous impetus which might be described as a "hungry joy." The phrase "brimming flood" suggests life at the full. The hungry joy, then, is a hunger for vivid life and the expectation of having found it. The horror of death and the hunger for life (which hunger, since it is a hunger for the passage of time, is in some sense a hunger for death) meet "in union by the brimming flood" of the boy's emotional growth.

"And Night devoured a hopeless loneliness" intensely conveys both the boy's identification with the dying man and the boy's own fear of death—perhaps with the added sense that it took a whole night for him to master the feeling which the story aroused in him. But also the line seems to say that the feeling was mastered, that the awesome finality of universal death, perhaps symbolized by the capitalized "Night," overwhelmed his sense of personal loneliness and fear and freed him of it.

At any rate, in the next lines the boat has passed out of the wood where the man died and the speaker's emotion subsides, but he still recalls the body as if it were lying there, its eyes reflecting the stars.

> Like mortal jaws, the alleys of the wood
> Fell-to behind us, caged upon a ghost
> That glimmered, hidden, with my gift of blood,
>
> Spreadeagled on a rack of leaves, almost
> Remembering. It searched among the skies,
> Calmly encountering the starry host,
>
> Meeting their silver eyes with silver eyes
> —An X of wavering flesh, a skull of light
> That dimmed in our wake and guttered to a close.

The "distress" of the man who "died in trouble" is over with his life. As the poet passes out of the woods where the death occurred, he sees in his mind's eye the dead man lying there, his eyes "Calmly encountering the starry host," and now that the death agony is over the dead man seems to reach that acceptance and reconciliation which was less realistically imagined in the boy's earlier immature dream in which the dead were "Scattered on starlit slopes with arms outspread/And eyes of silver . . ." The agony over, the dead man seems once again united with some kind of cosmic order. His dead eyes regard the stars calmly, "Meeting their silver eyes with silver eyes. . . ."

But what about those who are still alive? The next lines provide an image of a live surface trembling over an abyss to suggest the sense of danger and death which possesses the speaker. The dead are reconciled, the living tremble. The images suggest life above death.

> Then the current, pausing in its flight,
> Swerved on pliant muscle; we were sped
> Through sudden calm into a pit of night:
>
> The Mill-Hole, whose rocky fathoms fed
> On moss and pure depth and the cold fin
> Turning in its heart. The river bed
>
> Called to our flesh from under the watery skin
> And, breathless, our shell trembling across the abyss,
> We shipped our oars in dread. . . .

The phrase "our shell trembling across the abyss" gives the sense of life against death—"shell" can be taken as the boat itself or as a reference to the bodies of the speaker and his companion. (The word has been used earlier: "A man one night fell sick and left his shell/Collapsed, half-eaten, like a rotted thrush's/To frighten stumbling children.") The river bed, in this deep spot, seems hungry to swallow them. However, their fear is not of the death agony, the fear of dying; it is rather the fear of death itself—the abyss of infinite darkness which one imagines to ensue after the process of dying. We have moved from an evocation of the dying man's agony through a presentation of the way the calm after death seems to reconcile his pain with cosmic order, to this contemplation of the abyss of death—symbolized by the Mill-Hole—from the point of view of the living.

But within this "depth" of death there is life. The images of a fish ("the cold fin/Turning in its heart) and of a swan ("a quiet hiss . . . a folded crest") are evoked. The "cold fin" sounds ominous, perhaps partly by association with the phrase "cold fear." The swan, on the other hand, is made into an image of hope: "A soul of white with darkness for a nest." Utter blackness turns out to be a "nest" for utter whiteness. At the very heart of one's contemplation of death is the discovery of life. And not only of life but of life in keeping with purpose and divine order in the universe. Thus the presence of the swan somehow makes the poet look up and see the stars, their motions symbolic of that order.

> Some creature wore the night so tranquilly
> I lifted up my eyes. There without rest
>
> The phantoms of the overhanging sky
> Occupied their stations and descended. . . .

The phrase "without rest" is reminiscent of John Milton's well-known sonnet "On his Blindness" in which he reconciles himself to his inability to serve God actively because of the loss of his eyesight.

> [God's] state/Is kingly. Thousands at his bidding speed
> And post o'er land and ocean without rest;
> They also serve who only stand and wait.

But the stars are not seen as angels in Milton's poem, nor as "phantoms of the overhanging sky" which occupy their stations and descend. The stars are indeed identified with the heavenly host in a much later poem, George Meredith's "Lucifer in

Starlight," which may have been in the poet's mind. "On a starred night Prince Lucifer uprose" and, "Tired of his dark dominion" in Hell, soared above earth, which was, however, "Poor prey to his hot fit of pride," and flew higher, towards Heaven.

> Soaring through wider zones that pricked his scars
> With memory of the old revolt from Awe,
> He reached the middle height, and at the stars,
> Which are the brain of heaven, he looked, and sank.
> Around the ancient track marched, rank on rank,
> The army of unalterable law.

Whether these are deliberate allusions or chance similarities, it seems significant that in the three poems one moves from unquestioned faith in the "Thousands [that] at [God's] bidding speed," through the much more secularized, scientific, and deterministic conception of "The army of unalterable law," to the quite tenuous and tentative "phantoms of the overhanging sky." A phantom is something that has only an apparent existence, but it may be either completely illusory or it may refer to some reality—as, say, the ghost of Hamlet's father was in some sense real enough, even though Horatio called out to it, "Stay illusion!" The use of the word "phantoms" for what has earlier in the same poem been called "the starry host" implies a connection between the stars (and the cosmic order they represent) and the dead.

> But, for an instant, to the starlit eye,
>
> The slow, downstreaming dead, it seemed, were blended
> One with those silver hordes, and briefly shared
> Their order, glittering. . . .

Calling the stars "phantoms" already blends their "silver hordes" with the "downstreaming dead." At the same time, however, it underlines the tentative and provisional nature of any statement which the poem makes about the dead. "It seemed," at any rate, that, "briefly," those who die were seen by the speaker to be united to cosmic purpose. Death then may not be meaningless, although part of an order and a plan beyond man's comprehension.

Who are these "downstreaming dead"? All men, one supposes, especially those who were dying in the war. But since the "starlit eye" to which this brief vision appears is the speaker's own eye, and since he has spoken earlier of the eyes of the dead man, and of all the other dead, being silvered by the reflected starlight, the speaker himself, though still alive, becomes the representative of the dead. It is he and his companion who are literally boating down the stream as all men are figuratively streaming down to death. For a moment the wheeling of the heavens seems to give order and meaning to this mortal process and to descend mercifully to man.

This vision past, we return to actuality, and the speakers approach the shore where they intend to land and to take up their active lives again. In this return there will be no vision of cosmic order to sustain them. They return to a life something like the "barren earth obscurely lit" of an earlier stanza. As they approach shore a towering rock rises before them, shutting out the symbolic stars and presenting a barren and difficult front. Such is the exterior presented by the world in which they—and we—must find a *landing place.*

. . . And then impended

A barrier of rock that turned and bared
A varied barrenness as toward its base
We glided—blotting heaven as it towered—

Searching the darkness for a landing place.[1]

[1] In a letter the poet comments on the above analysis, finding in it "a shade too much of hopefulness at the end." He says, "In my own view the edifice of stars and order is (for the moment) *totally* blotted out by the rock and the things ends with a pang of more loss than doubt. Letter to David R. Clark, August 9, 1965.

In this analysis we have deliberately omitted calling attention to certain details, certain image patterns which we now wish you to investigate for yourself.

1. Point out *all* the images of hunger or thirst, eating or drinking in the poem and try to account fully for the author's purposes in dwelling on these images. Note that even the "cold fin" turning in the heart of the Mill-Hole is potentially something to be caught and eaten. And what about the word "mess"?
2. Do the same for the images of dying and of ghosts and phantoms.
3. Read something in an encyclopedia about the sacrament of the Eucharist. What images become more meaningful when considered against this background information?
4. What is communicated by the line, "An X of wavering flesh, a skull of light"? The "skull of light" may suggest that the dead man is for the speaker a kind of *memento mori* ("Remember that you have to die."). Skulls were frequently placed on the desks of medieval scholars and clerics to remind them constantly that their souls should be ready to meet death. But the X is puzzling. Of course, the spreadeagled body does make an X where it lies. But perhaps there is some meaning beyond the merely descriptive. Here are some uses of the letter X which the dictionary gives. See if any of them are relevant: the letter considered with regard to its shape, hence identified with a cross; in algebra, used as the symbol for an unknown or variable quantity, hence something unknown or undetermined; used to stand for a person's name when the name is unknown or to be left undetermined; in writing the name Christ, especially in abbreviations, X represents the first letter of Greek XPICTOC (Christos), hence it is used as an abbreviation of the syllable *Christ*.
4. Is there any special significance or allusion in these phrases: "You could tell . . . / . . . by the hands/He died in trouble" and "betraying with feathered kiss"?
5. Investigate the image of a "cage" throughout the poem and comment on its significance.
6. Investigate the symbolic use of the water and of the vegetation.

PETER

Marianne Moore

Strong and slippery, built for the midnight grass-party confronted
        by four cats,
  he sleeps his time away—the detached first claw on the foreleg,
        which corresponds

to the thumb, retracted to its tip; the small tuft of fronds
or katydid legs above each eye, still numbering the units
in each group;
the shadbones regularly set about the mouth, to droop or
rise. 5

in unison like the porcupine's quills—motionless. He lets himself
be flat-
tened out by gravity, as it were a piece of seaweed tamed and
weakened by
exposure to the sun; compelled when extended, to lie
stationary. Sleep is the result of his delusion that one must
do as
well as one can for oneself; sleep—epitome of
what is to 10

him as to the average person, the end of life. Demonstrate to him
how
the lady caught the dangerous southern snake, placing a
forked stick on either
side of its innocuous neck; one need not try to stir
him up; his prune-shaped head and alligator eyes are not
a party to the
joke. Lifted and handled, he may be dangled like an eel
or set 15

up on the forearm like a mouse; his eyes bisected by pupils of
a pin's
width, are flickeringly exhibited, then covered up. May be?
I should say
might have been; when he has been got the better of in a
dream—as in a fight with nature or with cats—we all know
it. Profound sleep is
not with him a fixed illusion. Springing about with
froglike ac- 20

curacy, emitting jerky cries when taken in the hand, he is
himself

again; to sit caged by the rungs of a domestic chair would be unprofit-
able—human. What is the good of hypocrisy? It
is permissible to choose one's employment, to abandon the wire nail, the
roly-poly, when it shows signs of being no longer a pleas- 25

ure, to score the adjacent magazine with a double line of strokes. He can
talk, but insolently says nothing. What of it? When one is frank, one's very
presence is a compliment. It is clear that he can see
the virtue of naturalness, that he is one of those who do not regard
the published fact as a surrender. As for the disposition 30

invariably to affront, an animal with claws wants to have to use
them; that eel-like extension of trunk into tail is not an accident. To
leap, to lengthen out, divide the air—to purloin, to pursue.
To tell the hen: fly over the fence, go in the wrong way in your perturba-
tion—this is life; to do less would be nothing but dishonesty. 35

1. This poem is an adroit combination of description and exposition, just as Miss Moore's "Poetry" (p. 286) skillfully combines argumentation and exposition. What portions of the poem are descriptive? What portions of the poem are expository? What characteristics of the subject of this poem are emphasized?
2. Make an analysis of the structure of the poem. Is the structure well calculated to get the effect at which Miss Moore is aiming? Why or why not?
3. List the metaphors and similes in this poem. What is the source of the majority of the figures in this poem? Are the figures at all comparable in nature and quality to those in Donne's "A Valediction: Forbidding Mourning" (p. 237)? Why or why not?

4. What devices of form or style differentiate this piece of writing from prose? Are you persuaded that this piece of writing is a poem? Why or why not?
5. Is the fact that the reader likes or dislikes cats really relevant to the effect of this poem? Give the reasons for your answer.

THE EXPRESS

Stephen Spender

After the first powerful plain manifesto
The black statement of pistons, without more fuss
But gliding like a queen, she leaves the station.
Without bowing and with restrained unconcern
She passes the houses which humbly crowd outside, 5
The gasworks and at last the heavy page
Of death, printed by gravestones in the cemetery.
Beyond the town there lies the open country
Where, gathering speed, she acquires mystery,
The luminous self-possession of ships on ocean. 10
It is now she begins to sing—at first quite low
Then loud, and at last with a jazzy madness—
The song of her whistle screaming at curves,
Of deafening tunnels, brakes, innumerable bolts.
And always light, aerial, underneath 15
Goes the elate metre of her wheels.
Steaming through metal landscape on her lines
She plunges new eras of wild happiness
Where speed throws up strange shapes, broad curves
And parallels clean like the steel of guns. 20
At last, further than Edinburgh or Rome,
Beyond the crest of the world, she reaches night
Where only a low streamline brightness
Of phosphorus on the tossing hills is white.
Ah, like a comet through flame she moves entranced 25
Wrapt in her music no bird song, no, nor bough
Breaking with honey buds, shall ever equal.

1. Make an analysis of the structure of the poem. Is the structure sufficiently strong to bear the weight of the descriptive details? Why or why not?
2. What characteristics of the subject of the poem does the poet emphasize? How?
3. Make an analysis of the meter of the last ten lines. Are there elements in the handling of the meter that seem to you to be non-traditional? Is the meter handled effectively? Why or why not?
4. Make an analysis of the imagery of the first ten lines of the poem. Contrast the imagery in these lines with that of the first stanza of Keats' "To Autumn" (p. 179).
5. Make a list of all the metaphors and similes used in this poem. Discuss the sources of the similes, their freshness, and their propriety. Are the metaphors or the similes of greater import to the effect of the poem? Why?
6. Has the poet succeeded in making poetry out of a subject that is commonly regarded as prosaic? Give the reasons for your answer.

Expression of Emotion in Poetry: Manner and Content

FULL FATHOM FIVE THY FATHER LIES

William Shakespeare

Full fathom five thy father lies:
  Of his bones are coral made;
Those are pearls that were his eyes;
  Nothing of him that doth fade
But doth suffer a sea-change 5
Into something rich and strange.
Sea-nymphs hourly ring his knell:
                    Ding-dong!
Hark! now I hear them,—Ding-dong, bell!

1. In Shakespeare's *The Tempest,* the playfully inhuman spirit, Ariel, sings this song to Prince Ferdinand, who thinks his father has been drowned in the shipwreck from which he himself has been saved. The audience, however, knows that the father has been saved. In the light of this situation, what is the purpose of the song? What is the relationship of the attitude toward death to this purpose?
2. Make an analysis of the imagery, and show how the imagery is calculated to express and communicate the feeling the song is intended to induce. Does the juxtaposition of pleasant and unpleasant images in lines 2 and 3 heighten or diminish the effect of the song?
3. What feeling is aroused by the last three lines? Is this feeling an appropriate one with which to terminate the song? Why or why not?
4. Is the effect at which Shakespeare is aiming here a more or less

complex effect than that at which he was aiming in the two songs discussed in the preceding section (pp. 173–174). Give the reasons for your answer.

Mourning the death of a loved or admired person provides one of the perpetual forms of poetry, as bereavement is a common experience of life. But the variety of kinds of grief and ways of expressing them is great. Here are two extremes.

ROSE AYLMER

Walter Savage Landor

Ah, what avails the sceptred race!
  Ah, what the form divine!
What every virtue, every grace!
  Rose Aylmer, all were thine.
Rose Aylmer, whom these wakeful eyes 5
  May weep, but never see,
A night of memories and of sighs
  I consecrate to thee.

COMPLAINT

James Wright

She's gone. She was my love, my moon or more.
She chased the chickens out and swept the floor,
Emptied the bones and nut-shells after feasts,
And smacked the kids for leaping up like beasts.
Now morbid boys have grown past awkwardness; 5
The girls let stitches out, dress after dress,
To free some swinging body's riding space
And form the new child's unimagined face.
Yet, while vague nephews, spitting on their curls,
Amble to pester winds and blowsy girls, 10
What arm will sweep the room, what hand will hold
New snow against the milk to keep it cold?

And who will dump the garbage, feed the hogs,
And pitch the chickens' heads to hungry dogs?
Not my lost hag who dumbly bore such pain: 15
Childbirth and midnight sassafras and rain.
New snow against her face and hands she bore,
And now lies down, who was my moon or more.

1. Is there any evidence that one of these laments is more sincere than the other?
2. Comment on what the second poem gains by including details like chasing chickens and sweeping floors, not to mention pitching the chickens' heads to hungry dogs. What is gained by using phrases like "smack the kids" and "dump the garbage"?
3. What does the first poem gain by excluding such details and such style?

IN THE CEMETERY

Thomas Hardy

"You see those mothers squabbling there?"
Remarks the man of the cemetery.
"One says in tears, '*Tis mine lies here!*'
Another, '*Nay, mine, you Pharisee!*'
Another, '*How dare you move my flowers* 5
And put your own on this grave of ours!'
But all their children were laid therein
At different times, like sprats in a tin.

"And then the main drain had to cross,
And we moved the lot some nights ago, 10
And packed them away in the general foss
With hundreds more. But their folks don't know,
And as well cry over a new-laid drain
As anything else, to ease your pain!"

1. Describe the attitude of the man of the cemetery, pointing to specific phrases that define that attitude.
2. Does the poet mean the reader to take the same attitude as the

man of the cemetery or a different attitude? If the latter, describe that attitude.

3. How much of the irony of this poem lies in the situation and how much in the expression?
4. Is this a successful poem?

THE DARKLING THRUSH

Thomas Hardy

I leant upon a coppice gate
  When Frost was spectre-gray,
And Winter's dregs made desolate
  The weakening eye of day.
The tangled bine-stems scored the sky 5
  Like strings of broken lyres,
And all mankind that haunted nigh
  Had sought their household fires.

The land's sharp features seemed to be
  The Century's corpse outleant, 10
His crypt the cloudy canopy,
  The wind his death-lament.
The ancient pulse of germ and birth
  Was shrunken hard and dry,
And every spirit upon earth 15
  Seemed fervourless as I.

At once a voice arose among
  The bleak twigs overhead
In a full-hearted evensong
  Of joy illimited; 20
An aged thrush, frail, gaunt, and small,
  In blast-beruffled plume,
Had chosen thus to fling his soul
  Upon the growing gloom.

So little cause for carolings 25
  Of such ecstatic sound

Was written on terrestrial things
Afar or nigh around,
That I could think there trembled through
His happy good-night air 30
Some blessed Hope, whereof he knew
And I was unaware.

1. Define the following terms: darkling, bine-stems, outleant, crypt, terrestrial.
2. What is the problem that faces the speaker in this poem? How is the problem established? What is the relation of the bird and his song to the problem? Does the poem present enough evidence to justify the conclusion to which the poet comes? Why or why not?
3. Outline the feelings and emotions experienced by the speaker in this poem. Discuss the means by which Hardy modulates from the feeling of the first two stanzas to that of the last stanza. Make an analysis of the imagery sufficiently detailed to show its relationship to this sequence of feelings and emotions.
4. Make an analysis of the meter and rhyme scheme of two of the stanzas. Do the meter and rhyme scheme seem appropriate to the subject and tone of the poem? Why or why not?
5. Do you think the personifications in the poem are successful? Give the reasons for your judgment.

SONG

Edmund Waller

Go, lovely rose,
Tell her that wastes her time and me
That now she knows,
When I resemble her to thee,
How sweet and fair she seems to be. 5

Tell her that's young,
And shuns to have her graces spied,
That hadst thou sprung
In deserts, where no men abide,
Thou must have uncommended died. 10

Small is the worth
Of beauty from the light retired;
Bid her come forth,
Suffer herself to be desired,
And not blush so to be admired. 15

Then die, that she
The common fate of all things rare
May read in thee;
How small a part of time they share,
That are so wondrous sweet and fair.

1. How would you describe the tone of the speaker's address to the rose? Is there anything unusual about his tone? Is it wryly humorous or sentimental or what? Is there anything ironic about the speaker's relation to the rose?
2. Mark the caesuras and the end-stopped and run-on lines in this poem. Has the poet accomplished anything special by variation in the treatment of pauses?
3. Is this poem metrically very strict? What are its basic metrical features?
4. Are there many repetitions in the poem?. What themes do they accent?
5. Is this poem remarkable for vivid imagery? Are there many striking metaphors? Do you think this poem is nearly perfect or simply banal? Why?

TO HIS COY MISTRESS

Andrew Marvell

Had we but world enough, and time,
This coyness, Lady, were no crime,
We would sit down and think which way
To walk and pass our long love's day.
Thou by the Indian Ganges' side 5
Shouldst rubies find; I by the tide
Of Humber would complain. I would
Love you ten years before the Flood,

And you should, if you please, refuse
Till the conversion of the Jews. 10
My vegetable love should grow
Vaster than empires, and more slow;
An hundred years should go to praise
Thine eyes and on thy forehead gaze;
Two hundred to adore each breast, 15
But thirty thousand to the rest;
An age at least to every part,
And the last age should show your heart.
For, Lady, you deserve this state,
Nor would I love at lower rate. 20

But at my back I always hear
Time's wingèd chariot hurrying near;
And yonder all before us lie
Deserts of vast eternity.
Thy beauty shall no more be found, 25
Nor, in thy marble vault, shall sound
My echoing song; then worms shall try
That long preserved virginity,
And your quaint honor turn to dust,
And into ashes all my lust: 30
The grave's a fine and private place,
But none, I think, do there embrace.

Now therefore, while the youthful hue
Sits on thy skin like morning dew,
And while thy willing soul transpires 35
At every pore with instant fires,
Now let us sport us while we may,
And now, like amorous birds of prey,
Rather at once our time devour
Than languish in his slow-chapt power. 40
Let us roll all our strength and all

Our sweetness up into one ball,
And tear our pleasures with rough strife
Thorough the iron gates of life:
Thus, though we cannot make our sun 45
Stand still, yet we will make him run.

1. What are the central themes of this poem? What is the relation of the title to these themes? What relation does the threefold division of the poem have to its structure? Make a summary of the content of the poem. To what type of discourse does this structure belong? Is the type of structure appropriate to the purpose of the poem? Why or why not?
2. What is the dominant tone of each part of the poem? Analyze enough of the imagery to show how it assists in creating each of these tones. Contrast the imagery of the second and third parts of the poem.
3. What is the metrical form of this poem called? How does Marvell attempt to minimize the effect of the rhymes? Are the meter and the rhyme scheme appropriate to the tone of this poem? Why or why not?
4. What contrast is emphasized by the antithesis of Ganges and Humber? Discuss the efficacy of the following phrases: vegetable love, quaint honor, amorous birds of prey, slow-chapt power. Use the best available library dictionary.
5. Compare the conception of love expressed in this poem and that expressed in Donne's "A Valediction: Forbidding Mourning." Does Marvell succeed in avoiding an effect of bad taste? Why or why not?

YOU, ANDREW MARVELL

Archibald MacLeish

And here face down beneath the sun
And here upon earth's noonward height
To feel the always coming on
The always rising of the night:

To feel creep up the curving east 5
The earthy chill of dusk and slow
Upon those under lands the vast
And ever climbing shadow grow

And strange at Ecbatan the trees
Take leaf by leaf the evening strange 10
The flooding dark about their knees
The mountains over Persia change

And now at Kermanshah the gate
Dark empty and the withered grass
And through the twilight now the late 15
Few travelers in the westward pass

And Baghdad darken and the bridge
Across the silent river gone
And through Arabia the edge
Of evening widen and steal on 20

And deepen on Palmyra's street
The wheel rut in the ruined stone
And Lebanon fade out and Crete
High through the clouds and overblown

And over Sicily the air 25
Still flashing with the landward gulls
And loom and slowly disappear
The sails above the shadowy hulls

And Spain go under and the shore
Of Africa the gilded sand 30
And evening vanish and no more
The low pale light across that land

Nor now the long light on the sea:

And here face downward in the sun
To feel how swift how secretly 35
The shadow of the night comes on . . .

Line 9. Ecbatan: capital of ancient Media (modern name, Hamadan)
Line 13. Kermanshah: city in southeastern Persia (Iran)
Line 21. Palmyra: city 130 miles northeast of Damascus; biblical name for it was Tamar

1. What are the effects of the nearly complete absence of punctuation in this poem?
2. Circle the repetitions and discuss their importance to the poem as a whole.
3. Compare this poem with Marvell's "To His Coy Mistress" with respect to meter, diction, and themes. What relations do you find between the two? State as carefully as you can the differences between the two with respect to themes.

AS I WALKED OUT ONE EVENING

W. H. Auden

As I walked out one evening,
  Walking down Bristol Street,
The crowds upon the pavement
  Were fields of harvest wheat.

And down by the brimming river 5
  I heard a lover sing
Under an arch of the railway:
  "Love has no ending.

I'll love you, dear, I'll love you
  Till China and Africa meet, 10
And the river jumps over the mountain
  And the salmon sing in the street.

I'll love you till the ocean
  Is folded and hung up to dry,
And the seven stars go squawking 15
  Like geese about the sky.

The years shall run like rabbits,
  For in my arms I hold
The Flower of the Ages,
  And the first love of the world." 20

But all the clocks in the city
  Began to whirr and chime:

"O let not Time deceive you,
  You cannot conquer Time.

In the burrows of the Nightmare 25
  Where Justice naked is,
Time watches from the shadow
  And coughs when you would kiss.

In headaches and in worry
  Vaguely life leaks away, 30
And Time will have his fancy
  Tomorrow or today.

Into many a green valley
  Drifts the appalling snow;
Time breaks the threaded dances 35
  And the diver's brilliant bow.

O plunge your hands in water,
  Plunge them in up to the wrist;
Stare, stare in the basin
  And wonder what you've missed. 40

The glacier knocks in the cupboard,
  The desert sighs in the bed,
And the crack in the tea-cup opens
  A lane to the land of the dead.

Where the beggars raffle the banknotes 45
  And the Giant is enchanting to Jack,
And the Lily-white Boy is a Roarer,
  And Jill goes down on her back.

O look, look in the mirror,
  O look in your distress; 50
Life remains a blessing
  Although you cannot bless.

O stand, stand at the window
  As the tears scald and start;
You shall love your crooked neighbor 55
  With your crooked heart."

It was late, late in the evening,
  The lovers they were gone;
The clocks had ceased their chiming,
  And the deep river ran on. 60

1. Would you call this poem a parody of popular love ballads? If so, what points of contact are there between Auden's poem and juke-box love lyrics?
2. What traditional verse form does this poem follow? Comment on the effect of the rhymes in stanzas 2, 5, and 7.
3. Which types of alliteration are illustrated in lines 12, 15, 28, 34–36, 45, and 57–58?
4. Does this poem rely more heavily on imagery or on metaphor for its effects? Is there a very wide range of imagery? Are the metaphors rather conventional or highly unusual?
5. Does this poem have the same basic themes as Waller's "Song" (p. 204)? In what respects are the themes of these two poems different?
6. Write a brief statement about the tone of Auden's poem. How does the tone of Auden's poem differ from that of Waller's poem? Which of these poems is more complex in tone?

THE LITTLE BLACK BOY
William Blake

My mother bore me in the southern wild,
And I am black, but O! my soul is white;
White as an angel is the English child,
But I am black, as if bereaved of light.

My mother taught me underneath a tree, 5
And sitting down before the heat of day,
She took me on her lap and kissèd me,
And pointing to the east, began to say:

"Look on the rising sun: there God does live,
And gives his light, and gives his heat away; 10
And flowers and trees and beasts and men receive
Comfort in morning, joy in the noonday.

"And we are put on earth a little space,
That we may learn to bear the beams of love;
And these black bodies and this sunburnt face 15
Is but a cloud, and like a shady grove.

"For when our souls have learned the heat to bear,
The cloud will vanish; we shall hear his voice,
Saying: 'Come out from the grove, my love and care,
And round my golden tent like lambs rejoice.'" 20

Thus did my mother say, and kissèd me;
And thus I say to little English boy.
When I from black and he from white cloud free,
And round the tent of God like lambs we joy,

I'll shade him from the heat, till he can bear 25
To lean in joy upon our father's knee;
And then I'll stand and stroke his silver hair,
And be like him, and he will then love me.

1. What does Blake gain by his choice of the speaker in this poem? What is the problem of the poem? What relation does the mother's speech have to the problem? How is the problem solved in the final stanza? Is the solution satisfactory to you? Why or why not?
2. Discuss the propriety or the impropriety of the diction to the persons of this poem.
3. Discuss the contribution of the meter to the tone of this poem.
4. Are the relatively numerous repetitions in this poem effective or ineffective? Why?
5. What view of life is implied in this poem? Is it appropriate to the mother of the little black boy? Why or why not?

CHANSONS INNOCENTES, I

E. E. Cummings

in Just-
spring when the world is mud-
luscious the little
lame balloonman

whistles far and wee 5

and eddieandbill come
running from marbles and
piracies and it's
spring

when the world is puddle-wonderful 10

the queer
old balloonman whistles
far and wee
and bettyandisbel come dancing

from hop-scotch and jump-rope and 15

it's
spring
and
the

goat-footed 20

balloonMan whistles
far
and
wee

1. What is the allusion in "goat-footed"? Read about Pan in an encyclopedia or dictionary of mythology. A good account of the use

of Pan in English poetry may be found in *Classical Myths in English Literature,* ed. Dan S. Norton and Peters Rushton (New York, Holt, Rinehart & Winston, 1952).

2. What effect is gained by capitalizing "Just" and not capitalizing "in" in the first line? What is "Just-spring," i.e., what does the word "just" mean here? What effect is gained by joining the two words "Just" and "spring" together as a compound? What effect is gained by making the line end divide the compound?
3. Are there other made-up compounds in the poem? List them and discuss the effect of each one.
4. What compounds are there in the poem which are not newly coined? Would the compounds "hop-scotch" and "jump-rope" originally have been coined by adults or by children? What point of view do the new compounds try to capture, that of adults or that of children?
5. Why is "Man" capitalized the third time "balloonman" is used and not the first two times? If you cannot find reasons for this immediately, come back to the question.
6. Contrast the three descriptions of the balloonman:

   the little
   lame balloonman

   the queer
   old balloonman

   and
   the
   goat-footed

   balloonMan

   Is the observer getting closer to the balloonMan or farther away from him as he notes these details?
7. Study the sentence structure of the poem. How many complete sentences are there? What is the effect of the repetition of "and"? Does the clause "when the world is puddle-wonderful" begin or end a sentence or is it impossible to tell? What is the purpose of this ambiguity of syntax?
8. Do the bare statements in the poem get anywhere? Take for example the first lines which inform us that "in Just-/spring" . . . "it's/spring"—a discovery which should cause no surprise to anyone! The whole poem seems to have this circularity. In spring the balloonman whistles, and boys come running, and it's spring, and the balloonman whistles, and girls come dancing, and it's spring, and the balloonMan whistles. On the other hand there

seems to be a certain recurrent order here: (1) The balloonman whistles; (2) the children come running or dancing; and then (3) it's spring. Are there causal connections among these items?

9. In *Paradise Lost* John Milton tells how "universal Pan,/Knit with the Graces and the Hours in dance,/Led on th' Eternal Spring" (Book IV, lines 266–268). Are there any parallels between Cummings' poem and the passage from Milton?
10. If one takes the first and last words of the poem only, "in Just-/spring" and "the/goat-footed/balloonMan whistles/far/and/wee," then a different order, a more naturalistic one, is evident: When spring comes the balloonman arrives to sell his wares. The 1,2,3, order indicated above, in which there may be a causal sequence, is tucked inside this more believable natural over-all order. But part of the effect of circularity in the poem is caused by the fact that these two orders coexist and work against each other. In spite of the effect of circularity, this poem does seem to progress and to arrive somewhere. What in the poem (besides the 1,2,3, order mentioned above) gives this effect of progression and change?
11. Whose point of view seems to be maintained throughout the poem? In whose words does the poem seem to be? Does the balloonman say anything? Do we know how he feels about spring? How many contrasts can you find between the balloonman and the children? How do the descriptions of the balloonman contrast with the children's exuberant love of spring? He is "lame" and "old." Can he be expected to run and dance as they do?
12. Does your attitude, or the attitude of the children, change toward the balloonman as we proceed through the poem? What would be the changing attitude toward "the little/lame balloonman"; "the queer/old balloonman"; and "the/goat-footed/balloonMan"? According to the lines quoted above from *Paradise Lost,* Pan's goat feet did not prevent him from cutting capers in dance. Whereas one might pity the "lame" and "old" balloonman who cannot run and dance like the children in spring, there is no point in pitying ageless and powerful Pan.
13. What movement of the balloonman's body does the arrangement of the lines suggest?

    and

        the

                goat-footed

    balloonMan

    What movement of the children's minds? What has happened to the old man's lameness?
14. Do you think that "goat-footed" is meant literally and that this

figure is really meant to be the god Pan or that "goat-footed" is merely metaphorical—perhaps meaning that the balloonman is a gay old man?

15. Is there anything sinister about the balloonman? Twice the poem runs through the pattern (1) balloonman whistles; (2) children run or dance; (3) it's spring. The third time the balloonman whistles he is simultaneously seen to be goat-footed. The pattern stops there. Though (1) has happened again, (2) and (3) do not recur. It is as if the children, now arrived where the balloonman is, stare in silence at his goat feet.
16. What, again, is the effect of the capitalization of "Man" in "balloonMan" in its final occurrence? Pan is goat-footed, but has the torso, arms and head of a man. Thus the juxtaposition of "goat-footed" and "balloonMan" may help us to visualize him. In any case, the stereotype "balloonman" (one of our compounds) is now broken down. This is a particular Man, remarkably worth noticing, at whom the children may well stare in awe now that they are close to him. There may be something too of the idea that the "*little* lame balloonman" is nevertheless a "Man," an adult, not a child like them. After the children run excitedly to share in the childlike gaiety of his balloons, they are confronted with an adult. A gay old adult, possibly, but nevertheless one shrouded in mystery and perhaps the terror of all sorts of things they do not yet understand. Pan, a god associated with growth, fertility, and sexual desire, would certainly be an enigma to young children—as, as a matter of fact, any adult would be. The children hear the balloonman's whistle and run gaily towards him. He looks little and lame to the boys, queer and old to the girls. And when they get there, they see a Man, an adult goat-footed with all the sexual mysteries of maturity. The children run and dance toward ageless Pan. He is lame and old, but dances on perpetually through the eternal recurrence of Nature. Adulthood is there unchangingly. It is the enigmatic threatening figure towards which the child runs in desire of the joy of life, only to stand in somewhat frightened awe when he finds what he has run toward. It is *youth* that passes away quickly. Age stays on. Having said these things, one feels that one has overemphasized them. This suggestion of a sinister quality in the old balloonman is probably a mere shadow of the dominant mood of the poem—which is the joy of spring. Perhaps this shadow of age and pain is necessary, however, to bring that dominant mood out by contrast. One must admit, in any case, that the fact that the balloonman is lame and old, and finally, has the legs of a beast, has its effect!
17. Consider the line which acts as a sort of refrain in the poem: "whistles far and wee." What is the sound of this line meant to

suggest? What familiar phrase does "far and wee" suggest? What is the relevance of this suggestion?

18. What literal and figurative meanings for "far" can you find in the poem? What kinds of distance in space or time are important in the poem? What literal and figurative meanings for "wee" can you find? What is the effect of the juxtaposition of "little" and "wee" early in the poem? Account for the three different ways in which this line is printed.

FROST AT MIDNIGHT

Samuel Taylor Coleridge

The Frost performs its secret ministry,
Unhelped by any wind. The owlet's cry
Came loud—and hark, again! loud as before.
The inmates of my cottage, all at rest,
Have left me to that solitude, which suits 5
Abstruser musings: save that at my side
My cradled infant slumbers peacefully.
'Tis calm indeed! so calm, that it disturbs
And vexes meditation with its strange
And extreme silentness. Sea, hill, and wood, 10
This populous village! Sea, and hill, and wood,
With all the numberless goings-on of life,
Inaudible as dreams! the thin blue flame
Lies on my low-burnt fire, and quivers not;
Only that film, which fluttered on the grate, 15
Still flutters there, the sole unquiet thing.
Methinks, its motion in this hush of nature
Gives it dim sympathies with me who live,
Making it a companionable form,
Whose puny flaps and freaks the idling Spirit 20
By its own moods interprets, every where
Echo or mirror seeking of itself,
And makes a toy of Thought.

But O! how oft,
How oft, at school, with most believing mind,

Presageful, have I gazed upon the bars, 25
To watch that fluttering *stranger!* and as oft
With unclosed lids already had I dreamt
Of my sweet birth-place, and the old church-tower,
Whose bells, the poor man's only music, rang
From morn to evening, all the hot Fair-day, 30
So sweetly, that they stirred and haunted me
With a wild pleasure, falling on mine ear
Most like articulate sounds of things to come!
So gazed I, till the soothing things, I dreamt,
Lulled me to sleep, and sleep prolonged my dreams! 35
And so I brooded all the following morn,
Awed by the stern preceptor's face, mine eye
Fixed with mock study on my swimming book:
Save if the door half-opened, and I snatched
A hasty glance, and still my heart leaped up, 40
For still I hoped to see the *stranger's* face,
Townsman, or aunt, or sister more beloved,
My play-mate when we both were clothed alike!

Dear Babe, that sleepest cradled by my side,
Whose gentle breathings, heard in this deep calm, 45
Fill up the interspersed vacancies
And momentary pauses of the thought!
My babe so beautiful! it thrills my heart
With tender gladness, thus to look at thee,
And think that thou shalt learn far other lore, 50
And in far other scenes! For I was reared
In the great city, pent 'mid cloisters dim,
And saw nought lovely but the sky and stars.
But *thou*, my babe! shalt wander like a breeze
By lakes and sandy shores, beneath the crags 55
Of ancient mountain, and beneath the clouds,
Which image in their bulk both lakes and shores
And mountain crags: so shalt thou see and hear

The lovely shapes and sounds intelligible
Of that eternal language, which thy God 60
Utters, who from eternity doth teach
Himself in all, and all things in himself.
Great universal Teacher! he shall mould
Thy spirit, and by giving make it ask.

Therefore all seasons shall be sweet to thee, 65
Whether the summer clothe the general earth
With greenness, or the redbreast sit and sing
Betwixt the tufts of snow on the bare branch
Of mossy apple-tree, while the nigh thatch
Smokes in the sun-thaw; whether the eave-drops fall 70
Heard only in the trances of the blast,
Or if the secret ministry of frost
Shall hang them up in silent icicles,
Quietly shining to the quiet Moon.

1. How do the four parts into which the poem is divided assist in defining the structure of the poem?
2. What elements in the setting described in the first stanza assist in creating the tone of that part of the poem? Is the return to this setting at the end of the poem effective or ineffective? Why?
3. Contrast the boyhoods described in the second and third parts of the poem.
4. The term "stranger" (line 26) is defined as a soot film the appearance of which is supposed "to portend the arrival of some absent friend." Is the pun on this word (line 41) effective or ineffective? Why?
5. Coleridge called this and similar poems of his "conversation poems." To whom is the speaker talking here? Is what he says appropriate or inappropriate to the situation he describes? Why? Is the situation more or less dramatic than that of Browning's "The Bishop Orders His Tomb"? Why?
6. Coleridge in his *Biographia Literaria* defines a good poem as one in which the component parts "mutually support and explain each other; all in their proportion harmonizing with and supporting the purpose and known influences of metrical arrangement." Discuss this poem in the light of this definition.

THE FUNERAL
John Donne

Whoever comes to shroud me, do not harm
    Nor question much
That subtle wreath of hair about mine arm;
The mystery, the sign you must not touch,
    For 'tis my outward soul, 5
Viceroy to that which, unto heaven being gone,
    Will leave this to control
And keep these limbs, her provinces, from dissolution.

For if the sinewy thread my brain lets fall
    Through every part 10
Can tie those parts, and make me one of all;
Those hairs, which upward grew, and strength and art
    Have from a better brain,
Can better do 't: except she meant that I
    By this should know my pain, 15
As prisoners then are manacled, when they're condemned to die.

Whate'er she meant by 't, bury it with me,
    For since I am
Love's martyr, it might breed idolatry
If into other hands these reliques came. 20
    As 't was humility
To afford to it all that a soul can do,
    So 't is some bravery
That, since you would have none of me, I bury some of you.

Line 23. bravery: a spirited act

1. Of what use is the title of the poem? What is the "subtle wreath of hair"? List the metaphors by which it is characterized. In each case, indicate the feeling toward the "wreath of hair" that is implied in the metaphor. Discuss the contrast which is built up by these

feelings. What is the final result of this sequence of contrasted feelings?

2. Compare the poet's attitude toward the "wreath of hair" and his attitude toward the lady who gave it to him. What is the functional relationship between these two attitudes?
3. Analyze closely the development of the metaphors: viceroy, thread, martyr. Do the metaphors in themselves seem to you to be far-fetched? Why or why not? Does the development of the metaphors seem to you to be overingenious? Why or why not?
4. Dr. Samuel Johnson defined the essence of "metaphysical poetry," of which this poem is an example, as the emphasis on the similarities between widely dissimilar things. What light does this definition throw on the metaphors in this poem?
5. Discuss the metrical effect of the short lines in this poem. By what means does Donne attempt to minimize their abruptness? Is he successful? Why or why not?

EPITAPH ON ELIZABETH, L. H.

Ben Jonson

Wouldst thou hear what man can say
In a little? Reader, stay.
Underneath this stone doth lie
As much beauty as could die;
Which in life did harbour give 5
To more virtue than doth live.
If at all she had a fault,
Leave it buried in this vault.
One name was *Elizabeth*,
Th'other, let it sleep with death: 10
Fitter, where it died, to tell
Than that it lived at all. Farewell.

The initials L. H. (*L* could stand for *Lady*) have never been satisfactorily or surely explained, and the lady's story, if any, is consequently unknown except for what Jonson has communicated in these lines. We have here a kind of poem within a poem: (1) the framework, implied in the first two lines, of a challenge to see how much can be told or implied in a short poem; (2) the lines 3–12 which refer directly to Elizabeth. "Farewell" in line 12 may work as part of both the framework and of the lines on Elizabeth.

1. Well, what has man been able to say "in little" here? Paraphrase lines 3–6. How much beauty could die? Is there some beauty that could not die? Where, if not under the stone, is that beauty now? Lines 3–4 seem to imply that all the beauty that could die did so. What advantage would there be to beauty in having as much of it as could die do so?
2. What are the implications of "to give harbour"? Harbour from what? What sort of thing needs to be harboured or sheltered? What happens when the harbour or shelter is taken away? On the other hand, a harbour may be entered and left again. The harbour and thing harboured are not necessarily coterminous. Does this virtue die with the body or is there some virtue, like some beauty, that cannot die? "In life" may mean "while alive," or "by means of (an exemplary) life." A third meaning would identify the harbour with life: Her beauty kept virtue alive, cherished it in the warm breathing life-process, did not let it become a dead abstraction.
3. Apparently more virtue died with Elizabeth than "doth live." What comment does line 6 make on the present age, including the reader and the speaker? Lines 7–8 seem possible to interpret in two ways: If she had any fault, it was mortality—the carnal weakness of the body which is buried here. Her fault would have been in beauty, not in virtue: the fault of having beauty, not lacking it. Do you think the poet suggests that she did have a fault? Is there any suggestion of what the fault, if any, is? Paraphrase lines 9–10. Is there a parallel between what is said in line 10 and what is said in line 8? In what sense could the lady's second or surname be a fault or a misfortune? "Fitter" (line 11) may be ambiguous syntactically. Does "fitter" modify "it" (the other name)? Or does it modify the infinitive "to tell," meaning that it would be a more fitting thing to do to tell where the surname dies, etc.? In the first reading, how does the surname tell where it died? In what ways has it died? How would it tell that it had lived at all? What effect does the repetition of "at all" in lines 7 and 12 have? If you feel that there is a story implied in lines 7–12, tell it in your own words.
4. Would the poem lose or gain if the first two lines were omitted? Who speaks the poem? Are the first two lines part of the epitaph, supposedly cut on a gravestone, or just lines 3–12? If the first, the reader is the reader of a book of poems; if the second, he is a reader of inscriptions on headstones.
5. What does "In a little" refer to? Small space? Few words? How much does the poet really tell you?
6. Who says "Farewell" and to whom? (There may be several possible answers.)
7. What effect does the use of Elizabeth's first name have in this context where the last name is not given?
8. Compare Jonson's poem with William Browne's "On the Countess Dowager of Pembroke" (p. 309).

ODE TO THE WEST WIND

Percy Bysshe Shelley

I

O wild West Wind, thou breath of Autumn's being,
Thou, from whose unseen presence the leaves dead
Are driven, like ghosts from an enchanter fleeing,

Yellow, and black, and pale, and hectic red,
Pestilence-stricken multitudes: O thou, 5
Who chariotest to their dark wintry bed

The wingèd seeds, where they lie cold and low,
Each like a corpse within its grave, until
Thine azure sister of the spring shall blow

Her clarion o'er the dreaming earth, and fill 10
(Driving sweet buds like flocks to feed in air)
With living hues and odours plain and hill:

Wild Spirit, which art moving everywhere;
Destroyer and preserver: hear, oh, hear!

II

Thou on whose stream, 'mid the steep sky's commotion, 15
Loose clouds like earth's decaying leaves are shed,
Shook from the tangled boughs of Heaven and Ocean,

Angels of rain and lightning: there are spread
On the blue surface of thine airy surge,
Like the bright hair uplifted from the head 20

Of some fierce Maenad, even from the dim verge
Of the horizon to the zenith's height
The locks of the approaching storm. Thou dirge

Of the dying year, to which this closing night
Will be the dome of a vast sepulcher, 25
Vaulted with all thy congregated might

Of vapours, from whose solid atmosphere
Black rain, and fire, and hail will burst: oh, hear!

III

Thou who didst waken from his summer dreams
  The blue Mediterranean, where he lay, 30
  Lulled by the coil of his crystàlline streams,

Beside a pumice isle in Baiae's bay,
  And saw in sleep old palaces and towers
  Quivering within the wave's intenser day,

All overgrown with azure moss and flowers 35
  So sweet, the sense faints picturing them! Thou
  For whose path the Atlantic's level powers

Cleave themselves into chasms, while far below
  The sea-blooms and the oozy woods which wear
  The sapless foliage of the ocean, know 40

Thy voice, and suddenly grow gray with fear,
And tremble and despoil themselves: oh, hear!

IV

If I were a dead leaf thou mightest bear;
  If I were a swift cloud to fly with thee;
  A wave to pant beneath thy power, and share 45

The impulse of thy strength, only less free
  Than thou, O, uncontrollable! If even
  I were as in my boyhood, and could be

The comrade of thy wanderings over Heaven,
  As then, when to outstrip thy skiey speed 50
  Scarce seemed a vision; I would ne'er have striven

As thus with thee in prayer in my sore need.
  Oh, lift me as a wave, a leaf, a cloud!
  I fall upon the thorns of life! I bleed!

A heavy weight of hours has chained and bowed 55
One too like thee: tameless, and swift, and proud.

V

Make me thy lyre, even as the forest is:
What if my leaves are falling like its own!
The tumult of thy mighty harmonies

Will take from both a deep, autumnal tone, 60
Sweet though in sadness. Be thou, Spirit fierce,
My spirit! Be thou me, impetuous one!

Drive my dead thoughts over the universe
Like withered leaves to quicken a new birth!
And, by the incantation of this verse, 65

Scatter, as from an unextinguished hearth
Ashes and sparks, my words among mankind!
Be through my lips to unawakened earth

The trumpet of a prophecy! O, Wind,
If Winter comes, can Spring be far behind? 70

Line 21. Maenad: a woman devoted to Dionysus; the Maenads danced and sang in honor of the god

1. State briefly some of the major themes of this poem. Make an analysis of the fivefold structure of the poem. How does the structure assist in expressing the themes effectively? What is the structural significance of the fourth section of the poem?
2. What is the poet's problem? Where is the problem stated? To what extent is the problem solved or unsolved? Give the reasons for your judgment.
3. Make an analysis of the imagery of the first three sections of the poem and discuss the propriety of the imagery to the aspect of the wind stressed in each of these sections. Show how the imagery of the final section echoes the imagery of the first three sections. Are those echoes effective? Why or why not?
4. Make an analysis of the rhyme scheme of the poem. What is the technical name of this particular rhyme scheme? Do you think that Shelley uses it skillfully? Why or why not?

5. What is the poet's attitude toward himself? How do you know? Do the following lines deepen or lessen your sympathy for the poet?

> I fall upon the thorns of life! I bleed!
> A heavy weight of hours has chained and bowed
> One too like thee: tameless, and swift, and proud.

6. Read a brief account of the life of Shelley. To what extent is the phrase which he uses of the wind, "destroyer and preserver," an appropriate description of the role Shelley hoped to play? Why?

ODE TO A NIGHTINGALE

John Keats

My heart aches, and a drowsy numbness pains
    My sense, as though of hemlock I had drunk,
Or emptied some dull opiate to the drains
    One minute past, and Lethe-wards had sunk:
'T is not through envy of thy happy lot, 5
    But being too happy in thine happiness,—
That thou, light-wingèd Dryad of the trees,
        In some melodious plot
    Of beechen green, and shadows numberless,
Singest of summer in full-throated ease. 10

O, for a draught of vintage! that hath been
    Cool'd a long age in the deep-delved earth,
Tasting of Flora and the country green,
    Dance, and Provençal song, and sunburnt mirth!
O for a beaker full of the warm South, 15
    Full of the true, the blushful Hippocrene,
With beaded bubbles winking at the brim,
        And purple-stained mouth;
    That I might drink, and leave the world unseen,
And with thee fade away into the forest dim: 20

Fade far away, dissolve, and quite forget
    What thou among the leaves hast never known,

The weariness, the fever, and the fret
  Here, where men sit and hear each other groan;
Where palsy shakes a few, sad, last gray hairs, 25
  Where youth grows pale, and specter-thin, and dies;
Where but to think is to be full of sorrow
    And leaden-eyed despairs,
  Where Beauty cannot keep her lustrous eyes,
Or new Love pine at them beyond tomorrow. 30

Away! away! for I will fly to thee,
  Not charioted by Bacchus and his pards,
But on the viewless wings of Poesy,
  Though the dull brain perplexes and retards:
Already with thee! tender is the night, 35
  And haply the Queen-Moon is on her throne,
Cluster'd around by all her starry Fays;
    But here there is no light,
  Save what from heaven is with the breezes blown
Through verdurous glooms and winding mossy ways. 40

I cannot see what flowers are at my feet,
  Nor what soft incense hangs upon the boughs,
But, in embalmed darkness, guess each sweet
  Wherewith the seasonable month endows
The grass, the thicket, and the fruit-tree wild; 45
  White hawthorn, and the pastoral eglantine;
Fast fading violets cover'd up in leaves;
    And mid-May's eldest child,
  The coming musk-rose, full of dewy wine,
The murmurous haunt of flies on summer eves. 50

Darkling I listen; and, for many a time
  I have been half in love with easeful Death,
Call'd him soft names in many a mused rhyme,
  To take into the air my quiet breath;
Now more than ever seems it rich to die, 55

To cease upon the midnight with no pain,
While thou art pouring forth thy soul abroad
In such an ecstasy!
Still wouldst thou sing, and I have ears in vain—
To thy high requiem become a sod. 60

Thou wast not born for death, immortal Bird!
No hungry generations tread thee down;
The voice I hear this passing night was heard
In ancient days by emperor and clown:
Perhaps the self-same song that found a path 65
Through the sad heart of Ruth, when, sick for home
She stood in tears amid the alien corn:
The same that oft-times hath
Charm'd magic casements, opening on the foam
Of perilous seas in faery lands forlorn. 70

Forlorn! the very word is like a bell
To toll me back from thee to my sole self!
Adieu! the fancy cannot cheat so well
As she is fam'd to do, deceiving elf,
Adieu! adieu! thy plaintive anthem fades 75
Past the near meadows, over the still stream,
Up the hill-side; and now 't is buried deep
In the next valley-glades:
Was it a vision, or a waking dream?
Fled is that music:—Do I wake or sleep? 80

Line 4. Lethe: the underworld river whose waters produce forgetfulness
Line 7. Dryad: tree nymph
Line 13. Flora: Roman goddess of flowers
Line 14. Provence: the part of southern France where the troubadours flourished
Line 16. Hippocrene: fountain on Mt. Helicon, a source of inspiration
Line 32. Bacchus and his pards: the chariot of the god of wine was drawn by leopards
Line 37. Fays: fairies
Line 51. Darkling: in the dark

1. What is the state of mind of the poet at the beginning of the poem? Where are the reasons given for this state of mind? By what means does the poet consider escaping from his depressed state? What means does he reject? What means does he accept? What effect does this choice have on the remainder of the poem? In which stanza is the poet's escape most complete? What happens to modify the sense of complete escape? In what state is the poet at the end of the poem? Why? Is the ambiguity of the final phrase effective or ineffective? Why?
2. Make an analysis of the structure of the poem. Of what structural value are the last six lines of the first stanza? Is the structure well designed to carry out the poet's intention? Why or why not?
3. By what means is the tone of the first four lines established? What is the tone of the second stanza? Is the tone effectively or ineffectively incongruous with the rest of the poem? Give the reasons for your judgment.
4. Make an analysis of the sound-pattern of the third and the seventh stanzas. In which lines is the sound-pattern a conspicuous element in their effectiveness?
5. As a matter of scientific fact, the life of the nightingale is much briefer than that of the poet. By what means does Keats endeavor to persuade the reader that the nightingale is immortal? Is he, within the limits of the poem, successful? Why or why not?
6. Compare the poet's attitude toward himself in this poem and that of Shelley to himself in the "Ode to the West Wind." Which poet is the more successful in arousing sympathy for himself? Why?

I THINK CONTINUALLY OF THOSE WHO WERE TRULY GREAT

Stephen Spender

I think continually of those who were truly great.
Who, from the womb, remembered the soul's history
Through corridors of light where the hours are suns
Endless and singing. Whose lovely ambition
Was that their lips, still touched with fire, 5
Should tell of the Spirit clothed from head to foot in song.
And who hoarded from the Spring branches
The desires falling across their bodies like blossoms.

What is precious is never to forget
The essential delight of the blood drawn from ageless
springs 10

Breaking through rocks in worlds before our earth.
Never to deny its pleasure in the simple morning light
Nor its grave evening demand for love.
Never to allow gradually the traffic to smother
With noise and fog the flowering of the spirit. 15

Near the snow, near the sun, in the highest fields
See how these names are feted by the waving grass
And by the streamers of white cloud,
And whispers of wind in the listening sky.
The names of those who in their lives fought for life 20
Who wore at their hearts the fire's centre.
Born of the sun they travelled a short while toward the sun,
And left the vivid air signed with their honour.

1. Summarize the content of "The Darkling Thrush" (p. 203) and of this poem. Which poem is more difficult to summarize? Why?
2. What are the feelings aroused by this poem? Does the poet succeed in avoiding an effect of monotony of feeling? Why or why not?
3. Analyze the meter of the last stanza of the poem. Is Spender's meter here more or less experimental than his meter in "The Express" (p. 198)? Give the reasons for your answer.
4. Mark the metaphors and similes in this poem and discuss their sources, their freshness, and the contribution they make to the tone of the poem.
5. Compare the attitude toward life expressed in this poem and that expressed in "The Darkling Thrush."

SHE DWELT AMONG THE UNTRODDEN WAYS

William Wordsworth

She dwelt among the untrodden ways
  Beside the springs of Dove,
A Maid whom there were none to praise
  And very few to love:

A violet by a mossy stone 5
  Half hidden from the eye!

—Fair as a star, when only one
Is shining in the sky.

She lived unknown, and few could know
When Lucy ceased to be; 10
But she is in her grave, and, oh,
The difference to me!

Line 2. Dove: a river
Line 10. Lucy: No one now knows whether Lucy was a real or an imaginary person.

(As a possibly useful example, the editors in this exercise provide answers to the questions.)

1. Summarize in your own words what the poem says.

(The poet tells us of a maiden named Lucy who died. Although she had lived unpraised and unknown, her death made a great difference to the poet.)

2. What is meant by "the springs of Dove"?

(The region of the source of the river.)

3. What would such a terrain be like? How thickly settled would the region be?

(It would be way up in the hills. As Wordsworth says, it would be untrodden, probably extremely rural, sparsely settled back-country.)

4. One of your editors had misremembered the first line to read "She dwelt among untrodden ways" instead of "among *the* untrodden ways." Does the addition of "the" make any difference in the meaning of these first two lines?

("Untrodden ways" is more general. "The untrodden ways" is a specific reference and points to actual roads or paths which the speaker knows about and which he also expects the reader to know about.)

5. Does the speaker himself dwell "among untrodden ways"? Does he live unknown?

(He does not speak of the place as if he dwelt there. If his life were untraveled and isolated as Lucy's he would not be likely to exclaim at how isolated hers was. He does not accept her isolation as the usual thing. He is a more traveled person than she and expects that the reader is too. That he exclaims about her being unknown also implies his being known. Moreover the very writing of the poem or uttering of the sentiment is an act of communication which implies being known. The speaker seems to expect us to share his standards and understand his feelings.)

6. Is the tone of the speaker's words in the first stanza that of one who is involved in the life he is describing or is it impersonal?

(Impersonal. He seems to be aloof, an observer.)

7. In what lines does this tone change? How?

(Although the second stanza contains images which probably show admiration, this admiration could be impersonal; it is not until the last two lines that we realize that the speaker is emotionally involved with Lucy.)

8. What seems to be the relation between Lucy and the speaker?

(He admired her and was deeply affected by her death. Perhaps she was his sweetheart.)

9. What items in the poem establish this relationship?

(She is a Maid, likened by him to a violet and said to be fair as a star. Her death has made a great difference to him personally. Yet he doesn't seem to be part of her family or group. Moreover a family member might say "What a difference to *us!*" The speaker seems alone in his grief—at least not to be concerned with any possible grief of the few who "could know/When Lucy ceased to be." Such unconscious selfishness is a mark of lovers!)

10. Why is there the distinction between "*none* to praise/And very *few* to love"?

(Your immediate family are more likely to love you than to praise you. If she is unknown to any but her immediate family and a few neighbors who have known her since birth she would simply be accepted. Another possibility is that in a culturally impoverished spot no one may appreciate her at her true worth—they may not have the standards to recognize her value by.)

11. Is the speaker among the few that love her?

(Yes.)

12. At what point in the poem are you sure of this answer?

(The last line.)

13. Does the speaker include himself when he says "there were none to praise" her?
14. If you say that he does, has this attitude changed by the end of the poem?

(In this case the exclamation "oh,/The difference to me" seems to show that he is surprised that Lucy's death moves him so much and that she now seems so entirely admirable and all-important.)

15. If he does not, what do the lines mean?

(Simply what we said in answer to 7.)

16. In stanza 2 we find the only figurative language in the poem: Two strong images telling us what Lucy is like—the metaphor "A violet by a mossy stone" and the simile "Fair as a star." Let's look at them, first separately and then together. What are the distinguishing characteristics which violets have which seem relevant here?

(Size: small and therefore unobtrusive; color: violet—which blends into surroundings; qualities: beauty, fragrance; physical characteristics: extreme delicacy; growing habits: it's common, wild, flourishes in a shady protected area, won't live in direct sunlight; life cycle: brief.)

17. Discuss the relevance of these qualities.

(Lucy is lovely but shy, unobtrusive, not a *striking* beauty, lives in an out-of-the-way spot, *has* lived there all her life; her type of beauty is suited to this humble natural environment.)

18. How long has the mossy stone been there in comparison to the life cycle of the violet? If the violet is a metaphor for Lucy, what does the mossy stone suggest?

(The former question is asked first because some students have responded to the latter question by saying that the stone represented the poet—apparently regarding Wordsworth as rather moss-grown. Since the discussion has now probably established that the poet-speaker is an outsider, pointing out that the rock has been there a long time and will probably continue there a long time will eliminate this misreading. The question points toward data establishing that the environment is solid, unchanging, quiet, its ruggedness overgrown with the softening effects of years of adjustment to the natural environment, and that, while it hides, or half-hides, Lucy, it also sets her off to good advantage. The stone shelters the violet, half-hides it, sets it off, in short, receives and accepts the violet, but it has no other relation to her—just as the people in Lucy's environment merely accept her without special recognition. And, of course, the stone suggests the continuity of the environment compared to her brief flourishing).

19. "Half hidden from the eye!" Whose eye?

(The eye of any chance passerby, particularly the poet speaker.)

What relation can exist between a passing observer and a violet by a mossy stone, that is, what probable choice of actions might be suggested to him?

(He can scarcely notice it; he can stop, bend down to admire it, and then can pass on; he can pluck it and put it in his buttonhole; or he can dig it up and transplant it. Goethe has a poem in which Christiane Vulpius, whom he took into his home and eventually married, is compared to a violet which he finds on a casual walk and which he transplants to his own garden. A translation of this poem might even be compared with the present one.)

20. Is a violet any the less beautiful for being half-hidden, or is this its natural and most flattering situation? What about a girl? Is there an appropriately feminine quality about being half-hidden? Is there anything denigrating to the girl here, any implication that she looked all the better for being only half-seen?

(Probably not.)

21. Now let's look at the star. "—Fair as a star, when only one/Is shining in the sky." When is there likely to be only one star shining in the sky and what star is it likely to be? When is this star most clearly visible and how long does the effect last?

(Probably the planet Venus, often called the Evening Star, which is most clearly seen in early evening, when it is the first prominently visible star to appear or in the early morning when it is the last star to disappear. The effect lasts only as briefly as evening or dawn.)

22. What are some of the qualities associated with stars? Are there any negative implications in "when only one/Is shining in the sky?"

(Beauty, coldness, unattainability, unchangingness or perpetual orderly recurrence, ideal perfection are qualities associated with stars. The negative implication is that Lucy would not show up as well in society as she does in this lonely rural setting where she is probably the only girl worth looking at, just as the Evening Star is diminished when the other stars come out.)

23. When you consider that the moments when only one star is shining in the sky are relatively brief and that it is only then that the star looks largest and brightest, what is the implication about

the poet-speaker's attitude toward Lucy—if, that is, we regard this stanza, or the first two stanzas, alone?

(That, while recognizing her loveliness, he is also conscious that she is a small, brief part of his life, and that under other circumstances and in other surroundings he might not think her extraordinary. At the same time, of course, he is conscious that while he is with her for this brief interlude, or these brief interludes, she fills his whole thought as the Evening Star dominates the evening sky.)

24. If now we read to the end of the poem, to the exclamation "oh,/ The difference to me!" is there a different implication in regard to the duration and intensity of Lucy's effect on the speaker?

(It seems now as if he'll never get over her loss, that it's made a total and lasting difference in his life.)

25. What meanings associated with stars (of those suggested in 17) seem relevant here?

(Unchangingness, everpresentness, unattainability, aloofness, apartness, coldness.)

26. Does the clause "when only one/Is shining in the sky," now have a different effect, relevant to the sense of bereavement?

(She was the only star in his sky, the only light in his life, and now that light is gone out with her death; or, she is forever there, the one star in the sky of his memory, but forever unattainable.)

27. With which of the answers in this extended series do you disagree? Why?

HERE LIES A LADY OF BEAUTY AND HIGH DEGREE

John Crowe Ransom

Here lies a lady of beauty and high degree.
Of chills and fever she died, of fever and chills,

The delight of her husband, her aunt, an infant of three,
And of medicos marvelling sweetly on her ills.

For either she burned, and her confident eyes would blaze, 5
And her fingers fly in a manner to puzzle their heads—
What was she making? Why, nothing; she sat in a maze
Of old scraps of laces, snipped into curious shreds—

Or this would pass, and the light of her fire decline
Till she lay discouraged and cold, like a stalk white and
blown, 10
And would not open her eyes, to kisses, to wine;
The sixth of these states was her last; the cold settled down.

Sweet ladies, long may ye bloom, and toughly I hope ye may thole,
But was she not lucky? In flowers and lace and mourning,
In love and great honor we bade God rest her soul 15
After six little spaces of chill, and six of burning.

1. Make a summary of the content of the poem. What is the purpose of the poem? What is the relationship between the expressed attitude toward death and the purpose of the poem?
2. Make an analysis of the meter of the poem. Do you see any justification for the apparently arbitrary differences in the number of heavy stresses per line?
3. The most subtle problem raised by this poem is that of its tone. What is the dominant element in the tone? What are the subordinate elements? Is the speaker as detached from his subject as the poem suggests? Why does he assume a detached attitude? Compare the attitude toward death expressed in this poem and that expressed in Shakespeare's "Full Fathom Five" (p. 200). Which attitude is the less human? Why?

A VALEDICTION: FORBIDDING MOURNING

John Donne

As virtuous men pass mildly away,
  And whisper to their souls, to go,
Whilst some of their sad friends do say,
  The breath goes now, and some say, No:

So let us melt, and make no noise, 5
No tear-floods, nor sigh-tempests move,
'Twere profanation of our joys
To tell the laity our love.

Moving of th' earth brings harms and fears,
Men reckon what it did and meant, 10
But trepidation of the spheres,
Though greater far, is innocent.

Dull sublunary lovers' love
(Whose soul is sense) cannot admit
Absence, because it doth remove 15
Those things which elemented it.

But we by a love, so much refined
That our selves know not what it is,
Inter-assurèd of the mind,
Care less, eyes, lips, and hands to miss. 20

Our two souls therefore, which are one,
Though I must go, endure not yet
A breach, but an expansion,
Like gold to airy thinness beat.

If they be two, they are two so 25
As stiff twin compasses are two;
Thy soul the fixed foot, makes no show
To move, but doth, if th' other do.

And though it in the center sit,
Yet when the other far doth roam, 30
It leans, and hearkens after it,
And grows erect as that comes home.

Such wilt thou be to me who must
Like th' other foot, obliquely run;

Thy firmness makes my circle just, 35
And makes me end, where I begun.

Line 11. trepidation of the spheres: measurable movements of celestial bodies the magnitude of which is not easily grasped
(See p. 74 for a discussion of some aspects of this poem.)

1. What are the central themes of this poem? What is the relationship of the title to these themes? Make a summary of the content of the poem. To what extent is the element of argument present in this poem? Is the combination of types of discourse effective or ineffective in the light of the purpose of this poem? Why?
2. What two kinds of love are contrasted in the first five stanzas? What metaphors are used to establish the differences between these two kinds of love? Make a close analysis of the metaphors in the third stanza. What is their source? Are they effective? What does the word "sublunary" contribute to the tone of the fourth stanza? Look up the word "element" in a reliable dictionary and decide which meaning contributes the most to the metaphor. What is the relation between "sense" and "element"?
3. Discuss the effectiveness of the simile, "Like gold to airy thinness beat."
4. Is the imagery or the sound-pattern the more important element in line 13?
5. Is the repetition in lines 25 and 26 overdone? Why or why not?
6. Compare Donne's attitude toward love in this poem with that expressed in "The Funeral" (p. 220). What two stages in the poet's experience of love do these poems reflect?

THE WINDHOVER:
To Christ our Lord
Gerard Manley Hopkins

I caught this morning morning's minion, kingdom of daylight's
dauphin, dapple-dawn-drawn Falcon, in his riding
Of the rolling level underneath him steady air, and striding
High there, how he rung upon the rein of a wimpling wing
In his ecstasy! then off, off forth on swing, 5
As a skate's heel sweeps smooth on a bow-bend: the hurl and
gliding

Rebuffed the big wind. My heart in hiding
Stirred for a bird,—the achieve of, the mastery of the thing!

Brute beauty and valour and act, oh, air, pride, plume, here
Buckle! AND the fire that breaks from thee then, a billion 10
Times told lovelier, more dangerous, O my chevalier!

No wonder of it: shéer plód makes plough down sillion
Shine, and blue-bleak embers, ah my dear,
Fall, gall themselves, and gash gold-vermilion.

1. What clue does the subtitle give to the themes of the poem? What are the themes? Make a summary of the content of the poem. What is the relationship between the content of the first and the second parts of the poem?
2. Make an analysis of the meter of the poem in accordance with the directions for the analysis of the meter of "Felix Randal" (p. 157). What does the meter of this poem contribute to the expression of the feeling Hopkins is attempting to communicate?
3. Make an analysis of the sound-pattern of this poem. Is the sound-pattern a more or less important element in the poem than in "Felix Randal"? Cite specific examples from your analysis in support of your answer.
4. Why does Hopkins capitalize Falcon and AND? To whom is the phrase "ah my dear" addressed? What does it contribute to the tone of the last three lines?
5. To what do you think the word "here" in line 9 refers? How does the imagery in the last three lines assist in resolving the conflict between the state of the falcon and the state of the poet?
6. The stylistic elements in this poem that raise the most difficult problems are the metaphors and similes, and these elements, therefore, deserve the closest study. Discuss the efficacy of the metaphor, "kingdom of daylight's dauphin," and of the simile, "As a skate's heel sweeps smooth on a bow-bend." What part of speech is "Buckle"? What comparison is implied? What comparisons are implied in the last three lines? Discuss their effectiveness.
7. What does Hopkins gain by the elimination of certain grammatical connectives and by the violent shifts of grammar in the first part of the poem?
8. Does the poem deserve the close analysis that you have given it? Why or why not?

TRANSPLANTING

Theodore Roethke

Watching hands transplanting,
Turning and tamping,
Lifting the young plants with two fingers,
Sifting in a palm-full of fresh loam,—
One swift movement,— 5
Then plumping in the bunched roots,
A single twist of the thumbs, a tamping and turning,
All in one,
Quick on the wooden bench,
A shaking down, while the stem stays straight, 10
Once, twice, and a faint third thump,—
Into the flat-box it goes,
Ready for the long days under the sloped glass:

The sun warming the fine loam,
The young horns winding and unwinding, 15
Creaking their thin spines,
The underleaves, the smallest buds
Breaking into nakedness,
The blossoms extending
Out into the sweet air, 20
The whole flower extending outward,
Stretching and reaching.

1. Make a study of the difference in rhythmical effect between stanza 1 and stanza 2, explaining how the difference is achieved and what the purpose of the difference is.

CHILD ON TOP OF A GREENHOUSE

Theodore Roethke

The wind billowing out the seat of my britches,
My feet crackling splinters of glass and dried putty,

The half-grown chrysanthemums staring up like accusers,
Up through the streaked glass, flashing with sunlight,
A few white clouds all rushing eastward, 5
A line of elms plunging and tossing like horses,
And everyone, everyone pointing up and shouting!

1. The boy's emotions and sensations are not reported directly but only implied by the details of the scene. What are his emotions and sensations?
2. What does each individual image and figure contribute to the general impression you have received?
3. Are the various details seen from one physical point of view? For example, would the clouds and the elms appear more violently in motion when seen from the boy's vantage point on the roof or from the onlookers' position on the ground?
4. Discuss the effect of the order of the details given. Suppose, for example, you should transpose lines 4 and 5 with lines 1 and 2. Would the effect be changed? In what way?
5. Pick out the present participles in the poem. Is there a main verb? What is gained by this syntax?
6. Discuss the effect of the unrhymed feminine endings, the primarily end-stopped lines, and the rhythms of these lines.

Ideas in Poetry

THE TYGER

William Blake

Tyger! Tyger! burning bright
In the forests of the night,
What immortal hand or eye
Could frame thy fearful symmetry?

In what distant deeps or skies 5
Burnt the fire of thine eyes?
On what wings dare he aspire?
What the hand dare seize the fire?

And what shoulder, & what art,
Could twist the sinews of thy heart? 10
And when thy heart began to beat,
What dread hand? & what dread feet?

What the hammer? what the chain?
In what furnace was thy brain?
What the anvil? what dread grasp 15
Dare its deadly terrors clasp?

When the stars threw down their spears,
And water'd heaven with their tears,
Did he smile his work to see?
Did he who made the Lamb make thee? 20

Tyger! Tyger! burning bright
In the forests of the night,
What immortal hand or eye
Dare frame thy fearful symmetry?

1. Herrick and Marvell were careful to select only such specific details as would emphasize the particular aspect of nature that would fulfill their purposes. What aspect of nature does Blake emphasize in this poem? Contrast the conventional prosaic view of the ostensible subject of Blake's poem with the fresh poetic view implied here.
2. What image-making words in this poem build up the idea of creative power? Does the phrase "burning bright" have any relation to these images?
3. Point out the repetitions in this poem and discuss their effectiveness, giving particular attention to Blake's triple use of the word "dread." Make an analysis of the rest of the sound-pattern. Is the sound-pattern more or less conspicuous than that in "The Little Black Boy" (p. 211)?
4. To what are the stars compared in the fifth stanza? Is the metaphor successful?
5. Discuss the propriety of the styles of this poem and "The Little Black Boy."
6. What are the major symbols in this poem? How are they related?

DOVER BEACH

Matthew Arnold

The sea is calm to-night.
The tide is full, the moon lies fair
Upon the straits;—on the French coast the light
Gleams and is gone; the cliffs of England stand,
Glimmering and vast, out in the tranquil bay. 5
Come to the window, sweet is the night-air!
Only, from the long line of spray
Where the sea meets the moon-blanch'd land,
Listen! you hear the grating roar
Of pebbles which the waves draw back, and fling, 10
At their return, up the high strand,
Begin, and cease, and then again begin,

With tremulous cadence slow, and bring
The eternal note of sadness in.

Sophocles long ago 15
Heard it on the Ægæan, and it brought
Into his mind the turbid ebb and flow
Of human misery; we
Find also in the sound a thought,
Hearing it by this distant northern sea. 20

The Sea of Faith
Was once, too, at the full, and round earth's shore
Lay like the folds of a bright girdle furled.
But now I only hear
Its melancholy, long, withdrawing roar, 25
Retreating, to the breath
Of the night-wind, down the vast edges drear
And naked shingles of the world.

Ah, love, let us be true
To one another! for the world, which seems 30
To lie before us like a land of dreams,
So various, so beautiful, so new,
Hath really neither joy, nor love, nor light,
Nor certitude, nor peace, nor help for pain;
And we are here as on a darkling plain 35
Swept with confused alarms of struggle and flight,
Where ignorant armies clash by night.

1. Like Wordsworth's "The World Is Too Much with Us" (p. 262), Arnold's poem sets forth a conflict and a suggested resolution of it. In what respects are the elements in Arnold's conflict like and unlike those in the conflict expressed in Wordsworth's poem? What light do Wordsworth's phrase "a creed outworn" and Arnold's phrase "the Sea of Faith" throw on the poets' attitudes toward life? Compare the major and the subordinate tones in these poems. Which poem expresses the more subdued or depressed feeling? Point out specific instances of imagery, sound-pattern, and figures of speech that contribute to creating the tone of "Dover Beach."

2. Make an analysis of the structure of the poem. What type of discourse predominates in it? What is the structural function of the first stanza? Of the second and third? What is the relationship between the third and the fourth stanzas?
3. Analyze the metrics and the rhyme scheme of the first stanza. Discuss the effectiveness or the ineffectiveness of the variation in line lengths.
4. Discuss the development of the metaphor of the sea in stanzas 2 and 3. Does the interpolated simile "like the folds of a bright girdle furled," seem to you to add to the effect of the third stanza or to detract from it? From what is the "northern sea" distant (line 20)?
5. What are the "ignorant armies" that "clash by night"?
6. Is the attitude expressed in this poem likely to have a special appeal to a reader living in the middle of the twentieth century? Why or why not?

A PRAYER FOR MY DAUGHTER

William Butler Yeats

Once more the storm is howling, and half hid
Under this cradle-hood and coverlid
My child sleeps on. There is no obstacle
But Gregory's wood and one bare hill
Whereby the haystack- and roof-levelling wind, 5
Bred on the Atlantic, can be stayed;
And for an hour I have walked and prayed
Because of the great gloom that is in my mind.

I have walked and prayed for this young child an hour
And heard the sea-wind scream upon the tower, 10
And under the arches of the bridge, and scream
In the elms above the flooded stream;
Imagining in excited reverie
That the future years had come,
Dancing to a frenzied drum, 15
Out of the murderous innocence of the sea.

May she be granted beauty and yet not
Beauty to make a stranger's eye distraught,

Or hers before a looking-glass, for such,
Being made beautiful overmuch, 20
Consider beauty a sufficient end,
Lose natural kindness and maybe
The heart-revealing intimacy
That chooses right, and never find a friend.

Helen being chosen found life flat and dull 25
And later had much trouble from a fool,
While that great Queen, that rose out of the spray,
Being fatherless could have her way
Yet chose a bandy-leggèd smith for man.
It's certain that fine women eat 30
A crazy salad with their meat
Whereby the Horn of Plenty is undone.

In courtesy I'd have her chiefly learned;
Hearts are not had as a gift but hearts are earned
By those that are not entirely beautiful; 35
Yet many, that have played the fool
For beauty's very self, has charm made wise,
And many a poor man that has roved,
Loved and thought himself beloved,
From a glad kindness cannot take his eyes. 40

May she become a flourishing hidden tree
That all her thoughts may like the linnet be,
And have no business but dispensing round
Their magnanimities of sound,
Nor but in merriment begin a chase, 45
Nor but in merriment a quarrel.
O may she live like some green laurel
Rooted in one dear perpetual place.

My mind, because the minds that I have loved,
The sort of beauty that I have approved, 50
Prosper but little, has dried up of late,

Yet knows that to be choked with hate
May well be of all evil chances chief.
If there's no hatred in a mind
Assault and battery of the wind 55
Can never tear the linnet from the leaf.

An intellectual hatred is the worst,
So let her think opinions are accursed.
Have I not seen the loveliest woman born
Out of the mouth of Plenty's horn, 60
Because of her opinionated mind
Barter that horn and every good
By quiet natures understood
For an old bellows full of angry wind?

Considering that, all hatred driven hence, 65
The soul recovers radical innocence
And learns at last that it is self-delighting,
Self-appeasing, self-affrighting,
And that its own sweet will is Heaven's will;
She can, though every face should scowl 70
And every windy quarter howl
Or every bellows burst, be happy still.

And may her bridegroom bring her to a house
Where all's accustomed, ceremonious;
For arrogance and hatred are the wares 75
Peddled in the thoroughfares.
How but in custom and in ceremony
Are innocence and beauty born?
Ceremony's a name for the rich horn,
And custom for the spreading laurel tree. 80

Line 10. the tower: Yeats bought and restored an old Norman tower, Thoor Ballylee, near his friend Lady Gregory's estate, and lived there summers

Line 25. Helen: Helen of Troy. Married to Menelaus of Sparta, she ran off with Paris, causing the Trojan War

Line 27. Queen: Aphrodite, goddess of love and beauty, was born from the sea; she married Hephaestus or Vulcan, the blacksmith of the gods, who was lame
Line 42. linnet: a small bird
Line 59. loveliest woman born: Yeats loved and admired the beautiful Irish nationalist Maude Gonne, but thought that her exclusive dedication to the political struggle narrowed and embittered her mind

1. Why is there a great gloom in his mind (line 8)?
2. Why is it "Out . . . of the sea" that he imagines "the future years" to have come (lines 13–16)?
3. What do you make of the phrase "murderous innocence"?
4. What does he mean when he says "fine women eat/A crazy salad with their meat" (lines 30–32)?
5. What is meant by the Horn of Plenty and how is it undone?
6. What is meant by "windy quarter" (line 71)?
7. What would you say the storm (line 1) is symbolic of?
8. Explain and develop briefly the thought implicit in "How but in custom and in ceremony/Are innocence and beauty born?" (lines 77–78).
9. What is the basic meaning of "radical" (line 66)? What is meant by "radical innocence"?
10. Can you relate the image of the laurel (lines 47–48 and 80) to this idea?
11. What is the difference between "murderous innocence" (line 16) and "radical innocence" (line 66)?
12. If innocence and beauty are born only in custom and ceremony (which seems to be implied in lines 77–78), how can one call the sea innocent (line 16)?
13. Would you make any connection between the ideas about innocence in this poem and the lines "and everywhere/The ceremony of innocence is drowned" in "The Second Coming" (p. 479)?
14. Discuss how the scene of "A Prayer for My Daughter" provides the basic metaphor or symbol for what the poet has to say.
15. Trace the image of wind through the poem. In lines 54–56 what do the wind, the linnet, and the leaf seem to stand for?
16. The poet calls the poem a prayer in the title and says he has walked and prayed (line 7). What traces do you find in the poem of his prayer? Do you think that the poem is basically a prayer in form? How much intensity of religious devotion do you find in the poem? Is there any thought in the poem of the god he is praying to?
17. Discuss the ideas in the next to the last stanza. Can you connect the thought that the soul's "own sweet will is Heaven's will" (line

69) with thoughts from other poems, such as "unless/Soul clap its hands and sing, and louder sing" ("Sailing to Byzantium," p. 267); Contrast the thought of this stanza with that of the first stanza of "The Second Coming." Contrast particularly the state of the soul which knows "its own sweet will is Heaven's will" with the state of the "best" who "lack all conviction."

SAY NOT THE STRUGGLE NOUGHT AVAILETH

Arthur Hugh Clough

Say not the struggle nought availeth,
  The labour and the wounds are vain,
The enemy faints not, nor faileth,
  And as things have been they remain.

If hopes were dupes, fears may be liars; 5
  It may be, in yon smoke concealed,
Your comrades chase e'en now the fliers,
  And, but for you, possess the field.

For while the tired waves, vainly breaking,
  Seem here no painful inch to gain, 10
Far back, through creeks and inlets making,
  Comes silent, flooding in, the main.

And not by eastern windows only,
  When daylight comes, comes in the light,
In front, the sun climbs slow, how slowly, 15
  But westward, look, the land is bright.

1. As we have pointed out (pp. 15–16), this is an argumentative poem, a poem that states a position and presents evidence in support of it. The arguments offered are what are technically called arguments by analogy. Discuss the effectiveness of each of the three arguments presented here. Are they presented in the most effective order or would the poem be strengthened by a rearrangement of the arguments? Give the reasons for your conclusion.
2. Make an analysis of the tone of the poem. Is the pattern of feelings

and emotions aroused by the poem an effective one? Why or why not?

3. In the light of your study of this poem and of Arnold's "Dover Beach" (p. 244), present evidence in support of your judgment as to the superiority of one poem to the other.

TO A FRIEND WHOSE WORK HAS COME TO NOTHING

William Butler Yeats

Now all the truth is out,
Be secret and take defeat
From any brazen throat,
For how can you compete,
Being honour bred, with one 5
Who, were it proved he lies,
Were neither shamed in his own
Nor in his neighbours' eyes?
Bred to a harder thing
Than Triumph, turn away 10
And like a laughing string
Whereon mad fingers play
Amid a place of stone,
Be secret and exult,
Because of all things known 15
That is most difficult.

1. State what the poem says in your own words. (You cannot, of course, know the specific story behind the poem, but what type of situation is referred to?)
2. What values do you find expressed here which you have found in other of Yeats' poems? Be specific in reference to other poems.
3. Comment on the paradox in "Now all the truth is out,/Be secret."
4. Comment on "brazen throat." Is there a latent musical metaphor in this phrase?
5. Comment on "honour bred."
6. What is the "harder thing/Than Triumph" to which the friend has been bred? What is the implication of "Bred to"?

7. Explain the simile in lines 10–13, showing how the elements of the simile relate to the elements of the situation.
8. Do the "mad fingers" relate to the friend or the brazen-throated mob? Explain.
9. To what in the situation does the "place of stone" relate? What effect would a "place of stone" have on a "laughing string"?
10. What should the friend "exult" about (line 14)?
11. What does "That" (line 16) refer to?
12. Comment on the kind of standards appealed to in the last two lines of the poem?
13. Comment on the verse form, on the rhetorical pattern, and on the appropriateness of these interrelated items to the subject. What effect is produced by the relationship of two long sentences to a verse form of very short, end-stopped lines?
14. Comment on the contrast between "brazen throat" and "laughing string." Could you relate the thought of this contrast to ideas in "A Prayer for My Daughter" (p. 246)?

THE FURY OF AERIAL BOMBARDMENT

Richard Eberhart

You would think the fury of aerial bombardment
Would rouse God to relent; the infinite spaces
Are still silent. He looks on shock-pried faces.
History, even, does not know what is meant.

You would feel that after so many centuries 5
God would give man to repent; yet he can kill
As Cain could, but with multitudinous will,
No farther advanced than in his ancient furies.

Was man made stupid to see his own stupidity?
Is God by definition indifferent, beyond us all? 10
Is the eternal truth man's fighting soul
Wherein the Beast ravens in its own avidity?

Of Van Wettering I speak, and Averill,
Names on a list, whose faces I do not recall
But they are gone to early death, who late in school 15
Distinguished the belt feed lever from the belt holding pawl.

1. Mark the rhyme scheme of the poem. Which types of rhyme are present? Discuss the role played by repetition, internal rhyme, assonance, and consonance. How is the sound of the *a*-rhyme used in the first two stanzas? Is the intricacy of the sound-pattern functional in relation to the poem's subject?
2. Write a one-paragraph statement of the poem's major themes.
3. Which of the following statements of the poem's themes would you reject? Why?
   a). The terrible destruction of a modern air raid calls into question both the ethical character of man and the providence of God.
   b). History seems to be a record of no progress, except in extension of mechanical capacity. Man himself has not changed at all.
   c). The destructiveness of modern warfare defies not only any moral ordering but even any meaningful analysis. The only concept that can fit our situation is that of the absurd.
   d). God has withdrawn from his creation. Deaths are not meaningful but merely pathetic.
   e). The will-to-death is superior to the will-to-life in man. Man has a compulsion to kill and to be killed, and this compulsion, associated with the now available mechanical means, will destroy us all.
   f). Man once had an individual identity—a name—and made personally his ultimate choices. Now man's individual identity has been wiped out, and, though he still technically has the choices, they have become mechanical distinctions, robbed of their meaning.

CORINNA'S GOING A-MAYING

Robert Herrick

Get up, get up for shame, the blooming morn
Upon her wings presents the god unshorn.
  See how Aurora throws her fair
  Fresh-quilted colors through the air:
  Get up, sweet slug-a-bed, and see 5
  The dew bespangling herb and tree.
Each flower has wept and bowèd toward the east
Above an hour since: yet you not dressed;
  Nay: not so much as out of bed?
  When all the birds have matins said 10
  And sung their thankful hymns, 'tis sin,

Nay, profanation, to keep in,
Whenas a thousand virgins on this day
Spring, sooner than the lark, to fetch in May.

Rise, and put on your foliage, and be seen 15
To come forth, like the spring-time, fresh and green,
And sweet as Flora. Take no care
For jewels for your gown or hair:
Fear not; the leaves will strew
Gems in abundance upon you: 20
Besides, the childhood of the day has kept,
Against you come, some orient pearls unwept;
Come and receive them while the light
Hangs on the dew-locks of the night:
And Titan on the eastern hill 25
Retires himself, or else stands still
Till you come forth. Wash, dress, be brief in praying:
Few beads are best when once we go a-Maying.

Come, my Corinna, come; and, coming mark
How each field turns a street, each street a park 30
Made green and trimmed with trees; see how
Devotion gives each house a bough
Or branch: each porch, each door ere this
An ark, a tabernacle is,
Made up of white-thorn, neatly interwove; 35
As if here were those cooler shades of love.
Can such delights be in the street
And open fields and we not see 't?
Come, we'll abroad; and let's obey
The proclamation made for May: 40
And sin no more, as we have done, by staying;
But, my Corinna, come, let's go a-Maying.

There's not a budding boy or girl this day
But is got up, and gone to bring in May.
A deal of youth, ere this, is come 45

Back, and with white-thorn laden home.
Some have despatched their cakes and cream
Before that we have left to dream:
And some have wept, and wooed, and plighted troth,
And chose their priest, ere we can cast off sloth: 50
Many a green-gown has been given;
Many a kiss, both odd and even:
Many a glance too has been sent
From out the eye, love's firmament;
Many a jest told of the keys betraying 55
This night, and locks picked, yet we're not a-Maying.

Come, let us go while we are in our prime;
And take the harmless folly of the time.
We shall grow old apace, and die
Before we know our liberty. 60
Our life is short, and our days run
As fast away as does the sun;
And, as a vapor or a drop of rain,
Once lost, can ne'er be found again,
So when or you or I are made 65
A fable, song, or fleeting shade,
All love, all liking, all delight
Lies drowned with us in endless night.
Then while time serves, and we are but decaying,
Come, my Corinna, come let's go a-Maying. 70

Line 3. Aurora: goddess of the dawn
Line 17. Flora: Roman goddess of flowers and gardens
Line 25. Titan: a name applied to the sun by Virgil and Ovid

1. What are the major themes of this poem? Where are they stated most clearly? How do they differ from those of Marvell's "To His Coy Mistress" (p. 205)?
2. Make an analysis of the structure of the poem. To what type of discourse does it belong? Discuss the relationship of the topic developed in each stanza to the themes of the poem.
3. Outline the sequence of feelings and emotions experienced by the

speaker in the poem. How does the order in which these feelings and emotions are presented contribute to the effect of the poem?
4. Since very little "happens" in this poem and since, consequently, its effect is rather static, discuss the means by which Herrick attempts to create, sustain, and intensify the interest of the reader.
5. Make an analysis of the meter of the first stanza of the poem and compare it with the meter of the first stanza of Wordsworth's "Intimations" ode (p. 269). Wordsworth, as we shall see later, varies the form from one part of the ode to the next. What does Herrick gain by using the same stanzaic form throughout the poem?
6. Make an analysis of the rhyme scheme of the last stanza. How does Herrick avoid the singsong effect that sometimes results from an amateurish use of this rhyme scheme?

THE GREEN SHEPHERD

Louis Simpson

Here sit a shepherd and a shepherdess,
He playing on his melancholy flute;
The sea wind ruffles up her simple dress
And shows the delicacy of her foot.

And there you see Constantinople's wall (5)
With arrows and Greek fire, molten lead;
Down from a turret seven virgins fall,
Hands folded, each one praying on her head.

The shepherd yawns and puts his flute away.
It's time, she murmurs, we were going back. (10)
He offers certain reasons she should stay—
But neither sees the dragon on their track.

A dragon like a car in a garage
Is in the wood, his long tail sticking out.
Here rides St. George, swinging his sword and targe, (15)
And sticks the grinning dragon in the snout.

Puffing a smoke ring, like the cigarette
Over Times Square, Sir Dragon snorts his last.
St. George takes off his armor in a sweat.
The Middle Ages have been safely passed. (20)

What is the sail that crosses the still bay,
Unnoticed by the shepherds? It could be
A caravel that's sailing to Cathay,
Westward from Palos on the unknown sea.

But the green shepherd travels in her eye 25
And whispers nothings in his lady's ear,
And sings a little song, that roses die,
Carpe diem, which she seems pleased to hear.

The vessel they ignored still sails away
So bravely on the water, Westward Ho! 30
And murdering, in a religious way,
Brings Jesus to the Gulf of Mexico.

Now Portugal is fading, and the state
Of Castile rising purple on Peru;
Now England, now America grows great— 35
With which these lovers have nothing to do.

What do they care if time, uncompassed, drift
To China, and the crew is a baboon?
But let him whisper always, and her lift
The oceans in her eyelids to the moon. 40

The dragon rises crackling in the air,
And who is god but Dagon? Wings careen,
Rejoicing, on the Russian hemisphere.
Meanwhile, the shepherd dotes upon her skin.

Old Aristotle, having seen this pass, 45
From where he studied in the giant's cave,
Went in and shut his book and locked the brass
And lay down with a shudder in his grave.

The groaning pole had gone more than a mile;
These shepherds did not feel it where they loved, 50
For time was sympathetic all the while
And on the magic mountain nothing moved.

Line 5. Constantinople: the ancient city of Byzantium, now Istanbul. Made the capital of the Roman empire by the Christian emperor Constantine; later capital of the Eastern empire

Line 6. Greek fire: the Byzantines used an inflammable mixture poured into pots and thrown burning into enemy ships to defeat an Arab fleet

Lines 17–18. cigarette/Over Times Square: a huge advertisement from which a mouth blew actual smoke rings

Line 19. St. George: Christian martyr and patron saint of England

Line 23. caravel: in the fifteenth and sixteenth centuries, a small vessel with broad bows, high poop, and lateen sails

Line 23. Cathay: China, so called formerly in Western Europe

Line 24. Palos: seaport in southwest Spain from which Columbus sailed in 1492

Line 28. *Carpe diem:* seize the day, take advantage of the present

Line 30. *Westward Ho!*: novel (1855) by Charles Kingsley (1819–1875) about the adventures of Elizabethan sailors in the Americas

Line 34. Castile: former kingdom in Spain

Line 42. Dagon: pagan god (of the Philistines) whose worship rivalled Jehovah's in the Old Testament

Line 45: Aristotle: the ancient Greek philosopher may be taken as the intelligence of Western man seeing the end, as it saw the beginning, of Western civilization

Line 46. The giant's cave: "In the next to the last stanza of "The Green Shepherd" the references to 'the giant's cave' and 'locked the brass' are merely imaginary details . . . I imagined Aristotle as having retired from the world to continue his studies—retired into a cave. The giant's cave would be a cave that was once occupied by heroes (the 'giants' of Vico). The book he wrote in would have a brass clasp and lock on it. Finally, as the world progresses, he gives up and locks his book shut." *

Line 49. The groaning pole: probably the North Pole, but one also thinks of the mast of a vessel

"The Green Shepherd" alludes indirectly to a traditional type of poem. Marlowe's "The Passionate Shepherd to His Love" (p. 405) gives us the classic situation. Robert Herrick's "To the Virgins, to Make Much of Time" (p. 374), Andrew Marvell's "To His Coy Mistress" (p. 205), and Edmund Waller's "Song" (p. 204) are all on the theme "that roses die" and that therefore the shepherdess should seize the day, *carpe diem,* and love the shepherd in the fast vanishing present. The theme of this

* Louis Simpson, letter to David R. Clark, September 22, 1965.

poem, however, is the opposite of these. On this magic mountain nothing moves, but out on the sea pass symbols of the whole course of western civilization which seems to go by while the lovers are wooing. In other words, civilizations come and go, but the whispering of lovers goes on forever.

1. What is the tone of this poem? Point out and comment upon the lines that define the poet's attitude toward the past, the present, and the future and toward the lovers. The latter is the most problematical. Contrast the poet's attitude to the lovers with his attitude to old Aristotle.

THE GARDEN

Andrew Marvell

How vainly men themselves amaze,
To win the palm, the oak, or bays,
And their incessant labors see
Crowned from some single herb or tree
Whose short and narrow-vergèd shade 5
Does prudently their toils upbraid,
While all the flowers and trees do close
To weave the garlands of repose!

Fair Quiet, have I found thee here,
And Innocence, thy sister dear? 10
Mistaken long, I sought you then
In busy companies of men.
Your sacred plants, if here below,
Only among the plants will grow;
Society is all but rude 15
To this delicious solitude.

No white nor red was ever seen
So amorous as this lovely green.
Fond lovers, cruel as their flame,
Cut in these trees their mistress' name. 20
Little, alas! they know or heed,

How far these beauties hers exceed!
Fair trees! wheres'e'er your barks I wound
No name shall but your own be found.

When we have run our passion's heat, 25
Love hither makes his best retreat.
The gods, that mortal beauty chase,
Still in a tree did end their race;
Apollo hunted Daphne so,
Only that she might laurel grow; 30
And Pan did after Syrinx speed,
Not as a nymph, but for a reed.

What wondrous life is this I lead!
Ripe apples drop about my head;
The luscious clusters of the vine 35
Upon my mouth do crush their wine;
The nectarine, and curious peach,
Into my hands themselves do reach;
Stumbling on melons, as I pass,
Insnared with flowers, I fall on grass. 40

Meanwhile the mind, from pleasure less,
Withdraws into its happiness;—
The mind, that ocean where each kind
Does straight its own resemblance find;
Yet it creates, transcending these, 45
Far other worlds, and other seas,
Annihilating all that's made
To a green thought in a green shade.

Here at the fountain's sliding foot,
Or at some fruit-tree's mossy root, 50
Casting the body's vest aside,
My soul into the boughs does glide:
There, like a bird, it sits and sings,

Then whets and combs its silver wings,
And, till prepared for longer flight, 55
Waves in its plumes the various light.

Such was that happy garden-state,
While man there walked without a mate:
After a place so pure and sweet,
What other help could yet be meet! 60
But 'twas beyond a mortal's share
To wander solitary there:
Two paradises 'twere in one,
To live in paradise alone.

How well the skilful gardener drew 65
Of flowers, and herbs, this dial new;
Where, from above, the milder sun
Does through a fragrant zodiac run;
And, as it works, the industrious bee
Computes its time as well as we! 70
How could such sweet and wholesome hours
Be reckoned but with herbs and flowers?

Line 29. Apollo and Daphne: Apollo's amorous pursuit of the reluctant river nymph, Daphne, caused her to call upon the gods for help; they changed her into a laurel; Apollo crowned his head with the leaves of the laurel

Line 31. Pan and Syrinx: the nymph Syrinx, escaping from the advances of Pan, was changed into a reed; Pan made himself a pipe of such reeds

1. Since a subtle and sophisticated mind is reacting here upon the chosen scene, the rich intellectual content of this poem deserves especially careful study. What contrast is worked out in each of the first three stanzas? Of what value to the contrast in the first stanza are the epithets "short and narrow-vergèd" and the phrase "garlands of repose"? Is the repetition of "plants" in the second stanza effective? Why or why not? In the third stanza, what does Marvell mean by "red and white"? How do you know?

2. Although there are ethical value judgments implied in Herrick's "Corinna's Going A-Maying," Marvell's poem is much more overtly philosophical and it would, therefore, be a mistake to regard this as a merely descriptive poem. Make an analysis of the structure of the poem and show how much of it is description and how much is exposition of the ideas suggested to Marvell by the garden. How does the order in which these elements appear contribute to the effectiveness of the poem?
3. Make an analysis of the imagery of the fifth stanza of the poem. Compare the imagery with that of the fifth stanza of Keats's "Ode to a Nightingale" (p. 227). Compare the over-all tones that the poets achieve by the kind and the amount of imagery they use.
4. In the sixth stanza, what does the phrase "from pleasure less" mean? To what does the word "these" in line 45 refer? What conception of the mind is set forth in this stanza?
5. Discuss the simile of the bird in the seventh stanza.
6. What comparison is developed in the eighth stanza? Why does Marvell use the words "help" and "meet" in line 60? Do you think that the play on words is effective? Why does Marvell believe that "Two paradises 'twere in one,/To live in paradise alone"?
7. What image is evoked by line 66? Why is the zodiac "fragrant"?
8. To what do "it" (line 69) and "its" (line 70) refer? In what sense does the industrious bee compute time?
9. Marianne Moore defines poetry as "imaginary gardens with real toads in them." Discuss Marvell's poem in the light of this definition.

THE WORLD IS TOO MUCH WITH US

William Wordsworth

The world is too much with us; late and soon,
Getting and spending, we lay waste our powers:
Little we see in Nature that is ours;
We have given our hearts away, a sordid boon!
This Sea that bares her bosom to the moon; 5
The winds that will be howling at all hours,
And are up-gathered now like sleeping flowers;
For this, for everything, we are out of tune;
It moves us not.—Great God! I'd rather be
A Pagan suckled in a creed outworn; 10
So might I, standing on this pleasant lea,
Have glimpses that would make me less forlorn;

Have sight of Proteus rising from the sea;
Or hear old Triton blow his wreathèd horn.

Line 13. Proteus: a son of Neptune who could change his shape at will
Line 14. Triton: a son of Neptune, the herald of the seas who had a conch shell for his trumpet

1. In the context of this poem what does Wordsworth mean by "the world"? By what means does he establish his attitude toward the world? What conception of nature is built up in the second half of the octave?
2. What is the problem the poet faces? Where is it set forth? What resolution of the conflict is suggested in the sestet?
3. Discuss repetitions in this sonnet. Analyze the sound-pattern of lines 5 and 6 and 13 and 14. Is alliteration or assonance the more conspicuous element in the sound-pattern of these lines? What does the rhyme scheme contribute to the tone of this sonnet?
4. What are the major symbols in the poem and what is their relationship? If Proteus and Triton are not to be considered merely as figures that appeal to the romantic imagination, what do they symbolize? What relationship do they have to the "creed outworn" and to Wordsworth's attitude toward "the world"?

Poetry's "teaching" includes the inculcation of traditional moral beliefs. If all other books were to go, most of the values of western civilization could be found in the works of Shakespeare. Unconventional attitudes too, however, are often subjects for poetry (including that of Shakespeare), because they make us look twice at conventional attitudes or at the world in which these attitudes are supposed to work but often do not. Shakespeare's sonnets No. 29 and No. 30 state the conventional idea that friendship is a higher value than worldly success.

SONNET 29

William Shakespeare

When, in disgrace with fortune and men's eyes,
I all alone beweep my outcast state,

And trouble deaf heaven with my bootless cries,
And look upon myself, and curse my fate,
Wishing me like to one more rich in hope 5
Featured like him, like him with friends possessed,
Desiring this man's art and that man's scope,
With what I most enjoy contented least;
Yet in these thoughts myself almost despising,
Haply I think on thee, and then my state, 10
Like to the lark at break of day arising
From sullen earth, sings hymns at heaven's gate;
For thy sweet love remembered such wealth brings
That then I scorn to change my state with kings.

SONNET 30

William Shakespeare

When to the sessions of sweet silent thought
I summon up remembrance of things past,
I sigh the lack of many a thing I sought,
And with old woes new wail my dear time's waste.
Then can I drown an eye, unused to flow, 5
For precious friends hid in death's dateless night,
And weep afresh love's long since cancelled woe,
And moan the expense of many a vanish'd sight.
Then can I grieve at grievances foregone,
And heavily from woe to woe tell o'er 10
The sad account of fore-bemoanèd moan,
Which I new pay as if not paid before.
But if the while I think on thee, dear friend,
All losses are restored, and sorrows end.

On the other hand, here is a poem which rejects friendship in favour of hard cash.

OF MONEY
Barnabe Googe

Give money me; take friendship whoso list!
  For friends are gone, come once adversity;
When money yet remaineth safe in chest,
  That quickly can thee bring from misery.
Fair face show friends, when riches do abound; 5
  Come time of proof, farewell, they must away!
Believe me well, they are not to be found
  If God but send thee once a louring day.
Gold never starts aside; but, in distress,
Finds ways enough to ease thine heaviness. 10

1. These are all successful poems. How is it possible to reconcile one's enjoyment of all three?
2. Is the last poem really an attack on the value of friendship?

ANYONE LIVED IN A PRETTY HOW TOWN
E. E. Cummings

anyone lived in a pretty how town
(with up so floating many bells down)
spring summer autumn winter
he sang his didn't he danced his did.

Women and men (both little and small) 5
cared for anyone not at all
they sowed their isn't they reaped their same
sun moon stars rain

children guessed (but only a few
and down they forgot as up they grew 10
autumn winter spring summer)
that noone loved him more by more

when by now and tree by leaf
she laughed his joy she cried his grief
bird by snow and stir by still 15
anyone's any was all to her

someones married their everyones
laughed their cryings and did their dance
(sleep wake hope and then) they
said their nevers they slept their dream 20

stars rain sun moon
(and only the snow can begin to explain
how children are apt to forget to remember
with up so floating many bells down)

one day anyone died i guess 25
(and noone stooped to kiss his face)
busy folk buried them side by side
little by little and was by was

all by all and deep by deep
and more by more they dream their sleep 30
noone and anyone earth by april
wish by spirit and if by yes.

Women and men (both dong and ding)
summer autumn winter spring
reaped their sowing and went their came 35
sun moon stars rain

This poem involves a difficulty we have not encountered in any of the poems we have studied. Even after you have made a serious attempt to discover the qualities of this poem, you may conclude that it is absurd rather than illuminating. The difficulty in this poem arises from what may seem at first to be an unjustifiable audacity in the use of language, as in the line "he sang his didn't he danced his did" where the verbs "didn't" and "did" are used as nouns. It is obvious that language is not used in this line as representationally as it is in Arnold's

Listen! you hear the grating roar
Of pebbles which the waves draw back, and fling,
At their return, up the high strand,
Begin, and cease, and then again begin,
With tremulous cadence slow.

And yet Cummings's poem is not meaningless. It is not completely abstract, that is, without any specific content, but semi-representational.

Probably the best way to get at the quality of this poem is to read it aloud several times, emphasizing the meter and the sound-pattern. If this procedure is followed, you should be in a position to answer the following questions.

1. The title of the poem indicates that its hero is named "anyone." What does Cummings gain by denoting his hero in this way? Summarize as clearly as you can what happens to "anyone" in the course of the poem. Is Cummings's attitude toward "anyone" simple or complex? How do the meter, the imagery, and the diction contribute to the expression of his attitude?
2. What is the major tone of the poem and what are its subordinate tones? Is the combination of tones agreeable or disagreeable? Why?
3. What justification can you see for the highly experimental use of language in this poem?
4. Compare the attitude toward life implied in Cummings's poem with that expressed in either Wordsworth's or Arnold's poem (p. 262 and 244).

SAILING TO BYZANTIUM

William Butler Yeats

I

That is no country for old men. The young
In one another's arms, birds in the trees
—Those dying generations—at their song,
The salmon-falls, the mackerel-crowded seas,
Fish, flesh, or fowl, commend all summer long 5
Whatever is begotten, born, and dies.

Caught in that sensual music all neglect
Monuments of unageing intellect.

II

An aged man is but a paltry thing,
A tattered coat upon a stick, unless 10
Soul clap its hands and sing, and louder sing
For every tatter in its mortal dress,
Nor is there singing school but studying
Monuments of its own magnificence;
And therefore I have sailed the seas and come 15
To the holy city of Byzantium.

III

O sages standing in God's holy fire
As in the gold mosaic of a wall,
Come from the holy fire, perne in a gyre,
And be the singing-masters of my soul. 20
Consume my heart away; sick with desire
And fastened to a dying animal
It knows not what it is; and gather me
Into the artifice of eternity.

IV

Once out of nature I shall never take 25
My bodily form from any natural thing,
But such a form as Grecian goldsmiths make
Of hammered gold and gold enamelling
To keep a drowsy Emperor awake;
Or set upon a golden bough to sing 30
To lords and ladies of Byzantium
Of what is past, or passing, or to come.

Line 16. Byzantium: Christian capital of the Eastern Roman Empire; famous for the development of a special style in painting and mosaics

Line 19. perne in a gyre: Yeats himself relates the movement here to the manner in which he saw thread wound onto a spool in a mill, a circular motion on a spiral shape

1. What types of structure are present in the poem? Which, if any, is the dominant type?
2. Compare and contrast stanzas I and IV with respect to the nature and arrangement of rhymes, metrics, tone (attitude of the speaker), and symbols.
3. What poetic devices does Yeats employ to give special vitality and value to soul, spirit, and intellect? Is there anything ironic about any of these devices?
4. Trace the symbolism of birds and of singing all the way through the poem. To what major themes does this symbolism give expression?

ODE

Intimations of Immortality from Recollections of Early Childhood

William Wordsworth

> *The Child is father to the Man;*
> *And I could wish my days to be*
> *Bound each to each by natural piety.*

I

There was a time when meadow, grove, and stream,
The earth, and every common sight,
To me did seem
Apparelled in celestial light,
The glory and the freshness of a dream. 5
It is not now as it hath been of yore;—
Turn wheresoe'er I may,
By night or day,
The things which I have seen I now can see no more.

II

The Rainbow comes and goes, 10
And lovely is the Rose,

The Moon doth with delight
Look round her when the heavens are bare,
Waters on a starry night
Are beautiful and fair; 15
The sunshine is a glorious birth;
But yet I know, where'er I go,
That there hath past away a glory from the earth.

III

Now, while the birds thus sing a joyous song,
And while the young lambs bound 20
As to the tabor's sound,
To me alone there came a thought of grief:
A timely utterance gave that thought relief,
And I again am strong:
The cataracts blow their trumpets from the steep; 25
No more shall grief of mine the season wrong;
I hear the Echoes through the mountains throng,
The Winds come to me from the fields of sleep,
And all the earth is gay;
Land and sea 30
Give themselves up to jollity,
And with the heart of May
Doth every Beast keep holiday;—
Thou Child of Joy,
Shout round me, let me hear thy shouts, thou happy Shepherd-
boy! 35

IV

Ye blessèd Creatures, I have heard the call
Ye to each other make; I see
The heavens laugh with you in your jubilee;
My heart is at your festival,
My head hath its coronal, 40

The fulness of your bliss, I feel—I feel it all.
Oh evil day! if I were sullen
While Earth herself is adorning,
This sweet May-morning,
And the Children are culling 45
On every side,
In a thousand valleys far and wide,
Fresh flowers; while the sun shines warm,
And the Babe leaps up on his Mother's arm:—
I hear, I hear, with joy I hear! 50
—But there's a Tree, of many, one,
A single Field which I have looked upon,
Both of them speak of something that is gone:
The Pansy at my feet
Doth the same tale repeat: 55
Whither is fled the visionary gleam?
Where is it now, the glory and the dream?

V

Our birth is but a sleep and a forgetting:
The Soul that rises with us, our life's Star,
Hath had elsewhere its setting, 60
And cometh from afar:
Not in entire forgetfulness,
And not in utter nakedness,
But trailing clouds of glory do we come
From God, who is our home: 65
Heaven lies about us in our infancy!
Shades of the prison-house begin to close
Upon the growing Boy,
But he beholds the light, and whence it flows,
He sees it in his joy; 70
The Youth, who daily farther from the east
Must travel, still is Nature's Priest,

And by the vision splendid
Is on his way attended;
At length the Man perceives it die away, 75
And fade into the light of common day.

VI

Earth fills her lap with pleasures of her own;
Yearnings she hath in her own natural kind,
And even with something of a Mother's mind,
And no unworthy aim, 80
The homely Nurse doth all she can
To make her Foster-child, her Inmate Man,
Forget the glories he hath known,
And that imperial palace whence he came.

VII

Behold the Child among his new-born blisses, 85
A six years' Darling of a pigmy size!
See, where 'mid work of his own hand he lies,
Fretted by sallies of his mother's kisses,
With light upon him from his father's eyes!
See, at his feet, some little plan or chart, 90
Some fragment from his dream of human life,
Shaped by himself with newly-learned art;
A wedding or a festival,
A mourning or a funeral;
And this hath now his heart, 95
And unto this he frames his song:
Then will he fit his tongue
To dialogues of business, love, or strife;
But it will not be long
Ere this be thrown aside, 100
And with new joy and pride
The little Actor cons another part;

Filling from time to time his "humorous stage"
With all the Persons, down to palsied Age,
That Life brings with her in her equipage; 105
As if his whole vocation
Were endless imitation.

VIII

Thou, whose exterior semblance doth belie
Thy soul's immensity;
Thou best Philosopher, who yet dost keep 110
Thy heritage, thou Eye among the blind,
That, deaf and silent, read'st the eternal deep,
Haunted for ever by the eternal mind,—
Mighty Prophet! Seer blest!
On whom those truths do rest, 115
Which we are toiling all our lives to find,
In darkness lost, the darkness of the grave;
Thou, over whom thy Immortality
Broods like the Day, a Master o'er a Slave,
A Presence which is not to be put by; 120
Thou little Child, yet glorious in the might
Of heaven-born freedom on thy being's height,
Why with such earnest pains dost thou provoke
The years to bring the inevitable yoke,
Thus blindly with thy blessedness at strife? 125
Full soon thy Soul shall have her earthly freight,
And custom lie upon thee with a weight,
Heavy as frost, and deep almost as life!

IX

Oh joy! that in our embers
Is something that doth live, 130
That nature yet remembers
What was so fugitive!

The thought of our past years in me doth breed
Perpetual benediction: not indeed
For that which is most worthy to be blest; 135
Delight and liberty, the simple creed
Of Childhood, whether busy or at rest,
With new-fledged hope still fluttering in his breast:—
Not for these I raise
The song of thanks and praise; 140
But for those obstinate questionings
Of sense and outward things,
Fallings from us, vanishings;
Blank misgivings of a Creature
Moving about in worlds not realized, 145
High instincts before which our mortal Nature
Did tremble like a guilty Thing surprised:
But for those first affections,
Those shadowy recollections,
Which, be they what they may, 150
Are yet the fountain light of all our day,
Are yet a master light of all our seeing;
Uphold us, cherish, and have power to make
Our noisy years seem moments in the being
Of the eternal Silence: truths that wake, 155
To perish never;
Which neither listlessness, nor mad endeavor,
Nor Man nor Boy,
Nor all that is at enmity with joy,
Can utterly abolish or destroy! 160
Hence in a season of calm weather
Though inland far we be,
Our Souls have sight of that immortal sea
Which brought us hither,
Can in a moment travel thither, 165
And see the Children sport upon the shore,
And hear the mighty waters rolling evermore.

X

Then sing, ye Birds, sing, sing a joyous song!
        And let the young Lambs bound
        As to the tabor's sound! 170
We in thought will join your throng,
        Ye that pipe and ye that play,
        Ye that through your hearts to-day
        Feel the gladness of the May!
What though the radiance which was once so bright 175
Be now for ever taken from my sight,
    Though nothing can bring back the hour
Of splendor in the grass, of glory in the flower;
        We will grieve not, rather find
        Strength in what remains behind; 180
        In the primal sympathy
        Which having been must ever be;
        In the soothing thoughts that spring
        Out of human suffering;
        In the faith that looks through death, 185
In years that bring the philosophic mind.

XI

And O, ye Fountains, Meadows, Hills, and Groves,
Forebode not any severing of our loves!
Yet in my heart of hearts I feel your might;
I only have relinquished one delight 190
To live beneath your more habitual sway.
I love the Brooks which down their channels fret,
Even more than when I tripped lightly as they;
The innocent brightness of a new-born Day
        Is lovely yet; 195
The Clouds that gather round the setting sun
Do take a sober colouring from an eye

That hath kept watch o'er man's mortality.
Another race hath been, and other palms are won.
Thanks to the human heart by which we live, 200
Thanks to its tenderness, its joys, and fears,
To me the meanest flower that blows can give
Thoughts that do often lie too deep for tears.

This poem is called an ode because it expresses in a lofty style and with considerable formality ideas that the poet considers worthy of such expression. Technically, it is an irregular rather than a formal ode, because it is written, not in a strict and recurrent stanzaic form and rhyme scheme, but in a form that permits unsystematic variations in line length and the placement of rhymes from stanza to stanza.

The chief problems here are the content of the poem and the adjustment of the form to the substance. You should consider the prose content of the poem first, although it cannot be isolated from your study of the structure of the poem, since the structure will throw light on the content. This poem is fundamentally expository in structure, but it differs from most expositions in prose in the extent to which the basic ideas are repeated. Perhaps the best analogy for the structure of this poem is that of a musical composition, in which themes are stated and then developed through a series of variations. Thus, the poem will be seen to fall into three fairly distinct sections or "movements," each of which develops a single theme.

1. The first section or "movement" of the poem includes Parts I to IV. State briefly the themes of this section of the poem. These themes receive an increasingly elaborate development. Show how the themes stated in Part I of the poem reappear in Parts III and IV.
2. The second movement of the poem includes Parts V to VIII. State briefly the themes of this "movement." Again these themes receive increasingly elaborate development. Show how Parts VII and VIII repeat with variations ideas that appear for the first time in Part V. Since it is this movement of the poem to which the subtitle "Intimations of Immortality in Early Childhood" is most relevant, it is necessary to define as clearly as possible the meaning Wordsworth attaches to the word "immortality," because his meaning differs fundamentally from the common definition of the term.

3. The third, and final, movement of the poem consists of Parts IX to XI. In this section—perhaps because the earlier sections have initiated us into most of the fundamental ideas in the poem—the themes are stated most fully in Part IX and then, with an effect of *diminuendo,* with less elaboration in Parts X and XI. State briefly the themes of this section. Note particularly the important connectives: "Not," "But," "But," in Part IX. Show how the last lines of Part XI repeat a motif that has been developed fully in the second movement of the poem. Of what value is this repetition?
4. Make an analysis of the meter and the rhyme scheme of Parts I, V, and IX. What elements make for a regularity of effect? What elements make for irregularity? Is the balance between these effects satisfactory? Why or why not? By what technical means does Wordsworth attempt to minimize the shock of shifting from groups of short lines to groups of longer lines? Is the attempt successful? Why or why not?
5. Coleridge criticized the poem on the ground that he had never encountered such an anomaly as the child-philosopher characterized in Part VIII. In another connection, while defining the nature of a poem, he suggested, in one of his most pregnant critical phrases, that a poem demands "a willing suspension of disbelief." Does his criticism of the concept of the child-philosopher accord or fail to accord with this critical doctrine? Why?
6. Read Jacques' speech on the "seven ages of man" in Shakespeare's *As You Like It,* Act II, Scene 7, lines 139–166. By what stylistic means does Wordsworth achieve a tone that is generally distinct from that with which Shakespeare invested his treatment of the common theme?

SONG IN AND OUT OF A COUNTRY CHURCHYARD

Robert Tucker

The black cat licked her whiskers and she sang:
I make my world, the dainty mouse made his,
The grey bitch, that great critic with her fang,
Makes hers, makes hers, and God makes all of this,
Creating in his own mysterious way. 5
I can tell the grey bitch from the mouse;
Both, from my Persian cousin; and I say
The sense of making order is here to stay.

And when that day, that day for which the grouse
Prepares, toward which I lope, that day arrives, 10

It seems to me that having had nine lives
As me, I'll really be as much myself
As I shall ever be; and God, Himself.

1. When does a cat lick its whiskers?
2. Why the distinction in tense between make and made in line 2?
3. Where is the cat?
4. Recall some of the themes and subject matter of Gray's "Elegy" to which the title of this poem obviously alludes.
5. Point out the significance of the differences between the title of this poem and that of Gray's poem.
6. What is the cat's special concern with the bitch's fang and why does he call her a "great critic"?
7. State in your own words the ideas the cat states in lines 2–8.
8. What is "that day" (line 9)?
9. The cat, with his nine lives, has nine times the opportunity to be himself, that the other animals have. How might the grey bitch's reflections differ from the cat's? Do you think that the mouse might philosophize about this matter in the same manner and to the same conclusions as the cat?
10. What does God do to be Himself?
11. What implication does the addition of the phrase "and God, Himself" (line 13) have in regard to the cat's sense of his own importance?
12. How are the ideas which the cat expresses qualified by the dramatic situation?
13. Discuss the total effect of the poem.

NOT MARBLE, NOR THE GILDED MONUMENTS

(Sonnet 55)

William Shakespeare

Not marble, nor the gilded monuments
Of princes, shall outlive this powerful rime;
But you shall shine more bright in these contents
Than unswept stone besmeared with sluttish time.
When wasteful war shall statues overturn, 5
And broils root out the work of masonry,
Nor Mars his sword nor war's quick fire shall burn
The living record of your memory.
'Gainst death and all-oblivious enmity
Shall you pace forth; your praise shall still find room 10

Even in the eyes of all posterity
That wear this world out to the ending doom.
  So, till the judgment that yourself arise,
  You live in this, and dwell in lovers' eyes.

1. Make a brief summary of the contents of this poem and of Landor's "Past Ruin'd Ilion" (p. 14). What do the contents of these poems have in common? To what extent are the ideas developed in similar ways? Which of the poems presents more convincing evidence in support of its themes? Why?
2. Make an analysis of the imagery of these two poems. In which is the imagery sharper and more definite? In which are there more unpleasant images? Does the poem that contains the more unpleasant images gain or lose by their inclusion? Why? Is the contrast built up in Shakespeare's sonnet a logical one? Why or why not? What element of contrast appears in Landor's poem?
3. Contrast the tone of these poems. If you consider one of these poems as better than the other, give specific reasons for your judgment. Do not be misled by the fact that one of the authors is Shakespeare.

MUSEUM PIECE

Richard Wilbur

The good grey guardians of art
Patrol the halls on spongy shoes,
Impartially protective, though
Perhaps suspicious of Toulouse.

Here dozes one against the wall, 5
Disposed upon a funeral chair.
A Degas dancer pirouettes
Upon the parting of his hair.

See how she spins! The grace is there,
But strain as well is plain to see. 10
Degas loved the two together:
Beauty joined to energy.

Edgar Degas purchased once
A fine El Greco, which he kept

Against the wall beside his bed 15
To hang his pants on while he slept.

Line 4. Toulouse: Toulouse-Lautrec

1. Compare the meter of this poem with that used by Eliot in "Sweeney Among the Nightingales" (p. 132). Is the meter equally effective in both poems? Why or why not?
2. How do the following details relate to over-all themes of Wilbur's poem: "spongy shoes," "impartially protective," "disposed," "a funeral chair," "beside his bed," "to hang his pants on"?
3. Is Wilbur serious about ideas in this poem? Compare Wilbur's attitude toward ideas here with Arnold's in "Dover Beach" (p. 244).

DEJECTION: AN ODE

Written 4 April, 1802

Samuel Taylor Coleridge

Late, late yestreen I saw the new Moon,
With the old Moon in her arms;
And I fear, I fear, my Master dear!
We shall have a deadly storm.
—Ballad of Sir Patrick Spence

I

Well, if the Bard was weather-wise, who made
The grand old ballad of Sir Patrick Spence,
This night, so tranquil now, will not go hence
Unroused by winds, that ply a busier trade
Than those which mould yon cloud in lazy flakes, 5
Or the dull sobbing draft, that moans and rakes
Upon the strings of this Aeolian lute,
Which better far were mute.
For lo! the New-moon winter-bright!
And overspread with phantom light, 10
(With swimming phantom light o'erspread
But rimmed and circled by a silver thread)
I see the old Moon in her lap, foretelling

The coming-on of rain and squally blast.
And oh! that even now the gust were swelling, 15
And the slant night-shower driving loud and fast!
Those sounds which oft have raised me, whilst they awed,
And sent my soul abroad,
Might now perhaps their wonted impulse give,
Might startle this dull pain, and make it move and live! 20

II

A grief without a pang, void, dark, and drear,
A stifled, drowsy, unimpassioned grief,
Which finds no natural outlet, no relief,
In word, or sigh, or tear—
O Lady! in this wan and heartless mood, 25
To other thoughts by yonder throstle wooed,
All this long eve, so balmy and serene,
Have I been gazing on the western sky,
And its peculiar tint of yellow green:
And still I gaze—and with how blank an eye! 30
And those thin clouds above, in flakes and bars,
That give away their motion to the stars;
Those stars, that glide behind them or between,
Now sparkling, now bedimmed, but always seen:
Yon crescent Moon, as fixed as if it grew 35
In its own cloudless, starless lake of blue;
I see them all so excellently fair,
I see, not feel, how beautiful they are!

III

My genial spirits fail;
And what can these avail 40
To lift the smothering weight from off my breast?
It were a vain endeavour,
Though I should gaze for ever

On that green light that lingers in the west:
I may not hope from outward forms to win 45
The passion and the life, whose fountains are within.

IV

O Lady! we receive but what we give,
And in our life alone does Nature live:
Ours is her wedding garment, ours her shroud!
And would we aught behold, of higher worth, 50
Than that inanimate cold world allowed
To the poor loveless ever-anxious crowd,
Ah! from the soul itself must issue forth
A light, a glory, a fair luminous cloud
Enveloping the Earth— 55
And from the soul itself must there be sent
A sweet and potent voice, of its own birth,
Of all sweet sounds the life and element!

V

O pure of heart! thou need'st not ask of me
What this strong music in the soul may be! 60
What, and wherein it doth exist,
This light, this glory, this fair luminous mist,
This beautiful and beauty-making power.
Joy, virtuous Lady! Joy that ne'er was given,
Save to the pure, and in their purest hour, 65
Life, and Life's effluence, cloud at once and shower,
Joy, Lady! is the spirit and the power,
Which wedding Nature to us gives in dower
A new Earth and new Heaven,
Undreamt of by the sensual and the proud— 70
Joy is the sweet voice, Joy the luminous cloud—
We in ourselves rejoice!
And thence flows all that charms or ear or sight,

All melodies the echoes of that voice,
All colours a suffusion from that light. 75

VI

There was a time when, though my path was rough,
This joy within me dallied with distress,
And all misfortunes were but as the stuff
Whence Fancy made me dreams of happiness:
For hope grew round me, like the twining vine, 80
And fruits, and foliage, not my own, seemed mine.
But now afflictions bow me down to earth:
Nor care I that they rob me of my mirth;
But oh! each visitation
Suspends what nature gave me at my birth, 85
My shaping spirit of Imagination.
For not to think of what I needs must feel,
But to be still and patient, all I can;
And haply by abstruse research to steal
From my own nature all the natural man— 90
This was my sole resource, my only plan:
Till that which suits a part infects the whole,
And now is almost grown the habit of my soul.

VII

Hence, viper thoughts, that coil around my mind,
Reality's dark dream! 95
I turn from you, and listen to the wind,
Which long has raved unnoticed. What a scream
Of agony by torture lengthened out
That lute sent forth! Thou Wind, that rav'st without,
Bare crag, or mountain-tairn, or blasted tree, 100
Or pine-grove whither woodman never clomb,
Or lonely house, long held the witches' home,
Methinks were fitter instruments for thee,

Mad Lutanist! who in this month of showers,
Of dark-brown gardens, and of peeping flowers, 105
Mak'st Devils' yule, with worse than wintry song,
The blossoms, buds, and timorous leaves among.
  Thou Actor, perfect in all tragic sounds!
Thou mighty Poet, e'en to frenzy bold!
    What tell'st thou now about? 110
    'Tis of the rushing of an host in rout,
  With groans of trampled men, with smarting wounds—
At once they groan with pain, and shudder with the cold!
But hush! there is a pause of deepest silence!
  And all that noise, as of a rushing crowd, 115
With groans, and tremulous shudderings—all is over—
  It tells another tale, with sounds less deep and loud!
    A tale of less affright,
    And tempered with delight,
As Otway's self had framed the tender lay,— 120
    'Tis of a little child
    Upon a lonesome wild,
Not far from home, but she hath lost her way:
And now moans low in bitter grief and fear,
And now screams loud, and hopes to make her mother hear. 125

VIII

'Tis midnight, but small thoughts have I of sleep:
Full seldom may my friend such vigils keep!
Visit her, gentle Sleep! with wings of healing,
  And may this storm be but a mountain-birth,
May all the stars hang bright above her dwelling, 130
  Silent as though they watched the sleeping Earth!
    With light heart may she rise,
    Gay fancy, cheerful eyes,
  Joy lift her spirit, joy attune her voice;
To her may all things live, from pole to pole, 135

Their life the eddying of her living soul!
O simple spirit, guided from above,
Dear Lady! friend devoutest of my choice,
Thus mayest thou ever, evermore rejoice.

1. There are reasons for believing that Coleridge saw the manuscript of at least a part of Wordsworth's ode at some stage during the long process of its composition. What elements of poetic form and what phrases in Coleridge's poem tend to substantiate such a connection?
2. The similarity between the two odes is, however, more than the superficial one of form and phrasing. There are also resemblances in subject matter and structure, and, as in the case of Wordsworth's ode, a study of the structure is the surest means of discovering what the poem says. Into what groups do the stanzas in this poem fall? What are the themes of the first group? Of the second group? Of the third? What is the logical relationship between the themes of the first group of stanzas and the second? What devices of coherence connect the first and the second stanzas? How does stanza I prepare the reader for stanza VII? Are stanzas IV, V, and VIII integral parts of the poem? Why or why not?
3. The most important ideas in the poem occur in the second group of stanzas. State these ideas as clearly as possible, paying especial attention to the meaning of the following phrases: "beauty-making power," "my shaping spirit of imagination," "abstruse research," "till that which suits a part infects the whole." Read a brief account of the career of Coleridge up to the time of composition of this poem (1802). What light does his career throw on the meaning of this stanza?
4. Does the third section of the poem furnish a solution to the problem that the poet is facing? Why or why not? Is this conclusion a more or less successful one than Wordsworth's? Why? Read a brief account of the career of Coleridge after 1802. Was he more or less successful in solving his problem in life than he was in this poem? Why?
5. Look up the meaning of Aeolian harp. This instrument is frequently referred to by Coleridge and other romantic poets. What was the source of its attraction to them?
6. Read a brief account of the life and career of Thomas Otway. Is the reference to Otway (line 120) appropriate or inappropriate? Why?
7. Make an analysis of the imagery of stanza VII, and discuss its contribution to the effect of this stanza.

POETRY

Marianne Moore

I, too, dislike it: there are things that are important beyond all
this fiddle.
Reading it, however, with a perfect contempt for it, one
discovers in
it after all, a place for the genuine.
Hands that can grasp, eyes
that can dilate, hair that can rise 5
if it must, these things are important not because a

high-sounding interpretation can be put upon them but because
they are
useful. When they become so derivative as to become unintelligible,
the same thing may be said for all of us, that we
do not admire what 10
we cannot understand: the bat
holding on upside down or in quest of something to

eat, elephants pushing, a wild horse taking a roll, a tireless
wolf under
a tree, the immovable critic twitching his skin like a horse
that feels a flea, the base-
ball fan, the statistician— 15
nor is it valid
to discriminate against 'business documents and
school-books'; all these phenomena are important. One must
make a distinction
however: when dragged into prominence by half poets, the
result is not poetry,
nor till the poets among us can be 20
'literalists of
the imagination'—above
insolence and triviality and can present

for inspection, imaginary gardens with real toads in them, shall
we have
it. In the meantime, if you demand on the one hand, 25
the raw material of poetry in
all its rawness and
that which is on the other hand
genuine, then you are interested in poetry.

Marianne Moore, like Sidney and Shelley before her, has written a defense of poetry; like them, she is concerned with defining poetry and with meeting some of the common objections to it. To a certain extent, therefore, the poem is exposition; to a certain extent, it is that portion of an argument that is called the rebuttal.

1. Since Miss Moore is concerned with persuading her readers of the soundness of her views on poetry, the devices by which she attempts to placate the reader and to ingratiate herself with him are especially worth noting. In this connection, what is the value of the first clause in the first sentence? What other concessions does the poet make in the remainder of the poem? Do these concessions seriously qualify the poet's sense of the importance of poetry? Why or why not? What effect on the reader is the final sentence intended to have?
2. What portions of the poem are devoted to defining poetry? Is Miss Moore well advised to alternate between definition and rebuttal? Why or why not? What does the poet mean by "literalists of the imagination"? What does she mean by "imaginary gardens with real toads in them"?
3. Contrast the over-all tone of this poem with that of Shapiro's "Poet" (p. 289). Which poet takes the more hopeful view of the fate of poetry? Does Miss Moore give any reasons for regarding poetry as useful or important?

YEAR'S-END

Richard Wilbur

Now winter downs the dying of the year,
And night is all a settlement of snow;
From the soft street the rooms of houses show

A gathered light, a shapen atmosphere,
Like frozen-over lakes whose ice is thin 5
And still allows some stirring down within.

I've known the wind by water banks to shake
The late leaves down, which frozen where they fell
And held in ice as dancers in a spell
Fluttered all winter long into a lake; 10
Graved on the dark in gestures of descent,
They seemed their own most perfect monument.

There was perfection in the death of ferns
Which laid their fragile cheeks against the stone
A million years. Great mammoths overthrown 15
Composedly have made their long sojourns,
Like palaces of patience, in the grey
And changeless lands of ice. And at Pompeii

The little dog lay curled and did not rise
But slept the deeper as the ashes rose 20
And found the people incomplete, and froze
The random hands, the loose unready eyes
Of men expecting yet another sun
To do the shapely thing they had not done.

These sudden ends of time must give us pause. 25
We fray into the future, rarely wrought
Save in the tapestries of afterthought.
More time, more time. Barrages of applause
Come muffled from a buried radio.
The New-year bells are wrangling with the snow. 30

1. Scan the second stanza and label the meter. What examples of functional variation do you find? How would you describe the function in each case?
2. "Downs" (line 1) and "settlement" (line 2) are denotatively ambiguous; they are a kind of pun. What other puns are there in the poem? Do they seem functional and justified? Why or why not?
3. Discuss the diction of the poem. Is it heavily dependent on imagery?

Are there many abstract words? How are abstract and concrete words related?

4. What are the most notable features of sound-pattern in the poem?
5. Would the following statement of the poem's major themes be complete or incomplete? Why? "Consciousness differentiates man from plants and among animals. Man is capable of being apprehensive about time and aware both of his achievement and of the incompleteness of his achievement."

POET

Karl Shapiro

Il arrive que l'esprit demande la poesie

Left leg flung out, head cocked to the right,
Tweed coat or army uniform, with book,
Beautiful eyes, who is this walking down?
Who, glancing at the pane of glass looks sharp
And thinks it is not he—as when a poet 5
Comes swiftly on some half-forgotten poem
And loosely holds the page, steady of mind,
Thinking it is not his?

And when will *you* exist?—Oh, it is I,
Incredibly skinny, stooped, and neat as pie, 10
Ignorant as dirt, erotic as an ape,
Dreamy as puberty—with dirty hair!
Into the room like kangaroo he bounds,
Ears flopping like the most expensive hound's;
His chin received all questions as he bows 15
Mouthing a green bon-bon.

Has no more memory than rubber. Stands
Waist-deep in heavy mud of thought and broods
At his own wetness. When he would get out,
To his surprise he lifts in air a phrase 20
As whole and clean and silvery as a fish,
Which jumps and dangles on his damned hooked grin,

But like a name-card on a man's lapel
Calls him a conscious fool.

And childlike he remembers all his life 25
And cannily constructs it, fact by fact,
As boys paste postage stamps in careful books,
Denoting pence and legends and profiles,
Nothing more valuable.—And like a thief,
His eyes glassed over and concealed with guilt, 30
Fondles his secrets like a case of tools,
And waits in empty doors.

By men despised for knowing what he is,
And by himself. But he exists for women.
As dolls to girls, as perfect wives to men, 35
So he to women. And to himself a thing,
All ages, epicene, without a trade.
To girls and wives always alive and fated;
To men and scholars always dead like Greek
And always mistranslated. 40

Towards exile and towards shame he lures himself,
Tongue winding on his arm, and thinks like Eve
By biting apple will become most wise.
Sentio ergo sum: he feels his way
And words themselves stand up for him like Braille 45
And punch and perforate his parchment ear.
All language falls like Chinese on his soul,
Image of song unsounded.

This is the coward's coward that in his dreams
Sees shapes of pain grow tall. Awake at night 50
He peers at sounds and stumbles at a breeze.
And none holds life less dear. For as a youth
Who by some accident observes his love
Naked and in some natural ugly act,
He turns with loathing and with flaming hands, 55
Seared and betrayed by sight.

He is the business man, on beauty trades,
Dealer in arts and thoughts who, like the Jew,
Shall rise from slums and hated dialects
A tower of bitterness. Shall be always strange, 60
Hunted and then sought after. Shall be sat
Like an ambassador from another race
At tables rich with music. He shall eat flowers,
Chew honey and spit out gall. They shall all smile
And love and pity him. 65

His death shall be by drowning. In that hour
When the last bubble of pure heaven's air
Hovers within his throat, safe on his bed,
A small eternal figurehead in terror,
He shall cry out and clutch his days of straw 70
Before the blackest wave. Lastly, his tomb
Shall list and founder in the troughs of grass.
And none shall speak his name.

In this poem as in the last three, a poet gives us his conception of the nature of poetry and its relationship to life. These are fundamental questions in aesthetics, and what any poet thinks of them is likely to condition and qualify the nature of his poetic products.

1. The title of the poem is equivocal since it may refer to a particular poet or the genus poet. It is an appropriately equivocal title since a portion of the poem seems to be portrait of a particular poet, and the remainder of the poem seems to treat his nature and fate as though they were the nature and fate of all poets. What portion of the poem sketches in the poet's portrait? What are the most individualizing details? What is the over-all tone of the portrait? What is the relationship between this tone and the poet's purpose?
2. On what topics does the poet express himself in the remainder of the poem? Is this series of topics coherently arranged? Why or why not?
3. Does Shapiro make an effective transition between the more specific and the more general portions of the poem? Why or why not?
4. Discuss the freshness and propriety of the similes and their contribution to the total effect of the poem.

5. Discuss the metaphors "tongue winding on his arm" and "by drowning." Analyze fully the metaphors of the last stanza.
6. Compare the attitude Shakespeare takes toward the fate of poetry with that Shapiro takes. Which attitude seems to you to be the more defensible? Why?
7. Do you consider this poem to be rich or poor in analytical value? Give the reasons for your judgment.

IN MY CRAFT OR SULLEN ART

Dylan Thomas

In my craft or sullen art
Exercised in the still night
When only the moon rages
And the lovers lie abed
With all their griefs in their arms, 5
I labour by singing light
Not for ambition or bread
Or the strut and trade of charms
On the ivory stages
But for the common wages 10
Of their most secret heart.

Not for the proud man apart
From the raging moon I write
On these spindrift pages
Nor for the towering dead 15
With their nightingales and psalms
But for the lovers, their arms
Round the griefs of the ages,
Who pay no praise or wages
Nor heed my craft or art. 20

1. Compare and contrast the rhyme scheme of lines 1–11 with that of lines 12–20. Are the intricacy and difficulty of the rhyme scheme justified or merely ingenious? Does the recurrence of rhyme sounds and words lead to unnatural distortion of word order?
2. Scan the poem. In what ways does the meter Thomas has chosen

assist in the expression of his themes? Comment on the treatment of end-stops.

3. List the metaphors and symbols in the poem. Which of these do you find most problematical? Why?
4. What is the significance of "or" in the first line?
5. How would you state the meanings of "sullen" in line 1?

PETER QUINCE AT THE CLAVIER

Wallace Stevens

I

Just as my fingers on these keys
Make music, so the selfsame sounds
On my spirit make a music, too.

Music is feeling, then, not sound;
And thus it is that what I feel, 5
Here in this room, desiring you,

Thinking of your blue-shadowed silk,
Is music. It is like the strain
Waked in the elders by Susanna.

Of a green evening, clear and warm, 10
She bathed in her still garden, while
The red-eyed elders watching, felt

The basses of their beings throb
In witching chords, and their thin blood
Pulse pizzicati of Hosanna. 15

II

In the green water, clear and warm,
Susanna lay.
She searched
The touch of springs,

And found 20

Concealed imaginings.
She sighed,
For so much melody.

Upon the bank, she stood
In the cool 25
Of spent emotions.
She felt, among the leaves,
The dew
Of old devotions.

She walked upon the grass, 30
Still quavering.
The winds were like her maids,
On timid feet,
Fetching her woven scarves,
Yet wavering. 35

A breath upon her hand
Muted the night.
She turned—
A cymbal crashed,
And roaring horns. 40

III

Soon, with a noise like tambourines,
Came her attendant Byzantines.

They wondered why Susanna cried
Against the elders by her side;

And as they whispered, the refrain 45
Was like a willow swept by rain.

Anon, their lamps' uplifted flame
Revealed Susanna and her shame.

And then, the simpering Byzantines
Fled, with a noise like tambourines. 50

IV

Beauty is momentary in the mind—
The fitful tracing of a portal;
But in the flesh it is immortal.
The body dies; the body's beauty lives.
So evenings die, in their green going, 55
A wave, interminably flowing.
So gardens die, their meek breath scenting
The cowl of winter, done repenting.
So maidens die, to the auroral
Celebration of a maiden's choral. 60
Susanna's music touched the bawdy strings
Of those white elders; but, escaping,
Left only Death's ironic scraping.
Now, in its immortality, it plays
On the clear viol of her memory, 65
And makes a constant sacrament of praise.

1. What is a clavier? What does Stevens gain by the use of this word rather than the word "piano"? Read the scenes in Shakespeare's *A Midsummer Night's Dream* in which the character Peter Quince appears. Why did Stevens give his hero this name? Read in the Biblical Apocrypha the story of Susanna and the Elders. Would "Susanna and the Elders" have been a more suitable title for this poem? Why or why not?
2. What are the main themes of this poem? Do you see any connection between the themes of this poem and those of Landor's "Past Ruin'd Ilion" (p. 14)? Make an analysis of the structure of the poem. What is the type of structure? Discuss the relationship of each section of the poem to its theme.
3. What words in the poem refer to music? What does this emphasis on musical terminology contribute to the poem? Are there any other noteworthy devices of coherence in the poem?
4. Make an analysis of the meter and rhyme scheme to show the nature of the variations from one part to another. Is the shift in meter and rhyme scheme from one part of the poem to another disturbing or pleasurable? Why? If you were to indicate the tempo of each section of the poem by means of a musical term, such as

andante or *allegretto,* what term would you choose for each section?

5. In what sense is beauty immortal in the flesh? In what sense does the body's beauty live? How does this poem illustrate the truth of this idea?
6. Was the introduction of the lady in "blue-shadowed silk" advisable or inadvisable? Why?

PART IV

An Anthology of Poems

BACK AND SIDE GO BARE

Anonymous

Back and side go bare, go bare,
Both foot and hand go cold;
But, belly, God send thee good ale enough,
Whether it be new or old.

I cannot eat but little meat, 5
My stomach is not good;
But sure I think that I can drink
With him that wears a hood.
Though I go bare, take ye no care,
I am nothing a-cold; 10
I stuff my skin so full within
Of jolly good ale and old.

Back and side go bare, go bare,
Both foot and hand go cold;
But, belly, God send thee good ale enough, 15
Whether it be new or old.

I love no roast but a nutbrown toast,
And a crab laid in the fire;
A little bread shall do me stead,
Much bread I not desire. 20
No frost nor snow, no wind, I trow,
Can hurt me if I would,
I am so wrapped, and throughly lapped
Of jolly good ale and old.

Back and side go bare, &c. 25

And Tib my wife, that as her life
  Loveth well good ale to seek,
Full oft drinks she, till ye may see
  The tears run down her cheeks.
Then doth she troll to me the bowl, 30
  Even as a maltworm should,
And saith, Sweetheart, I took my part
  Of this jolly good ale and old.

Back and side go bare, &c.

Now let them drink, till they nod and wink, 35
  Even as good fellows should do;
They shall not miss to have the bliss
  Good ale doth bring men to;
And all poor souls that have scoured bowls
  Or have them lustily trolled, 40
God save the lives of them and their wives,
  Whether they be young or old.

Back and side go bare, &c.

WEEP YOU NO MORE, SAD FOUNTAINS

Anonymous

Weep you no more, sad fountains;
  What need you flow so fast?
Look how the snowy mountains
  Heaven's sun doth gently waste.
  But my sun's heavenly eyes 5
    View not your weeping,
    That now lie sleeping
  Softly, now softly lies
      Sleeping.

Sleep is a reconciling, 10
  A rest that peace begets.

Doth not the sun rise smiling
When fair at even he sets?
Rest you then, rest, sad eyes,
Melt not in weeping 15
While she lies sleeping
Softly, now softly lies
Sleeping.

REQUIESCAT

Matthew Arnold (1822–1888)

Strew on her roses, roses,
And never a spray of yew.
In quiet she reposes:
Ah! would that I did too.

Her mirth the world required: 5
She bathed it in smiles of glee.
But her heart was tired, tired,
And now they let her be.

Her life was turning, turning,
In mazes of heat and sound. 10
But for peace her soul was yearning,
And now peace laps her round.

Her cabin'd, ample Spirit,
It flutter'd and fail'd for breath.
To-night it doth inherit 15
The vasty hall of Death.

THE FOOLISH CAT THAT DIED ON HALLOWE'EN

Leon Barron (1923–)

Under the final straw of this light loss
The summer's bridge has fallen down,

And like this cat that played about our legs
Lies buried in bright leaves.

Soft children who once cradled her 5
And vaguely sang their infant love
Observe the make-shift ritual
Without a word.

One dreams of pumpkins carved and lit
Against the horror of his Hallowe'en; 10
This older boy, my arrow aimed at time,
Is stonily withdrawn.

At ankle height, the brother of this cat
Of fuzzy frailties and sudden strengths
Storms straws at every wind. 15
The breezy cosmos blows him steady good.

Well may they share the mansions of their house,
For they who promise nothing are not bound
By blood to mourn a loss.
But above this natural scene the old leaves twist. 20

BIG BUSINESS

Leon Barron (1923–)

Relinquishing the lion's chair and voice
The Head of a Department Now Absorbed
Remains perplexed.

For time that took him fast
And smiling through the years allowed no choice, 5
Forming within his eager grasp of hands
This living thing.

Now Galatea grown to mortal size
Has smiles no longer for Pygmalion's eyes.

She sees in him a former generation, 10
Needs no pretense to miss his consternation,
And rustles off to meet her latest spark.
Pygmalion gropes in rooms of sudden dark.

So he now frightened hears
A mingling of well-wishing and farewell, 15
And his victorious moment somehow gone.

Congratulating hands thus shake farewell
In greeting fathers of dynastic bliss
Who feel, amazed, death's very quiet kiss.

FROM MILTON

William Blake (1757–1827)

And did those feet in ancient time
Walk upon England's mountains green?
And was the holy Lamb of God
On England's pleasant pastures seen?

And did the Countenance Divine 5
Shine forth upon our clouded hills?
And was Jerusalem builded here
Among these dark Satanic Mills?

Bring me my bow of burning gold!
Bring me my arrows of desire! 10
Bring me my spear! O clouds, unfold!
Bring me my chariot of fire!

I will not cease from mental fight,
Nor shall my sword sleep in my hand,
Till we have built Jerusalem 15
In England's green and pleasant land.

NEVER SEEK TO TELL THY LOVE

William Blake (1757–1827)

Never seek to tell thy love,
Love that never told can be;
For the gentle wind does move
Silently, invisibly.

I told my love, I told my love, 5
I told her all my heart;
Trembling, cold, in ghastly fears,
Ah! she doth depart.

Soon as she was gone from me,
A traveller came by, 10
Silently, invisibly:
He took her with a sigh.

LONDON

William Blake (1757–1827)

I wander thro' each charter'd street,
Near where the charter'd Thames does flow,
And mark in every face I meet
Marks of weakness, marks of woe.

In every cry of every Man, 5
In every Infant's cry of fear,
In every voice, in every ban,
The mind-forg'd manacles I hear.

How the chimney-sweeper's cry
Every black'ning church appals; 10
And the hapless soldier's sigh
Runs in blood down palace walls.

But most thro' midnight streets I hear
How the youthful harlot's curse
Blasts the new-born infant's tear, 15
And blights with plagues the marriage hearse.

A POISON TREE

William Blake (1757–1827)

I was angry with my friend:
I told my wrath, my wrath did end.
I was angry with my foe:
I told it not, my wrath did grow.

And I water'd it in fears, 5
Night and morning with my tears;
And I sunnèd it with smiles,
And with soft deceitful wiles.

And it grew both day and night,
Till it bore an apple bright; 10
And my foe beheld it shine,
And he knew that it was mine,

And into my garden stole
When the night had veil'd the pole:
In the morning glad I see 15
My foe outstretch'd beneath the tree.

THE SICK ROSE

William Blake (1757–1827)

O Rose, thou art sick!
The invisible worm,
That flies in the night,
In the howling storm,

Has found out thy bed 5
Of crimson joy;
And his dark secret love
Does thy life destroy.

SONG

William Blake (1757–1827)

My silks and fine array,
My smiles and languish'd air,
By love are driv'n away;
And mournful lean Despair
Brings me yew to deck my grave; 5
Such end true lovers have.

His face is fair as heav'n
When springing buds unfold;
O why to him was't giv'n
Whose heart is wintry cold? 10
His breast is love's all-worshipp'd tomb,
Where all love's pilgrims come.

Bring me an axe and spade,
Bring me a winding-sheet;
When I my grave have made 15
Let winds and tempests beat:
Then down I'll lie as cold as clay.
True love doth pass away!

SONG

William Blake (1757–1827)

How sweet I roam'd from field to field
And tasted all the summer's pride,
Till I the Prince of Love beheld
Who in the sunny beams did glide!

He show'd me lilies for my hair, 5
And blushing roses for my brow;
He led me through his gardens fair
Where all his golden pleasures grow.

With sweet May dews my wings were wet,
And Phoebus fir'd my vocal rage; 10
He caught me in his silken net,
And shut me in his golden cage.

He loves to sit and hear me sing,
Then, laughing, sports and plays with me;
Then stretches out my golden wing, 15
And mocks my loss of liberty.

HERON

Philip Booth (1925–)

In the copper marsh
I saw a stilted heron
wade the tidal wash

and I, who caught no fish,
thought the grass barren 5
and that jade inlet harsh

until the quick-billed splash
of the long-necked heron
fulfilled my hunter's wish.

Then in the rising rush 10
of those great wings, far on
I saw the herring flash

and drop. And the dash
of lesser wings in the barren
marsh flew through my flesh. 15

THE OWL

Philip Booth (1925–)

I thought he'd gone, that owl,
to wherever owls winter at.
But no, he's out there still,
hooing the cold, awake
to what small things an owl 5
can hear under those big fake
horns. My eyes blink shut,
but his are full of the dark,
and see. I saw him once,
at noon, when they wouldn't work, 10
and he sat sleeping, up
in a deadwood oak, looking more
like a displaced giant moth
than a bird of prey. Except
for his triple talons, which tore 15
at the branch, or at dreams, while he slept,
he sat unruffled, and aloof.
I tried to stone him off,
but I missed; his dreams were remote,
and swaying, he never woke. 20
Or say he waited me out.
That was ten days ago,
and I'm still unsure of us both.
By our different lights, we're blind
two ways to our different stake 25
in these woods. I hear him hoo,
again, and think of the beak
those dove sounds issue from.
I'm frozen, too. I'd sleep
if I could, while he hunts, 30

but I've got a mind to outlast him.
And this time, but not to cast
stones, I stretch and walk out,
to find what he's hunting for.
Not that I think this first snow 35
will be full of tracks to identify;
that owl, from whatever tree
he looks down, has only an eye
for what's warm, and shivering
still, with a need to run free. 40
Awake where my eyes adjust
to the dark, I stand frozen now,
and I begin to see.

ON THE COUNTESS DOWAGER OF PEMBROKE

William Browne (1591–1643)

Underneath this sable hearse
Lies the subject of all verse:
Sidney's sister, Pembroke's mother.
Death, ere thou hast slain another
Fair and learn'd and good as she, 5
Time shall throw a dart at thee.

Marble piles let no man raise
To her name, for after-days
Some kind woman, born as she,
Reading this, like Niobe 10
Shall turn marble, and become
Both her mourner and her tomb.

"CHILDE ROLAND TO THE DARK TOWER CAME"

(See Edgar's song in "Lear")

Robert Browning (1812–1889)

I

My first thought was, he lied in every word,
  That hoary cripple, with malicious eye
  Askance to watch the working of his lie
On mine, and mouth scarce able to afford
Suppression of the glee, that pursed and scored 5
  Its edge, at one more victim gained thereby.

II

What else should he be set for, with his staff?
  What, save to waylay with his lies, ensnare
  All travellers who might find him posted there,
And ask the road? I guessed what skull-like laugh 10
Would break, what crutch 'gin write my epitaph
  For pastime in the dusty thoroughfare,

III

If at his counsel I should turn aside
  Into that ominous tract which, all agree,
  Hides the Dark Tower. Yet acquiescingly 15
I did turn as he pointed: neither pride
Nor hope rekindling at the end descried,
  So much as gladness that some end might be.

IV

For, what with my whole world-wide wandering,
  What with my search drawn out thro' years, my hope 20
  Dwindled into a ghost not fit to cope

With that obstreperous joy success would bring,
I hardly tried now to rebuke the spring
  My heart made, finding failure in its scope.

V

As when a sick man very near to death 25
  Seems dead indeed, and feels begin and end
  The tears and takes the farewell of each friend,
And hears one bid the other go, draw breath
Freelier outside, ("since all is o'er," he saith,
  "And the blow fallen no grieving can amend;") 30

VI

While some discuss if near the other graves
  Be room enough for this, and when a day
  Suits best for carrying the corpse away,
With care about the banners, scarves and staves:
And still the man hears all, and only craves 35
  He may not shame such tender love and stay.

VII

Thus, I had so long suffered in this quest,
  Heard failure prophesied so oft, been writ
  So many times among "The Band"—to wit,
The knights who to the Dark Tower's search addressed 40
Their steps—that just to fail as they, seemed best,
  And all the doubt was now—should I be fit?

VIII

So, quiet as despair, I turned from him,
  That hateful cripple, out of his highway
  Into the path he pointed. All the day 45
Had been a dreary one at best, and dim

Was settling to its close, yet shot one grim
  Red leer to see the plain catch its estray.

IX

For mark! no sooner was I fairly found
  Pledged to the plain, after a pace or two, 50
  Than, pausing to throw backward a last view
O'er the safe road, 'twas gone; grey plain all round:
Nothing but plain to the horizon's bound.
  I might go on; nought else remained to do.

X

So, on I went. I think I never saw 55
  Such starved ignoble nature; nothing throve:
  For flowers—as well expect a cedar grove!
But cockle, spurge, according to their law
Might propagate their kind, with none to awe,
  You'd think; a burr had been a treasure-trove. 60

XI

No! penury, inertness and grimace,
  In some strange sort, were the land's portion. "See
  Or shut your eyes," said Nature peevishly,
"It nothing skills: I cannot help my case:
'Tis the Last Judgment's fire must cure this place, 65
  Calcine its clods and set my prisoners free."

XII

If there pushed any ragged thistle-stalk
  Above its mates, the head was chopped; the bents
  Were jealous else. What made those holes and rents
In the dock's harsh swarth leaves, bruised as to baulk 70

All hope of greenness? 'tis a brute must walk
Pashing their life out, with a brute's intents.

XIII

As for the grass, it grew as scant as hair
In leprosy; thin dry blades pricked the mud
Which underneath looked kneaded up with blood. 75
One stiff blind horse, his every bone a-stare,
Stood stupefied, however he came there:
Thrust out past service from the devil's stud!

XIV

Alive? he might be dead for aught I know,
With that red gaunt and colloped neck a-strain, 80
And shut eyes underneath the rusty mane;
Seldom went such grotesqueness with such woe;
I never saw a brute I hated so;
He must be wicked to deserve such pain.

XV

I shut my eyes and turned them on my heart. 85
As a man calls for wine before he fights,
I asked one draught of earlier, happier sights,
Ere fitly I could hope to play my part.
Think first, fight afterwards—the soldier's art:
One taste of the old time sets all to rights. 90

XVI

Not it! I fancied Cuthbert's reddening face
Beneath its garniture of curly gold,
Dear fellow, till I almost felt him fold
An arm in mine to fix me to the place,

That way he used. Alas, one night's disgrace! 95
Out went my heart's new fire and left it cold.

XVII

Giles then, the soul of honour—there he stands
Frank as ten years ago when knighted first.
What honest man should dare (he said) he durst.
Good—but the scene shifts—faugh! what hangman hands 100
Pin to his breast a parchment? His own bands
Read it. Poor traitor, spit upon and curst!

XVIII

Better this present than a past like that;
Back therefore to my darkening path again!
No sound, no sight as far as eye could strain. 105
Will the night send a howlet or a bat?
I asked: when something on the dismal flat
Came to arrest my thoughts and change their train.

XIX

A sudden little river crossed my path
As unexpected as a serpent comes. 110
No sluggish tide congenial to the glooms;
This, as it frothed by, might have been a bath
For the fiend's glowing hoof—to see the wrath
Of its black eddy bespate with flakes and spumes.

XX

So petty yet so spiteful! All along, 115
Low scrubby alders kneeled down over it;
Drenched willows flung them headlong in a fit
Of mute despair, a suicidal throng:

The river which had done them all the wrong,
  Whate'er that was, rolled by, deterred no whit. 120

XXI

Which, while I forded,—good saints, how I feared
  To set my foot upon a dead man's cheek,
  Each step, or feel the spear I thrust to seek
For hollows, tangled in his hair or beard!
—It may have been a water-rat I speared, 125
  But, ugh! It sounded like a baby's shriek.

XXII

Glad was I when I reached the other bank.
  Now for a better country. Vain presage!
  Who were the strugglers, what war did they wage,
Whose savage trample thus could pad the dank 130
Soil to a plash? Toads in a poisoned tank,
  Or wild cats in a red-hot iron cage—

XXIII

The fight must so have seemed in that fell cirque.
  What penned them there, with all the plain to choose?
  No foot-print leading to that horrid mews, 135
None out of it. Mad brewage set to work
Their brains, no doubt, like galley-slaves the Turk
  Pits for his pastime, Christians against Jews.

XXIV

And more than that—a furlong on—why, there!
  What bad use was that engine for, that wheel, 140
  Or brake, not wheel—that harrow fit to reel
Men's bodies out like silk? with all the air

Of Tophet's tool, on earth left unaware,
Or brought to sharpen its rusty teeth of steel.

XXV

Then came a bit of stubbed ground, once a wood, 145
Next a marsh, it would seem, and now mere earth
Desperate and done with; (so a fool finds mirth,
Makes a thing and then mars it, till his mood
Changes and off he goes!) within a rood—
Bog, clay and rubble, sand and stark black dearth. 150

XXVI

Now blotches rankling, coloured gay and grim,
Now patches where some leanness of the soil's
Broke into moss or substances like boils;
Then came some palsied oak, a cleft in him
Like a distorted mouth that splits its rim 155
Gaping at death, and dies while it recoils.

XXVII

And just as far as ever from the end!
Nought in the distance but the evening, nought
To point my footstep further! At the thought,
A great black bird, Apollyon's bosom-friend, 160
Sailed past, nor beat his wide wing dragon-penned
That brushed my cap—perchance the guide I sought.

XXVIII

For, looking up, aware I somehow grew,
'Spite of the dusk, the plain had given place
All round to mountains—with such name to grace 165
Mere ugly heights and heaps now stolen in view.

How thus they had surprised me,—solve it, you!
  How to get from them was no clearer case.

XXIX

Yet half I seemed to recognize some trick
  Of mischief happened to me, God knows when— 170
  In a bad dream perhaps. Here ended, then,
Progress this way. When, in the very nick
Of giving up, one time more, came a click
  As when a trap shuts—you're inside the den!

XXX

Burningly it came on me all at once, 175
  This was the place! those two hills on the right,
  Crouched like two bulls locked horn in horn in fight;
While to the left, a tall scalped mountain . . . Dunce,
Dotard, a-dozing at the very nonce,
  After a life spent training for the sight! 180

XXXI

What in the midst lay but the Tower itself?
  The round squat turret, blind as the fool's heart,
  Built of brown stone, without a counterpart
  In the whole world. The tempest's mocking elf
Points to the shipman thus the unseen shelf 185
  He strikes on, only when the timbers start.

XXXII

Not see? because of night perhaps?—why, day
  Came back again for that! before it left,
  The dying sunset kindled through a cleft:
The hills, like giants at a hunting, lay, 190

Chin upon hand, to see the game at bay,—
"Now stab and end the creature—to the heft!"

XXXIII

Not hear? when noise was everywhere! it tolled
Increasing like a bell. Names in my ears
Of all the lost adventurers my peers,— 195
How such a one was strong, and such was bold,
And such was fortunate, yet each of old
Lost, lost! one moment knelled the woe of years.

XXXIV

There they stood, ranged along the hillsides, met
To view the last of me, a living frame 200
For one more picture! in a sheet of flame
I saw them and I knew them all. And yet
Dauntless the slug-horn to my lips I set
And blew. *"Childe Roland to the Dark Tower came."*

TAM O'SHANTER

Robert Burns (1759–1796)

When chapman billies leave the street,
And drouthy neibors neibors meet,
As market days are wearin' late,
And folk begin to tak the gate;
While we sit bousing at the nappy, 5
And gettin' fou and unco happy,
We think na on the lang Scots miles,

Line 1. chapman billies: pedlars
Line 2. drouthy: thirsty
Line 4. gate: road
Line 5. nappy: ale

The mosses, waters, slaps, and stiles,
That lie between us and our hame,
Whare sits our sulky sullen dame, 10
Gathering her brows like gathering storm,
Nursing her wrath to keep it warm.

This truth fand honest Tam o'Shanter,
As he frae Ayr ae night did canter,
(Auld Ayr, wham ne'er a town surpasses 15
For honest men and bonny lasses.)

O Tam! hadst thou but been sae wise
As ta'en thy ain wife Kate's advice!
She tauld thee weel thou wast a skellum,
A blethering, blustering, drunken blellum; 20
That frae November till October,
Ae market day thou wasna sober;
That ilka melder, wi' the miller
Thou sat as lang as thou hadst siller;

That every naig was ca'd a shoe on, 25
The smith and thee gat roaring fou on;
That at the Lord's house, even on Sunday,
Thou drank wi' Kirkton Jean till Monday.
She prophesied that, late or soon,
Thou wouldst be found deep drown'd in Doon! 30
Or catch'd wi' warlocks i' the mirk,
By Alloway's auld haunted kirk.

Ah, gentle dames! it gars me greet
To think how mony counsels sweet,

Line 8. stiles: breaches in hedges or walls
Line 19. skellum: worthless fellow
Line 20. blellum: talker of nonsense, boaster, drunken fool
Line 24. siller: money
Line 25. naig: horse
Line 31. mirk: dark
Line 33. gars me greet: makes me weep

How mony lengthen'd sage advices, 35
The husband frae the wife despises!

But to our tale:—Ae market night,
Tam had got planted unco right
Fast by an ingle, bleezing finely,
Wi' reaming swats that drank divinely; 40
And at his elbow, Souter Johnny,
His ancient, trusty, drouthy crony;
Tam lo'ed him like a vera brither—
They had been fou for weeks thegither!
The night drave on wi' sangs and clatter 45
And aye the ale was growing better:
The landlady and Tam grew gracious,
Wi' favours secret, sweet, and precious;
The Souter tauld his queerest stories,
The landlord's laugh was ready chorus: 50
The storm without might rair and rustle—
Tam didna mind the storm a whistle.

Care, mad to see a man sae happy,
E'en drown'd himsel amang the nappy!
As bees flee hame wi' lades o' treasure. 55
The minutes wing'd their way wi' pleasure:
Kings may be blest, but Tam was glorious,
O'er a' the ills o' life victorious!

But pleasures are like poppies spread,
You seize the flower, its bloom is shed! 60
Or like the snowfall in the river,
A moment white—then melts for ever;
Or like the borealis race,

Line 38. unco: unusually
Line 39. ingle: fire
Line 40. swats: foaming ale
Line 51. rair: roar
Line 55. lades: loads

That flit ere you can point their place;
Or like the rainbow's lovely form, 65
Evanishing amid the storm.
Nae man can tether time or tide;
The hour approaches Tam maun ride;
That hour, o'night's black arch the keystane,
That dreary hour he mounts his beast in; 70
And sic a night he taks the road in
As ne'er poor sinner was abroad in.

The wind blew as 'twad blawn its last;
The rattling showers rose on the blast;
The speedy gleams the darkness swallow'd; 75
Loud, deep, and lang, the thunder bellow'd:
That night, a child might understand
The deil had business on his hand.

Weel mounted on his gray mare, Meg,
A better never lifted leg, 80
Tam skelpit on through dub and mire,
Despising wind, and rain, and fire;
Whiles holding fast his guid blue bonnet,
Whiles crooning o'er some auld Scots sonnet;
Whiles glowering round wi' prudent cares, 85
Lest bogles catch him unawares:
Kirk-Alloway was drawing nigh,
Whare ghaists and houlets nightly cry.

By this time he was 'cross the foord,
Whare in the snaw the chapman smoor'd; 90
And past the birks and meikle stane

Line 71. sic: such
Line 81. skelpit: rode with careless speed
Line 84. crooning: humming
Line 85. glowering: staring
Line 86. bogles: spirits
Line 88. ghaists and houlets: ghosts and owls
Line 90. smoor'd: smothered

Where drunken Charlie brak's neck-bane:
And through the whins, and by the cairn
Whare hunters fand the murder'd bairn;
And near the thorn, aboon the well, 95
Whare Mungo's mither hang'd hersel.
Before him Doon pours a' his floods;
The doubling storm roars through the woods;
The lightnings flash frae pole to pole;
Near and more near the thunders roll; 100
When, glimmering through the groaning trees,
Kirk-Alloway seem'd in a bleeze;
Through ilka bore the beams were glancing,
And loud resounded mirth and dancing.

Inspiring bold John Barleycorn! 105
What dangers thou canst mak us scorn!
Wi' tippenny, we fear nae evil;
Wi' usquebae, we'll face the devil!—
The swats sae ream'd in Tammie's noddle,
Fair play, he cared na deils a boddle. 110
But Maggie stood right sair astonish'd,
Till, by the heel and hand admonish'd,
She ventured forward on the light;
And, wow! Tam saw an unco sight!
Warlocks and witches in a dance; 115
Nae cotillon brent-new frae France,
But hornpipes, jigs, strathspeys, and reels,
Put life and mettle i' their heels:

Line 93. cairn: stone-heap
Line 103. ilka bore: every hole in the wall
Line 107. tippenny: twopenny ale
Line 108. usquebae: whiskey
Line 109. sae ream'd in Tammie's noddle: so wrought in Tammie's head
Line 110. boddle: small coin
Line 116. brent-new: brand-new

At winnock-bunker, i' the east,
There sat auld Nick, in shape o' beast; 120
A towzie tyke, black, grim, and large,
To gie them music was his charge;
He screw'd the pipes, and gart them skirl,
Till roof and rafters a' did dirl.
Coffins stood round, like open presses, 125
That shaw'd the dead in their last dresses;
And by some devilish cantrip slight
Each in its cauld hand held a light,—
By which heroic Tam was able
To note upon the haly table, 130
A murderer's banes in gibbet airns;
Twa span-lang, wee, unchristen'd bairns;
A thief, new-cutted frae a rape,
Wi' his last gasp his gab did gape;
Five tomahawks, wi' bluid red-rusted; 135
Five scimitars, wi' murder crusted;
A garter, which a babe had strangled;
A knife, a father's throat had mangled,
Whom his ain son o' life bereft,
The gray hairs yet stack to the heft: 140
Wi' mair o' horrible and awfu',
Which even to name wad be unlawfu'.

As Tammie glower'd, amazed and curious,
The mirth and fun grew fast and furious:
The piper loud and louder blew, 145

Line 119. winnock-bunker: kind of window seat
Line 121. towzie tyke: rough dog
Line 123. gart them skirl: made them scream
Line 124. dirl: vibrate
Line 127. cantrip slight: magic trick or spell
Line 131. airns: irons
Line 134. gab: mouth
Line 140. heft: handle

The dancers quick and quicker flew;
They reel'd, they set, they cross'd, they cleekit,
Till ilka carlin swat and reekit,
And coost her duddies to the wark,
And linket at it in her sark. 150

Now Tam! O Tam! had thae been queans,
A' plump and strappin' in their teens,
Their sarks, instead o' creeshie flannen,
Been snaw-white seventeen-hunder linen!
Thir breeks o' mine, my only pair, 155
That ance were plush, o' guid blue hair,
I wad hae gien them aff my hurdies,
For ae blink o' the bonny burdies!

But wither'd beldams, auld and droll,
Rigwoodie hags, wad spean a foal, 160
Lowpin' and flingin' on a cummock,
I wonder didna turn thy stomach.

But Tam kenn'd what was what fu'brawlie,
"There was ae winsome wench and walie."
That night enlisted in the core, 165
(Lang after kenn'd on Carrick shore;
For mony a beast to dead she shot,
And perish'd mony a bonny boat,

Line 148. ilka carlin swat and reekit: each old crone smoked with sweat
Line 149. coost her duddies: stript her clothes
Line 150. linket: tripped; sark: shirt or shift
Line 151. queans: young girls
Line 153. creeshie flannen: greasy flannel
Line 155. thir breeks: these breeches
Line 157. hurdies: hams
Line 158. blink: look; burdies: lasses
Line 160. rigwoodie: gallows-worthy; spean: wean
Line 161. lowpin' and flingin' on a cummock: jumping and capering on a staff
Line 163. kenn'd . . . fu'brawlie: knew . . . full well
Line 164. winsome wench and walie: hearty girl and jolly

And shook baith meikle corn and bear,
And kept the country-side in fear.) 170
Her cutty sark, o' Paisley harn,
That, while a lassie, she had worn,
In longitude though sorely scanty,
It was her best, and she was vauntie.

Ah! little kenn'd thy reverend grannie, 175
That sark she coft for her wee Nannie,
Wi' twa pund Scots, ('twas a'her riches,)
Wad ever graced a dance o' witches!

But here my Muse her wing maun cour,
Sic flights are far beyond her power; 180
To sing how Nannie lap and flang,
(A souple jade she was, and strang,)
And how Tam stood, like ane bewitch'd,
And thought his very een enrich'd;
Even Satan glower'd, and fidged fu' fain, 185
And hotch'd and blew wi' might and main:
Till first ae caper, syne anither,
Tam tint his reason a' thegither,
And roars out, "Weel done, Cutty-sark!"
And in an instant a' was dark: 190
And scarcely had he Maggie rallied,
When out the hellish legion sallied.
As bees bizz out wi' angry fyke,
When plundering herds assail their byke,

Line 171. cutty: short
Line 174. vauntie: proud of it
Line 176. coft: bought
Line 179. cour: lower
Line 181. lap and flang: jumped and kicked
Line 182. jade: girl; strang: strong
Line 186. hotch'd: hitched
Line 187. syne: then
Line 188. tint: lost
Line 193. fyke: fuss
Line 194. byke: hive

As open pussie's mortal foes, 195
When, pop! she starts before their nose;
As eager runs the market-crowd,
When "Catch the thief!" resounds aloud;
So Maggie runs, the witches follow,
Wi' mony an eldritch screech and hollow. 200

Ah, Tam! ah, Tam! thou'lt get thy fairin'!
In hell they'll roast thee like a herrin'!
In vain thy Kate awaits thy comin'!
Kate soon will be a woefu' woman!
Now, do thy speedy utmost, Meg, 205
And win the keystane of the brig;
There at them thou thy tail may toss,
A running stream they darena cross;
But ere the keystane she could make,
The fient a tail she had to shake! 210
For Nannie, far before the rest,
Hard upon noble Maggie prest,
And flew at Tam wi' furious ettle;
But little wist she Maggie's mettle—
Ae spring brought off her master hale, 215
But left behind her ain gray tail:
The carlin claught her by the rump,
And left poor Maggie scarce a stump.

Now, wha this tale o' truth shall read,
Ilk man and mother's son, take heed: 220
Whane'er to drink you are inclined,
Or cutty-sarks run in your mind,
Think! ye may buy the joys owre dear—
Remember Tam o'Shanter's mare.

Line 200. eldritch: unearthly
Line 201. fairin': deserts
Line 210. fient: fiend
Line 213. ettle: design
Line 214. wist: knew

THERE IS A GARDEN
Thomas Campion (1567–1620)

There is a garden in her face,
Where roses and white lilies grow;
A heav'nly paradise is that place,
Wherein all pleasant fruits do flow.
There cherries grow which none may buy 5
Till cherry-ripe themselves do cry.

Those cherries fairly do enclose
Of orient pearl a double row,
Which when her lovely laughter shows,
They look like rosebuds filled with snow. 10
Yet them nor peer nor prince can buy,
Till cherry-ripe themselves do cry.

Her eyes like angels watch them still;
Her brows like bended bows do stand,
Threat'ning with piercing frowns to kill 15
All that attempt with eye or hand
Those sacred cherries to come nigh,
Till cherry-ripe themselves do cry.

WHEN THOU MUST HOME
Thomas Campion (1567–1620)

When thou must home to shades of underground,
And there arrived, a new admirèd guest,
The beauteous spirits do engirt thee round,
White Iope, blithe Helen, and the rest,
To hear the stories of thy finished love 5
From that smooth tongue whose music hell can move,

Then wilt thou speak of banqueting delights,
  Of masks and revels which sweet youth did make,
Of tourneys and great challenges of knights,
  And all these triumphs for thy beauty's sake: 10
When thou hast told these honors done to thee,
Then tell, O tell, how thou didst murder me.

O SING UNTO MY ROUNDELAY

Thomas Chatterton (1752–1770)

O sing unto my roundelay,
O drop the briny tear with me;
Dance no more at holyday,
Like a running river be:
    My love is dead, 5
    Gone to his death-bed
All under the willow-tree.

Black his cryne as the winter night,
White his rode as the summer snow,
Red his face as the morning light, 10
Cold he lies in the grave below:
    My love is dead,
    Gone to his death-bed
All under the willow-tree.

Sweet his tongue as the throstle's note, 15
Quick in dance as thought can be,
Deft his tabor, cudgel stout;
O he lies by the willow-tree!
    My love is dead,
    Gone to his death-bed 20
All under the willow-tree.

Hark! the raven flaps his wing
In the brier'd dell below;

Hark! the death-owl loud doth sing
To the nightmares, as they go: 25
    My love is dead,
    Gone to his death-bed
All under the willow-tree.

See! the white moon shines on high;
Whiter is my true-love's shroud: 30
Whiter than the morning sky,
Whiter than the evening cloud:
    My love is dead,
    Gone to his death-bed
All under the willow-tree. 35

Here upon my true-love's grave
Shall the barren flowers be laid;
Not one holy saint to save
All the coldness of a maid:
    My love is dead, 40
    Gone to his death-bed
All under the willow-tree.

With my hands I'll dent the briers
Round his holy corse to gre:
Ouph and fairy, light your fires, 45
Here my body still shall be:
    My love is dead,
    Gone to his death-bed
All under the willow-tree.

Come, with acorn-cup and thorn, 50
Drain my heartès blood away;
Life and all its good I scorn,
Dance by night, or feast by day:
    My love is dead,
    Gone to his death-bed 55
All under the willow-tree.

ANCIENT LIGHTS

Austin Clarke (1896–)

When all of us wore smaller shoes
And knew the next world better than
The knots we broke, I used to hurry
On missions of my own to Capel
Street, Bolton Street and Granby Row 5
To see what man has made. But darkness
Was roomed with fears. Sleep, stripped by woes
I had been taught, beat door, leaped landing,
Lied down the bannisters of naught.

Being sent to penance, come Saturday, 10
I shuffled slower than my sins should.
My fears were candle-spiked at side-shrines,
Rays lengthened them in stained-glass. Confided
To night again, my grief bowed down,
Heard hand on shutter-knob. Did I 15
Take pleasure, when alone—how much—
In a bad thought, immodest look
Or worse, unnecessary touch?

Closeted in the confessional,
I put on flesh, so many years 20
Were added to my own, attempted
In vain to keep Dominican
As much i' the dark as I was, mixing
Whispered replies with his low words;
Then shuddered past the crucifix, 25
The feet so hammered, daubed-on blood-drip,
Black with lip-scrimmage of the damned.

Once as I crept from the church-steps,
Beside myself, the air opened
On purpose. Nature read in a flutter 30

An evening lesson above my head.
Atwirl beyond the leadings, corbels,
A cage-bird came among sparrows
(The moral inescapable)
Plucked, roof-mired, all in mad bits. O 35
The pizzicato of its wires!

Goodness of air can be proverbial:
That day, by the kerb at Rutland Square,
A bronze bird fabled out of trees,
Mailing the spearheads of the railings, 40
Sparrow at nails, I hailed the skies
To save the tiny dropper, found
Appetite gone. A child of clay
Has blustered it away. Pity
Could raise some littleness from dust. 45

What Sunday clothes can change us now
Or humble orders in black and white?
Stinking with centuries the act
Of thought. So think, man, as Augustine
Did, dread the ink-bespattered ex-monk, 50
And keep your name. No, let me abandon
Night's jakes. Self-persecuted of late
Among the hatreds of rent Europe,
Poetry burns at a different stake.

Still, still I remember aweful downpour 55
Cabbing Mountjoy Street, spun loneliness
Veiling almost the Protestant church,
Two backyards from my very home.
I dared to shelter at locked door.
There, walled by heresy, my fears 60
Were solved. I had absolved myself:
Feast-day effulgence, as though I gained
For life a plenary indulgence.

The sun came out, new smoke flew up,
The gutters of the Black Church rang 65
With services. Waste water mocked
The ballcocks: down-pipes sparrowing,
And all around the spires of Dublin
Such swallowing in the air, such cowling
To keep high offices pure: I heard 70
From shore to shore, the iron gratings
Take half our heavens with a roar.

THE SCHOLAR

Austin Clarke (1896–)

Summer delights the scholar
With knowledge and reason.
Who is happy in hedgerow
Or meadow as he is?

Paying no dues to the parish, 5
He argues in logic
And has no care of cattle
But a satchel and stick.

The showery airs grow softer,
He profits from his ploughland 10
For the share of the schoolmen
Is a pen in hand.

When midday hides the reaping,
He sleeps by a river
Or comes to the stone plain 15
Where the saints live.

But in winter by the big fires,
The ignorant hear his fiddle,
And he battles on the chessboard,
As the land lords bid him. 20

AT MELVILLE'S TOMB

Hart Crane (1899–1932)

Often beneath the wave, wide from this ledge
The dice of drowned men's bones he saw bequeath
An embassy. Their numbers as he watched,
Beat on the dusty shore and were obscured.

And wrecks passed without sound of bells, 5
The calyx of death's bounty giving back
A scattered chapter, livid hieroglyph,
The portent wound in corridors of shells.

Then in the circuit calm of one vast coil,
Its lashings charmed and malice reconciled, 10
Frosted eyes there were that lifted altars:
And silent answers crept across the stars.

Compass, quadrant and sextant contrive
No farther tides . . . High in the azure steeps
Monody shall not wake the mariner. 15
This fabulous shadow only the sea keeps.

THE RIVER (*from* THE BRIDGE)

Hart Crane (1899–1932)

. . . and past the din and slogans of the year—

Stick your patent name on a signboard
brother—all over—going west—young man
Tintex—Japalac—Certain-teed Overalls ads
and lands sakes! under the new playbill ripped
in the guaranteed corner—see Bert Williams what? 5
Minstrels when you steal a chicken just
save me the wing for if it isn't
Erie it ain't for miles around a
Mazda—and the telegraphic night coming on Thomas

a Ediford—and whistling down the tracks 10
a headlight rushing with the sound—can you
imagine—while an EXPRESS makes time like
SCIENCE—COMMERCE and the HOLYGHOST
RADIO ROARS IN EVERY HOME WE HAVE THE NORTHPOLE
WALLSTREET AND VIRGINBIRTH WITHOUT STONES OR 15
WIRES OR EVEN RUNning brooks connecting ears
and no more sermons windows flashing roar
Breathtaking—as you like it . . . eh?

So the 20th Century—so
whizzed the Limited—roared by and left 20
three men, still hungry on the tracks, ploddingly
watching the tail lights wizen and converge, slipping gimleted and neatly out of sight.

*

The last bear, shot drinking in the Dakotas
Loped under wires that span the mountain stream. 25
Keen instruments, strung to a vast precision
Bind town to town and dream to ticking dream. *to those whose addresses are never near*
But some men take their liquor slow—and count
—Though they'll confess no rosary nor clue—
The river's minute by the far brook's year. 30
Under a world of whistles, wires and steam
Caboose-like they go ruminating through
Ohio, Indiana—blind baggage—
To Cheyenne tagging . . . Maybe Kalamazoo.

Time's rendings, time's blendings they construe 35
As final reckonings of fire and snow;
Strange bird-wit, like the elemental gist
Of unwalled winds they offer, singing low
My Old Kentucky Home and *Casey Jones,*
Some Sunny Day. I heard a road-gang chanting so. 40
And afterwards, who had a colt's eyes—one said,

"Jesus! Oh I remember watermelon days!" And sped
High in a cloud of merriment, recalled
"—And when my Aunt Sally Simpson smiled," he drawled—
"It was almost Louisiana, long ago." 45

"There's no place like Booneville though, Buddy,"
One said, excising a last burr from his vest,
"—For early trouting." Then peering in the can,
"—But I kept on the tracks." Possessed, resigned,
He trod the fire down pensively and grinned, 50
Spreading dry shingles of a bread . . . .

Behind
My father's cannery works I used to see
Rail-squatters ranged in nomad raillery,
The ancient men—wifeless or runaway
Hobo-trekkers that forever search 55
An empire wilderness of freight and rails.
Each seemed a child, like me, on a loose perch,
Holding to childhood like some termless play.
John, Jake or Charley, hopping the slow freight
—Memphis to Tallahassee—riding the rods, 60
Blind fists of nothing, humpty-dumpty clods.

Yet they touch something like a key perhaps.
From pole to pole across the hills, the states
—They know a body under the wide rain;
Youngsters with eyes like fjords, old reprobates 65
With racetrack jargon,—dotting immensity
They lurk across her, knowing her yonder breast
Snow-silvered, sumac-stained or smoky blue—
Is past the valley-sleepers, south or west.
—As I have trod the rumorous midnights, too, 70

but who have touched her, knowing her without name

And past the circuit of the lamp's thin flame
(O Nights that brought me to her body bare!)
Have dreamed beyond the print that bound her name.

Trains sounding the long blizzards out—I heard
Wail into distances I knew were hers. 75
Papooses crying on the wind's long mane
Screamed redskin dynasties that fled the brain,
—Dead echoes! But I knew her body there,
Time like a serpent down her shoulder, dark,
And space, an eaglet's wing, laid on her hair. 80

Under the Ozarks, domed by Iron Mountain,
The old gods of the rain lie wrapped in pools
Where eyeless fish curvet a sunken fountain — nor the myths of her fathers
And re-descend with corn from querulous crows.
Such pilferings make up their timeless eatage, 85
Propitiate them for their timber torn
By iron, iron—always the iron dealt cleavage!
They doze now, below axe and powder horn.

And Pullman breakfasters glide glistening steel
From tunnel into field—iron strides the dew— 90
Straddles the hill, a dance of wheel on wheel.
You have a half-hour's wait at Siskiyou,
Or stay the night and take the next train through.
Southward, near Cairo passing, you can see
The Ohio merging,—borne down Tennessee; 95
And if it's summer and the sun's in dusk
Maybe the breeze will lift the River's musk
—As though the waters breathed that you might know
Memphis Johnny, Steamboat Bill, Missouri Joe.
Oh, lean from the window, if the train slows down, 100
As though you touched hands with some ancient clown,
—A little while gaze absently below
And hum *Deep River* with them while they go.

Yes, turn again and sniff once more—look see,
O Sheriff, Brakeman, and Authority— 105
Hitch up your pants and crunch another quid,
For you, too, feed the River timelessly.

And few evade full measure of their fate;
Always they smile out eerily what they seem.
I could believe he joked at heaven's gate— 110
Dan Midland—jolted from the cold brake-beam.

Down, down—born pioneers in time's despite,
Grimed tributaries to an ancient flow—
They win no frontier by their wayward plight,
But drift in stillness, as from Jordan's brow. 115

You will not hear it as the sea; even stone
Is not more hushed by gravity . . . But slow,
As loth to take more tribute—sliding prone
Like one whose eyes were buried long ago

The River, spreading, flows—and spends your dream. 120
What are you, lost within this tideless spell?
You are your father's father, and the stream—
A liquid theme that floating niggers swell.

Damp tonnage and alluvial march of days—
Nights turbid, vascular with silted shale 125
And roots surrendered down of moraine clays:
The Mississippi drinks the farthest dale.

O quarrying passion, undertowed sunlight!
The basalt surface drags a jungle grace
Ochreous and lynx-barred in lengthening might; 130
Patience! and you shall reach the biding place!

Over De Soto's bones the freighted floors
Throb past the City storied of three thrones.
Down two more turns the Mississippi pours
(Anon tall ironsides up from salt lagoons) 135

And flows within itself, heaps itself free.
All fades but one thin skyline 'round . . . Ahead
No embrace opens but the stinging sea;
The River lifts itself from its long bed,

Poised wholly on its dream, a mustard glow 140
Tortured with history, its one will—flow!
—The Passion spreads in wide tongues, choked and slow,
Meeting the Gulf, hosannas silently below.

[it's over a(see just over this)wall]

E. E. Cummings (1894–1962)

it's over a(see just
over this)wall
the apples are(yes
they're gravensteins)all
as red as to lose 5
and as round as to find.

Each why of a leaf says
(floating each how)
you're which as to die
(each green of a new) 10
you're who as to grow
but you're he as to do

what must(whispers)be must
be(the wise fool)
if living's to give 15
so breathing's to steal—
five wishes are five
and one hand is a mind

then over our thief goes
(you go and i) 20
has pulled(for he's we)
such fruit from what bough
that someone called they
made him pay with his now.

But over a(see just
over this)wall
the red and the round
(they're gravensteins)fall
with kind of a blind
big sound on the ground 30

DROWNING WITH OTHERS

James Dickey (1923–)

There are moments a man turns from us
Whom we have all known until now.
Upgathered, we watch him grow,
Unshipping his shoulder bones

Like human, everyday wings 5
That he has not ever used,
Releasing his hair from his brain,
A kingfisher's crest, confused

By the God-tilted light of Heaven.
His deep, window-watching smile 10
Comes closely upon us in waves,
And spreads, and now we are

At last within it, dancing.
Slowly we turn and shine
Upon what is holding us, 15
As under our feet he soars,

Struck dumb as the angel of Eden,
In wide, eye-opening rings.
Yet the hand on my shoulder fears
To feel my own wingblades spring, 20

To feel me sink slowly away
In my hair turned loose like a thought

Of a fisherbird dying in flight.
If I opened my arms, I could hear

Every shell in the sea find the word 25
It has tried to put into my mouth.
Broad flight would become of my dancing,
And I would obsess the whole sea,

But I keep rising and singing
With my last breath. Upon my back, 30
With his hand on my unborn wing,
A man rests easy as sunlight

Who has kept himself free of the forms
Of the deaf, down-soaring dead,
And me laid out and alive 35
For nothing at all, in his arms.

A DOG SLEEPING ON MY FEET

James Dickey (1923–)

Being his resting place,
I do not even tense
The muscles of a leg
Or I would seem to be changing.
Instead, I turn the page 5
Of the notebook, carefully not

Remembering what I have written,
For now, with my feet beneath him
Dying like embers,
The poem is beginning to move 10
Up through my pine-prickling legs
Out of the night wood,

Taking hold of the pen by my fingers.
Before me the fox floats lightly,
On fire with his holy scent. 15

All, all are running.
Marvelous is the pursuit,
Like a dazzle of nails through the ankles,

Like a twisting shout through the trees
Sent after the flying fox 20
Through the holes of logs, over streams
Stock-still with the pressure of moonlight.
My killed legs,
My legs of a dead thing, follow,

Quick as pins, through the forest, 25
And all rushes on into dark
And ends on the brightness of paper.
When my hand, which speaks in a daze
The hypnotized language of beasts,
Shall falter, and fail 30

Back into the human tongue,
And the dog gets up and goes out
To wander the dawning yard,
I shall crawl to my human bed
And lie there smiling at sunrise, 35
With the scent of the fox

Burning my brain like an incense,
Floating out of the night wood,
Coming home to my wife and my sons
From the dream of an animal, 40
Assembling the self I must wake to,
Sleeping to grow back my legs.

THE FLEA

John Donne (1572–1631)

Mark but this flea, and mark in this
How little that which thou deny'st me is;
It suck'd me first, and now sucks thee,

And in this flea, our two bloods mingled be;
Thou know'st that this cannot be said 5
A sin, nor shame, nor loss of maidenhead,
    Yet this enjoys before it woo,
    And pamper'd swells with one blood made of two,
    And this, alas, is more than we would do.

O stay, three lives in one flea spare, 10
Where we almost, yea more than married are.
This flea is you and I and this
Our marriage bed, and marriage temple is;
Though parents grudge, and you, w'are met,
And cloister'd in these living walls of jet. 15
    Though use make you apt to kill me,
    Let not to that, self-murder added be,
    And sacrilege, three sins in killing three.

Cruel and sudden, hast thou since
Purpled thy nail, in blood of innocence? 20
Wherein could this flea guilty be,
Except in that drop which it suck'd from thee?
Yet thou triumph'st, and say'st that thou
Find'st not thyself, nor me the weaker now;
    'Tis true, then learn how false, fears be; 25
    Just so much honor, when thou yield'st to me,
    Will waste, as this flea's death took life from thee.

THE GOOD-MORROW

John Donne (1572–1631)

I wonder by my troth, what thou, and I
Did, till we lov'd? Were we not wean'd till then?
But suck'd on country pleasures, childishly?
Or snorted we in the Seven Sleepers' den?
'Twas so; but this, all pleasures fancies be. 5

If ever any beauty I did see,
Which I desir'd and got, 'twas but a dream of thee.

And now good morrow to our waking souls,
Which watch not one another out of fear;
For love, all love of other sights controls, 10
And makes one little room, an everywhere.
Let sea-discoverers to new worlds have gone,
Let maps to others, worlds on worlds have shown,
Let us possess one world, each hath one, and is one.

My face in thine eye, thine in mine appears, 15
And true plain hearts do in the faces rest,
Where can we find two better hemispheres
Without sharp North, without declining West?
Whatever dies, was not mix'd equally;
If our two loves be one, or thou and I 20
Love so alike, that none do slacken, none can die.

SONG

John Donne (1572–1631)

Go, and catch a falling star,
  Get with child a mandrake root,
Tell me, where all past years are,
  Or who cleft the devil's foot,
Teach me to hear mermaids singing, 5
  Or to keep off envy's stinging,
        And find
        What wind
Serves to advance an honest mind.

If thou be'st born to strange sights, 10
  Things invisible to see,
Ride ten thousand days and nights,
  Till age snow white hairs on thee;

Thou, when thou return'st, wilt tell me
All strange wonders that befell thee, 15
And swear
Nowhere
Lives a woman true, and fair.

If thou find'st one, let me know,
Such a pilgrimage were sweet; 20
Yet do not, I would not go,
Though at next door we might meet;
Though she were true, when you met her,
And last, till you write your letter,
Yet she 25
Will be
False, ere I come, to two, or three.

THE CANONIZATION

John Donne (1572–1631)

For God's sake hold your tongue, and let me love!
Or chide my palsy, or my gout,
My five gray hairs, or ruin'd fortune flout,
With wealth your state, your mind with arts improve,
Take you a course, get you a place, 5
Observe his Honor, or his Grace,
Or the king's real, or his stampèd face
Contemplate, what you will, approve,
So you will let me love.

Alas, alas, who's injur'd by my love? 10
What merchant's ships have my sighs drown'd?
Who says my tears have overflowed his ground?
When did my colds a forward spring remove?
When did the heats which my veins fill
Add one man to the plaguy bill? 15

Soldiers find wars, and lawyers find out still
  Litigious men, which quarrels move,
  Though she and I do love.

Call us what you will, we are made such by love;
  Call her one, me another fly, 20
We're tapers too, and at our own cost die.
  And we in us find th' eagle and the dove.
    The phoenix riddle hath more wit
    By us; we two being one, are it.
So to one neutral thing both sexes fit, 25
  We die and rise the same, and prove
  Mysterious by this love.

We can die by it, if not live by love,
  And if unfit for tombs and hearse
Our legend be, it will be fit for verse; 30
  And if no piece of chronicle we prove,
    We'll build in sonnets pretty rooms;
    As well a well-wrought urn becomes
The greatest ashes, as half-acre tombs
  And by these hymns, all shall approve 35
  Us canoniz'd for love.

And thus invoke us: "You whom reverent love
  Made one another's hermitage;
You, to whom love was peace, that now is rage;
  Who did the whole world's soul contract, and drove 40
    Into the glasses of your eyes
    (So made such mirrors, and such spies,
That they did all to you epitomize)
  Countries, towns, courts: Beg from above
  A pattern of your love!" 45

THE UNDERTAKING
John Donne (1572–1631)

I have done one braver thing
  Than all the Worthies did,
And yet a braver thence doth spring,
  Which is, to keep that hid.

It were but madness now t' impart   5
  The skill of specular stone,
When he which can have learn'd the art
  To cut it, can find none.

So, if I now should utter this,
  Others (because no more   10
Such stuff to work upon there is)
  Would love but as before.

But he who loveliness within
  Hath found, all outward loathes,
For he who color loves, and skin,   15
  Loves but their oldest clothes.

If, as I have, you also do
  Virtue'attir'd in woman see,
And dare love that, and say so too,
  And forget the He and She;   20

And if this love, though placèd so,
  From profane men you hide,
Which will no faith on this bestow,
  Or, if they do, deride:

Then you have done a braver thing   25
  Than all the Worthies did;
And a braver thence will spring,
  Which is, to keep that hid.

THE SUN RISING

John Donne (1572–1631)

Busy old fool, unruly Sun
Why dost thou thus,
Through windows, and through curtains call on us?
Must to thy motions lovers's seasons run?
Saucy pedantic wretch, go chide 5
Late schoolboys, and sour prentices,
Go tell court huntsmen that the king will ride,
Call country ants to harvest offices;
Love, all alike, no season knows, nor clime,
Nor hours, days, months, which are the rags of time. 10

Thy beams, so reverend, and strong
Why shouldst thou think?
I could eclipse and cloud them with a wink,
But that I would not lose her sight so long:
If her eyes have not blinded thine, 15
Look, and tomorrow late, tell me,
Whether both th'Indias of spice and mine
Be where thou left'st them, or lie here with me.
Ask for those kings whom thou saw'st yesterday,
And thou shalt hear: All here in one bed lay. 20

She's all states, and all princes, I,
Nothing else is.
Princes do but play us; compar'd to this,
All honor's mimic, all wealth alchemy.
Thou, sun, art half as happy's we, 25
In that the world's contracted thus;
Thine age asks ease, and since thy duties be
To warm the world, that's done in warming us.
Shine here to us, and thou art everywhere;
This bed thy center is, these walls, thy sphere. 30

SONG

John Donne (1572–1631)

Sweetest love, I do not go,
  For weariness of thee,
Nor in hope the world can show
  A fitter love for me;
    But since that I   5
Must die at last, 'tis best,
To use myself in jest
  Thus by feign'd deaths to die.

Yesternight the sun went hence,
  And yet is here today;   10
He hath no desire nor sense,
  Nor half so short a way:
    Then fear not me,
But believe that I shall make
Speedier journeys, since I take   15
  More wings and spurs than he.

O how feeble is man's power,
  That if good fortune fall,
Cannot add another hour,
  Nor a lost hour recall!   20
    But come bad chance,
And we join to'it our strength,
And we teach it art and length,
  Itself o'er us t' advance.

When thou sigh'st, thou sigh'st not wind   25
  But sigh'st my soul away,
When thou weep'st, unkindly kind,
  My life's blood doth decay.
    It cannot be

That thou lov'st me, as thou say'st, 30
If in thine my life thou waste,
Thou art the best of me.

Let not thy divining heart
Forethink me any ill,
Destiny may take thy part, 35
And may thy fears fulfill;
But think that we
Are but turn'd aside to sleep;
They who one another keep
Alive, ne'er parted be. 40

THE ANNIVERSARY

John Donne (1572–1631)

All kings, and all their favorites,
All glory of honors, beauties, wits,
The sun itself, which makes times, as they pass,
Is elder by a year, now, than it was
When thou and I first one another saw: 5
All other things, to their destruction draw,
Only our love hath no decay;
This, no tomorrow hath, nor yesterday,
Running it never runs from us away,
But truly keeps his first, last, everlasting day. 10

Two graves must hide thine and my corse.
If one might, death were no divorce.
Alas, as well as other princes, we,
(Who prince enough in one another be)
Must leave at last in death, these eyes, and ears, 15
Oft fed with true oaths, and with sweet salt tears;
But souls where nothing dwells but love
(All other thoughts being inmates) then shall prove

This, or a love increasèd there above,
When bodies to their graves, souls from their graves remove. 20

And then we shall be thoroughly blest,
But we no more, than all the rest;
Here upon earth we're kings, and none but we
Can be such kings, nor of such, subjects be.
Who is so safe as we, where none can do 25
Treason to us, except one of us two?
True and false fears let us refrain,
Let us love nobly, and live, and add again
Years and years unto years, till we attain
To write threescore: this is the second of our reign. 30

THE ECSTASY

John Donne (1572–1631)

Where, like a pillow on a bed,
A pregnant bank swell'd up, to rest
The violet's reclining head,
Sat we two, one another's best.
Our hands were firmly cemented 5
With a fast balm, which thence did spring,
Our eye-beams twisted, and did thread
Our eyes, upon one double string;
So t' intergraft our hands, as yet
Was all the means to make us one, 10
And pictures in our eyes to get
Was all our propagation.
As 'twixt two equal armies, fate
Suspends uncertain victory,
Our souls (which to advance their state, 15
Were gone out) hung 'twixt her, and me.
And whilst our souls negotiate there,
We like sepulchral statues lay;

All day, the same our postures were,
  And we said nothing, all the day. 20
If any, so by love refin'd,
  That he soul's language understood,
And by good love were grown all mind,
  Within convenient distance stood,
He (though he knew not which soul spake, 25
  Because both meant, both spake the same)
Might thence a new concoction take,
  And part far purer than he came.
This ecstasy doth unperplex
  (We said) and tell us what we love, 30
We see by this, it was not sex,
  We see, we saw not what did move:
But as all several souls contain
  Mixture of things, they know not what,
Love, these mixt souls, doth mix again, 35
  And makes both one, each this and that.
A single violet transplant,
  The strength, the color, and the size
(All which before was poor, and scant)
  Redoubles still, and multiplies. 40
When love, with one another so
  Interinanimates two souls,
That abler soul, which thence doth flow,
  Defects of loneliness controls.
We then, who are this new soul, know, 45
  Of what we are compos'd, and made,
For, th' atomies of which we grow,
  Are souls, whom no change can invade.
But O alas, so long, so far
  Our bodies why do we forbear? 50
They're ours, though they're not we: we are
  Th' intelligences, they the sphere.
We owe them thanks, because they thus

Did us, to us, at first convey,
Yielded their forces, sense, to us, 55
Nor are dross to us, but allay.
On man heaven's influence works not so,
But that it first imprints the air,
So soul into the soul may flow,
Though it to body first repair. 60
As our blood labors to beget
Spirits, as like souls as it can,
Because such fingers need to knit
That subtile knot, which makes us man,
So must pure lovers' souls descend 65
T' affections, and to faculties,
Which sense may reach and apprehend,
Else a great prince in prison lies.
T' our bodies turn we then, that so
Weak men on love reveal'd may look; 70
Love's mysteries in souls do grow,
But yet the body is his book.
And if some lover, such as we,
Have heard this dialogue of one,
Let him still mark us; he shall see 75
Small change, when we're to bodies gone.

LOVE'S DEITY

John Donne (1572–1631)

I long to talk with some old lover's ghost,
Who died before the god of love was born:
I cannot think that he, who then lov'd most,
Sunk so low, as to love one which did scorn.
But since this god produc'd a destiny, 5
And that vice-nature, custom, lets it be,
I must love her, that loves not me.

Sure, they which made him god, meant not so much,
  Nor he, in his young godhead practis'd it;
But when an even flame two hearts did touch, 10
  His office was indulgently to fit
Actives to passives. Correspondency
Only his subject was. It cannot be
  Love, till I love her, that loves me.

But every modern god will now extend 15
  His vast prerogative, as far as Jove.
To rage, to lust, to write to, to commend,
  All is the purlieu of the god of love.
O were we waken'd by this tyranny
T' ungod this child again, it could not be 20
  I should love her, who loves not me.

Rebel and atheist too, why murmur I,
  As though I felt the worst that love could do?
Love might make me leave loving, or might try
  A deeper plague, to make her love me too, 25
Which, since she loves before, I'm loath to see;
Falsehood is worse than hate; and that must be
  If she whom I love, should love me.

THE RELIC

John Donne (1572–1631)

When my grave is broke up again
Some second guest to entertain,
(For graves have learn'd that womanhead
To be to more than one a bed)
  And he that digs it, spies 5
A bracelet of bright hair about the bone,
  Will he not let'us alone,
And think that there a loving couple lies,
Who thought that this device might be some way

To make their souls, at the last busy day, 10
Meet at this grave, and make a little stay?

If this fall in a time, or land,
Where mis-devotion doth command,
Then, he that digs us up, will bring
Us, to the Bishop, and the King, 15
To make us relics; then
Thou shalt be a Mary Magdalen, and I
A something else thereby;
All women shall adore us, and some men;
And since at such time, miracles are sought, 20
I would have that age by this paper taught
What miracles we harmless lovers wrought.

First, we lov'd well and faithfully,
Yet knew not what we lov'd, nor why;
Difference of sex no more we knew, 25
Than our guardian angels do;
Coming and going, we
Perchance might kiss, but not between those meals;
Our hands ne'er touch'd the seals,
Which nature, injur'd by late law, sets free: 30
These miracles we did; but now alas,
All measure, and all language, I should pass,
Should I tell what a miracle she was.

HOLY SONNETS

John Donne (1572–1631)

7

At the round earth's imagin'd corners, blow
Your trumpets, angels, and arise, arise
From death, you numberless infinities
Of souls, and to your scatter'd bodies go,
All whom the flood did, and fire shall o'erthrow, 5

All whom war, dearth, age, agues, tyrannies,
Despair, law, chance hath slain, and you whose eyes
Shall behold God, and never taste death's woe.
But let them sleep, Lord, and me mourn a space,
For, if above all these, my sins abound 10
'Tis late to ask abundance of thy grace,
When we are there; here on this lowly ground,
Teach me how to repent; for that's as good
As if thou'dst seal'd my pardon, with thy blood.

10

Death be not proud, though some have called thee
Mighty and dreadful, for, thou art not so,
For, those, whom thou think'st, thou dost overthrow,
Die not, poor death, nor yet canst thou kill me;
From rest and sleep, which but thy pictures be, 5
Much pleasure, then from thee, much more must flow;
And soonest our best men with thee do go,
Rest of their bones, and soul's delivery.
Thou'rt slave to fate, chance, kings, and desperate men,
And dost with poison, war, and sickness dwell, 10
And poppy, or charms can make us sleep as well,
And better than thy stroke; why swell'st thou then?
One short sleep past, we wake eternally,
And death shall be no more. Death, thou shalt die.

14

Batter my heart, three-person'd God; for you
As yet but knock, breathe, shine, and seek to mend;
That I may rise, and stand, o'erthrow me, 'nd bend
Your force, to break, blow, burn and make me new.
I, like an usurp'd town, t' another due, 5
Labor t' admit you, but O, to no end!
Reason, your viceroy in me, me should defend,
But is captiv'd, and proves weak or untrue.

Yet dearly'I love you, and would be lov'd fain,
But am bethroth'd unto your enemy. 10
Divorce me, untie, or break that knot again,
Take me to you, imprison me, for I
Except y' enthrall me, never shall be free,
Nor ever chaste, except you ravish me.

A HYMN TO GOD THE FATHER

John Donne (1572–1631)

Wilt thou forgive that sin where I begun,
  Which is my sin, though it were done before?
Wilt thou forgive those sins through which I run,
  And do them still: though still I do deplore?
    When thou hast done, thou hast not done, 5
      For, I have more.

Wilt thou forgive that sin by which I won
  Others to sin? and, made my sin their door?
Wilt thou forgive that sin which I did shun
  A year, or two: but wallow'd in, a score? 10
    When thou hast done, thou hast not done,
      For, I have more.

I have a sin of fear, that when I have spun
  My last thread, I shall perish on the shore;
Swear by thy self, that at my death thy Sun 15
Shall shine as it shines now, and heretofore;
    And, having done that, thou hast done,
      I have no more.

SINCE THERE'S NO HELP

Michael Drayton (1563–1631)

Since there's no help, come let us kiss and part;
Nay, I have done, you get no more of me,

And I am glad, yea glad with all my heart
That thus so cleanly I myself can free;
Shake hands forever, cancel all our vows, 5
And when we meet at any time again,
Be it not seen in either of our brows
That we one jot of former love retain.
Now at the last gasp of love's latest breath,
When, his pulse failing, passion speechless lies, 10
When faith is kneeling by his bed of death,
And innocence is closing up his eyes,
  Now if thou wouldst, when all have given him over,
  From death to life thou mightst him yet recover.

TO THE MEMORY OF MR. OLDHAM

John Dryden (1631–1700)

Farewell, too little, and too lately known,
Whom I began to think and call my own:
For sure our souls were near allied, and thine
Cast in the same poetic mold with mine.
One common note on either lyre did strike, 5
And knaves and fools we both abhorr'd alike.
To the same goal did both our studies drive;
The last set out the soonest did arrive.
Thus Nisus fell upon the slippery place,
While his young friend perform'd and won the race. 10
O early ripe! to thy abundant store
What could advancing age have added more?
It might (what nature never gives the young)
Have taught the numbers of thy native tongue.
But satire needs not those, and wit will shine 15
Thro' the harsh cadence of a rugged line:
A noble error, and but seldom made,
When poets are by too much force betray'd.
Thy generous fruits, tho' gather'd ere their prime,

Still shew'd a quickness; and maturing time 20
But mellows what we write to the dull sweets of rhyme.
Once more, hail and farewell; farewell, thou young,
But ah too short, Marcellus of our tongue;
Thy brows with ivy, and with laurels bound;
But fate and gloomy night encompass thee around. 25

THE GROUNDHOG

Richard Eberhart (1904–)

In June, amid the golden fields,
I saw a groundhog lying dead.
Dead lay he; my senses shook,
And mind outshot our naked frailty.
There lowly in the vigorous summer 5
His form began its senseless change,
And made my senses waver dim
Seeing nature ferocious in him.
Inspecting close his maggots' might
And seething cauldron of his being, 10
Half with loathing, half with a strange love,
I poked him with an angry stick.
The fever arose, became a flame
And Vigour circumscribed the skies,
Immense energy in the sun, 15
And through my frame a sunless trembling.
My stick had done nor good nor harm.
Then stood I silent in the day
Watching the object, as before;
And kept my reverence for knowledge 20
Trying for control, to be still,
To quell the passion of the blood;
Until I had bent down on my knees
Praying for joy in the sight of decay.
And so I left; and I returned 25

In Autumn strict of eye, to see
The sap gone out of the groundhog,
But the bony sodden hulk remained.
But the year had lost its meaning,
And in intellectual chains 30
I lost both love and loathing,
Mured up in the wall of wisdom.
Another summer took the fields again
Massive and burning, full of life,
But when I chanced upon the spot 35
There was only a little hair left,
And bones bleaching in the sunlight
Beautiful as architecture;
I watched them like a geometer,
And cut a walking stick from a birch. 40
It has been three years, now.
There is no sign of the groundhog.
I stood there in the whirling summer,
My hand capped a withered heart,
And thought of China and of Greece, 45
Of Alexander in his tent;
Of Montaigne in his tower,
Of Saint Theresa in her wild lament.

MARINA

T. S. Eliot (1888–1965)

Quis hic locus, quae regio, quae mundi plaga?

What seas what shores what grey rocks and what islands
What water lapping the bow
And scent of pine and the woodthrush singing through the fog
What images return
O my daughter. 5

Those who sharpen the tooth of the dog, meaning
Death
Those who glitter with the glory of the hummingbird, meaning
Death
Those who sit in the stye of contentment, meaning 10
Death
Those who suffer the ecstasy of the animals, meaning
Death

Are become unsubstantial, reduced by a wind,
A breath of pine, and the woodsong fog 15
By this grace dissolved in place

What is this face, less clear and clearer
The pulse in the arm, less strong and stronger—
Given or lent? more distant than stars and nearer than the eye

Whispers and small laughter between leaves and
  hurrying feet 20
Under sleep, where all the waters meet.

Bowsprit cracked with ice and paint cracked with heat.
I made this, I have forgotten
And remember.
The rigging weak and the canvas rotten 25
Between one June and another September.
Made this unknowing, half conscious, unknown, my own.
The garboard strake leaks, the seams need caulking.
This form, this face, this life
Living to live in a world of time beyond me; let me 30
Resign my life for this life, my speech for that unspoken,
The awakened, lips parted, the hope, the new ships.

What seas what shores what granite islands towards my timbers
And woodthrush calling through the fog
My daughter. 35

HIDE-AND-SEEK

Robert Francis (1901–)

Here where the dead lie hidden
Too well ever to speak,
Three children unforbidden
Are playing hide-and-seek.

What if for such a hiding 5
These stones were not designed?
The dead are far from chiding;
The living need not mind.

Too soon the stones that hid them
Anonymously in play 10
Will learn their names and bid them
Come back to hide to stay.

FARM BOY AFTER SUMMER

Robert Francis (1901–)

A seated statue of himself he seems.
A bronze slowness becomes him. Patently
The page he contemplates he doesn't see.

The lesson, the long lesson, has been summer.
His mind holds summer as his skin holds sun. 5
For once the homework, all of it, was done.

What were the crops, where were the fiery fields
Where for so many days so many hours
The sun assaulted him with glittering showers?

Expect a certain absence in his presence. 10
Expect all winter long a summer scholar,
For scarcely all its snows can cool that color.

SWIMMER

Robert Francis (1901–)

I

Observe how he negotiates his way
With trust and the least violence, making
The stranger friend, the enemy ally.
The depth that could destroy gently supports him.
With water he defends himself from water. 5
Danger he leans on, rests in. The drowning sea
Is all he has between himself and drowning.

II

What lover ever lay more mutually
With his beloved, his always-reaching arms
Stroking in smooth and powerful caresses? 10
Some drown in love as in dark water, and some
By love are strongly held as the green sea
Now holds the swimmer. Indolently he turns
To float.—The swimmer floats, the lover sleeps.

HIGH DIVER

Robert Francis (1901–)

How deep is his duplicity who in a flash
Passes from resting bird to flying bird to fish,

Who momentarily is sculpture, then all motion,
Speed and splash, then climbs again to contemplation.

He is the archer who himself is bow and arrow. 5
He is the upper-under-world-commuting hero.

His downward going has the air of sacrifice
To some dark seaweed-bearded seagod face to face

Or goddess. Rippling and responsive lies the water
For him to contemplate, then powerfully to enter. 10

PITCHER

Robert Francis (1901–)

His art is eccentricity, his aim
How not to hit the mark he seems to aim at,

His passion how to avoid the obvious,
His technique how to vary the avoidance.

The others throw to be comprehended. He 5
Throws to be a moment misunderstood.

Yet not too much. Not errant, arrant, wild,
But every seeming aberration willed.

Not to, yet still, still to communicate
Making the batter understand too late. 10

'OUT, OUT—'

Robert Frost (1875–1963)

The buzz saw snarled and rattled in the yard
And made dust and dropped stove-length sticks of wood,
Sweet-scented stuff when the breeze drew across it.
And from there those that lifted eyes could count
Five mountain ranges one behind the other 5
Under the sunset far into Vermont.
And the saw snarled and rattled, snarled and rattled,
As it ran light, or had to bear a load.
And nothing happened: day was all but done.
Call it a day, I wish they might have said 10
To please the boy by giving him the half hour
That a boy counts so much when saved from work.

His sister stood beside them in her apron
To tell them 'Supper.' At the word, the saw,
As if to prove saws knew what supper meant, 15
Leaped out at the boy's hand, or seemed to leap—
He must have given the hand. However it was,
Neither refused the meeting. But the hand!
The boy's first outcry was a rueful laugh,
As he swung toward them holding up the hand 20
Half in appeal, but half as if to keep
The life from spilling. Then the boy saw all—
Since he was old enough to know, big boy
Doing a man's work, though a child at heart—
He saw all spoiled. 'Don't let him cut my hand off— 25
The doctor, when he comes. Don't let him, sister!'
So. But the hand was gone already.
The doctor put him in the dark of ether.
He lay and puffed his lips out with his breath.
And then—the watcher at his pulse took fright. 30
No one believed. They listened at his heart.
Little—less—nothing!—and that ended it.
No more to build on there. And they, since they
Were not the one dead, turned to their affairs.

HOUSE FEAR

Robert Frost (1875–1963)

Always—I tell you this they learned—
Always at night when they returned
To the lonely house from far away
To lamps unlighted and fire gone gray,
They learned to rattle the lock and key 5
To give whatever might chance to be
Warning and time to be off in flight:
And preferring the out- to the in-door night,

They learned to leave the house-door wide
Until they had lit the lamp inside. 10

THE OFT-REPEATED DREAM

Robert Frost (1875–1963)

She had no saying dark enough
  For the dark pine that kept
Forever trying the window-latch
  Of the room where they slept.

The tireless but ineffectual hands 5
  That with every futile pass
Made the great tree seem as a little bird
  Before the mystery of glass!

It never had been inside the room,
  And only one of the two 10
Was afraid in an oft-repeated dream
  Of what the tree might do.

IN THE MOONLIGHT

Thomas Hardy (1840–1928)

"O lonely workman, standing there
In a dream, why do you stare and stare
At her grave, as no other grave there were?

"If your great gaunt eyes so importune
Her soul by the shine of this corpse-cold moon, 5
Maybe you'll raise her phantom soon!"

"Why, fool, it is what I would rather see
Than all the living folk there be;
But alas, there is no such joy for me!"

"Ah—she was one you loved, no doubt, 10
Through good and evil, through rain and drought,
And when she passed, all your sun went out?"

"Nay: she was the woman I did not love,
Whom all the others were ranked above,
Whom during her life I thought nothing of." 15

SAMUEL SEWALL
Anthony Hecht (1923–)

Samuel Sewall, in a world of wigs,
Flouted opinion in his personal hair;
For foppery he gave not any figs,
But in his right and honor took the air.

Thus in his naked style, though well attired, 5
He went forth in the city, or paid court
To Madam Winthrop, whom he much admired,
Most godly, but yet liberal with the port.

And all the town admired for two full years
His excellent address, his gifts of fruit, 10
Her gracious ways and delicate white ears,
And held the course of nature absolute.

But yet she bade him suffer a peruke,
"That One be not distinguished from the All;"
Delivered of herself this stern rebuke 15
Framed in the resonant language of St. Paul.

"Madam," he answered her, "I have a Friend
Furnishes me with hair out of His strength,
And He requires only I attend
Unto His charity and to its length." 20

And all the town was witness to his trust:
On Monday he walked out with the Widow Gibbs,

A pious lady of charm and notable bust,
Whose heart beat tolerably beneath her ribs.

On Saturday he wrote proposing marriage, 25
And closed, imploring that she be not cruel,
"Your favorable answer will oblige,
Madam, your humble servant, Samuel Sewall."

REDEMPTION

George Herbert (1593–1633)

Having been tenant long to a rich lord,
Not thriving, I resolvèd to be bold,
And make a suit unto him, to afford
A new small-rented lease, and cancel th'old.
In heaven at his manor I him sought: 5
They told me there, that he was lately gone
About some land, which he had dearly bought
Long since on earth, to take possession.
I straight return'd, and knowing his great birth,
Sought him accordingly in great resorts; 10
In cities, theaters, gardens, parks, and courts:
At length I heard a ragged noise and mirth
Of thieves and murderers: there I him espied,
Who straight, "Your suit is granted" said, and died.

VIRTUE

George Herbert (1593–1633)

Sweet day, so cool, so calm, so bright,
The bridal of the earth and sky:
The dew shall weep thy fall tonight,
For thou must die.

Sweet rose, whose hue angry and brave 5
Bids the rash gazer wipe his eye:

Thy root is ever in its grave,
And thou must die.

Sweet spring, full of sweet days and roses,
A box where sweets compacted lie; 10
My music shows ye have your closes,
And all must die.

Only a sweet and virtuous soul,
Like season'd timber, never gives;
But though the whole world turn to coal, 15
Then chiefly lives.

THE COLLAR

George Herbert (1593–1633)

I struck the board, and cried, "No more!
I will abroad!
What? Shall I ever sigh and pine?
My lines and life are free; free as the road,
Loose as the wind, as large as store. 5
Shall I be still in suit?
Have I no harvest but a thorn
To let me blood, and not restore
What I have lost with cordial fruit?
Sure there was wine 10
Before my sighs did dry it: there was corn
Before my tears did drown it.
Is the year only lost to me?
Have I no bays to crown it?
No flowers, no garlands gay? All blasted? 15
All wasted?
Not so, my heart: but there is fruit,
And thou hast hands.
Recover all thy sigh-blown age
On double pleasures: leave thy cold dispute 20

Of what is fit, and not. Forsake thy cage,
Thy rope of sands,
Which petty thoughts have made, and made to thee
Good cable, to enforce and draw,
And be thy law, 25
While thou didst wink and wouldst not see.
Away! Take heed!
I will abroad!
Call in thy death's head there: tie up thy fears.
He that forbears 30
To suit and serve his need,
Deserves his load."
But as I raved and grew more fierce and wild
At every word,
Methoughts I heard one calling, "Child!" 35
And I replied, "My Lord!"

THE PULLEY

George Herbert (1593–1633)

When God at first made man,
Having a glass of blessings standing by,
"Let us," said He, "pour on him all we can;
Let the world's riches, which dispersèd lie,
Contract into a span. 5

So strength first made a way;
Then beauty flow'd, then wisdom, honor, pleasure:
When almost all was out, God made a stay,
Perceiving that alone of all His treasure
Rest in the bottom lay. 10

"For if I should," said He,
"Bestow this jewel also on My creature,
He would adore My gifts instead of Me,

And rest in Nature, not the God of Nature:
So both should losers be. 15

"Yet let him keep the rest,
But keep them with repining restlessness:
Let him be rich and weary, that at least,
If goodness lead him not, yet weariness
May toss him to My breast." 20

LOVE

George Herbert (1593–1633)

Love bade me welcome: yet my soul drew back,
Guilty of dust and sin.
But quick-eyed Love, observing me grow slack
From my first entrance in,
Drew nearer to me, sweetly questioning, 5
If I lack'd anything.

"A guest," I answer'd, "worthy to be here."
Love said, "You shall be he."
"I, the unkind, ungrateful? Ah my dear,
I cannot look on Thee." 10
Love took my hand, and smiling did reply,
"Who made the eyes but I?"

"Truth, Lord, but I have marr'd them: let my shame
Go where it doth deserve."
"And know you not," says Love, "who bore the
blame?" 15
"My dear, then I will serve."
"You must sit down," says Love, "and taste my meat."
So I did sit and eat.

DISCIPLINE

George Herbert (1593–1633)

Throw away Thy rod,
Throw away Thy wrath:
O my God,
Take the gentle path.

For my heart's desire 5
Unto Thine is bent:
I aspire
To a full consent.

Not a word or look
I affect to own, 10
But by book,
And Thy book alone.

Though I fail, I weep:
Though I halt in pace,
Yet I creep 15
To the throne of grace.

Then let wrath remove,
Love will do the deed:
For with love
Stony hearts will bleed. 20

Love is swift of foot;
Love's a man of war,
And can shoot,
And can hit from far.

Who can 'scape his bow? 25
That which wrought on Thee,
Brought Thee low,
Needs must work on me.

Throw away Thy rod;
Though man frailties hath, 30
Thou art God:
Throw away Thy wrath.

UPON JULIA'S CLOTHES

Robert Herrick (1591–1674)

When as in silks my Julia goes,
Then, then (methinks) how sweetly flows
That liquefaction of her clothes.

Next, when I cast mine eyes and see
That brave vibration each way free: 5
O how that glittering taketh me!

TO DAFFODILS

Robert Herrick (1591–1674)

Fair daffodils, we weep to see
You haste away so soon:
As yet the early-rising sun
Has not attain'd his noon.
Stay, stay, 5
Until the hasting day
Has run
But to the even-song;
And, having pray'd together, we
Will go with you along. 10

We have short time to stay, as you,
We have as short a spring;
As quick a growth to meet decay,
As you, or any thing.
We die, 15
As your hours do, and dry
Away,

Like to the summer's rain;
Or as the pearls of morning's dew
Ne'er to be found again. 20

Nair

THE NIGHT PIECE, TO JULIA
Robert Herrick (1591–1674)

Her eyes the glow-worm lend thee,
The shooting stars attend thee
And the elves also,
Whose little eyes glow,
Like the sparks of fire, befriend thee. 5

No will-o'-th'-wisp mis-light thee,
Nor snake, or slow-worm bite thee:
But on, on thy way
Not making a stay,
Since ghost there's none to affright thee. 10

Let not the dark thee cumber;
What though the moon does slumber?
The stars of the night
Will lend thee their light,
Like tapers clear without number. 15

Then, Julia, let me woo thee,
Thus, thus to come unto me:
And when I shall meet
Thy silv'ry feet,
My soul I'll pour into thee. 20

DELIGHT IN DISORDER
Robert Herrick (1591–1674)

A sweet disorder in the dress
Kindles in clothes a wantonness:
A lawn about the shoulders thrown

Into a fine distraction;
An erring lace, which here and there 5
Enthralls the crimson stomacher;
A cuff neglectful, and thereby
Ribands to flow confusedly;
A winning wave (deserving note)
In the tempestuous petticoat; 10
A careless shoe-string, in whose tie
I see a wild civility;
Do more bewitch me, than when art
Is too precise in every part.

TO THE VIRGINS, TO MAKE MUCH OF TIME

Robert Herrick (1591–1674)

Gather ye rosebuds while ye may,
Old Time is still a-flying:
And this same flower that smiles today,
Tomorrow will be dying.

The glorious lamp of heaven, the sun, 5
The higher he's a getting,
The sooner will his race be run,
And nearer he's to setting.

That age is best, which is the first,
When youth and blood are warmer; 10
But being spent, the worse, and worst
Times, still succeed the former.

Then be not coy, but use your time;
And while ye may, go marry:
For having lost but once your prime, 15
You may for ever tarry.

SPRING AND FALL:
To a Young Child
Gerard Manley Hopkins (1844–1889)

MARGARÉT, are you gríeving
Over Goldengrove unleaving?
Leáves, líke the things of man, you
With your fresh thoughts care for, can you?
Áh! ás the heart grows older 5
It will come to such sights colder
By and by, nor spare a sigh
Though worlds of wanwood leafmeal lie;
And yet you wíll weep and know why.
Now no matter, child, the name: 10
Sórrow's spríngs áre the same.
Nor mouth had, no nor mind, expressed
What heart heard of, ghost guessed:
It ís the blight man was born for,
It is Margaret you mourn for. 15

ON WENLOCK EDGE THE WOOD'S IN TROUBLE
A. E. Housman (1859–1936)

On Wenlock Edge the wood's in trouble;
His forest fleece the Wrekin heaves;
The gale, it plies the saplings double,
And thick on Severn snow the leaves.

'Twould blow like this through holt and hanger 5
When Uricon the city stood:

'Tis the old wind in the old anger,
  But then it threshed another wood.

Then, 'twas before my time, the Roman
  At yonder heaving hill would stare: 10
The blood that warms an English yeoman,
  The thoughts that hurt him, they were there.

There, like the wind through woods in riot,
  Through him the gale of life blew high;
The tree of man was never quiet: 15
  Then 'twas the Roman, now 'tis I.

The gale, it plies the saplings double,
  It blows so hard, 'twill soon be gone:
To-day the Roman and his trouble
  Are ashes under Uricon. 20

DEATH OF A VERMONT FARM WOMAN

Barbara Howes (1914–)

Is it time now to go away?
July is nearly over; hay
Fattens the barn, the herds are strong,
Our old fields prosper; these long
Green evenings will keep death at bay. 5

Last winter lingered; it was May
Before a flowering lilac spray
Barred cold for ever. I was wrong.
          Is it time now?

Six decades vanished in a day!
I bore four sons: one lives; they 10
Were all good men; three dying young
Was hard on us. I have looked long
For these hills to show me where peace lay . . .
          Is it time now?

THE ROSES OF SA'ADI

Marceline Desbordes-Valmore
trans. by Barbara Howes (1914–)

I wanted this morning to bring you a gift of roses,
But I took so many in my wide belt
The tightened knots could not contain them all

And burst asunder. The roses taking wing
In the wind were all blown out to sea, 5
Following the water, never to return;

The waves were red with them as if aflame.
This evening my dress bears the perfume still:
You may take from it now their fragrant souvenir.

EL DESDICHADO

Gérard de Nerval
trans. by Barbara Howes (1914–)

The dark one am I, the widowed, unconsoled,
Prince of Aquitania whose tower lies ruined,
My one star is dead, and my radiant lute
Renders only the black sun of Melancholy.

In the night of the tomb, oh, you, my consoler, 5
Give me back Posilipo and the Italian sea,
The flower which delighted my desolate heart,
And the trellis where the vine and the roses marry.

Am I Eros or Phoebus, Lusignan or Biron?
My brow is still red with the kiss of the Queen; 10
I have dreamed in the grotto where the siren swims . . .

And twice have I, victor, crossed the Acheron:
Passing, in turn, on Orpheus' lyre
From the sighs of a saint to a fairy's cries.

THE LOST WINE

Paul Valéry

trans. by Barbara Howes (1914–)

One day into the sea I cast
(But where I cannot now divine)
As offering to oblivion,
My small store of precious wine . . .

What, oh rare liquor, willed your loss? 5
Some oracle half-understood?
Some hidden impulse of the heart
That made the poured wine seem like blood?

From this infusion of smoky rose
The sea regained its purity, 10
Its usual transparency . . .

Lost was the wine, and drunk the waves!
I saw high in the briny air
Forms unfathomed leaping there.

MEETING

Ted Hughes (1930–)

He smiles in a mirror, shrinking the whole
Sun-swung zodiac of light to a trinket shape
On the rise of his eye: it is a role

In which he can fling a cape,
And outloom life like Faustus. But once when 5
On an empty mountain slope

A black goat clattered and ran
Towards him, and set forefeet firm on a rock
Above and looked down

A square-pupilled yellow-eyed look, 10
The black devil head against the blue air,
What gigantic fingers took

Him up and on a bare
Palm turned him close under an eye
That was like a living hanging hemisphere 15

And watched his blood's gleam with a ray
Slow and cold and ferocious as a star
Till the goat clattered away.

THE THOUGHT-FOX

Ted Hughes (1930–)

I imagine this midnight moment's forest:
Something else is alive
Beside the clock's loneliness
And this blank page where my fingers move.

Through the window I see no star: 5
Something more near
Though deeper within darkness
Is entering the loneliness:

Cold, delicately as the dark snow,
A fox's nose touches twig, leaf; 10
Two eyes serve a movement, that now
And again now, and now, and now

Sets neat prints into the snow
Between trees, and warily a lame
Shadow lags by stump and in hollow 15
Of a body that is bold to come

Across clearings, an eye,
A widening deepening greenness,
Brilliantly, concentratedly,
Coming about its own business 20

Till, with a sudden sharp hot stink of fox
It enters the dark hole of the head.
The window is starless still; the clock ticks,
The page is printed.

THE JAGUAR

Ted Hughes (1930–   )

The apes yawn and adore their fleas in the sun.
The parrots shriek as if they were on fire, or strut
Like cheap tarts to attract the stroller with the nut.
Fatigued with indolence, tiger and lion

Lie still as the sun. The boa-constrictor's coil 5
Is a fossil. Cage after cage seems empty, or
Stinks of sleepers from the breathing straw.
It might be painted on a nursery wall.

But who runs like the rest past these arrives
At a cage where the crowd stands, stares,
  mesmerized, 10
As a child at a dream, at a jaguar hurrying enraged
Through prison darkness after the drills of his eyes

On a short fierce fuse. Not in boredom—
The eye satisfied to be blind in fire,
By the bang of blood in the brain deaf the ear— 15
He spins from the bars, but there's no cage to him

More than to the visionary his cell:
His stride is wildernesses of freedom:
The world rolls under the long thrust of his heel.
Over the cage floor the horizons come. 20

SLOW, SLOW, FRESH FOUNT

Ben Jonson (1573?–1637)

Slow, slow, fresh fount, keep time with my salt tears;
  Yet slower yet, oh faintly, gentle springs;
List to the heavy part the music bears,
  Woe weeps out her division when she sings.
    Droop herbs and flowers, 5
    Fall grief in showers:
    Our beauties are not ours;
      Oh, I could still,
Like melting snow upon some craggy hill,
  Drop, drop, drop, drop, 10
Since nature's pride is now a withered daffodil.

QUEEN AND HUNTRESS

Ben Jonson (1573?–1637)

Queen and huntress, chaste and fair,
Now the sun is laid to sleep,
Seated in thy silver chair
State in wonted manner keep;
  Hesperus entreats thy light, 5
  Goddess excellently bright.

Earth, let not thy envious shade
Dare itself to interpose;
Cynthia's shining orb was made
Heaven to clear, when day did close; 10
  Bless us then with wishèd sight,
  Goddess excellently bright.

Lay thy bow of pearl apart,
And thy crystal shining quiver;

Give unto the flying hart 15
Space to breathe, how short soever,
  Thou that mak'st a day of night,
  Goddess excellently bright.

HIS EXCUSE FOR LOVING

Ben Jonson (1573?–1637)

Let it not your wonder move,
Less your laughter, that I love.
Though I now write fifty years,
I have had, and have, my peers;
Poets though divine are men, 5
Some have loved as old again.
And it is not always face,
Clothes, or fortune, gives the grace,
Or the feature, or the youth;
But the language and the truth, 10
With the ardor and the passion,
Gives the lover weight and fashion.
If you then will read the story,
First prepare you to be sorry
That you never knew till now 15
Either whom to love, or how;
But be glad, as soon with me,
When you know that this is she
Of whose beauty it was sung:
She shall make the old man young, 20
Keep the middle age at stay,
And let nothing high decay;
Till she be the reason why
All the world for love may die.

HER TRIUMPH

Ben Jonson (1573?–1637)

See the chariot at hand here of love,
  Wherein my lady rideth!
Each that draws is a swan or a dove,
  And well the car love guideth.
As she goes all hearts do duty 5
    Unto her beauty,
And enamoured do wish so they might
    But enjoy such a sight,
That they still were to run by her side,
Through swords, through seas, whither she would ride. 10

Do but look on her eyes; they do light
  All that love's world compriseth!
Do but look on her hair; it is bright
  As love's star when it riseth!
Do but mark, her forehead's smoother 15
    Than words that soothe her;
And from her arched brows, such a grace
    Sheds itself through the face,
As alone there triumphs to the life
All the gain, all the good of the elements' strife. 20

Have you seen but a bright lily grow
  Before rude hands have touched it?
Ha' you marked but the fall o' the snow
  Before the soil hath smutched it?
Ha' you felt the wool of beaver, 25
    Or swan's down ever?
Or have smelt o' the bud o' the briar?
    Or the nard in the fire?
Or have tasted the bag of the bee?
O so white! O so soft! O so sweet is she! 30

TO PENSHURST

Ben Jonson (1573?–1637)

Thou art not, Penshurst, built to envious show
  Of touch or marble, nor canst boast a row
Of polished pillars, or a roof of gold;
  Thou hast no lantern whereof tales are told,
Or stairs or courts; but stand'st an ancient pile, 5
  And these, grudged at, art reverenced the while.
Thou joy'st in better marks, of soil, of air,
  Of wood, of water; therein thou art fair.
Thou hast thy walks for health as well as sport;
  Thy mount, to which the Dryads do resort, 10
Where Pan and Bacchus their high feasts have made
  Beneath the broad beech, and the chestnut shade,
That taller tree, which of a nut was set
  At his great birth, where all the Muses met.
There in the writhèd bark are cut the names 15
  Of many a sylvan, taken with his flames;
And thence the ruddy satyrs oft provoke
  The lighter fauns to reach thy Lady's oak.
Thy copse too, named of Gamage, thou hast there,
  That never fails to serve thee seasoned deer 20
When thou wouldst feast, or exercise thy friends.
  The lower land, that to the river bends,
Thy sheep, thy bullocks, kine, and calves do feed;
  The middle grounds thy mares and horses breed.
Each bank doth yield thee conies; and the tops, 25
  Fertile of wood, Ashore and Sidney's copse,
To crown thy open table, doth provide
  The purpled pheasant with the speckled side;
The painted partridge lies in every field,
  And, for thy mess, is willing to be killed. 30
And if the high-swollen Medway fail thy dish,

Thou hast thy ponds that pay thee tribute fish,
Fat agèd carps that run into thy net,
And pikes, now weary their own kind to eat,
As loath the second draught or cast to stay, 35
Officiously at first themselves betray;
Bright eels that emulate them, and leap on land
Before the fisher, or into his hand.
Then hath thy orchard fruit, thy garden flowers
Fresh as the air, and new as are the hours. 40
The early cherry, with the later plum,
Fig, grape, and quince, each in his time doth come;
The blushing apricot and woolly peach
Hang on thy walls, that every child may reach.
And though thy walls be of the country stone, 45
They'are reared with no man's ruin, no man's groan;
There's none that dwell about them wish them down,
But all come in, the farmer and the clown,
And no one empty handed, to salute
Thy lord and lady, though they have no suit. 50
Some bring a capon, some a rural cake,
Some nuts, some apples; some that think they make
The better cheeses bring 'em, or else send
By their ripe daughters whom they would commend
This way to husbands, and whose baskets bear 55
An emblem of themselves in plum or pear.
But what can this, more than express their love,
Add to thy free provisions, far above
The need of such, whose liberal board doth flow
With all that hospitality doth know? 60
Where comes no guest but is allowed to eat
Without his fear, and of thy lord's own meat;
Where the same beer and bread, and self-same wine
That is his lordship's shall be also mine.
And I not fain to sit, as some this day 65
At great men's tables, and yet dine away.

Here no man tells my cups, nor, standing by,
  A waiter doth my gluttony envý,
But gives me what I call and lets me eat;
  He knows below he shall find plenty of meat. 70
Thy tables hoard not up for the next day,
  Nor when I take my lodging need I pray
For fire or lights or livery; all is there
  As if thou then wert mine, or I reigned here;
There's nothing I can wish, for which I stay. 75
  That found King James, when hunting late this way
With his brave son, the prince, they saw thy fires
  Shine bright on every hearth as the desires
Of thy Penates had been set on flame
  To entertain them, or the country came 80
With all their zeal to warm their welcome here.
  What great I will not say, but sudden cheer
Didst thou then make 'em! and what praise was heaped
  On thy good lady then! who therein reaped
The just reward of her high huswifery; 85
  To have her linen, plate, and all things nigh
When she was far, and not a room but dressed
  As if it had expected such a guest!
These, Penshurst, are thy praise, and yet not all.
  Thy lady's noble, fruitful, chaste withal; 90
His children thy great lord may call his own,
  A fortune in this age but rarely known.
They are and have been taught religion; thence
  Their gentler spirits have sucked innocence.
Each morn and even they are taught to pray 95
  With the whole household, and may every day
Read, in their virtuous parents' noble parts,
  The mysteries of manners, arms, and arts.
Now, Penshurst, they that will proportion thee
  With other edifices when they see 100

Those proud, ambitious heaps and nothing else,
May say, their lords have built, but thy lord dwells.

Line 1. Penshurst: the Sidney country place in Kent
Line 2. touch: touchstone
Line 4. lantern: light tower
Line 14. his: Sir Philip Sidney
Line 19. Gamage: Barbara Gamage, wife of the owner of Penshurst, Sir Robert Sidney, younger brother of Sir Philip
Line 48. clown: rustic
Line 67. tells: counts

ANNIVERSARIES

Donald Justice (1925–)

Great Leo roared at my birth,
The windowpanes were lit
With stars' applausive light,
And I have heard that the earth
As far away as Japan 5
Was shaken again and again
The morning I came forth.
Many drew round me then,
Admiring. Beside my bed
The tall aunts prophesied, 10
And cousins from afar,
Predicting a great career.

At ten there came an hour
When, waking out of ether
Into an autumn weather 15
Inexpressibly dear,
I was wheeled superb in a chair
Past vacant lots in bloom
With goldenrod and with broom,
In secret proud of the scar 20

Dividing me from life,
Which I could admire like one
Come down from Mars or the moon,
Standing a little off.

By seventeen I had guessed 25
That the "really great loneliness"
Of James's governess
Might account for the ghost
On the other side of the lake.
Oh, all that year was lost 30
Somewhere among the black
Keys of Chopin! I sat
All afternoon after school,
Fingering his ripe heart,
While boys outside in the dirt 35
Kicked, up and down, their ball.

Thirty today, I saw
The trees flare briefly like
The candles upon a cake
As the sun went down the sky, 40
A momentary flash,
Yet there was time to wish
Before the light could die,
If I had known what to wish,
As once I must have known, 45
Bending above the clean,
Candlelit tablecloth
To blow them out with a breath.

LANDSCAPE WITH LITTLE FIGURES

Donald Justice (1925–)

There once were some pines, a canal, a piece of sky.
The pines are the houses now of the very poor,

Huddled together, in a blue, ragged wind.
Children go whistling their dogs, down by the mudflats,
Once the canal. There's a red ball lost in the weeds. 5
It's winter, it's after supper, it's goodbye.
O goodbye to the houses, the children, the little red ball,
And the pieces of sky that will go on falling for days.

A DREAM SESTINA

Donald Justice (1925–)

I woke by first light in a wood
Right in the shadow of a hill
And saw about me in a circle
Many I knew, the dear faces
Of some I recognized as friends. 5
I knew that I had lost my way.

I asked if any knew the way.
They stared at me like blocks of wood.
They turned their backs on me, those friends,
And struggled up the stubborn hill 10
Along that road which makes a circle.
No longer could I see their faces.

But there were trees with human faces.
Afraid, I ran a little way
But must have wandered in a circle. 15
I had not left that human wood;
I was no farther up the hill.
And all the while I heard my friends

Discussing me, but not like friends.
Through gaps in trees I glimpsed their faces. 20
(The trees grow crooked on that hill.)
Now all at once I saw the way:

Above a clearing in the wood
A lone bird wheeling in a circle,

And in that shadowed space the circle 25
Of those I thought of still as friends.
I drew near, calling, and the wood
Rang and they turned their deaf faces
This way and that, but not my way.
They rose and danced upon the hill. 30

And it grew dark. Behind the hill
The sun slid down, a fiery circle;
Screeching, the bird flew on her way.
It was too dark to see my friends.
But then I saw them, and their faces 35
Were leaning above me like a wood.

Round me they circle on the hill.
But what is wrong with my friends' faces?
Why have they changed that way to wood?

COUNTING THE MAD

Donald Justice (1925–)

This one was put in a jacket,
This one was sent home,
This one was given bread and meat
But would eat none,
And this one cried No No No No 5
All day long.

This one looked at the window
As though it were a wall,
This one saw things that were not there,
This one things that were, 10
And this one cried No No No No
All day long.

This one thought himself a bird,
This one a dog,
And this one thought himself a man, 15
An ordinary man,
And cried and cried No No No No
All day long.

FISHING HARBOUR TOWARDS EVENING

Richard Kell (1927–)

Slashed clouds leak gold. Along the slurping wharf
The snugged boats creak and seesaw. Round the masts

Abrasive squalls flake seagulls off the sky:
Choppy with wings the rapids of shrill sound.

Wrapt in spliced airs of fish and tar, 5
Light wincing on their knives, the clockwork men

Incise and scoop the oily pouches, flip
The soft guts overboard with blood-wet fingers.

Among three rhythms the slapping silver turns
To polished icy marble upon the deck. 10

THE SWAN

Richard Kell (1927–)

Nothing more serene than the fluid neck,
The body curved like snow on foliage,
And split reflection moving smooth as oil.

But something wrecks the tranquil certainty:
The clean-cut shape unfolds; an evil wind 5
Tears its roots out of the fertile water.

The pattern's tugged awry—the neck rammed stiff,
Cumbrous wings whacking the startled air—
And terror swirls the surface of the lake.

NOTE UPON A MANNER OF LIVING

Arnold Kenseth (1915–   )

Earth-bound and dragged by body to the feast,
The Smiths enjoy snug comfort at the table,
Imbibe their drinks, attend the current fable
At the Orpheum. Happy is the beast
When the blood purrs, happy when belly heat 5
Mounts from the body's furnace to the chin;
When sex, sly and with padded house-cat feet,
Walks on the maiden membranes of the skin.

And now arouse the napping bones and drive
Home to the old adventure of the bed, 10
To stroke the animal to sleep, to wed
Forgetfulness again, and so survive.
For midnight at the corner is alive
And sky is falling inward overhead.

ELEGY

Arnold Kenseth (1915–   )

It was there I went
In the hot summer
To the dried field
Behind spruces, intent

On the priest cry 5
Of the mourning doves.
O the amen, the amen,
Low and sad in that field

Dried and withered
Like the world, 10

Where the doves shook joy
From the dust in the hollows.

But never a dove was seen.
Only the amen's fall
And its fade-away 15
Far among trees.

O STAND ME MASSIVE, THEN

Arnold Kenseth (1915–)

O stand me massive, then,
Against all mortal evil;
Against my midnights when
My amorous devil

Shrives me as white as bone 5
And shrewdly winks me in
To the rituals that condone,
To the magic of more sin.

Or, when he shoulders over me,
Let heaven's tumbling dove 10
With bright wings hover over me
And put between us love.

From bread of stone and power,
The eucharist of mammon,
Defend me at each hour 15
In penitential famine.

And should I like old Faust
Against You tower me,
Or money-lend my ghost
For science on a tree: 20

Scatter me in anger,
Let my tongues bell wild;

Church me in the manger
Save me in the Child.

THE BLUE UMBRELLA

Stanley Koehler (1915–)

From tide to tide
we lay under a blue shade.
The water's edge crept up: we slept
by children at their play,

and not one thought 5
of ocean took us.
No notion of the done undoing
in the green wave

till hours older
I stepped where I could 10
on wider sand, and watched.
Never a castle

we had bent to
or wryly wrought shadowed
the shining plain, yet there 15
between the loose sand

and the sea, how
far from me my children
built again.
Sun, that will
drive them thence, 20

these hours undo me.
I think of a blue umbrella set
at flood, pitched close
to what was dark

and under tide, 25
it may be, for a mark

they could make out, whatever ebbs
they knelt beside.

TWO BY THE FORSYTHIA

Stanley Koehler (1915–)

Black bird, alighting, moves
wing shadows on the green lawn.
For a moment, a minor statue, then
slur, in a blur of legs.

By the drapery of a bush 5
the watcher hides his motion, all
but the tail; the brittle legs
pause again, black neighboring black.

Stiller is a cat's breath
than worms, or insect's clamor. 10
I will take on a stick
the flesh he lets rot

to be fragrant in some other
spring, and on these same boughs.
Is it hate or hunger 15
that keeps this beast well-fed?

He is here for beauty;
the effect is made
by shadow and sharp motion where
these yellow blossoms fall. 20

WAR

Joseph Langland (1917–)

When my young brother was killed
By a mute and dusty shell in the thorny brush
Crowning the boulders of the Villa Verde Trail
On the island of Luzon,

I laid my whole dry body down, 5
Dropping my face like a stone in a green park
On the east banks of the Rhine;

On an airstrip skirting the Seine
His sergeant brother sat like a stick in his barracks
While cracks of fading sunlight 10
Caged the dusty air;

In the rocky rolling hills west of the Mississippi
His father and mother sat in a simple Norwegian parlor
With a photograph smiling between them on the table
And their hands fallen into their laps 15
Like sticks and dust;

And still other brothers and sisters,
Linking their arms together,
Walked down the dusty road where once he ran
And into the deep green valley 20
To sit on the stony banks of the stream he loved
And let the murmuring waters
Wash over their blood-hot feet with a springing crown of tears.

CRANE

Joseph Langland (1917–)

One day when childhood tumbled the spongy tufts
Banking the naked edge of our bottomlands
A shadowy sand-hill crane
Arose from Rocky Spring with a flipping fish,
A speckled rainbow, 5
Speared in her slim black bill.
She offered her wings in sluggish waves,
Wading impossibly up the slapping waters,
And ascended the crystal floods.

Under that dark ark 10
Two grappling anchors of dangling legs
Rolled away so smoothly the eye forgot them
Until that tall ungainly crane
Lay in the sky like a dream.
Her snaking head 15
Pivoted vaguely over our deep, green valley
And straightened to kiss the horizon.
Fish and crane
Swam through the white bowl of blue air,
Spinning outward upon 20
Mountainous heights and their soft mysterious pulleys.

My naked shoulders ached for the tumbling clouds,
And my shivering legs
Thrashed through those mossy fishing meadows,
Over the rose-pebbled bottoms, 25
And churned in the chilled and iridescent spawn
Of the crane's pool.
Clamped and flexed in the vise of her beating wings
Now flaring astride the brassy eye of the sun,
I gasped like a fish 30
Hung out in the harsh and sudden air
And flipped, past sparkling regions, underground.

SACRIFICE OF A GUNNYSACK OF CATS

Joseph Langland (1917–)

The quick small bubbles popping from the gunnysack,
Hooked by a pitchfork braced in the cattle tank,
Almost unhinged my heart and made me drop
The stick with which I forced the young cats down.

A population explosion, that's what it was. 5
With twelve mother cats and a year of visiting toms

We met September with the wildest host
Of squinting eyes behind our milking cows.

We divvied them up among the brothers and sisters,
And each had only six. But since we were nine 10
My father thought things were getting out of hand.
Next day I received my melancholy orders.

"You'll have to catch the most of them and drown them.
Just tidy up the place and make it normal.
Fifty-four cats! Why, that's an infernal nuisance. 15
Think what would happen next year!" What could I tell him?

So there I was dashing with my gunnysack
Into the bins and under the stalls and mangers.
The wild ones scratched me, but I thrust them in.
The tame ones? Oh, I brushed them with my cheek, 20

Sighed and kissed them, then I thrust them in.
I climbed the ladders to the highest mows,
Ran through the orchard under the heavy apples
And crept among the tall weeds by the granary,

Until I thought I could not bear that cross. 25
I dropped it once; that made it twice as hard
To lure them once again into that womb
And bear it backward to the spermal waters.

But there I was: filthy, bleeding, and sick,
Tired and thirsty, my cord pulled at its neck, 30
The undulating coffin on my waggon,
Trudging down to the sea, my cross upon me.

The thorny dissonance of dying song
Over the squealing of the waggon wheels
Ran up a cloud of dust that nearly drowned me. 35
It is one thing to think, and one to do.

I wanted to avoid the thinking in the doing
And, quick, be done with it and off to play.

But you can see this didn't work too well. . . .
Thirty-three years to get that cord untied. 40

I stood in the dust manure at my feet,
The green scum in the corners of the tank
Eyeing my smothering conscience toward a size
My body could not hold. Good God, I seized

That squirming sepulchre, that crying tomb, 45
That leaping heart familiar as myself,
And heaved it from my homemade hearse and plunged
It back to evolution. Hooking the fork,

I ticked five awful minutes by the hours,
Damned by the furious bubbles where they broke 50
Among my unwashed hands. And then I went
Up to the barn to find my mother cat.

We sat in a beam of sunlight on the floor
Petting and purring, while out of a knothole eye
Hung in the roof of God the motes of dust 55
Sang of our comforts and our curious loves.

A HAPPENING

Denise Levertov (1923–)

Two birds, flying East, hit the night
at 3 in the afternoon; stars came out
over the badlands, and the billowy
snowlands; they floundered on
resolving not to turn back in search 5
of lost afternoon; continuing
through cotton wildernesses
through the stretched night
and caught up with dawn in a rainstorm
in the City, where they fell 10

in semblance of torn paper sacks
to the sidewalk on 42nd St., and resumed
their human shape, and separated:
one turned uptown, to follow
the Broadway river to its possible source, 15
the other downtown, to see
the fair and goodly harbor; but each,
accosted by shadows that muttered to him
pleading mysteriously, half-hostile, was drawn
into crosstown streets, into 20
revolving doorways, into nameless
small spaces back of buildings,
airless airshafts, till no more
was known of man, bird, nor paper.

TO THE SNAKE

Denise Levertov (1923–)

Green Snake, when I hung you round my neck
and stroked your cold, pulsing throat
  as you hissed to me, glinting
arrowy gold scales, and I felt
  the weight of you on my shoulders, 5
and the whispering silver of your dryness
  sounded close at my ears—

Green Snake—I swore to my companions that certainly
  you were harmless! But truly
I had no certainty, and no hope, only desiring 10
  to hold you, for that joy,
                which left
a long wake of pleasure, as the leaves moved
and you faded into the pattern
of grass and shadows, and I returned
smiling and haunted, to a dark morning. 15

THE DEPARTURE

Denise Levertov (1923–   )

Have you got the moon safe?
Please, tie those strings a little tighter.
This loaf, push it down further
the light is crushing it—such a baguette
golden brown and so white inside 5
you don't see every day
nowadays. And for god's sake
don't let's leave in the end
without the ocean! Put it
in there among the shoes, and 10
tie the moon on behind. It's time!

ROSALIND'S MADRIGAL

Thomas Lodge (1558–1625)

Love in my bosom like a bee
  Doth suck his sweet;
Now with his wings he plays with me,
  Now with his feet.
Within mine eyes he makes his nest, 5
His bed amidst my tender breast,
My kisses are his daily feast,
And yet he robs me of my rest—
  Ah, wanton, will ye?

And if I sleep, then percheth he 10
  With pretty flight,
And makes his pillow of my knee
  The livelong night.
Strike I my lute, he tunes the string,

He music plays if so I sing, 15
He lends me every lovely thing,
Yet cruel he my heart doth sting—
  Whist, wanton, still ye!

Else I with roses every day
  Will whip you hence, 20
And bind you, when you long to play,
  For your offence.
I'll shut mine eyes to keep you in,
I'll make you fast it for your sin,
I'll count your power not worth a pin; 25
Alas! what hereby shall I win
  If he gainsay me?

What if I beat the wanton boy
  With many a rod?
He will repay me with annoy, 30
  Because a god.
Then sit thou safely on my knee,
And let thy bower my bosom be,
Lurk in mine eyes, I like of thee.
O Cupid, so thou pity me, 35
  Spare not, but play thee!

TO LUCASTA,

Going to the wars

Richard Lovelace (1618–1657)

Tell me not, Sweet, I am unkind,
  That from the nunnery
Of thy chaste breast, and quiet mind,
  To war and arms I fly.

True, a new mistress now I chase, 5
  The first foe in the field;

And with a stronger faith embrace
  A sword, a horse, a shield.

Yet this inconstancy is such,
  As you too shall adore; 10
I could not love thee, Dear, so much,
  Lov'd I not honor more.

TO ALTHEA, FROM PRISON

Richard Lovelace (1618–1657)

When Love with unconfinèd wings
  Hovers within my gates;
And my divine Althea brings
  To whisper at the grates:
When I lie tangled in her hair, 5
  And fetter'd to her eye;
The gods that wanton in the air,
  Know no such liberty.

When flowing cups run swiftly round
  With no allaying Thames, 10
Our careless heads with roses bound,
  Our hearts with loyal flames;
When thirsty grief in wine we steep,
  When healths and draughts go free,
Fishes that tipple in the deep, 15
  Know no such liberty.

When, like committed linnets, I
  With shriller throat shall sing
The sweetness, mercy, majesty,
  And glories of my King; 20
When I shall voice aloud, how good
  He is, how great should be;

Enlargèd winds that curl the flood,
Know no such liberty.

Stone walls do not a prison make, 25
Nor iron bars a cage;
Minds innocent and quiet take
That for an hermitage;
If I have freedom in my love,
And in my soul am free; 30
Angels alone that soar above
Enjoy such liberty.

CHRISTMAS EVE UNDER HOOKER'S STATUE

Robert Lowell (1917–)

Tonight a blackout. Twenty years ago
I hung my stocking on the tree, and hell's
Serpent entwined the apple in the toe
To sting the child with knowledge. Hooker's heels
Kicking at nothing in the shifting snow, 5
A cannon and a cairn of cannon balls
Rusting before the blackened Statehouse, know
How the long horn of plenty broke like glass
In Hooker's gauntlets. Once I came from Mass;

Now storm-clouds shelter Christmas, once again 10
Mars meets his fruitless star with open arms,
His heavy sabre flashes with the rime,
The war-god's bronzed and empty forehead forms
Anonymous machinery from raw men;
The cannon on the Common cannot stun 15
The blundering butcher as he rides on Time—
The barrel clinks with holly. I am cold:
I ask for bread, my father gives me mould;

His stocking is full of stones, Santa in red
Is crowned with wizened berries. Man of war, 20
Where is the summer's garden? In its bed

The ancient speckled serpent will appear,
And black-eyed susan with her frizzled head.
When Chancellorsville mowed down the volunteer,
"All wars are boyish," Herman Melville said; 25
But we are old, our fields are running wild:
Till Christ again turn wanderer and child.

THE PASSIONATE SHEPHERD TO HIS LOVE

Christopher Marlowe (1564–1593)

Come live with me and be my love,
And we will all the pleasures prove
That valleys, groves, hills, and fields,
Woods, or steepy mountain yields.

And we will sit upon the rocks, 5
Seeing the shepherds feed their flocks,
By shallow rivers to whose falls
Melodious birds sing madrigals.

And I will make thee beds of roses
And a thousand fragrant posies, 10
A cap of flowers, and a kirtle
Embroidered all with leaves of myrtle;

A gown made of the finest wool
Which from our pretty lambs we pull;
Fair linèd slippers for the cold, 15
With buckles of the purest gold;

A belt of straw and ivy buds,
With coral clasps and amber studs:
And if these pleasures may thee move,
Come live with me, and be my love. 20

The shepherds' swains shall dance and sing
For thy delight each May morning:
If these delights thy mind may move,
Then live with me and be my love.

THE MOWER TO THE GLOW-WORMS

Andrew Marvell (1621–1678)

I

Ye living lamps, by whose dear light
The nightingale does sit so late,
And studying all the summer night,
Her matchless songs does meditate;

II

Ye country comets, that portend 5
No war nor prince's funeral,
Shining unto no higher end
Than to presage the grass's fall;

III

Ye glow-worms, whose officious flame
To wandering mowers shows the way, 10
That in the night have lost their aim,
And after foolish fires do stray;

IV

Your courteous lights in vain you waste,
Since JULIANA here is come,
For she my mind hath so displaced, 15
That I shall never find my home.

THE DEFINITION OF LOVE

Andrew Marvell (1621–1678)

My love is of a birth as rare
As 'tis for object strange and high;

It was begotten by despair
Upon impossibility.

Magnanimous despair alone 5
Could show me so divine a thing,
Where feeble hope could ne'er have flown,
But vainly flapped its tinsel wing.

And yet I quickly might arrive
Where my extended soul is fixed, 10
But fate does iron wedges drive,
And always crowds itself betwixt.

For fate with jealous eye does see
Two perfect loves, nor lets them close;
Their union would her ruin be, 15
And her tyrannic power depose.

And therefore her decrees of steel
Us as the distant poles have placed,
Though love's whole world on us doth wheel,
Not by themselves to be embraced; 20

Unless the giddy heaven fall,
And earth some new convulsion tear,
And, us to join, the world should all
Be cramped into a planisphere.

As lines, so loves, oblique may well 25
Themselves in every angle greet;
But ours so truly parallel,
Though infinite, can never meet.

Therefore the love which us doth bind,
But fate so enviously debars, 30
Is the conjunction of the mind,
And opposition of the stars.

SHILOH

A Requiem (April, 1862)

Herman Melville (1819–1891)

Skimming lightly, wheeling still,
  The swallows fly low
Over the field in clouded days,
  The forest-field of Shiloh—
Over the field where April rain 5
Solaced the parched ones stretched in pain
Through the pause of night
That followed the Sunday fight
  Around the church of Shiloh—
The church so lone, the log-built one, 10
That echoed to many a parting groan
    And natural prayer
  Of dying foemen mingled there—
Foemen at morn, but friends at eve—
  Fame or country least their care: 15
(What like a bullet can undeceive!)
  But now they lie low,
While over them the swallows skim,
  And all is hushed at Shiloh.

MONODY

Herman Melville (1819–1891)

To have known him, to have loved him
  After loneness long;
And then to be estranged in life,
  And neither in the wrong;
And now for death to set his seal— 5
  Ease me, a little ease, my song!

By wintry hills his hermit-mound
  The sheeted snow-drifts drape,
And houseless there the snow-bird flits
  Beneath the fir-trees' crape: 10
Glazed now with ice the cloistral vine
  That hid the shyest grape.

ON THE LATE MASSACRE IN PIEDMONT

John Milton (1608–1674)

Avenge, O Lord, thy slaughtered saints, whose bones
  Lie scattered on the Alpine mountains cold;
  Even them who kept thy truth so pure of old,
  When all our fathers worshiped stocks and stones,
Forget not: in thy book record their groans 5
  Who were thy sheep, and in their ancient fold
  Slain by the bloody Piemontese, that rolled
  Mother with infant down the rocks. Their moans
The vales redoubled to the hills, and they
  To heaven. Their martyred blood and ashes sow 10
  O'er all the Italian fields, where still doth sway
The triple Tyrant; that from these may grow
  A hundredfold, who, having learnt thy way,
  Early may fly the Babylonian woe.

ON HIS DECEASED WIFE

John Milton (1608–1674)

Methought I saw my late espousèd saint
  Brought to me like Alcestis from the grave,
  Whom Jove's great son to her glad husband gave,
  Rescued from Death by force, though pale and faint.
Mine, as whom washed from spot of childbed taint 5
  Purification in the Old Law did save,

And such as yet once more I trust to have
Full sight of her in Heav'n without restraint,
Came vested all in white, pure as her mind.
Her face was veiled; yet to my fancied sight 10
Love, sweetness, goodness, in her person shined
So clear as in no face with more delight.
But, O! as to embrace me she inclined,
I waked, she fled, and day brought back my night.

THE FIRST INVASION OF IRELAND

For Michael Walsh

John Montague (1929–)

According to Leabhar Gabhala, The Book of Conquests, the first invasion of Ireland was by relatives of Noah, just before the Flood. Refused entry into the Ark, they consulted an idol which told them to flee to Ireland. There were three men and fifty-one women in the party and their behaviour had so little in common with subsequent tradition in Ireland that one must take the story to be mythological.

Fleeing from threatened flood, they sailed,
Seeking the fair island, without serpent or claw;
From the deck of their hasty windjammer watched
The soft edge of Ireland nearward draw.

A sweet confluence of waters, a trinity of rivers, 5
Was their first resting place:
They unloaded the women and the sensual idol,
Guiding image of their disgrace.

Division of damsels they did there,
The slender, the tender, the dimpled, the round, 10
It was the first just bargain in Ireland,
There was enough to go around.

Lightly they lay and pleasured
In the green grass of that guileless place:

Ladhra was the first to die; 15
He perished of an embrace.

Bith was buried in a stone heap,
Riot of mind, all passion spent.
Fintan fled from the ferocious women
Before he, too, by love was rent. 20

Great primitive princes of our line
They were the first, with stately freedom
To sleep with women in Ireland:
Soft the eternal bed they lie upon.

On a lonely headland the women assembled, 25
Chill as worshippers in a nave,
And watched the eastern waters gather
Into a great virile flooding wave.

THE DROWNING OF A NOVICE

Richard Murphy (1927–   )

At Easter he came
with a March wind blowing,
A lapsed Benedictine
whose mind was fabling

An island where the monks 5
like cormorants
Fished from the rocks
in black garments.

He thought he could quietly
with his own boat 10
Be fed by the sea;
and with a spade

In winter find cockles
and clams to eat.

But for her novice
the sea grew white 15

Flowers in her garden
petalled with spray.
He had brought no chart
and he lost his way. 20

Where was the pebbled cove
and the famine cottage?
His fingers piano soft
ached at the oars.

Book-disputes that he dreaded 25
reared up in waves,
His catechized head
was coldly doused.

Now his feet were washed
in the sluicing bilges. 30
For his last swim
there were no prizes.

When his dinghy went down
at a sheer shore
And the swell slogging, 35
his arms opened

As if to his mother,
and he drowned.
An island beachcomber
picked up an oar. 40

TO ROBERT EARL OF OXFORD AND EARL MORTIMER

Alexander Pope (1688–1744)

Such were the notes thy once-loved poet sung,
Till death untimely stopped his tuneful tongue.

Oh just beheld, and lost! admired and mourned!
With softest manners, gentlest arts adorned!
Blest in each science, blest in every strain! 5
Dear to the Muse! to Harley dear—in vain!
For him, thou oft hast bid the world attend,
Fond to forget the statesman in the friend;
For Swift and him, despised the farce of state,
The sober follies of the wise and great; 10
Dexterous, the craving, fawning crowd to quit,
And pleased to 'scape from flattery to wit.
Absent or dead, still let a friend be dear,
(A sigh the absent claims, the dead a tear)
Recall those nights that closed thy toilsome days, 15
Still hear thy Parnell in his living lays,
Who, careless now of interest, fame, or fate,
Perhaps forgets that *Oxford* e'er was great;
Or deeming meanest what we greatest call,
Beholds thee glorious only in thy fall. 20
And sure, if aught below the seats divine
Can touch immortals, 'tis a soul like thine:
A soul supreme, in each hard instance tried,
Above all pain, all passion, and all pride,
The rage of power, the blast of public breath, 25
The lust of lucre, and the dread of death.
In vain to deserts thy retreat is made;
The Muse attends thee to the silent shade:
'Tis hers the brave man's latest steps to trace,
Rejudge his acts, and dignify disgrace. 30
When interest calls off all her sneaking train,
And all th' obliged desert, and all the vain;
She waits, or to the scaffold, or the cell,
When the last lingering friend has bid farewell.
Even now, she shades thy evening-walk with bays 35
(No hireling she, no prostitute to praise)
Even now, observant of the parting ray,
Eyes the calm sunset of thy various day,

Through fortune's cloud one truly great can see,
Nor fears to tell, that MORTIMER is he. 40

A VIRGINAL

Ezra Pound (1885–)

No, no! Go from me. I have left her lately.
I will not spoil my sheath with lesser brightness,
For my surrounding air hath a new lightness;
Slight are her arms, yet they have bound me straitly
And left me cloaked as with a gauze of aether; 5
As with sweet leaves, as with subtle clearness.
Oh, I have picked up magic in her nearness
To sheathe me half in half the things that sheathe her.
No, no! Go from me. I have still the flavour,
Soft as spring wind that's come from birchen bowers. 10
Green come the shoots, aye April in the branches,
As winter's wound with her sleight hand she staunches,
Hath of the trees a likeness of the savour:
As white their bark, so white this lady's hours.

THE RETURN

Ezra Pound (1885–)

See, they return; ah, see the tentative
Movements, and the slow feet,
The trouble in the pace and the uncertain
Wavering!

See, they return, one, and by one, 5
With fear, as half-awakened;
As if the snow should hesitate
And murmur in the wind,
                    and half turn back;

These were the "Wing'd-with-Awe," 10
Inviolable.

Gods of the wingèd shoe!
With them the silver hounds,
sniffing the trace of air!

Haie! Haie! 15
These were the swift to harry;
These the keen-scented;
These were the souls of blood.

Slow on the leash,
pallid the leash-men! 20

ENVOI

Ezra Pound (1885–)

Go, dumb-born book,
Tell her that sang me once that song of Lawes:
Hadst thou but song
As thou hast subjects known,
Then were there cause in thee that should condone 5
Even my faults that heavy upon me lie,
And build her glories their longevity.

Tell her that sheds
Such treasure in the air,
Recking naught else but that her graces give 10
Life to the moment,
I would bid them live
As roses might, in magic amber laid,
Red overwrought with orange and all made
One substance and one colour 15
Braving time.

Tell her that goes
With song upon her lips

But sings not out the song, nor knows
The maker of it, some other mouth, 20
May be as fair as hers,
Might, in new ages, gain her worshippers,
When our two dusts with Waller's shall be laid,
Siftings on siftings in oblivion,
Till change hath broken down 25
All things save Beauty alone.

THE TALL GIRL

John Crowe Ransom (1888–)

The Queens of Hell had lissome necks to crane
At the tall girl approaching with long tread
And, when she was caught up even with them, nodded:
"If the young miss with gold hair might not disdain,
We would esteem her company over the plain, 5
To profit us all where the dogs will be out barking;
And we'll walk by the windows where the young men are working
And to-morrow we will all come home again."

But the Queen of Heaven on the other side of the road
In the likeness, I hear, of a fine motherly woman 10
Made a wry face, despite it was so common
To be worsted by the smooth ladies of hell,
And crisped her sweet tongue: "This never will come to good!
Just an old woman, my pet, that wishes you well."

WINTER REMEMBERED

John Crowe Ransom (1888–)

Two evils, monstrous either one apart,
Possessed me, and were long and loath at going:
A cry of Absence, Absence, in the heart,
And in the wood the furious winter blowing.

Think not, when fire was bright upon my bricks, 5
And past the tight boards hardly a wind could enter,
I glowed like them, the simple burning sticks,
Far from my cause, my proper heat and centre.

Better to walk forth in the murderous air
And wash my wound in the snows; that would be
healing; 10
Because my heart would throb less painful there,
Being caked with cold, and past the smart of feeling.

And where I went, the hugest winter blast
Would have this body bowed, these eyeballs streaming,
And though I think this heart's blood froze not fast, 15
It ran too small to spare one drop for dreaming.

Dear love, these fingers that had known your touch,
And tied our separate forces first together,
Were ten poor idiot fingers not worth much,
Ten frozen parsnips hanging in the weather. 20

BELLS FOR JOHN WHITESIDE'S DAUGHTER

John Crowe Ransom (1888–)

There was such speed in her little body,
And such lightness in her footfall,
It is no wonder that her brown study
Astonishes us all.

Her wars were bruited in our high window. 5
We looked among orchard trees and beyond,
Where she took arms against her shadow,
Or harried unto the pond

The lazy geese, like a snow cloud
Dripping their snow on the green grass, 10
Tricking and stopping, sleepy and proud,
Who cried in goose, Alas,

For the tireless heart within the little
Lady with rod that made them rise
From their noon apple dreams, and scuttle 15
Goose-fashion under the skies!

But now go the bells, and we are ready;
In one house we are sternly stopped
To say we are vexed at her brown study,
Lying so primly propped. 20

LESSONS OF THE WAR

To Alan Michell

Henry Reed (1914–)

Vixi duellis nuper idoneus
Et militavi non sine gloria

I. Naming of Parts

Today we have naming of parts. Yesterday,
We had daily cleaning. And tomorrow morning,
We shall have what to do after firing. But today,
Today we have naming of parts. Japonica
Glistens like coral in all of the neighboring gardens, 5
And today we have naming of parts.

This is the lower sling swivel. And this
Is the upper sling swivel, whose use you will see,
When you are given your slings. And this is the piling swivel,
Which in your case you have not got. The branches 10
Hold in the gardens their silent, eloquent gestures,
Which in our case we have not got.

This is the safety-catch, which is always released
With an easy flick of the thumb. And please do not let me
See anyone using his finger. You can do it quite easy 15
If you have any strength in your thumb. The blossoms

Are fragile and motionless, never letting anyone see
    Any of them using their finger.

And this you can see is the bolt. The purpose of this
Is to open the breech, as you see. We can slide it 20
Rapidly backwards and forwards: we call this
Easing the spring. And rapidly backwards and forwards
The early bees are assaulting and fumbling the flowers:
    They call it easing the Spring.

They call it easing the Spring: it is perfectly easy 25
If you have any strength in your thumb: like the bolt,
And the breech, and the cocking-piece, and the point of balance,
Which in our case we have not got; and the almond-blossom
Silent in all of the gardens and the bees going backwards and
    forwards,
    For today we have naming of parts. 30

FOR A DEAD LADY

Edwin Arlington Robinson (1869–1935)

No more with overflowing light
Shall fill the eyes that now are faded,
Nor shall another's fringe with night
Their woman-hidden world as they did.
No more shall quiver down the days 5
The flowing wonder of her ways,
Whereof no language may requite
The shifting and the many-shaded.

The grace, divine, definitive,
Clings only as a faint forestalling; 10
The laugh that love could not forgive
Is hushed, and answers to no calling;
The forehead and the little ears
Have gone where Saturn keeps the years;

The breast where roses could not live 15
Has done with rising and with falling.

The beauty, shattered by the laws
That have creation in their keeping,
No longer trembles at applause,
Or over children that are sleeping; 20
And we who delve in beauty's lore
Know all that we have known before
Of what inexorable cause
Makes Time so vicious in his reaping.

MR. FLOOD'S PARTY

Edwin Arlington Robinson (1869–1935)

Old Eben Flood, climbing alone one night
Over the hill between the town below
And the forsaken upland hermitage
That held as much as he should ever know
On earth again of home, paused warily. 5
The road was his with not a native near;
And Eben, having leisure, said aloud,
For no man else in Tilbury Town to hear:

"Well, Mr. Flood, we have the harvest moon
Again, and we may not have many more; 10
The bird is on the wing, the poet says,
And you and I have said it here before.
Drink to the bird." He raised up to the light
The jug that he had gone so far to fill,
And answered huskily: "Well, Mr. Flood, 15
Since you propose it, I believe I will."

Alone, as if enduring to the end
A valiant armor of scarred hopes outworn,
He stood there in the middle of the road

Like Roland's ghost winding a silent horn. 20
Below him, in the town among the trees,
Where friends of other days had honored him,
A phantom salutation of the dead
Rang thinly till old Eben's eyes were dim.

Then, as a mother lays her sleeping child 25
Down tenderly, fearing it may awake,
He set the jug down slowly at his feet
With trembling care, knowing that most things break;
And only when assured that on firm earth
It stood, as the uncertain lives of men 30
Assuredly did not, he paced away,
And with his hand extended paused again:

"Well, Mr. Flood, we have not met like this
In a long time; and many a change has come
To both of us, I fear, since last it was 35
We had a drop together. Welcome home!"
Convivially returning with himself,
Again he raised the jug up to the light;
And with an acquiescent quaver said:
"Well, Mr. Flood, if you insist, I might. 40

"Only a very little, Mr. Flood—
For auld lang syne. No more, sir; that will do."
So, for the time, apparently it did,
And Eben evidently thought so too;
For soon amid the silver loneliness 45
Of night he lifted up his voice and sang,
Secure, with only two moons listening,
Until the whole harmonious landscape rang—

"For auld lang syne." The weary throat gave out,
The last word wavered, and the song was done. 50
He raised again the jug regretfully
And shook his head, and was again alone.

There was not much that was ahead of him,
And there was nothing in the town below—
Where strangers would have shut the many doors 55
That many friends had opened long ago.

RICHARD CORY

Edwin Arlington Robinson (1869–1935)

Whenever Richard Cory went down town,
We people on the pavement looked at him:
He was a gentleman from sole to crown,
Clean favored, and imperially slim.

And he was always quietly arrayed, 5
And he was always human when he talked;
But still he fluttered pulses when he said,
"Good-morning," and he glittered when he walked.

And he was rich—yes, richer than a king—
And admirably schooled in every grace: 10
In fine, we thought that he was everything
To make us wish that we were in his place.

So on we worked, and waited for the light,
And went without the meat, and cursed the bread;
And Richard Cory, one calm summer night, 15
Went home and put a bullet through his head.

EROS TURANNOS

Edwin Arlington Robinson (1869–1935)

She fears him, and will always ask
What fated her to choose him;
She meets in his engaging mask
All reasons to refuse him;
But what she meets and what she fears 5

Are less than are the downward years,
Drawn slowly to the foamless weirs
Of age, were she to lose him.

Between a blurred sagacity
That once had power to sound him, 10
And Love, that will not let him be
The Judas that she found him,
Her pride assuages her almost,
As if it were alone the cost.—
He sees that he will not be lost, 15
And waits and looks around him.

A sense of ocean and old trees
Envelops and allures him;
Tradition, touching all he sees,
Beguiles and reassures him; 20
And all her doubts of what he says
Are dimmed with what she knows of days—
Till even prejudice delays
And fades, and she secures him.

The falling leaf inaugurates 25
The reign of her confusion;
The pounding wave reverberates
The dirge of her illusion;
And home, where passion lived and died,
Becomes a place where she can hide, 30
While all the town and harbor side
Vibrate with her seclusion.

We tell you, tapping on our brows,
The story as it should be,—
As if the story of a house 35
Were told, or ever could be;
We'll have no kindly veil between
Her visions and those we have seen,—

As if we guessed what hers have been,
  Or what they are or would be. 40

Meanwhile we do no harm; for they
  That with a god have striven,
Not hearing much of what we say,
  Take what the god has given;
Though like waves breaking it may be, 45
Or like a changed familiar tree,
Or like a stairway to the sea
  Where down the blind are driven.

MINIVER CHEEVY

Edwin Arlington Robinson (1869–1935)

Miniver Cheevy, child of scorn,
  Grew lean while he assailed the seasons;
He wept that he was ever born,
  And he had reasons.

Miniver loved the days of old 5
  When swords were bright and steeds were prancing;
The vision of a warrior bold
  Would set him dancing.

Miniver sighed for what was not,
  And dreamed, and rested from his labors; 10
He dreamed of Thebes and Camelot,
  And Priam's neighbors.

Miniver mourned the ripe renown
  That made so many a name so fragrant;
He mourned Romance, now on the town, 15
  And Art, a vagrant.

Miniver loved the Medici,
  Albeit he had never seen one;

He would have sinned incessantly
  Could he have been one. 20

Miniver cursed the commonplace
  And eyed a khaki suit with loathing;
He missed the mediæval grace
  Of iron clothing.

Miniver scorned the gold he sought, 25
  But sore annoyed was he without it;
Miniver thought, and thought, and thought,
  And thought about it.

Miniver Cheevy, born too late,
  Scratched his head and kept on thinking; 30
Miniver coughed, and called it fate,
  And kept on drinking.

LUKE HAVERGAL

Edwin Arlington Robinson (1869–1935)

Go to the western gate, Luke Havergal,
There where the vines cling crimson on the wall,
And in the twilight wait for what will come.
The leaves will whisper there of her, and some,
Like flying words, will strike you as they fall; 5
But go, and if you listen she will call.
Go to the western gate, Luke Havergal—
Luke Havergal.

No, there is not a dawn in eastern skies
To rift the fiery night that's in your eyes; 10
But there, where western glooms are gathering,
The dark will end the dark, if anything:
God slays Himself with every leaf that flies,
And hell is more than half of paradise.

No, there is not a dawn in eastern skies— 15
In eastern skies.

Out of a grave I come to tell you this,
Out of a grave I come to quench the kiss
That flames upon your forehead with a glow
That blinds you to the way that you must go. 20
Yes, there is yet one way to where she is,
Bitter, but one that faith may never miss.
Out of a grave I come to tell you this—
To tell you this.

There is the western gate, Luke Havergal, 25
There are the crimson leaves upon the wall.
Go, for the winds are tearing them away,—
Nor think to riddle the dead words they say,
Nor any more to feel them as they fall;
But go, and if you trust her she will call. 30
There is the western gate, Luke Havergal—
Luke Havergal.

A FIELD OF LIGHT

Theodore Roethke (1908–1963)

1

Came to lakes; came to dead water,
Ponds with moss and leaves floating,
Planks sunk in the sand.

A log turned at the touch of a foot;
A long weed floated upward; 5
An eye tilted.

Small winds made
A chilly noise;
The softest cove
Cried for sound. 10

Reached for a grape
And the leaves changed;
A stone's shape
Became a clam.

A fine rain fell 15
On fat leaves;
I was there alone
In a watery drowse.

2

Angel within me, I asked,
Did I ever curse the sun? 20
Speak and abide.

Under, under the sheaves,
Under the blackened leaves,
Behind the green viscid trellis,
In the deep grass at the edge of a field, 25
Along the low ground dry only in August,—

Was it dust I was kissing?
A sigh came far.
Alone, I kissed the skin of a stone;
Marrow-soft, danced in the sand. 30

3

The dirt left my hand, visitor.
I could feel the mare's nose.
A path went walking.
The sun glittered on a small rapids.
Some morning thing came, beating its wings. 35
The great elm filled with birds.

Listen, love,
The fat lark sang in the field;
I touched the ground, the ground warmed by the killdeer,

The salt laughed and the stones; 40
The ferns had their ways, and the pulsing lizards,
And the new plants, still awkward in their soil,
The lovely diminutives.

I could watch! I could watch!
I saw the separateness of all things! 45
My heart lifted up with the great grasses;
The weeds believed me, and the nesting birds.
There were clouds making a rout of shapes crossing a windbreak of cedars,
And a bee shaking drops from a rain-soaked honeysuckle.
The worms were delighted as wrens. 50
And I walked, I walked through the light air;
I moved with the morning.

ELEGY FOR JANE

My Student, Thrown by a Horse

Theodore Roethke (1908–1963)

I remember the neckcurls, limp and damp as tendrils;
And her quick look, a sidelong pickerel smile;
And how, once startled into talk, the light syllables leaped for her,
And she balanced in the delight of her thought,
A wren, happy, tail into the wind, 5
Her song trembling the twigs and small branches.
The shade sang with her;
The leaves, their whispers turned to kissing;
And the mold sang in the bleached valleys under the rose.

Oh, when she was sad, she cast herself down into such a pure depth, 10
Even a father could not find her:
Scraping her cheek against straw;
Stirring the clearest water.

My sparrow, you are not here,
Waiting like a fern, making a spiny shadow. 15
The sides of wet stones cannot console me,
Nor the moss, wound with the last light.

If only I could nudge you from this sleep,
My maimed darling, my skittery pigeon.
Over this damp grave I speak the words of my love: 20
I, with no rights in this matter,
Neither father nor lover.

SONG FOR THE SQUEEZE-BOX

Theodore Roethke (1908–1963)

It wasn't Ernest; it wasn't Scott—
The boys I knew when I went to pot;
They didn't boast; they didn't snivel,
But stepped right up and swung at the Devil;
And after exchanging a punch or two, 5
They all sat down like me and you
—And began to drink up the money.

It wasn't the Colony; it wasn't the Stork;
It wasn't the joints in New York, New York;
But me and a girl friend learned a lot 10
In Ecorse, Toledo, and Wyandotte
—About getting rid of our money.

It was jump-in-the-hedge; it was wait-in-the-hall;
It was "Would you believe it—*fawther's* tall!"
(It turned out she hadn't a father at all) 15
—But how she could burn up the money!

A place I surely did like to go
Was the underbelly of Cicero;
And East St. Louis and Monongahela

Had the red-hot spots where you feel a 20
—Lot like losing some money.

Oh, the Synco Septet played for us then,
And even the boys turned out to be men
As we sat there drinking that bathtub gin
—And loosened up with our money. 25

It was Samoots Matuna and Bugs Moran;
It was Fade me another and Stick out your can;
It was Place and Show and Also Ran
—For you never won with that money.

Oh, it wasn't a crime, it wasn't a sin, 30
And nobody slipped me a Mickey Finn,
For whenever I could, I dealt them all in
—On that chunk of Grandpa's money.

It was Dead Man's Corner, it was Kelly's Stable;
It was Stand on your feet as long as you're able, 35
But many a man rolled under the table
—When he tried to drink up the money.

To some it may seem a sad thing to relate,
The dough I spent on Chippewa Kate,
For she finally left town on the Bay City freight 40
—When she thought I'd run out of money.

The doctors, the lawyers, the cops are all paid—
So I've got to get me a rich ugly old maid
Who isn't unwilling, who isn't afraid
—To help me eat up her money. 45

BIG WIND

Theodore Roethke (1908–1963)

Where were the greenhouses going,
Lunging into the lashing
Wind driving water

So far down the river
All the faucets stopped?— 5
So we drained the manure-machine
For the steam plant,
Pumping the stale mixture
Into the rusty boilers,
Watching the pressure gauge 10
Waver over to red,
As the seams hissed
And the live steam
Drove to the far
End of the rose-house, 15
Where the worst wind was,
Creaking the cypress window-frames,
Cracking so much thin glass
We stayed all night,
Stuffing the holes with burlap; 20
But she rode it out,
That old rose-house,
She hove into the teeth of it,
The core and pith of that ugly storm,
Ploughing with her stiff prow, 25
Bucking into the wind-waves
That broke over the whole of her,
Flailing her sides with spray,
Flinging long strings of wet across the roof-top,
Finally veering, wearing themselves out, merely 30
Whistling thinly under the wind-vents;
She sailed until the calm morning,
Carrying her full cargo of roses.

MY PAPA'S WALTZ

Theodore Roethke (1908–1963)

The whiskey on your breath
Could make a small boy dizzy;

But I hung on like death:
Such waltzing was not easy.

We romped until the pans 5
Slid from the kitchen shelf;
My mother's countenance
Could not unfrown itself.

The hand that held my wrist
Was battered on one knuckle; 10
At every step you missed
My right ear scraped a buckle.

You beat time on my head
With a palm caked hard by dirt,
Then waltzed me off to bed 15
Still clinging to your shirt.

IN THE NAKED BED, IN PLATO'S CAVE

Delmore Schwartz (1913–1966)

In the naked bed, in Plato's cave,
Reflected headlights slowly slid the wall,
Carpenters hammered under the shaded window,
Wind troubled the window curtains all night long.
A fleet of trucks strained uphill, grinding, 5
Their freights covered, as usual.
The ceiling lightened again, the slanting diagram
Slid slowly forth.
Hearing the milkman's chop,
His striving up the stair, the bottle's chink,
I rose from bed, lit a cigarette, 10
And walked to the window. The stony street
Displayed the stillness in which buildings stand,
The street-lamp's vigil and the horse's patience.
The winter sky's pure capital
Turned me back to bed with exhausted eyes. 15

Strangeness grew in the motionless air. The loose
Film grayed. Shaking wagons, hooves' waterfalls,
Sounded far off, increasing, louder and nearer.
A car coughed, starting. Morning, softly
Melting the air, lifted the half-covered chair 20
From underseas, kindled the looking-glass,
Distinguished the dresser and the white wall.
The bird called tentatively, whistled, called,
Bubbled and whistled, so! Perplexed, still wet
With sleep, affectionate, hungry and cold. So, so, 25
O son of man, the ignorant night, the travail
Of early morning, the mystery of beginning
Again and again,
while History is unforgiven.

SOCRATES' GHOST MUST HAUNT ME NOW

Delmore Schwartz (1913–1966)

Socrates' ghost must haunt me now,
Notorious death has let him go,
He comes to me with a clumsy bow,
Saying in his disusèd voice,
That I do not know I do not know, 5
The mechanical whims of appetite
Are all that I have of conscious choice,
The butterfly caged in electric light
Is my only day in the world's great night,
Love is not love, it is a child 10
Sucking his thumb and biting his lip,
But grasp it all, there may be more!
From the topless sky to the bottomless floor
With the heavy head and the fingertip:
All is not blind, obscene, and poor. 15
Socrates stands by me stockstill,
Teaching hope to my flickering will,

Pointing to the sky's inexorable blue
—Old Noumenon, come true, come true!

SONNET 33

William Shakespeare (1564–1616)

Full many a glorious morning have I seen
Flatter the mountain-tops with sovereign eye,
Kissing with golden face the meadows green,
Gilding pale streams with heavenly alchemy;
Anon permit the basest clouds to ride 5
With ugly rack on his celestial face,
And from the forlorn world his visage hide,
Stealing unseen to west with this disgrace:
Even so my sun one early morn did shine
With all-triumphant splendour on my brow; 10
But out, alack! he was but one hour mine;
The region cloud hath masked him from me now.
Yet him for this my love no whit disdaineth;
Suns of the world may stain when heaven's sun staineth.

SCYROS

Karl Shapiro (1913–)

Snuffle and sniff and handkerchief

The doctor punched my vein
The captain called me Cain
Upon my belly sat the sow of fear
With coins on either eye
The President came by 5
And whispered to the braid what none could hear

High over where the storm
Stood steadfast cruciform

The golden eagle sank in wounded wheels
  White Negroes laughing still 10
  Crept fiercely on Brazil
Turning the navies upward on their keels

  Now one by one the trees
  Stripped to their naked knees
To dance upon the heaps of shrunken dead 15
  The roof of England fell
  Great Paris tolled her bell
And China staunched her milk and wept for bread

  No island singly lay
  But lost its name that day 20
The Ainu dived across the plunging sands
  From dawn to dawn to dawn
  King George's birds came on
Strafing the tulips from his children's hands

  Thus in the classic sea 25
  Southeast from Thessaly
The dynamited mermen washed ashore
  And tritons dressed in steel
  Trolled heads with rod and reel
And dredged potatoes from the Aegean floor 30

  Hot is the sky and green
  Where Germans have been seen
The moon leaks metal on the Atlantic fields
  Pink boys in birthday shrouds
  Loop lightly through the clouds 35
Or coast the peaks of Finland on their shields

  That prophet year by year
  Lay still but could not hear
Where scholars tapped to find his new remains
  Gog and Magog ate pork 40
  In vertical New York
And war began next Wednesday on the Danes

LEAVE ME, O LOVE

Sir Philip Sidney (1554–1586)

Leave me, O love which reachest but to dust;
And thou, my mind, aspire to higher things;
Grow rich in that which never taketh rust,
Whatever fades but fading pleasure brings.
Draw in thy beams, and humble all thy might 5
To that sweet yoke where lasting freedoms be;
Which breaks the clouds and opens forth the light,
That doth both shine and give us sight to see.
O take fast hold; let that light be thy guide
In this small course which birth draws out to death, 10
And think how evil becometh him to slide,
Who seeketh heav'n, and comes of heav'nly breath.
  Then farewell, world, thy uttermost I see;
  Eternal Love, maintain thy life in me.

THOU BLIND MAN'S MARK

Sir Philip Sidney (1554–1586)

Thou blind man's mark, thou fool's self-chosen snare,
Fond fancy's scum, and dregs of scattered thought;
Band of all evils, cradle of causeless care;
Thou web of will, whose end is never wrought;
Desire, desire! I have too dearly bought, 5
With price of mangled mind, thy worthless ware;
Too long, too long, asleep thou hast me brought,
Who should my mind to higher things prepare.
But yet in vain thou hast my ruin sought;
In vain thou madest me to vain things aspire; 10
In vain thou kindlest all thy smoky fire;
For virtue hath this better lesson taught,—

Within myself to seek my only hire,
Desiring nought but how to kill desire.

FROM ASTROPHEL AND STELLA

Sir Philip Sidney (1554–1586)

I

Loving in truth, and fain in verse my love to show,
That she, dear she, might take some pleasure of my pain,
Pleasure might cause her read, reading might make her know,
Knowledge might pity win, and pity grace obtain,—
I sought fit words to paint the blackest face of woe; 5
Studying inventions fine, her wits to entertain,
Oft turning others' leaves to see if thence would flow
Some fresh and fruitful showers upon my sun-burned brain.
But words came halting forth, wanting invention's stay;
Invention, nature's child, fled step-dame Study's blows, 10
And others' feet still seemed but strangers in my way.
Thus, great with child to speak, and helpless in my throes,
Biting my truant pen, beating myself for spite,
Fool, said my muse to me, look in thy heart and write.

THE TROIKA

Louis Simpson (1923–   )

Troika, troika! The snow moon
whirls through the forest.

Where lamplight like a knife
gleams through a door, I see two graybeards bending.
They're playing chess, it seems. And then one rises 5
and stands in silence. Does he hear me passing?

Troika, troika! In the moonlight
his spirit hears my spirit passing.

I whip the horses on. The houses vanish.
The moon looks over fields   10
littered with debris. And there in trenches
the guardsmen stand, wind fluttering their rags.

And there were darker fields without a moon.
I walk across a field, bound on an errand.
The errand's forgotten—something depended on it.   15
A nightmare! I have lost my father's horses!

And then a white bird rises
and goes before me, hopping through the forest.

I held the bird—it vanished with a cry,
and on a branch a girl sat sideways, combing   20
her long black hair. The dew
shone on her lips; her breasts were white as roses.

Troika, troika! Three white horses,
a whip of silver, and my father's sleigh . . .

When morning breaks, the sea   25
gleams through the branches,
and the white bird, enchanted,
is flying through the world, across the sea.

AMERICAN POETRY

Louis Simpson (1923–)

Whatever it is, it must have
A stomach that can digest
Rubber, coal, uranium, moons, poems.

Like the shark, it contains a shoe.
It must swim for miles through the desert   5
Uttering cries that are almost human.

A STORY ABOUT CHICKEN SOUP

Louis Simpson (1923–)

In my grandmother's house there was always chicken soup
And talk of the old country—mud and boards,
Poverty,
The snow falling down the necks of lovers.

Now and then, out of her savings 5
She sent them a dowry. Imagine
The rice-powdered faces!
And the smell of the bride, like chicken soup.

But the Germans killed them.
I know it's in bad taste to say it, 10
But it's true. The Germans killed them all.

*

In the ruins of Berchtesgaden
A child with yellow hair
Ran out of a doorway.

A German girl-child— 15
Cuckoo, all skin and bones—
Not even enough to make chicken soup.
She sat by the stream and smiled.

Then as we splashed in the sun
She laughed at us. 20
We had killed her mechanical brothers,
So we forgave her.

*

The sun is shining.
The shadows of the lovers have disappeared.
They are all eyes; they have some demand on me— 25
They want me to be more serious than I want to be.

They want me to stick in their mudhole
Where no one is elegant.
They want me to wear old clothes,
They want me to be poor, to sleep in a room with many others— 30

Not to walk in the painted sunshine
To a summer house,
But to live in the tragic world forever.

THE REDWOODS

Louis Simpson (1923–)

Mountains are moving, rivers
are hurrying. But we
are still.

We have the thoughts of giants—
clouds, and at night the stars. 5

And we have names—guttural, grotesque—
Hamet, Og—names with no syllables.

And perish, one by one, our roots
gnawed by the mice. And fall.
And are too slow for death, and change 10

to stone. Or else too quick,

like candles in a fire. Giants
are lonely. We have waited long

for someone. By our waiting, surely
there must be someone at whose touch 15

our boughs would bend; and hands
to gather us; a spirit

to whom we are light as the hawthorn tree.
O if there is a poet

let him come now! We stand at the Pacific 20
like great unmarried girls,

turning in our heads the stars and clouds,
considering whom to please.

ASS-FACE

Dame Edith Sitwell (1887–1964)

Ass-Face drank
The asses' milk of the stars . . .
The milky spirals as they sank
From heaven's saloons and golden bars,
Made a gown 5
For Columbine,
Spirting down
On sands divine
By the asses' hide of the sea
(With each tide braying free). 10
And the beavers building Babel
Beneath each tree's thin beard,
Said, 'Is it Cain and Abel
Fighting again we heard?'
It is Ass-Face, Ass-Face, 15
Drunk on the milk of the stars,
Who will spoil their houses of white lace—
Expelled from the golden bars!

HERON

Robin Skelton (1925–)

Stoop-shouldered heron, head awry,
stick-legged fisher in the stream,
stands alone as destiny;
we see him as we cross the fields,

a figure carved of reed and briar 5
native to the chill thin air
below the lock whose silver shoals
scatter through his agate stare

that sifts their nature, waiting for
the golden fin, the feathered tail, 10
of some irradiant star-crossed fish,
patiently as daylight fails,

and as we cross this lover's field
we see him standing grey and still,
and sudden through our shoal of talk 15
death's image arrows to the kill.

A BALLAD OF DESPAIR

Robin Skelton (1925–)

Mercy, Pity, Peace, and Love.
  I met a walking man.
He walked each street towards despair
  and stared up at the sun.

This way he walked. A sawdust head 5
  knocked on his coughing chest.
A hand twitched like an empty glove.
  A boot scratched at the dust.

That way he was. He walked that way.
  Flame throbbed within his head. 10
The wax mouths of his five children
  spoke like they were dead.

'The Lamb that died' the preacher said.
  He saw the Lamb that died.
There was a black cloud round its head, 15
  a law book at its side.

'Love your neighbour', said the preacher,
  'and obey the Law.'
He saw the blinded fishermen
  die on the green shore. 20

He saw his brother spitting sand
  with barbed wire round his head.
His hands like rags turned his door key.
  His mouth shone like lead.

He climbed the stair. At the first step 25
  He saw a city burn.
Children with flesh like trailing rags
  watched him from the turn.

The second step he took, the sea
  delivered up its dead. 30
The shoals of miles shone their white bellies
  at his staring head.

And the third step he climbed, he stopped.
  He stood stiff as a door.
A thousand blinded tongueless creatures 35
  coupled on the floor.

He stopped, then climbed. He went into
  the room his children lay.
He knew that he was mad as truth
  to take their lives away. 40

He knew that truth was mad. He walked
  the darkness of the street,
cried, 'Suffer the little children
  to die in a clean sheet.'

He climbed the headline steps outside 45
  the black industrial hall,
cried, 'Though the children ask for bread,
  what bread is there not stone?'

What bread not stone? I met him dressed
in pity and in blood. 50
I met him knelt in Calvary Place
beside his children's bed.

Mercy, Pity, Peace, and Love,
I saw him lift his gun.
He lay like logic in the street 55
and stared at the blind sun.

PROTHALAMION

Edmund Spenser (1552?–1599)

1

Calm was the day, and through the trembling air
Sweet breathing Zephyrus did softly play,
A gentle spirit, that lightly did delay
Hot Titan's beams, which then did glister fair;
When I (whom sullen care, 5
Through discontent of my long fruitless stay
In princes' court, and expectation vain
Of idle hopes, which still do fly away,
Like empty shadows, did afflict my brain)
Walked forth to ease my pain 10
Along the shore of silver streaming Thames;
Whose rutty bank, the which his river hems,
Was painted all with variable flowers,
And all the meads adorned with dainty gems
Fit to deck maidens' bowers, 15
And crown their paramours,
Against the bridal day, which is not long.
Sweet Thames, run softly, till I end my song.

2

There, in a meadow, by the river's side,
A flock of nymphs I chancèd to espy, 20

All lovely daughters of the flood thereby,
With goodly greenish locks, all loose untied,
As each had been a bride;
And each one had a little wicker basket,
Made of fine twigs entrailèd curiously, 25
In which they gathered flowers to fill their flasket,
And with fine fingers cropped full feateously
The tender stalks on high.
Of every sort which in that meadow grew
They gathered some; the violet pallid blue, 30
The little daisy, that at evening closes,
The virgin lily, and the primrose true,
With store of vermeil roses,
To deck their bridegroom's posies
Against the bridal day, which was not long. 35
Sweet Thames, run softly, till I end my song.

3

With that I saw two swans of goodly hue
Come softly swimming down along the Lee.
Two fairer birds I yet did never see;
The snow which doth the top of Pindus strew 40
Did never whiter shew,
Not Jove himself, when he a swan would be
For love of Leda, whiter did appear;
Yet Leda was, they say, as white as he,
Yet not so white as these, not nothing near; 45
So purely white they were
That even the gentle stream, the which them bare,
Seemed foul to them, and bade his billows spare
To wet their silken feathers, lest they might
Soil their fair plumes with water not so fair, 50
And mar their beauties bright,
That shone as heaven's light,
Against their bridal day, which was not long.
Sweet Thames, run softly, till I end my song.

4

Eftsoons the nymphs, which now had flowers their fill, 55
Ran all in haste to see that silver brood,
As they came floating on the crystal flood;
Whom when they saw, they stood amazèd still,
Their wondering eyes to fill;
Them seemed they never saw a sight so fair 60
Of fowls so lovely, that they sure did deem
Them heavenly born, or to be that same pair
Which through the sky draw Venus' silver team;
For sure they did not seem
To be begot of any earthly seed, 65
But rather angels, or of angels' breed;
Yet were they bred of summer's heat, they say,
In sweetest season, when each flower and weed
The earth did fresh array;
So fresh they seemed as day, 70
Even as their bridal day, which was not long.
Sweet Thames, run softly, till I end my song.

5

Then forth they all out of their baskets drew
Great store of flowers, the honor of the field,
That to the sense did fragrant odors yield, 75
All which upon those goodly birds they threw,
And all the waves did strew,
That like old Peneus' waters they did seem,
When down along by pleasant Tempe's shore,
Scatt'rèd with flowers, through Thessaly they stream, 80
That they appear, through lilies' plenteous store,
Like a bride's chamber floor.
Two of those nymphs meanwhile two garlands bound
Of freshest flowers which in that mead they found,
The which presenting all in trim array, 85

Their snowy foreheads therewithal they crowned,
Whilst one did sing this lay,
Prepared against that day,
Against their bridal day, which was not long:
  Sweet Thames, run softly, till I end my song. 90

6

"Ye gentle birds, the world's fair ornament,
And heaven's glory, whom this happy hour
Doth lead unto your lovers' blissful bower,
Joy may you have, and gentle hearts' content
Of your love's couplement: 95
And let fair Venus, that is queen of love,
With her heart-quelling son, upon you smile,
Whose smile, they say, hath virtue to remove
All love's dislike, and friendship's faulty guile
For ever to assoil. 100
Let endless peace your steadfast hearts accord,
And blessèd plenty wait upon your board;
And let your bed with pleasures chaste abound,
That fruitful issue may to you afford,
Which may your foes confound, 105
And make your joys redound
Upon your bridal day, which is not long."
  Sweet Thames, run softly, till I end my song.

7

So ended she; and all the rest around
To her redoubled that her undersong, 110
Which said their bridal day should not be long;
And gentle Echo from the neighbor ground
Their accents did resound.
So forth those joyous birds did pass along,
Adown the Lee, that to them murmured low, 115
As he would speak, but that he lacked a tongue,

Yet did by signs his glad affection show,
Making his stream run slow.
And all the fowl which in his flood did dwell
Gan flock about these twain, that did excel 120
The rest, so far as Cynthia doth shend
The lesser stars. So they, enranged well,
Did on those two attend,
And their best service lend,
Against their wedding day, which was not long. 125
Sweet Thames, run softly, till I end my song.

8

At length they all to merry London came,
To merry London, my most kindly nurse,
That to me gave this life's first native source,
Though from another place I take my name, 130
An house of ancient fame.
There when they came, whereas those bricky towers
The which on Thames' broad, agèd back do ride,
Where now the studious lawyers have their bowers,
There whilom wont the Templar Knights to bide, 135
Till they decayed through pride;
Next whereunto there stands a stately place,
Where oft I gainèd gifts and goodly grace
Of that great lord which therein wont to dwell,
Whose want too well now feels my friendless case— 140
But ah! here fits not well
Old woes, but joys, to tell,
Against the bridal day, which is not long.
Sweet Thames, run softly, till I end my song.

9

Yet therein now doth lodge a noble peer, 145
Great England's glory, and the world's wide wonder,
Whose dreadful name late through all Spain did thunder,

And Hercules' two pillars standing near
Did make to quake and fear.
Fair branch of honor, flower of chivalry, 150
That fillest England with thy triumph's fame,
Joy have thou of thy noble victory,
And endless happiness of thine own name,
That promiseth the same;
That through thy prowess and victorious arms 155
Thy country may be freed from foreign harms;
And great Eliza's glorious name may ring
Through all the world, filled with thy wide alarms,
Which some brave muse may sing
To ages following, 160
Upon the bridal day, which is not long.
Sweet Thames, run softly, till I end my song.

10

From those high towers this noble lord issuing,
Like radiant Hesper, when his golden hair
In the ocean billows he hath bathèd fair, 165
Descended to the river's open viewing,
With a great train ensuing.
Above the rest were goodly to be seen
Two gentle knights of lovely face and feature,
Beseeming well the bower of any queen, 170
With gifts of wit, and ornaments of nature,
Fit for so goodly stature,
That like the twins of Jove they seemed in sight,
Which deck the baldrick of the heavens bright.
They two, forth pacing to the river's side 175
Received those two fair brides, their love's delight;
Which, at the appointed tide,
Each one did make his bride,
Against their bridal day, which is not long.
Sweet Thames, run softly, till I end my song. 180

SONG

Sir John Suckling (1609–1642)

Out upon it, I have lov'd,
  Three whole days together;
And am like to love three more,
  If it prove fair weather.

Time shall moult away his wings   5
  Ere he shall discover
In the whole wide world again
  Such a constant lover.

But the spite on't is, no praise
  Is due at all to me: 10
Love with me had made no stays,
  Had it any been but she.

Had it any been but she
  And that very face,
There had been at least ere this   15
  A dozen dozen in her place.

SONG

Sir John Suckling (1609–1642)

Why so pale and wan fond lover?
  Prithee why so pale?
Will, when looking well can't move her,
  Looking ill prevail?
  Prithee why so pale?   5

Why so dull and mute young sinner?
  Prithee why so mute?
Will, when speaking well can't win her,

Saying nothing do't?
Prithee why so mute? 10

Quit, quit, for shame, this will not move,
This will not take her;
If of herself she will not love,
Nothing can make her:
The devil take her. 15

A REFUSAL TO MOURN THE DEATH, BY FIRE, OF A CHILD IN LONDON

Dylan Thomas (1914–1953)

Never until the mankind making
Bird beast and flower
Fathering and all humbling darkness
Tells with silence the last light breaking
And the still hour 5
Is come of the sea tumbling in harness

And I must enter again the round
Zion of the water bead
And the synagogue of the ear of corn
Shall I let pray the shadow of a sound 10
Or sow my salt seed
In the least valley of sackcloth to mourn

The majesty and burning of the child's death.
I shall not murder
The mankind of her going with a grave truth 15
Nor blaspheme down the stations of the breath
With any further
Elegy of innocence and youth.

Deep with the first dead lies London's daughter,
Robed in the long friends, 20
The grains beyond age, the dark veins of her mother,

Secret by the unmourning water
Of the riding Thames.
After the first death, there is no other.

DO NOT GO GENTLE INTO THAT GOOD NIGHT

Dylan Thomas (1914–1953)

Do not go gentle into that good night,
Old age should burn and rave at close of day;
Rage, rage against the dying of the light.

Though wise men at their end know dark is right,
Because their words had forked no lightning they 5
Do not go gentle into that good night.

Good men, the last wave by, crying how bright
Their frail deeds might have danced in a green bay,
Rage, rage against the dying of the light.

Wild men who caught and sang the sun in flight, 10
And learn, too late, they grieved it on its way,
Do not go gentle into that good night.

Grave men, near death, who see with blinding sight
Blind eyes could blaze like meteors and be gay,
Rage, rage against the dying of the light. 15

And you, my father, there on the sad height,
Curse, bless, me now with your fierce tears, I pray.
Do not go gentle into that good night.
Rage, rage against the dying of the light.

PRAYER

Robert Tucker (1921–)

Nourish, where slowly it wakes, a strong seed.
Advance the urgent massing in the core,

The dark vigor groping, unhusking.
At the burst be. Be to the first sure,
To the second shoot, the third, sure. Choose, 5
Love, root's will to sink root,
Sprout's to lift sprout. No filament fail.
Though heaven spill, let bud compose
Stalk and twig, trunk, branches, the panoply.
Foster bloom-savor, the full fruit, 10
Mist-smoke, fleck, rose-cheek. Bear
In my touch gleam, to my eyes form.
When teeth tear the taut skin,
Salvage a strong seed. Arise, descend to my taste.

THE RETREAT

Henry Vaughan (1622–1695)

Happy those early days! when I
Shin'd in my angel-infancy.
Before I understood this place
Appointed for my second race,
Or taught my soul to fancy aught 5
But a white, celestial thought,
When yet I had not walked above
A mile, or two, from my first love,
And looking back (at that short space)
Could see a glimpse of His bright face; 10
When on some gilded cloud, or flow'r
My gazing soul would dwell an hour,
And in those weaker glories spy
Some shadows of eternity;
Before I taught my tongue to wound 15
My conscience with a sinful sound,
Or had the black art to dispense
A sev'ral sin to ev'ry sense,

But felt through all this fleshly dress
Bright shoots of everlastingness. 20
O how I long to travel back
And tread again that ancient track!
That I might once more reach that plain
Where first I left my glorious train,
From whence th'enlight'ned spirit sees 25
That shady city of palm trees;
But, ah! my soul with too much stay
Is drunk, and staggers in the way.
Some men a forward motion love,
But I by backward steps would move, 30
And when this dust falls to the urn
In that state I came return.

THEY ARE ALL GONE INTO THE WORLD OF LIGHT

Henry Vaughan (1622–1695)

They are all gone into the world of light!
And I alone sit ling'ring here;
Their very memory is fair and bright,
And my sad thoughts doth clear.

It glows and glitters in my cloudy breast 5
Like stars upon some gloomy grove,
Or those faint beams in which this hill is dress'd
After the sun's remove.

I see them walking in an air of glory,
Whose light doth trample on my days: 10
My days, which are at best but dull and hoary,
Mere glimmering and decays.

O holy hope! and high humility,
High as the heavens above!

These are your walks, and you have show'd them me 15
To kindle my cold love,

Dear, beauteous death! the jewel of the just,
Shining nowhere, but in the dark;
What mysteries do lie beyond thy dust;
Could man outlook that mark! 20

He that hath found some fledg'd bird's nest, may know
At first sight, if the bird be flown;
But what fair well, or grove he sings in now,
That is to him unknown.

And yet, as angels in some brighter dreams 25
Call to the soul, when man doth sleep:
So some strange thoughts transcend our wonted themes,
And into glory peep.

If a star were confin'd into a tomb
Her captive flames must needs burn there; 30
But when the hand that locked her up, gives room,
She'll shine through all the sphere.

O Father of eternal life, and all
Created glories under Thee!
Resume Thy spirit from this world of thrall 35
Into true liberty.

Either disperse these mists, which blot and fill
My pèrspective, still, as they pass,
Or else remove me hence unto that hill,
Where I shall need no glass. 40

ON A GIRDLE

Edmund Waller (1606–1687)

That which her slender waist confined
Shall now my joyful temples bind;

No monarch but would give his crown
His arms might do what this has done.

It was my heaven's extremest sphere, 5
The pale which held that lovely deer.
My joy, my grief, my hope, my love,
Did all within this circle move!

A narrow compass, and yet there
Dwelt all that's good and all that's fair; 10
Give me but what this riband bound,
Take all the rest the sun goes round.

TO A FAIR LADY, PLAYING WITH A SNAKE

Edmund Waller (1606–1687)

Strange! that such horror and such grace
Should dwell together in one place;
A fury's arm, an angel's face!

'Tis innocence, and youth, which makes
In Chloris' fancy such mistakes, 5
To start at love, and play with snakes.

By this and by her coldness barred,
Her servants have a task too hard;
The tyrant has a double guard!

Thrice happy snake! that in her sleeve 10
May boldly creep; we dare not give
Our thoughts so unconfined a leave.

Contented in that nest of snow
He lies, as he his bliss did know,
And to the wood no more would go. 15

Take heed, fair Eve! you do not make
Another tempter of this snake;
A marble one so warmed would speak.

OF THE LAST VERSES IN THE BOOK

Edmund Waller (1606–1687)

When we for age could neither read nor write,
The subject made us able to indite;
The soul, with nobler resolutions decked,
The body stooping, does herself erect.
No mortal parts are requisite to raise 5
Her that, unbodied, can her Maker praise.
The seas are quiet when the winds give o'er;
So, calm are we when passions are no more!
For then we know how vain it was to boast
Of fleeting things, so certain to be lost. 10
Clouds of affection from our younger eyes
Conceal that emptiness which age descries.
The soul's dark cottage, battered and decayed,
Lets in new light through chinks that time has made;
Stronger by weakness, wiser men become, 15
As they draw near to their eternal home.
Leaving the old, both worlds at once they view,
That stand upon the threshold of the new.

ON AN ITALIAN HILLSIDE

Richard Weber (1932–)

On a hillside in Italy
The air shook like a single grass
In a secret morning wind
That moves no other about it
And moves it only, 5
Awaiting the waiting thoughts and themes of the day.

From a hillside in Italy
The sea was a child's blue slate

With toy craft signing their furrows
In chalk-marks, moved 10
By no child's hand, appearing,
Scratching in silence the tilted slate of the sea.

Above a hillside in Italy
The sun sank like a paper rose
Through water, dyeing it red, 15
Or like a drop of scarlet
Watercolour falling and softening
Into the yellow on already wet watercolour paper.

Below a hillside in Italy
The darkness filled the bay 20
Like flood-water, pushing
Down all opposition, submerging
The ships, the olive trees, the town,
The little gripping houses, the slipping rocks.

On a hillside in Italy 25
The lights came out like stars, steadied
In the net of haze over the sea.
And night climbed the hill to the top
To sit watching the twinkling fishboats
On the secret, slate-dark, flowering, flooded sea. 30

ADVICE TO A PROPHET

Richard Wilbur (1921–)

When you come, as you soon must, to the streets of our city,
Mad-eyed from stating the obvious,
Not proclaiming our fall but begging us
In God's name to have self-pity,

Spare us all word of the weapons, their force and range, 5
The long numbers that rocket the mind;

Our slow, unreckoning hearts will be left behind,
Unable to fear what is too strange.

Nor shall you scare us with talk of the death of the race.
How should we dream of this place without us?— 10
The sun mere fire, the leaves untroubled about us,
A stone look on the stone's face?

Speak of the world's own change. Though we cannot conceive
Of an undreamt thing, we know to our cost
How the dreamt cloud crumbles, the vines are blackened
by frost, 15
How the view alters. We could believe,

If you told us so, that the white-tailed deer will slip
Into perfect shade, grown perfectly shy,
The lark avoid the reaches of our eye,
The jack-pine lose its knuckled grip 20

On the cold ledge, and every torrent burn
As Xanthus once, its gliding trout
Stunned in a twinkling. What should we be without
The dolphin's arc, the dove's return,

These things in which we have seen ourselves and spoken? 25
Ask us, prophet, how we shall call
Our natures forth when that live tongue is all
Dispelled, that glass obscured or broken

In which we have said the rose of our love and the clean
Horse of our courage, in which beheld 30
The singing locust of the soul unshelled,
And all we mean or wish to mean.

Ask us, ask us whether with the worldless rose
Our hearts shall fail us; come demanding
Whether there shall be lofty or long standing 35
When the bronze annals of the oak-tree close.

THE PARDON

Richard Wilbur (1921–)

My dog lay dead five days without a grave
In the thick of summer, hid in a clump of pine
And a jungle of grass and honeysuckle-vine.
I who had loved him while he kept alive

Went only close enough to where he was 5
To sniff the heavy honeysuckle-smell
Twined with another odour heavier still
And hear the flies' intolerable buzz.

Well, I was ten and very much afraid.
In my kind world the dead were out of range 10
And I could not forgive the sad or strange
In beast or man. My father took the spade

And buried him. Last night I saw the grass
Slowly divide (it was the same scene
But now it glowed a fierce and mortal green) 15
And saw the dog emerging. I confess

I felt afraid again, but still he came
In the carnal sun, clothed in a hymn of flies,
And death was breeding in his lively eyes.
I started in to cry and call his name, 20

Asking forgiveness of his tongueless head.
. . . I dreamt the past was never past redeeming:
But whether this was false or honest dreaming
I beg death's pardon now. And mourn the dead.

CEREMONY

Richard Wilbur (1921–)

A striped blouse in a clearing by Bazille
Is, you may say, a patroness of boughs
Too queenly kind toward nature to be kin.
But ceremony never did conceal,
Save to the silly eye, which all allows, 5
How much we are the woods we wander in.

Let her be some Sabrina fresh from stream,
Lucent as shallows slowed by wading sun,
Bedded on fern, the flowers' cynosure:
Then nymph and wood must nod and strive to dream 10
That she is airy earth, the trees, undone,
Must ape her languor natural and pure.

Ho-hum. I am for wit and wakefulness,
And love this feigning lady by Bazille.
What's lightly hid is deepest understood, 15
And when with social smile and formal dress
She teaches leaves to curtsey and quadrille,
I think there are most tigers in the wood.

THE RED WHEELBARROW

William Carlos Williams (1883–1963)

so much depends
upon

a red wheel
barrow

glazed with rain 5
water

beside the white
chickens

THE BOTTICELLIAN TREES

William Carlos Williams (1883–1963)

The alphabet of
the trees

is fading in the
song of the leaves

the crossing   5
bars of the thin

letters that spelled
winter

and the cold
have been illumined   10

with
pointed green

by the rain and sun—
The strict simple

principles of   15
straight branches

are being modified
by pinched out

ifs of color, devout
conditions   20

the smiles of love—

. . . . . .

until the stript
sentences

move as a woman's
limbs under cloth   25

and praise from secrecy
with hot ardor

love's ascendancy
in summer—

In summer the song 30
sings itself

above the muffled words—

POEM

William Carlos Williams (1883–1963)

As the cat
climbed over
the top of

the jamcloset
first the right 5
forefoot

carefully
then the hind
stepped down

into the pit of 10
the empty
flowerpot

THIS IS JUST TO SAY

William Carlos Williams (1883–1963)

I have eaten
the plums
that were in
the icebox

and which 5
you were probably
saving
for breakfast

Forgive me
they were delicious 10
so sweet
and so cold

LUCY GRAY

Or, Solitude

William Wordsworth (1770–1850)

Oft I had heard of Lucy Gray:
And, when I crossed the wild,
I chanced to see at break of day
The solitary child.

No mate, no comrade Lucy knew; 5
She dwelt on a wide moor,
—The sweetest thing that ever grew
Beside a human door!

You yet may spy the fawn at play,
The hare upon the green; 10
But the sweet face of Lucy Gray
Will never more be seen.

"To-night will be a stormy night—
You to the town must go;
And take a lantern, Child, to light 15
Your mother through the snow."

"That, Father! will I gladly do:
'Tis scarcely afternoon—
The minster-clock has just struck two,
And yonder is the moon!" 20

At this the Father raised his hook,
And snapped a faggot-band;
He plied his work;—and Lucy took
The lantern in her hand.

Not blither is the mountain roe: 25
With many a wanton stroke
Her feet disperse the powdery snow,
That rises up like smoke.

The storm came on before its time:
She wandered up and down; 30
And many a hill did Lucy climb:
But never reached the town.

The wretched parents all that night
Went shouting far and wide;
But there was neither sound nor sight 35
To serve them for a guide.

At day-break on a hill they stood
That overlooked the moor;
And thence they saw the bridge of wood,
A furlong from their door. 40

They wept—and, turning homeward, cried,
"In heaven we all shall meet;"
—When in the snow the mother spied
The print of Lucy's feet.

Then downwards from the steep hill's edge, 45
They tracked the footmarks small;
And through the broken hawthorn hedge,
And by the long stone-wall;

And then an open field they crossed;
The marks were still the same; 50
They tracked them on, nor ever lost;
And to the bridge they came.

They followed from the snowy bank
Those footmarks, one by one,
Into the middle of the plank; 55
And further there were none!

—Yet some maintain that to this day
She is a living child;
That you may see sweet Lucy Gray
Upon the lonesome wild. 60

O'er rough and smooth she trips along,
And never looks behind;
And sings a solitary song
That whistles in the wind.

A SLUMBER DID MY SPIRIT SEAL

William Wordsworth (1770–1850)

A slumber did my spirit seal;
  I had no human fears:
She seemed a thing that could not feel
  The touch of earthly years.

No motion has she now, no force; 5
  She neither hears nor sees;
Rolled round in earth's diurnal course,
  With rocks, and stones, and trees.

A DREAM OF BURIAL

James Wright (1927–)

Nothing was left of me
But my right foot
And my left shoulder.
They lay white as the skein of a spider floating
In a field of snow toward a dark building 5

Tilted and stained by wind.
Inside the dream, I dreamed on.

A parade of old women
Sang softly above me,
Faint mosquitoes near still water. 10

So, I waited, in my corridor.
I listened for the sea
To call me.
I knew that, somewhere outside, the horse
Stood saddled, browsing in grass, 15
Waiting for me.

MILKWEED

James Wright (1927–)

While I stood here, in the open, lost in myself,
I must have looked a long time
Down the corn rows, beyond grass,
The small house,
White walls, animals lumbering toward the barn. 5
I look down now. It is all changed.
Whatever it was I lost, whatever I wept for
Was a wild, gentle thing, the small dark eyes
Loving me in secret.
It is here. At a touch of my hand, 10
The air fills with delicate creatures
From the other world.

A BLESSING

James Wright (1927–)

Just off the highway to Rochester, Minnesota,
Twilight bounds softly forth on the grass.

And the eyes of those two Indian ponies
Darken with kindness.
They have come gladly out of the willows 5
To welcome my friend and me.
We step over the barbed wire into the pasture
Where they have been grazing all day, alone.
They ripple tensely, they can hardly contain their happiness
That we have come. 10
They bow shyly as wet swans. They love each other.
There is no loneliness like theirs.
At home once more,
They begin munching the young tufts of spring in the darkness.
I would like to hold the slenderer one in my arms, 15
For she has walked over to me
And nuzzled my left hand.
She is black and white,
Her mane falls wild on her forehead,
And the light breeze moves me to caress her long ear 20
That is delicate as the skin over a girl's wrist.
Suddenly I realize
That if I stepped out of my body I would break
Into blossom.

AUTUMN BEGINS IN MARTINS FERRY, OHIO

James Wright (1927–)

In the Shreve High football stadium,
I think of Polacks nursing long beers in Tiltonsville,
And gray faces of Negroes in the blast furnace at Benwood,
And the ruptured night watchman of Wheeling Steel,
Dreaming of heroes. 5

All the proud fathers are ashamed to go home.
Their women cluck like starved pullets,
Dying for love.

Therefore,
Their sons grow suicidally beautiful 10
At the beginning of October,
And gallop terribly against each other's bodies.

PAUL

James Wright (1927–)

I used to see her in the door,
Lifting up her hand to wave
To citizens, or pass the hour
With neighboring wives who did not have
Anything more than time to say. 5

I used to see her in the door,
Simple and quiet woman, slim;
And so, I think, Paul cared the more
The night they carried her from him,
The night they carried her away. 10

The doctor did not even ask
For any neighborly advice;
He knew he had a simple task,
And it was obvious from his eyes
There was not anything to say. 15

The doctor had a word for Paul;
He said that she was resting now,
And would not wake, and that was all.
And then he walked into the snow,
Into the snow he walked away. 20

And did Paul shriek and curse the air,
And did he pummel with his fist
Against the wall, or tear his hair
And rush outside to bite the mist
That did not have a thing to say? 25

He sat upon her ruffled bed
And did not even look at me.
She was lovely, she was dead.
Some sparrows chirruped on a tree
Outside, and then they flew away. 30

OLD MAN DRUNK

James Wright (1927–)

He sits before me now, reptilian, cold,
Worn skeletal with sorrow for his child.
He would have lied to her, were he not old:
An old man's fumbling lips are not defiled
By the sweet lies of love. Yet one must be 5
Skillful to bring it off; that treachery
Whips back to lash the bungler of its art.
He curses his ineptitude of heart.

He knows the quivering eye of youth is blind.
The pale ears, roaring deep as shell, are deaf 10
To the half-drowning cry of love behind
The skull. His daughter struck him in her grief
Across the face, hearing her lover dead.
He stood behind her chair, he bowed his head,
Knowing that even death cannot prolong 15
The quick hysteric angers of the young.

I can say nothing. I will see him sit
Under the vacant clock, till I grow old.
The barkeep's wife returns to throw her fit
And pitch us out into the early cold. 20
I touch his shoulder, but he does not move,
Lost in the blind bewilderment of love,
The meaningless despair that could not keep
His daughter long from falling off to sleep.

Meanwhile, the many faces of old age 25
Flutter before me in the tavern haze.
He cannot let me see him weep and rage
Into his wrinkled pillow. Face by face,
He grins to entertain, he fills my glass,
Cold to the gestures of my vague *alas,* 30
Gay as a futile god who cannot die
Till daylight, when the barkeep says goodbye.

THE LOVER SHOWETH HOW HE IS FORSAKEN OF SUCH AS HE SOMETIME ENJOYED

Sir Thomas Wyatt (1503–1542)

They flee from me, that sometime did me seek,
With naked foot stalking within my chamber.
Once have I seen them gentle, tame, and meek,
That now are wild, and do not once remember
That sometime they have put themselves in danger 5
To take bread at my hand; and now they range,
Busily seeking in continual change.
Thanked be fortune it hath been otherwise,
Twenty times better; but once especïal,
In thin array, after a pleasant guise, 10
When her loose gown did from her shoulders fall,
And she me caught in her arms long and small,
And therewithal so sweetly did me kiss
And softly said, Dear heart, how like you this?
It was no dream, for I lay broad awaking. 15
But all is turned now, through my gentleness,
Into a bitter fashion of forsaking;
And I have leave to go, of her goodness,
And she also to use newfangleness.
But since that I unkindly so am served, 20
How like you this? what hath she now deserved?

JOHN KINSELLA'S LAMENT FOR MRS. MARY MOORE

William Butler Yeats (1865–1939)

A bloody and a sudden end,
  Gunshot or a noose,
For Death who takes what man would keep,
  Leaves what man would lose.
He might have had my sister, 5
  My cousins by the score,
But nothing satisfied the fool
  But my dear Mary Moore,
None other knows what pleasures man
  At table or in bed. 10
What shall I do for pretty girls
  Now my old bawd is dead?

Though stiff to strike a bargain,
  Like an old Jew man,
Her bargain struck we laughed and talked 15
  And emptied many a can;
And O! but she had stories,
  Though not for the priest's ear,
To keep the soul of man alive,
  Banish age and care, 20
And being old she put a skin
  On everything she said.
What shall I do for pretty girls
  Now my old bawd is dead?

The priests have got a book that says 25
  But for Adam's sin
Eden's Garden would be there
  And I there within.
No expectation fails there,

No pleasing habit ends, 30
No man grows old, no girl grows cold,
But friends walk by friends.
Who quarrels over halfpennies
That plucks the trees for bread?
What shall I do for pretty girls 35
Now my old bawd is dead?

A WOMAN'S BEAUTY

William Butler Yeats (1865–1939)

A woman's beauty is like a white
Frail bird, like a white sea-bird alone
At daybreak after stormy night
Between two furrows upon the ploughed land:
A sudden storm, and it was thrown 5
Between dark furrows upon the ploughed land.
How many centuries spent
The sedentary soul
In toils of measurement
Beyond eagle or mole, 10
Beyond hearing or seeing,
Or Archimedes' guess,
To raise into being
That loveliness?

A strange, unserviceable thing, 15
A fragile, exquisite, pale shell,
That the vast troubled waters bring
To the loud sands before day has broken.
The storm arose and suddenly fell
Amid the dark before day had broken. 20
What death? what discipline?
What bonds no man could unbind,
Being imagined within

The labyrinth of the mind,
What pursuing or fleeing, 25
What wounds, what bloody press,
Dragged into being
This loveliness?

FROM THE 'ANTIGONE'

William Butler Yeats (1865–1939)

Overcome—O bitter sweetness,
Inhabitant of the soft cheek of a girl—
The rich man and his affairs,
The fat flocks and the fields' fatness,
Mariners, rough harvesters; 5
Overcome gods upon Parnassus;

Overcome the Empyrean; hurl
Heaven and Earth out of their places,
That in the same calamity
Brother and brother, friend and friend, 10
Family and family,
City and city may contend,
By that great glory driven wild.

Pray I will and sing I must,
And yet I weep—Oedipus' child 15
Descends into the loveless dust.

MOHINI CHATTERJEE

William Butler Yeats (1865–1939)

I asked if I should pray,
But the Brahmin said,
'Pray for nothing, say
Every night in bed,

"I have been a king, 5
I have been a slave,
Nor is there anything,
Fool, rascal, knave,
That I have not been,
And yet upon my breast 10
A myriad heads have lain." '

That he might set at rest
A boy's turbulent days
Mohini Chatterjee
Spoke these, or words like these. 15
I add in commentary,
'Old lovers yet may have
All that time denied—
Grave is heaped on grave
That they be satisfied— 20
Over the blackened earth
The old troops parade,
Birth is heaped on birth
That such cannonade
May thunder time away, 25
Birth-hour and death-hour meet,
Or, as great sages say,
Men dance on deathless feet.'

ON A POLITICAL PRISONER

William Butler Yeats (1865–1939)

She that but little patience knew,
From childhood on, had now so much
A grey gull lost its fear and flew
Down to her cell and there alit,
And there endured her fingers' touch 5
And from her fingers ate its bit.

Did she in touching that lone wing
Recall the years before her mind
Became a bitter, an abstract thing,
Her thought some popular enmity: 10
Blind and leader of the blind
Drinking the foul ditch where they lie?

When long ago I saw her ride
Under Ben Bulben to the meet,
The beauty of her country-side 15
With all youth's lonely wildness stirred,
She seemed to have grown clean and sweet
Like any rock-bred, sea-borne bird:

Sea-borne, or balanced on the air
When first it sprang out of the nest 20
Upon some lofty rock to stare
Upon the cloudy canopy,
While under its storm-beaten breast
Cried out the hollows of the sea.

THE MAGI

William Butler Yeats (1865–1939)

Now as at all times I can see in the mind's eye,
In their stiff, painted clothes, the pale unsatisfied ones
Appear and disappear in the blue depth of the sky
With all their ancient faces like rain-beaten stones,
And all their helms of silver hovering side by side, 5
And all their eyes still fixed, hoping to find once more,
Being by Calvary's turbulence unsatisfied,
The uncontrollable mystery on the bestial floor.

THE COLD HEAVEN

William Butler Yeats (1865–1939)

Suddenly I saw the cold and rook-delighting heaven
That seemed as though ice burned and was but the more ice,
And thereupon imagination and heart were driven
So wild that every casual thought of that and this
Vanished, and left but memories, that should be out of season 5
With the hot blood of youth, of love crossed long ago;
And I took all the blame out of all sense and reason,
Until I cried and trembled and rocked to and fro,
Riddled with light. Ah! when the ghost begins to quicken,
Confusion of the death-bed over, is it sent 10
Out naked on the roads, as the books say, and stricken
By the injustice of the skies for punishment?

THAT THE NIGHT COME

William Butler Yeats (1865–1939)

She lived in storm and strife,
Her soul had such desire
For what proud death may bring
That it could not endure
The common good of life, 5
But lived as 'twere a king
That packed his marriage day
With banneret and pennon,
Trumpet and kettledrum,
And the outrageous cannon, 10
To bundle time away
That the night come.

LEDA AND THE SWAN

William Butler Yeats (1865–1939)

A sudden blow: the great wings beating still
Above the staggering girl, her thighs caressed
By the dark webs, her nape caught in his bill,
He holds her helpless breast upon his breast.

How can those terrified vague fingers push 5
The feathered glory from her loosening thighs?
And how can body, laid in that white rush,
But feel the strange heart beating where it lies?

A shudder in the loins engenders there
The broken wall, the burning roof and tower 10
And Agamemnon dead.

Being so caught up,
So mastered by the brute blood of the air,
Did she put on his knowledge with his power
Before the indifferent beak could let her drop?

'I AM OF IRELAND'

William Butler Yeats (1865–1939)

'I am of Ireland,
And the Holy Land of Ireland,
And time runs on,' cried she.
'Come out of charity,
Come dance with me in Ireland.' 5

One man, one man alone
In that outlandish gear,
One solitary man
Of all that rambled there
Had turned his stately head. 10

'That is a long way off,
And time runs on,' he said,
'And the night grows rough.'

'I am of Ireland,
And the Holy Land of Ireland, 15
And time runs on,' cried she.
'Come out of charity
And dance with me in Ireland.'

'The fiddlers are all thumbs,
Or the fiddle-string accursed, 20
The drums and the kettledrums
And the trumpets all are burst,
And the trombone,' cried he,
'The trumpet and trombone,'
And cocked a malicious eye, 25
'But time runs on, runs on.'

'I am of Ireland,
And the Holy Land of Ireland,
And time runs on,' cried she.
'Come out of charity 30
And dance with me in Ireland.'

THE SECOND COMING

William Butler Yeats (1865–1939)

Turning and turning in the widening gyre
The falcon cannot hear the falconer;
Things fall apart; the centre cannot hold;
Mere anarchy is loosed upon the world,
The blood-dimmed tide is loosed, and everywhere 5
The ceremony of innocence is drowned;
The best lack all conviction, while the worst
Are full of passionate intensity.

Surely some revelation is at hand;
Surely the Second Coming is at hand. 10
The Second Coming! Hardly are those words out
When a vast image out of *Spiritus Mundi*
Troubles my sight: somewhere in sands of the desert
A shape with lion body and the head of a man,
A gaze blank and pitiless as the sun, 15
Is moving its slow thighs, while all about it
Reel shadows of the indignant desert birds.
The darkness drops again; but now I know
That twenty centuries of stony sleep
Were vexed to nightmare by a rocking cradle, 20
And what rough beast, its hour come round at last,
Slouches towards Bethlehem to be born?

APPENDIX

The Values of Poetry

A poem is not the result of the imposition of technique upon subject matter; it is the *offspring of the union of substance and form,* of subject matter and technique. This offspring, like every human being, is a unique organism. It cannot properly be considered as the addition of form to substance, or of technique to subject matter. If this were the case, the form and substance, technique and subject matter, would be separable. But since a poem, like an organism, is the product of the complex fusion of substance and form, of subject matter and technique, it has an indestructible uniqueness. There is, besides, a functional relationship between form and substance, between subject matter and technique, just as there is a functional relationship between mind and body. Destroy the vital connection between mind and body, and you destroy a living human being. Ignore the vital connection between substance and form, between the subject matter and the technique of a poem, and you destroy the life of the poem.

There is a common critical heresy that analyzing a poem destroys any pleasure it might give, if not analyzed. But just as the uncritical life, in Socrates' phrase, is the life of a beast, so the unanalyzed pleasure induced by a poem is crude and coarse. The pleasure such heretics lose is that which arises from their fantasies concerning a work they have imperfectly comprehended. That such fantasies have their psychological utility cannot be denied, but the use of a poem as a stimulus to egocentric daydreaming is a perversion of its real function. The method of intensive analysis set forth in this book is intended to bring about, first, the student's accurate and detailed comprehension of the work under analysis and, second, an understanding of the means by which the artist has achieved the effect that the student has, through the process of analysis, really grasped. There is no comparison between the rewards of casual reading accompanied by vague personal associations and the rewards of attentive reading free from illegitimate associations.

What, then, are the values that the reader may derive from the aesthetic-critical approach to poetry and from the process of intensive analysis?

If we make a thoroughgoing analysis of our experience when we really read a poem, we shall discover in it a number of distinct elements, any one of which may be agreeable or instructive to experience. These elements may be designated as "factual," psychological, technical, symbolical, and ideational. They constitute the different values that are inherent in the aesthetic experience of poetry. To define and illustrate them may make clear how the study of poetry can be both pleasant and profitable.

"Factual" Values[1]

"Factual" values are the values of the raw material of the work. They are evident in a simple prose summary of the substance of a work. These are the most elementary of literary values, because they arise from the substance forcibly separated from the form. For instance, the "factual" values of "Sir Patrick Spens" or of "The Eve of St. Agnes" are those that might be felt if one read an accurate summary of the action in these works. But these values, though elementary, are not, for that reason, unimportant. They are the base on which the more subtle pleasures that the work may give us are built.

Now, how is it that we can get pleasure from even a summary of a poem? Such a summary can give us a pleasure of one of two kinds, or a pleasure that involves both kinds. One kind of pleasure is that of recognition. The pleasure of recognition arises from our finding elements in the substance of a poem familiar to us either because they are part and parcel of our personal experience or because they echo our literary experi-

[1] Quotation marks are used around the word factual to distinguish a "fact" in a poem from a fact in life. It is unnecessary, here, to do more than hint at the philosophical implications of this distinction.

ences. The possible intensity of the pleasure of recognition may explain the behavior of persons who select poems on the basis of their subject matter. They would feel unhappy if forced to read poems the subject matter of which they had not encountered repeatedly.

But pleasure is quite as likely to come to us because the substance of a poem is unfamiliar. The strange, the unknown, the exotic may be much more alluring than that which has become familiar to us in either our daily lives or our habitual reading. The history of literature furnishes numerous examples of the vogue of exotic subject matters and their exploitation. Italy at the time of the English Renaissance, the American Indian in the late eighteenth and nineteenth centuries, the South Sea Islands in the late nineteenth and early twentieth centuries are instances of exotic material that stirred the imagination and excited the feelings of both writers and audiences.

Most poems blend familiar and unfamiliar elements. In poetry about the life with which the reader is most familiar, some novel observation or fresh insight prevents its being disappointingly banal. On the other hand, poetry of the most fantastic sort—if it is to be acceptable—must have something in common with life as we know it or it will be well-nigh unintelligible to us.

These "factual" values are implicit in the raw material of the poem, the condensed prose meaning of its content. The other values—psychological, technical, symbolical, and ideational—all grow out of the fusion of substance and form in a unique organism; they cannot properly be experienced apart from the total effect of that product.

Psychological Values

The psychological values of a poem may be classified as sensory, emotional, empathetic, and analytical.

By the sensory values in a poem, we mean the experience of a rich and vivid series of images. Some words evoke images (in the reader endowed with a normal apparatus of sense perception), and others do not evoke specific images. Words like *red, hot, saline, soft, crunch, bludgeon* are image-making words; words like *thought, soul, enumerate, sociological, ideal* may evoke associations that involve images, but they do not evoke images directly. Psychologists distinguish six types of images: visual (sight), auditory (sound), tactile (touch), gustatory (taste), olfactory (smell), and kinesthetic (the sensation of tension or relaxation in muscles, tendons, or joints).

It is possible to discover in any poem the words that make images, the words that do not, and the proportion of image-making to non-image-making words. Writing in which the proportion of image-making words is high makes an impact on our senses only slightly less sharp and distinct than actual sense perceptions. Writing in which the proportion of non-image-making words is high obviously has a limited sensory appeal and makes considerable demands on the reader's power to conceive abstract terms easily and clearly.

Words have other powers, however, than those of evoking images and denoting abstract ideas. They also have the power of arousing feelings and emotions. Feelings can be roughly distinguished from emotions by their vagueness and lack of intensity. Love and hate are emotions; anxiety, serenity, melancholy, and lassitude are feelings. Words that represent universal elements in simple human experience—words like *home, mother, war, death*—arouse emotional responses that are practically identical for persons conditioned by the same culture. It is on the power of such words that writers—both popular and sophisticated—rely to manipulate the emotions of the reader. (The cold-blooded exploitation of such emotions is obvious in the American commercialization of "Mother's Day.") Not all words that arouse feelings, however, arouse the same feelings in all readers; such a common word as *cat* evokes very different emotions in those who "love" cats and those who are afraid of them. Although the word *snake* evokes for most readers a feeling of vague distaste, if not of fear, there are a few persons who devote their lives to a study of the genus, and a snake charmer hardly shares the normal distaste for this creature. Lovers of dogs might very well resent the fact—if they were aware of it—that Shakespeare never mentions a dog except to attach a disagreeable or distasteful feeling to this usually unobjectionable animal.

One particular complex feeling, that of empathy, may be distinguished from simple feelings of distaste or fondness. Empathy, as the roots of the word indicate, means the experience of "feeling oneself into" a character or emotion or situation. It is brought about in poetry by the accumulation of a complex series of images and feelings that lure the reader into identifying himself with a character or emotion or situation. Probably any poem which we experience intimately gives us the beginnings of the feeling of empathy, but some works manifest the power of empathy to a very high degree. Any situation that arouses basic human emotions is likely to lure even the experienced reader into feeling, temporarily, one or more of the emotions appropriate to the situation. But the experience of empathy depends very decidedly on the nature and experience of the reader. Some readers whose feelings and emotions are easily stirred will experience empathy much more rapidly and vividly than readers whose feelings and emotions are sluggish or who have a strong sense of their own identity. Naïve or relatively inexperienced readers certainly achieve empathy more easily than experienced or sophisticated readers.

The final kind of psychological value to be defined and discussed here is the analytical. It is the most complex and, therefore, perhaps the least tangible of the psychological values that inhere in literature but its presence is essential to all literature of quality. It is the power manifested by the author in his analysis of character and his understanding of the motivation of human beings. The analysis of character may be made explicitly, or the results of the analysis may be presented and the analysis itself left implicit. Older writers were inclined to make explicit analyses of their characters; modern writers prefer to give the results of their analysis and to leave the analyzing to their readers. Thus, the modern writer is making demands on his reader that the earlier writer did not always make; he is asking of his reader a capacity for analysis that is roughly equivalent to his own. The reader's ability to meet the responsibility means that he, like the writer, is unusually able to observe and analyze human beings, collect evidence from their appearance, speech, manners, and conduct, and weigh accurately the significance of that evidence. On occasions when the reader cooperates happily with the author in discovering the personality pattern of a character, he is experiencing the special psychological value that we have called analytical.

Technical Values

Since most of the chapters in this volume have been devoted to the technical elements of the short poem, here we need do no more than define this value and differentiate it from the "factual," psychological, symbolical, and ideational values that we are discussing. The technical values of a poem are those that belong to its formal aspects, to the properties it has as a result of the fusion of a particular subject matter and a particular form, or, to put it differently, as a result of giving a particular subject matter the form that will express most satisfactorily its potential values. Any reader who is at all conscious of the rhythm and rhyme scheme of a poem, is responding, however modestly, to the technical values of the work he is reading. It has been the purpose of this book to make the reader intensely conscious of the technical values of the types of poetry we have been studying and of the functional relationship between the subject matter of a poem and its technique, in other words, of the use of a particular technique as a means to the end of giving maximum expressiveness to a particular subject matter.

Symbolical Values

Through the elements the writer treats as symbols, a poem achieves a significance for its readers beyond the merely "factual" and literal. The words of which poetry is composed are technically called *signs*. Words are combinations of sounds that point to an actual or an absent or an imagined person, action, object, or idea. The omnipresence of verbal signs—words—needs no illustration, although the creation of language is perhaps man's most spectacular achievement. But the world of nature is no less full of signs than the mind of man is full of words. Certainly no dweller in the country passes a day without attempting to interpret the signs that point to the weather of the rest of the day or the next day. So, birds flying high, smoke rising straight in the air, and a clear sunset are commonly regarded as signs pointing to clear weather, whereas leaves blown wrong-side out or smoke hanging low are commonly regarded as signs pointing to bad weather. But these are, as Mrs. Langer shows in *Philosophy in a New Key,* "natural signs," and, just as nature produces natural signs, man seems to have an uncontrollable impulse to produce artificial signs. Thus, a wedding ring is a sign of a particular personal and social relationship, just as a black band on the coat sleeve is a sign of a particular emotional state. But both the wedding ring and the black band are not only signs but symbols; that is to say, they not only *point* to something fairly specific, but they *stand* for a wide range of significant acts or attitudes. The wedding ring is intrinsically of very slight value; extrinsically, it takes on the values of the relationship toward which it points. Certainly we all know of persons whose overvaluation of a wedding ring is so great that they would hesitate to remove it from the finger, and who would regard the loss of a wedding ring as at least ominous and possibly disastrous.

The fact of the matter is that man finds it impossible to express the values that he finds most significant, except through tangible physical symbols or relatively intangible verbal symbols. Intrinsically, many of these symbols may be valueless; extrinsically, they are beyond price. Two sticks crossed or a pattern of colored bunting cost little or nothing; actually, they may stand for values for which men have died the most painful of deaths.[2]

The artist, like man generally, must, if he is to precipitate and communicate his most precious values, choose and present symbols that will convey to the reader the values he holds dear. The symbols may be national or racial or universal; what he attempts to do is to present them in such a way, arrange them in such a pattern that the reader will catch the particular values that he attaches to them. Psychoanalysts have shown through the analysis of dreams that certain symbols are almost universal, and such symbols, if the artist uses them, are likely to make the deepest—because sometimes unconscious—appeal to the reader. But the artist, on the other hand, may reject universal or even common symbols and create his own symbols. In the use of such symbols, his task is indeed difficult, because he must persuade the reader to accept the symbolical significance he attaches to persons, actions, objects, or words. Thus Eliot's use of the personality of Sweeney may be regarded as a personal symbol that it is his business to persuade the reader to accept on the writer's terms.[3]

[2] Of course, there is a common tendency to increase the intrinsic value of a symbol in order to suggest its great extrinsic value. Thus, we may explain the creation of monetarily very valuable (and incidentally very beautiful) religious symbolic objects, and of engagement rings that are intended to suggest by their size and brilliance the "overvaluation" of the beloved person that is implied in the bestowal of the ring.

[3] A symbol may be profitably compared and contrasted with a simile on the one hand and a metaphor on the other. All three—simile, metaphor, and symbol—resemble each other in that they indicate a kind of relationship between one object, entity, or concept and another object, entity, or

The significance of symbols in poetry may now become apparent. It is possible for a poem to take on a greater significance than a nonimaginative work like an encyclopedia article on Borneo or a demonstration of a geometrical proposition, largely because the artist utilizes words not only as signs but also as symbols. In fact, if he wishes the poem to have a wide significance, he embodies in it a pattern of symbols that points to the meaning he wishes to communicate. "The arts are our storehouse of recorded values," as I. A. Richards says, because artists are especially skilled in the use of symbols to express the values they find most significant.

Ideational Values

The somewhat formidable term "ideational" is used to suggest the philosophical or ethical values in poetry. Every poem implicitly, and many poems explicitly, express the philosophical, ethical, or religious attitudes of the writer. He chooses and presents his subject in the light of, and against the background of,

---

concept, of a different sort. They differ from each other in the nature of the relationship. The simplest of these relationships is that of the simile, the verbal form of which—"like" or "as"—indicates that the relationship is that of comparison. A slightly more complex type of relationship is the metaphor, which involves a momentary identification of the two elements in the comparison; thus, the metaphor, "dripping wisteria" suggests a momentary but imaginatively illuminating identification between the pendant flowers of the wisteria and a little shower of raindrops. The symbol represents the most potentially complicated kind of comparison; it may be indicated by the phrase "stands for." This loose phrase makes it clear why a symbol is capable of an almost indefinite expansion of meaning, since the symbol may be made by a man or a race to stand for a very considerable variety of significances. Thus, a nation's flag is a symbol that stands for the whole range of emotions and ideas that are associated by an individual or a people with the country to which they belong. Since it admits of a wide variety of significances, it is easy to see why the symbolic significance of a flag ranges from the casually to the tragically meaningful. In wartime, this particular symbol is most potent, as one realizes when he recalls the great emotion stirred in the American people by the photograph of the flag being planted by a group of Marines on Iwo Jima. Similarly, the symbol of the national anthem permits of varying significances. When it is played at the beginning of a concert or the performance of a play in wartime, only the most insensitive person remains quite unmoved by patriotic emotion. It is astonishing that the habit of playing the national anthem under such circumstances should lapse rapidly after the end of a war.

his total intellectual experience. The attitude he takes toward his subject is part and parcel of his general attitude toward the world and the values or absence of values in that world.

It may be well to indicate as simply and specifically as possible what is meant by the terms, philosophical, ethical, or religious views. Philosophical views are views of the nature of reality, the nature of the world, the nature of man, and the relationship between man and the universe in which he finds himself. Ethical views are ideas as to what constitutes good and what constitutes evil. Religious views are ideas concerning the nature of the power behind the universe, whether that power be a personal deity, immanent or transcendent, or an impersonal force, and man's relationship to that power or force. If in a short poem, the reader is unable to see ideas relevant to these great intellectual problems, he should remember that the poet's choice of a subject implies that he feels that the subject is worth treating, and his preference for this subject implies his rejection of other subjects as less important. And almost no work is so brief as not to suggest what the writer regards as good and what he regards as less good or evil. A writer's views of the world often change, however, and he should not be expected to express or suggest the same ethical or philosophical views in every work he produces during his lifetime.

The attentive reader will watch for the ideational overtones in a given poem and will not be satisfied until he has grasped and understood them, particularly when they are antithetical to his own philosophical, ethical, or religious views.[4]

Imaginative poetry is the embodiment by the artist, in alluring and enduring words, of substances that have for him explicit or implicit values. The substance thus alluringly embodied may vivify, clarify, and make meaningful experiences that the reader has had, or make compelling and illuminating experiences he has not had. Poetry may stimulate and enrich the reader's imaginative experience on its sensory and emotional planes. Poetry

[4] The distinction between the philosophical-ethical approach to poetry and the discrimination of the ideational values in a poem may be difficult to keep in mind, but it nevertheless exists. Quite simply, the philosophical-ethical approach removes the ideas from their context and considers their validity in a philosophical framework. The discrimination of the ideational values in a poem does not divorce the ideas from their context, does not concern itself with their validity, and weighs them as only one—and often not the most important—of the aesthetic values of the poem.

may, by its presentation of the author's philosophical, ethical, or religious views, clarify and order the reader's views or may give him the temporary experience of philosophical, ethical, or religious views that are not his own. The reader's temporary acceptance of unfamiliar views may deepen and broaden the whole stream of his ideas, may encourage him continually to modify his own view of life in the light of views that he only partially accepts, and may—in the long run—increase the store of wisdom he may garner from the insights of greater and more penetrating intellects. Poetry in its technical aspects may give the reader an intense experience of the infinite variety and wonder of human creativity, of the artist's godlike power to give a peculiar permanence to fleeting and transitory experience through the immensely evocative patterns made by words.

Indexes

Index

Index of First Lines

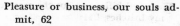

Set in Linotype Baskerville
Format by Frances Torbert Tilley
Composition by V & M Typographical, Inc.
Printed by The Murray Printing Co.
Manufactured by The Murray Printing Co.

67 68 69 70 7 6 5 4 3 2 1